DEER
OF BRITAIN
AND IRELAND

THEIR ORIGINS AND DISTRIBUTION

DEER
OF BRITAIN
AND IRELAND

THEIR ORIGINS AND DISTRIBUTION

PETER CARNE

SWAN·HILL
PRESS

First published in the UK in 2000
by Swan Hill Press, an imprint of Airlife Publishing Ltd

British Library Cataloguing-in-Publication Data
A catalogue record for this book
is available from the British Library

ISBN 1 84037 091 2

Typeset by Rowland Phototypesetting Ltd, Bury St
Edmunds, Suffolk.
Printed in England by Butler & Tanner Ltd, London and
Frome.

Swan Hill Press
an imprint of Airlife Publishing Ltd

101 Longden Road, Shrewsbury, SY3 9EB, England
E-mail: airlife@airlifebooks.com
Website: www.airlifebooks.com

ACKNOWLEDGMENTS

This book could not have been written without help from many quarters. It was made possible in the first place by the encouragement I received from Christopher Borthen, publisher-editor of *Stalking Magazine*, in which the substance of this volume originally appeared in a series of monthly articles over a recent three-year period. I am further indebted to Christopher for finding time in a busy life to read the proofs, for which his knowledge of deer and his professional expertise stood him in exceptionally good stead.

I also acknowledge a special debt to the late Gerald Johnstone, a founder member and Vice-President of the British Deer Society, who did much to stimulate my interest in the study of deer distribution in the early 1950s, when little was known about the subject.

In order to present an up-to-date and comprehensive picture of the distribution of the various deer species I have been in touch with landowners, estate managers, factors and agents, local authorities, forest officials, gamekeepers and many others throughout these islands, and would like to thank them for the information they have given. I am also grateful to those who have afforded me hospitality and have shared their local knowledge with me during more than half a century of watching and studying deer in almost all parts of Britain and Ireland. Irish friends who have been particularly helpful include Tom Brown of the Ulster branch of the British Deer Society, John McCurdy of the Northern Ireland Deer Society, Liam McGarry of the Irish Deer Society and Liam Nolan of the Wicklow Deer Group.

My own photographs have been generously augmented by others loaned or obtained for me by Michael Baxter Brown, Norma Chapman, Peter Delap, John K. Fawcett, Veronica Heath, Jochen Langbein, R. P. Lawrence, Jonathan Lucas, Michael MacNally on behalf of his father, the late Lea MacNally, BEM, Sean Ryan, Steve Smith and Marc Thole, to all of whom I am very grateful. Contributing photographers are acknowledged in each instance and their copyright is reserved.

I also thank Henry R. Arnold, Database Manager, Biological Records Centre, Institute of Terrestrial Ecology, as well as Andy Miles Illustration of Tankerton, Whitstable, Kent and David Muttock of Northampton for advice and help with maps. Brenda Mayle of Forest Research and Peter Watson, Deer Officer for the British Association for Shooting and Conservation, supplied me with relevant literature and I am grateful to them for this.

John and Nichola Fletcher of Reediehill Deer Farm, Auchtermuchty, Fifeshire, Jonathan Lucas of Warnham Park, Horsham, West Sussex, and the British Deer Farmers' Association updated me on deer-farming developments in Britain and abroad, and for this I thank them.

My very special thanks go to my wife, Gladys, for her help and support in countless ways and for her patience and forbearance in once again allowing part of our mutual living space to double as a writer's den over the fairly extended period when this book was in preparation.

Peter Carne
February, 2000.

PREFACE

Deer are the largest wild land mammals existing today in Great Britain and Ireland. One or more species are present in almost every county or other geographical or administrative region, and yet in many ways deer are among the least well-understood members of our wild fauna. Throughout the twentieth century, and particularly during its second half, deer of all the six species which are resident in the wild state in these islands have greatly increased in both numbers and range, at the same time as much other wildlife has been diminishing largely due to the influence of human activity with its ever-increasing impact upon wild habitat of all descriptions.

The place in nature of deer in general, the characteristics and lifestyles of species present in Britain and Ireland and how their dramatic increase and spread have come about are explored in this book. More specifically, the historical background and current status of deer in the various regions and counties are examined in detail, discussing which species are present in different areas and how they have come to be there.

G. Kenneth Whitehead's classic work on this subject, *The Deer of Great Britain and Ireland*, was published in 1964 and is long out of print, but is an indispensable reference source, of which full use has been made in this book. However, since the 1960s the distribution of deer, in Great Britain especially, has undergone many changes. The provision of up-to-date information on this and on likely future developments is one of the main purposes of the present volume.

Many of our wild deer populations originated as deer-park escapees. No study of free-living deer would be complete without some basic information about those confined in deer parks, wildlife parks, deer farms and zoological collections, many of which are dealt with in these pages although no claim is made to present an all-embracing account of these establishments or of the deer they contained at the start of the twenty-first century.

About This Book

If you wish to learn about a species of deer found in Britain and Ireland go to Chapter 1. If you wish to know where a species can be found study the distribution maps from page 184 onwards and then go to the relevant chapter between numbers 2 to 13. If you want to know what types of deer can be found in certain areas go to the relevant chapter between numbers 2 to 13. The Index contains the names of estates, parkland and forests, so consult this if you wish to find out more about a specific location and its deer population. There are two colour-plate sections in this book and a list of the photographs included can be found on page 8.

CONTENTS

List of colour plates

1
THE DEER AND THEIR HABITAT

Deer are members of the order Artiodactyla or even-toed ungulates, which also includes pigs, peccaries, hippopotamuses, camels, llamas and, in the same suborder (Ruminanta) chevrotains, giraffes, okapis, porcupines, cattle, bison, buffalo, goats, musk-oxen and sheep. Deer comprise two separate families, the Moschidae or musk deer and the Cervidae, comprising in turn seventeen genera. As at present recognised, there are reckoned to be between 42 and 45 deer species in all, including one, Schomburkg's deer (*Cervus schomburkgi*) of Thailand, which is now probably extinct and two subspecies of wapiti which became extinct within historic times. These in turn embrace around 200 subspecies. New species are still being identified, and expert opinion tends to differ over whether some supposed species should be more correctly classified as subspecies, and vice versa.

Unique to deer is the capacity of nearly all species to grow antlers. Whereas the horns of ungulates such as cattle, antelopes, sheep and goats remain with their owners for life, antlers are deciduous, normally being shed and regrown annually. Typically they first develop as mere spikes or buttons, becoming larger and more complex in terms of tines, or number of points, with each successive year until the deer reaches its prime, after which they begin to decline or go back.

As a general rule only male deer grow antlers. Exceptions are reindeer and caribou, from the Arctic and sub-Arctic regions of the Old and New Worlds respectively, in which both sexes grow antlers, although those grown by females are smaller. Antlers are sometimes grown abnormally by females of other species, particularly roe deer. At the other extreme there are two deer species, Chinese water deer and tufted deer, which do not grow antlers at all. Male deer of other species sometimes fail to grow antlers while normal in all other respects. In the case of red deer in Scotland these aberrant males are called 'hummels'. In south-west England they are called 'notts'.

Antlers grow from bony projections from the skull known as pedicles. During growth they are covered by skin and hair and nurtured by blood vessels. If antlers are damaged during this period their owner is likely to suffer pain and distress, and subsequent growth will be deformed. If the pedicle itself suffers damage, malformed antlers are likely during the remainder of the animal's life. Undersized antlers in relation to the deer's age may stem from some hereditary deficiency, but much more probably reflect poor health or poor nutrition.

Antler growth is a rapid process, being completed in four to five months. The enveloping blood vessels and protective skin, called velvet, then die and are rubbed off by the deer against any handy shrub or tree, during which process the animal looks untidy and slightly bizarre, with shreds of partly shed velvet dangling from the antlers. When the cleaning of antlers is complete, there is a greater or lesser interval before the onset of the mating season or rut, following which the antlers are retained until the annual cycle starts all over again, the whole sequence being governed by the secretion or abatement of the male sex hormone testosterone. In females the breeding cycle is regulated by the hormone oestrogen, which controls ovulation and receptivity to conception.

Antlers vary enormously in shape and size, according to species, extremes being the massive palmated appendages of the North American moose, the largest of all living deer, and the modest 7.5 cm (3 in) or possibly 10 cm (4 in) ones of the little muntjac from south-east Asia, now well distributed in England. 'Horns' is not an acceptable synonym for antlers as they have quite different characteristics, although it is frequently used in that context, sometimes by people who ought to know better!

The different parts of an antler have their own accepted terminology. The broad, bony circlet at the base is the coronet, the main antler stem is the beam and the various branches, as I have said, are called tines, adding up to so many points. Taking red deer as an example, the first branch, directly above the coronet, is the brow tine, the second one the bez, or bay tine and the third one the trez, or tray tine. Terminal tines are points on top, comprising the crown. It is erroneous to suppose that the number of points on both antlers equates to the age of the deer in years. As I have said, antler size and complexity as regards numbers of points can vary enormously, dependent largely upon local conditions, especially quality of feed, and on the physical health of the animal. The best that can be said about the value of antlers as indicators of age is that the antlers of most young male deer are relatively thin and short, with few points; that those of middle-aged beasts in their prime are biggest and best, with most points, and that those of ageing animals tend to thicken and be blunt at the tips.

As ruminants dependent upon a large daily intake of greenstuff of relatively poor nutritional value, deer divide much of their time between eating and processing what they have ingested while lying down to cud at leisure. Food passes initially into the rumen, the first and largest of four stomachs, there to begin digestion. As cellulose, the food has to be broken down by rumen micro-organisms. Fermented rumen contents in due course rise as a succession of boluses, to be masticated and swallowed again for the next stage of digestion. The passage of boluses up the throat is externally visible at close quarters.

Deer normally sleep in snatches. As prey species they cannot afford to be taken unawares, and among resting groups there are always individuals which are wide awake and alert for possible danger. When fleeing from a potential enemy, deer will raise their tails or expand their rear ends to reveal a white or light-coloured rump patch, known as the caudal patch or speculum, as a signal for others to follow and thus quit the scene of apparent peril as quickly as possible.

Many deer species are highly gregarious, occasionally, as in the case of migrating caribou in Arctic North America, congregating in assemblages of several hundreds or even thousands. In most static situations sexually separate social groupings are the rule, although aggregations of females are likely to include a few male yearlings as well as male young of the year. Some deer species are territorial and normally limit association to family groups of a female with her young of the year, with or without an attendant male. Outside of the breeding season there may be some loose social linkage between different family groups, but without any cohesive herd structure.

Although deer are normally fairly silent, males of most species are conspicuously vocal during the rut. Barks or cries of alarm are often uttered when disturbed, and among groups of females with young, subdued 'conversational' exchanges can sometimes be heard if one is able to approach sufficiently closely.

Deer of all species present in the wild state in Britain and Ireland shed their winter coats in spring in favour of a less dense, differently coloured summer pelage. While the shedding process is under way the deer concerned look decidedly tatty and unkempt. Tufts or clumps of hair on barbed-wire fences or in bedding places plainly advertise their movements or close proximity. The winter coat reappears in autumn by growing through the summer one.

The approximate age of deer may be estimated by various body characteristics in addition to antler size and shape. Even when almost fully grown and otherwise hard to distinguish from adult deer, young of the preceding summer have a tell-tale baby-faced appearance. Young adults are more slender in build than their slightly older congeners. Animals in their prime reflect this fact in their general physique and all-round appearance of robust maturity, while older animals often look sleepy and less obviously alert, more obese and slacker in muscle, and with their heads carried at a lower angle in relation to their body.

Few deer live out their natural span. Most are culled, predated or die prematurely from accident, disease or some other cause. Most of the remainder die well before the age of twenty from the effects of malnutrition brought about by advanced tooth wear.

Deer occur naturally throughout North and South America, continental Europe and Asia and most of the larger adjacent islands including those of Indonesia and the Philippines, as well as in Africa north of the Sahara. They are absent from sub-Saharan Africa, Australasia, Antarctica and nearly all the islands of the West Indies, but have been introduced by man to many of these places.

Red Deer (*Cervus elaphus*)

Red deer are the larger of the two deer species which are native to Great Britain and are the only living species native to Ireland. Adult males (stags) stand up to about 120 cm (4 ft) high at the shoulder, with a weight of about 150 kg (330 lb). Adult females (hinds) are about 15 cm (6 in) shorter and weigh about one-third less than

A yearling red deer stag with its first head of antlers, exceptionally small ones in this case.

A prime-quality red deer stag in late summer, shortly after cleaning the velvet from its new antlers.

stags. The body weights of deer living on the open hill in Scotland are lower on average than those of animals enjoying more congenial conditions of food and climate, and antler quality varies in proportion.

Coat colour varies from a warm reddish-brown on the back and flanks in summer to a duller greyish-brown in winter, with lighter undersides and a buffish rump patch surmounted by a wedge-shaped tail. Stags grow a mane which thickens with the approach of the rut in autumn. Hoofprints, or slots, are almost heifer-like in size, squarish in outline if made by a fully mature stag or more oval in shape in the case of hinds.

Red deer are opportunistic feeders. Although primarily grazers, they will also browse tree foliage and sometimes cause quite serious forestry damage by stripping off bark, especially in winter. Acorns, beech-mast and a wide variety of wild and cultivated fruits are eaten in due season, not to mention market-garden produce, especially turnips, where available.

The cast antler of a mature red deer stag.

Antlers are cast between March and early May, with the older stags casting first, and regrowth is complete by the end of August or early September. Stag groups then break up as individual animals disperse in preparation for the rut. This lasts from late September until early November, the peak being during the first half of October, when well-matched stags compete for harems of hinds in traditional rutting areas. Harems tend to be larger on the open hill than in woodland, and the characteristic roaring by master stags is much more evident in open situations. Fighting between rival stags involves much clashing of antlers but rarely results in serious injury.

After the rut, stags return to their normal home areas to consort with their own kind in loose assemblages while hinds and their young of the year (calves) live separately in herds dominated by a matriarch and with a distinctive peck order of age and seniority. Individual deer of both sexes have well-defined home ranges from which they very rarely wander. Calves are mostly born in June and are almost always single, although twins occur occasionally. Calves are dappled white on the flanks during their first few weeks of life, and are able to follow their mothers from a very early stage. A gruff bark is the characteristic alarm call of this species.

Although red deer have adapted well to life on the open hill in Scotland, wherever woodland is available it will be used for food and shelter, especially in winter. Fossil evidence makes it clear that these deer were once widespread in these islands, with human settlement and the spread of agriculture later depriving them of much habitat and restricting their range and numbers.

Wild red deer and their shrinking sanctuaries were saved from early oblivion by the intervention of kings and other privileged individuals who set aside substantial areas of land for their preservation. William the Conqueror is said to have 'loved the talle deere as if he were their father', earmarking numerous forests for their total preservation apart from hunting by himself, his guests and his heirs. Forest Law was promulgated, Draconian penalties being imposed for unlawful encroachment upon the vert or designated forest areas, and for venison trespass in particular.

Parallel measures to those in England helped save red deer elsewhere in Britain and also in Ireland. In England, apart from the royal forests, sixty in number at one period, numerous chases were established. These functioned in much the same way as forests except that the hunting rights were reserved not for the sovereign but for some privileged individual such as a bishop or other oligarch. Some of these chases adjoined royal forests and so were able to benefit from any natural overflow of the deer living in those forests.

A third type of deer habitat was parks, which differed from forests and chases in being enclosed within walls and palings so that the deer, instead of enjoying free range, were confined. If a park was adjacent to a forest, the owner might sometimes obtain royal sanction for the installation of a saltory or deer leap, enabling deer from the forest to augment the stock in the park but designed in such a way as to prevent them from returning to a free life in the woods if they found the park not quite to their liking.

Deer parks were first created as readily available sources of protein. They were also used for the sport of hunting; Queen Elizabeth I was not averse to loosing arrows at park deer driven past her for the purpose. Not until later centuries did deer begin to be kept in parks almost solely for ornamental purposes. The Victorian era was the heyday of deer parks of this kind. Twentieth-century taxation and two world wars reduced their number very substantially, with many of the deer they once held escaping into the wild.

As for the wild deer proper, increasing human population and declining interest by monarchs in hunting brought about a steady reduction in the number and size of forests and chases and of the numbers of deer these held. By the end of the eighteenth century few wild red deer remained in England and Ireland, and none in Wales. Their one remaining significant stronghold was Highland Scotland, and even there their numbers and range had been progressively contracting under the impact of social changes.

During the nineteenth century the fortunes of Highland red deer were dramatically reversed, and there were some improvements elsewhere, as we shall see in later chapters. The twentieth century brought more changes to the status of red deer in Britain and Ireland, notably the development of deer farming, which has mainly involved this species and has brought a new dimension to livestock husbandry in these islands and in a number of other countries around the world.

Roe Deer (*Capreolus capreolus*)

Roe deer are indigenous to Great Britain but not to Ireland. Fourth in order of size of the six deer species found wild in Britain, mature roe have a shoulder height of between about 60 cm (2 ft) and 75 cm (2 ft 6 in). Mature males (bucks) weigh up to about 30 kg (66 lb), mature females (does) being about 5 kg (11 lb) lighter. Coat colour is a warm foxy-red on the back and flanks with a buffish rump patch in summer, changing in autumn to a winter pelage of grey-brown with an expandable white rump patch. There are black and white markings about the nose, and roe have no externally visible tail.

A roebuck in winter pelage, showing the kidney-shaped white rump patch of a male roe at that season. (Lea MacNally, BEM)

Small in relation to overall body size, the antlers of a mature roebuck of good quality will rarely exceed 30 cm (12 in) in length, and 25 cm (10 in) is better than average in most areas. In addition to the beam there is normally a front tine and a rear tine, adding up to a six-point head. Occasionally there may be a vestigial third antler growing from a separate pedicle alongside one of the normal antlers or from a shared pedicle. Hormonal imbalance sometimes causes roe does to grow antlers, which are permanently in velvet and are usually never shed.

The slots of roe are heart shaped. Except when splayed through movement at speed or across soft ground, their imprints are about 5 cm (2 in) long and 3.75 cm (1½ in) across the heel.

The most familiar vocal utterance by roe is their bark of alarm, emitted singly when the roe concerned is stationary, contemplating what to do next, or as a series of strident 'bough–bough–bough' barks as the animal bounds away, a fresh bark seemingly being 'punched out' every time the deer's hooves hit the ground. Does in season for mating will summon a buck with soft, plaintive calls, while somewhat higher-pitched calls by a youngster (kid) will usually bring its mother running, and she will respond with still greater alacrity to a scream of alarm by her offspring. These vocal intercommunications are simulated artificially by calls designed to lure roe within close range of human observers, especially stalkers.

Roe are basically woodland dwellers. They have a particular liking for woods with a generous shrub layer and abundant ground vegetation, and will live in all types of cover from large forestry plantations to coppices and spinneys of very small size, and even hedgerows. They will also lie up by day in field crops and even in garden shrubberies. In some areas they appear to have taken to living permanently in the open, and are quite often seen at lower altitudes on the open hill in Scotland.

This versatility reflects the highly pragmatic adaptability of a species whose recent history is one of the most outstanding wildlife success stories of the twentieth century.

Roe are browsers first and foremost, bramble being a winter mainstay where the choice is otherwise limited. They will browse fresh leaves in spring and bite off the leading shoots of saplings where these are unprotected by 'dead hedges' or plastic tree shelters. They will graze spring grass and young cereals, raid market gardens for soft fruit and clear domestic gardens of roses. In times of plenty in particular they are highly selective feeders, constantly moving from one delicacy to another and consuming only the best. Fungi and the wild fruits of autumn figure as largely in their diet as in that of other deer species. In short, roe can find a living in almost every type of habitat: one of the reasons for their success. As will be clear, they can also cause significant damage, especially to forestry and in gardens, and their numbers need to be controlled accordingly.

In contrast to the gregarious red deer, roe are territorial, but after the bucks cast their antlers in late autumn this territoriality breaks down for the months of winter, when loose assemblages of bucks, does and kids are quite often seen. New antlers are fully developed and cleaned of velvet over a period extending from April well into May, with individual yearlings sometimes cleaning as late as June. Once their antlers are clean of velvet, mature bucks again become mutually intolerant, each staking out its own territory, defending this against rivals and scent-marking its boundaries.

Does chase off their young of the previous year prior to giving birth to new ones, for the most part in late May. Except where feeding conditions are poor and in the case of young does giving birth for the first time, twins are more common than singletons, and triplets by no means rare.

The rutting season for roe is in late July and early August, with a further brief spell of rutting activity sometimes noted in October. Contrary to common belief, roe deer are not monogamous. A buck will mate with any available doe when it comes into season, and does are equally promiscuous. Like badgers, pine martens and some others, roe experience the phenomenon of delayed implantation. The fertilised egg or eggs are kept in a state of suspended animation for several months, active development usually commencing around 28 December. Growth of the foetuses then proceeds normally.

Roe have had a chequered history. At one time widespread in mainland Britain, they were never as highly regarded as red deer and at an early date were deprived of the full protection of Forest Law. They disappeared from Wales and from most of England but retained a foothold in Scotland, from which they later staged a recovery by a combination of natural spread and reintroduction to former haunts. The expansion of their range continues, its momentum maintained by the continuous outward pressure in search of new ground to colonise by a territorial species whose members are mutually intolerant of living at too high densities.

Fallow Deer (*Dama dama*)

Second in order of size among wild deer species present in Britain and Ireland, fallow deer stand about 90 cm (3 ft) at the shoulder when mature in the case of males (bucks) and weigh up to about 80 kg (175 lb), the females (does) being marginally shorter and lighter in body weight. They occur in four main colour varieties. The so-called common variety is light brown on the back and flanks in summer, densely dappled with white spots in a pattern distinctive to each individual deer. A mid-flank dividing line separates a relatively darker base colour above from a lighter one below, the undersides being white. A black dorsal stripe goes with a prominent tail, about 15 cm (6 in) long, which is black on the upper surface and white underneath, being raised under impetus of alarm to expose a shield-shaped white rump patch surmounted by a black 'horseshoe'.

This changes to a winter coat of dark mulberry brown on the back and flanks, with the spots only faintly discernible – one of the features distinguishing the common and menil colour varieties. Besides being light-spotted all year round, menil fallow are lighter in colour overall and normally have a brown rather than black horseshoe-shaped stripe above the white rump. Seen in half-light, at a distance, menil fallow look almost white. So-called white fallow, on the other hand, are creamy-white rather than pure white, being distinctly buffish in colour during their first year or so of life. These white deer are not albinos and retain full body pigmentation.

Black fallow are dark all over and have no white rump patch, although there is some variation of shade between the very dark back and upper flanks and the slightly less dark

A West Sussex fallow buck with the palmated antlers characteristic of this species.

underparts, the coat overall being darker in summer than in winter. Flank spots are only faintly visible. These colour varieties intermix freely in many wild and park populations, and there are intergradations between them, although there are also some fallow herds all of one particular colour as well as some in which one colour predominates but is not exclusive. As with deer of other species, newly born young (fawns) are brightly dappled during their first few weeks of life, irrespective of their ultimate colour variety.

The antlers of a mature fallow buck are highly distinctive. Typically about 60 cm (2 ft) in length, they have a brow tine and a trez tine but no bez tine, and broaden out towards the tips in the form of palms fringed at the rear with short points known as spellers. Antler development ranges from single spikes in the case of yearlings to the fully palmed head of maturity, usually attained at the age of six or seven.

Different stages of development are identified in ancient royal forest terminology by names which are supposed to correspond with the age of the deer concerned: pricket for a yearling, sorel for a two-year-old, sore for a three-year-old, bare buck for a four-year-old, buck for a five-year-old and great buck for one which is six years old or older, but these definitions may not always be biologically accurate.

A crisp, brief bark is the characteristic alarm call of a fallow deer. Among themselves, especially when fawns are present, they sometimes carry on a subdued conversational chatter. They are otherwise vocally silent for the most part except during the rut, when bucks utter belching grunts or 'groan', whilst patrolling their rutting stands, when continual chivvying stimulates low-level peevish bleats from the does involved.

The rut takes place around mid-October, stand bucks advertising their presence to in-season does by scent as well as sight and sound. Fights between bucks are short, sharp and noisy, but the shape of the antlers helps ensure that serious injury is rare. Like red deer, fallow are gregarious. After the rut they mostly separate into herds of one sex or the other, the members of which circulate around interlocking home ranges. Bucks cast their antlers in late spring, regrowth and cleaning of velvet being complete by early September. Bucks then disperse in preparation for the rut a few weeks later. Most fawns are born in June and are almost always singletons, although twin births are not unknown. Doe herds break up for fawning but soon reunite, with their fawns accompanying them.

Fallow like woods of moderate size. Deciduous ones are their favourite, although conifer plantations are not spurned. Around dawn and dusk they will often emerge from cover to feed on farmland and they sometimes lie out in fields or other open ground all day where not disturbed. Although fundamentally grazers, their dietary range is extensive and can yield surprises when rumen contents are examined. They will even browse yew in small quantities without apparent ill effect, although too large an intake of this highly toxic greenery will invariably prove fatal. Like red deer, they will sometimes browse the leading shoots of saplings and cause serious forestry damage by bark-stripping.

Slot impressions made by fallow, like their rump patches, are shield shaped, being relatively straight-sided. If made by a mature animal they are about 7.5 cm (3 in) long and 5 cm (2 in) across the heel. The slots of bucks are larger and more rectangular than those of does.

Fallow deer of the common subspecies *Dama dama dama* have been moved around much by man over the ages. Originally from the Mediterranean region, with the possible exception of some remnant populations in Asia Minor the present world distribution of *D. d. dama* is entirely the result of artificial introductions at various times. An allied subspecies, the Persian fallow (*D. d. mesopotamica*), was once common in regions bordering the Persian Gulf and elsewhere in south-west Asia, but may now be extinct in the wild state in Iran. There is, however, a captive stock, and because of the larger size of this subspecies it is sometimes crossed with *D. d. dama* for deer-farming purposes.

When the ancestors of present-day fallow first came to Britain, and who brought them, is uncertain. Archaeological evidence shows that a closely related but slightly larger species, the Clacton fallow (*D. clactoniana*), named after one of the areas where its remains were first discovered, existed in Britain in Pleistocene times and was probably hunted by Palaeolithic man. There is also some evidence that fallow indistinguishable from *D. d. dama* were present here before the last glaciation, but many millennia passed before their modern counterparts arrived on the scene. There were some here before the Norman Conquest, but it was after that event that written records of the occurrence of fallow in England in particular began to proliferate.

Throughout the Middle Ages fallow were present in forests, chases and parks throughout much of England, as well as more widely. They have always been held in particular favour as deer-park denizens. As the royal forests and chases were whittled down in size and number and wild deer came close to vanishing with them, fallow continued to flourish in countless parks all over Britain and Ireland. It was these that were to provide foundation stocks for a fallow revival as feral animals on a truly spectacular scale within the last hundred years or less.

Sika Deer (*Cervus nippon*)

Sika are native to eastern Asia including Japan, Taiwan and the intervening Ryukyu Islands, and there is considerable variation in size between the largest and the smallest of the thirteen named subspecies. The sika which are now feral in Britain and Ireland are thought to be mainly of one of the Japanese subspecies *C. n. nippon*. They are somewhat smaller than fallow and therefore third in order of size among the wild deer of these islands. There is, however, considerable doubt about the provenance of some sika populations and there has certainly been a measure of interbreeding between different subspecies, especially under captive conditions. It has also been suggested by G. Kenneth Whitehead that sika living wild in the Bowland area of eastern Lancashire are of one of the larger subspecies from the Asiatic mainland, probably Manchurian sika (*C. n. mantchuricus*), which are equal in size to fallow or even larger.

weight within sika populations of doubtful subspecies and uncertain antecedents is further complicated by the proneness of these deer to hybridisation with red deer where the two species overlap. Not all hybrids are visually obvious as such. They are likely to be bigger than the smaller subspecies of sika, but this by itself is insufficient to identify them as hybrids.

The antlers of sika are simple in structure, a maximum of eight points being usual in maturity. A typical sika antler is characteristically ridged along the inner edge of the beam and has a brow tine, a trez tine but no bez tine, and an inner tine two-thirds of the way along its length. Stags of exceptional quality occasionally grow antlers with additional points, usually located between the inner tine and the beam tip to form a crown. Average antler length overall is about 45 cm (18 in) to 50 cm (20 in). As well as being shorter, the antlers of slightly immature stags, and of lesser-quality mature ones, may lack the inner tine.

A sika stag still in unspotted winter pelage in early spring, with newly developing antlers in velvet.

The summer coat of Japanese sika is a warm chestnut with a black dorsal stripe extending around a white rump patch surmounted by a short tail which frequently has a black dorsal stripe of its own. Except when agitated to repel insects the tail is normally inconspicuous, being held flat against the rump patch, which is expandable under the impetus of fear to present a broad white 'target' shaped like a large powder-puff for other deer to see and follow. The flanks are dappled with white spots and shade off into paler underparts. The males (stags) are slightly darker than the females (hinds) in summer and more markedly so in winter, when the flank spots almost disappear and the coat in general looks almost black when seen in poor light or from a distance. Hinds, by contrast, are a fairly uniform pale grey in their winter pelage. Stags grow a mane which thickens in autumn, and both sexes have a distinctive V-shaped eyebrow stripe of light coloration as well as a pale patch on the hock marking the location of the scent gland there.

A fully grown Japanese sika stag (*C. n. nippon*) stands about 80 cm (2 ft 6 in) high at the shoulder and weighs between 75 kg and 90 kg (160 lb and 200 lb), hinds being slightly shorter in stature and weighing up to one-third less. The assessment of average stature and body

The ears of sika are short and stubby, giving

A Formosan sika stag. These sika retain some dappling in their flank pelage all year round.

them a somewhat teddy-bear-like appearance as they turn their heads to face a human intruder. They are of compact build and often display a characteristic 'rocking-horse' gait when running away from disturbance before pausing to look back, and, not infrequently, then cautiously retracing their steps for a short distance while assessing the cause of the disturbance and the possible need for a full-scale retreat.

Sika slots are marginally smaller and less angular in shape than those of fallow deer.

Like red deer and fallow, sika are gregarious, single-sex groupings being the rule except during the rut, when individual mature stags take up stands where they announce their availability to in-season hinds by thrashing bushes with their antlers, 'going to soil' in favourite mud wallows (as also do red deer in similar circumstances) and proclaiming their presence by various calls. The most characteristic of these calls is a series of 'whistles' or high-pitched moaning cries, each rising quickly to a crescendo and then declining down the scale. Uttered in quick succession, the whistles are usually three in number, sometimes just two or occasionally four, and there are often quite long intervals between one series of calls and another.

Fatalities sometimes result from the quite severe fights between rival stags. The first rutting whistles are often heard at the end of August and they continue, with the rut itself, through September and October into November. Hinds coming into season as late as January are likely to be served. Stags cast their antlers between March and early May, new growth being complete by the end of August for all except a few young animals. The young (calves) are almost always singletons and are born in May or June.

Sika are basically woodland dwellers which do particularly well in commercial conifer plantations as well as in hardwood areas. They will also live out in the open above the treeline in suitable weather and sometimes on farmland if they are undisturbed. They can cause quite serious forestry damage, not least by bole-scoring – gouging the boles of trees with the brow tines of their antlers. Mainly crepuscular and nocturnal, they are primarily grazers, although some populations also browse extensively.

Individual sika circulate within well-defined, mutually overlapping home ranges. Most never travel far from their birthplace. In expanding populations stags live around the range periphery and are the first to colonise new ground.

Sika first came to these islands in the mid-nineteenth century, when some were introduced to Ireland as deer-park stock. As well as being decorative they proved hardy and adaptable. Although their propensity for hybridising with red deer soon became manifest, this did nothing to discourage their more widespread introduction, both in Ireland and Great Britain, mostly to deer parks in the first place. Escapes occurred in a number of areas. There were also some deliberate releases into the wild. As a result, flourishing feral populations of these deer have been established in Scotland and England as well as in Ireland.

As I have said, most of these sika, both park and wild, are believed to be of Japanese origin. Other subspecies are, or have been, kept in various zoos and in a few parks, but the two most widely maintained behind park fences and on deer farms are Manchurian sika (*C. n. mantchuricus*) and Formosan sika (*C. n. taiouanus*). All are larger than *C. n. nippon*, and Formosan sika, which are almost certainly now extinct in the wild state in their native Taiwan, retain some white dappling on the flanks in their winter pelage, this being more pronounced and yellowish-white rather than pure white in summer.

Reeves's Muntjac (*Muntiacus reevesi*)

Muntjac are small, primitive, forest-dwelling deer native to tropical and sub-tropical south and south-east Asia. Several species and numerous subspecies have been described, new ones having been added to the list as recently as the 1990s. Towards the end of the nineteenth century two species, namely the Indian muntjac (*Muntiacus muntjak*) and Reeves's muntjac (*M. reevesi*) were introduced by the eleventh Duke of Bedford to Woburn Park, Bedfordshire, and a few years later some of these were released into the neighbouring woods. Over the course of time it became clear that only Reeves's muntjac survived, both in the park itself and outside it, and it is from this foundation stock that the muntjac now living wild in Britain are all believed to be descended.

Muntjac rarely tolerate each other's company except when feeding or mating, or with dependent young.

A captive Reeves's muntjac buck.

Reeves's muntjac are indigenous to south-east China, with a subspecies (*M. r. micrurus*) in nearby Taiwan. This species is smaller than the Indian muntjac, standing about 43 cm (17 in) to 46 cm (18 in) at the shoulder and weighing 14 kg (30 lb) to 16 kg (35 lb). Females (does) are often heavier than males (bucks) as a result of being almost always pregnant. The rump is higher than the forequarters, the back being curved and the head carried low.

The summer coat of chestnut-bay changes in autumn to a winter one of greyish-brown on the back, flanks and upper tail surface. The undersides are lighter in colour and there is white along the belly. When a muntjac is fleeing from disturbance the prominent tail, about 15 cm (6 in) long, is raised to reveal a white underside. There is a light patch on the throat and dark brown and sometimes yellowish streaks on the head. Rarely longer than about 5 cm (2 in) and often lacking the vestigial brow tine which some possess, the antlers of the bucks grow from long, hairy pedicles which extend well down the forehead. Fawns, which are nearly always singletons, are light-spotted on the flanks during the first few weeks of life.

Muntjac slots are about the size of a man's thumbnail. Bucks normally cast their antlers in late spring, regrowing them during the summer. Does have no annual breeding cycle but come into season within days of giving birth after a seven-month pregnancy; consequently, fawns are born all year round.

Muntjac are territorial animals which communicate by scent-marking and barking, hence their alternative name of barking deer. The bark of a muntjac is short and crisp, often being uttered at intervals of about seven seconds for as long as ten or fifteen minutes, or even longer. Bucks disputing over a doe in oestrus will fight fiercely, sometimes with fatal consequences. The mutual antipathy of muntjac except for purposes of breeding and rearing their young has been a major factor in bringing about their dispersal over the British countryside during the course of the twentieth century, and this process is continuing. Individual animals sometimes turn up many miles from others of their species, well in advance of full-scale colonisation of the areas concerned.

Muntjac are lovers of thick cover with a warm, sheltering understorey, dense bramble being particularly favoured. They are browsers rather than grazers, feeding on a wide variety of woodland fruits and foliage. They will also eat market-garden produce and can cause significant forestry damage where they are numerous.

Chinese Water Deer
(*Hydropotes inermis*)

These small east Asian deer are of two subspecies: *Hydropotes inermis inermis*, which is native to north-east China; and *H. i. argyropus*, which originated in Korea, where they inhabit riverine reedbeds and other wetlands. In the early twentieth century these deer were introduced to Woburn Park and, at a later date, to Whipsnade Zoo – now known as Whipsnade Wild Animal Park – in Bedfordshire, as well as to parks, paddocks and other enclosed areas in counties as far apart as Hampshire, Shropshire, Norfolk and Yorkshire.

Despite being subject to heavy mortality during severe winters, Chinese water deer have proved resilient and adaptable to park conditions in Britain. During the Second World War some escaped, and the species has established itself in the wild state in parts of Bedfordshire, Cambridgeshire and Norfolk, either on farmland or, to a limited extent, in woodland or in wetlands corresponding to those with which it was ancestrally familiar.

Confusion with muntjac has made it difficult to determine with any degree of certainty just how widely Chinese water deer are established ferally in Britain. There are, however, many points of difference between the two species which should make identification easy. Chinese water deer are the larger species, the shoulder height of a mature male (buck) being about 50 cm (20 in) and its weight around 11–13.5 kg (20–25 lb). Females (does) are slightly smaller and lighter. In contrast with the conspicuous tail of the muntjac, the very short tail of the Chinese water deer is barely visible externally, and the upright carriage of the head, with its rounded ears, dark, round eyes and button nose, is strikingly characteristic. Even more so, in the case of the buck, is the lack of antlers. Instead it grows prominent canine teeth in the shape of tusks, which may be as much as 7 cm (2¾ in) long. The canines of does are much shorter. Muntjac also grow elongated canines but these are much smaller and less conspicuous than those of Chinese water deer. The coat colour of Chinese water deer is reddish-brown in summer, changing to dull brown flecked with grey in winter, infants (fawns) being dappled on the flanks during their first few weeks. Slots of this species are about 3.75 cm (1½ in) long and 2.5 cm (1 in) wide across the heel.

The peak month for the rut of Chinese water deer is December, most of the young being born in June. It is not unusual for there to be two or three young at a birth, and as many as seven foetuses have been found in a single female. Multiple births commonly correlate with a higher than average death rate in infancy, and this is as true of Chinese water deer as of many other species.

In deer-park conditions Chinese water deer will flourish at quite high densities, but they are not a gregarious species. In the wild state they are characteristically dispersed in discrete territories, each of which accommodates a buck and a doe with their young of the year. A number of deer may sometimes be observed feeding in fairly close proximity but without any obvious social interaction of any kind.

Water deer are primarily grazers, grass and other ground herbage being their mainstay, but they will also browse bramble leaves and the like, especially in winter. They are said to be fond of carrot tops and harvested potatoes and so may cause problems in market gardens but cause no known damage to forestry interests.

Other Species

Wild reindeer (*Rangifer tarandus*) were present in Scotland until about the ninth century and are said to have been hunted in Caithness in Viking

Père David's deer from China are flourishing in many deer parks and zoological collections in Britain, where they were saved from worldwide extinction in the late nineteenth century when the eleventh Duke of Bedford gathered together at Woburn Park in Bedfordshire most of the known captive specimens in Europe. They bred successfully and some have been returned to China.

to flourish – five of the original eight animals, and a calf born to one of them, died within the first year – but reindeer of the forest-dwelling type brought over later did rather better. A breeding population was eventually established and continues to be maintained. Some of these reindeer spend part of their time on high ground while others remain in the fenced enclosure where they are accessible to public viewing. There are no plans to allow them to become feral or to instigate any measures to re-establish wild reindeer in Scotland.

As well as the six deer species now to be found in the wild state in Britain a number of others are kept in parks and zoos. One of these, Père David's deer (*Elaphurus davidianus*) from China, was saved from world extinction by the eleventh Duke of Bedford when he gathered together individuals from various European zoos to establish a breeding stock at Woburn after the species had been wiped out in its native country. There are now several flourishing herds of these animals and stock from Britain has been sent back to China to re-establish the species there.

Other deer species bred in confinement in Britain include axis deer or chital (*Axis axis*), hog deer or para (*Axis porcinus*), swamp deer or barasingha (*Cervus duvauceli*) and rusa deer (*Cervus timorensis*), all from tropical and sub-tropical south or south-east Asia or Indonesia. Deer of several of these species have escaped from time to time but, so far as is known, have never established feral breeding populations. Deer from North and South America have rarely been bred in British parks although white-tailed deer (*Odocoileus virginianus*) were at one time at large in the woods at Woburn and have also been kept at Whipsnade.

American wapiti (*Cervus canadensis*) have been crossed with European red deer (*C. elaphus*) at

times by the jarls of Orkney. Why they became extinct is uncertain, but destruction of the original forest cover may have been at least partly responsible. Several attempts to reintroduce these animals have come to naught, but a few years after the Second World War further efforts met with some success. The object this time was to acclimatise domestic reindeer for experimental breeding, the area chosen for this purpose being a specially prepared enclosure near Loch Morlich, on the northern edge of the Cairngorm Mountains in Inverness-shire.

A first consignment of mountain reindeer from Sweden arrived in 1952 following arrangements put in hand by the late Mikel Utsi, a Lapp reindeer herder. Another key figure was Utsi's wife, the late Dr Ethel Lindgren of Cambridge University, in her role as honorary secretary of the body set up to administer the whole project, the Reindeer Council of the United Kingdom. The initial introduction failed various times and places to produce bigger beasts with heavier trophies as well as by deer farmers for the enhancement of venison yields. From the standpoint of trophy improvement results have been less than satisfactory and cross-breeding experiments have been short-lived, but indications of wapiti influence have persisted in some red deer populations.

Deer of the prehistoric past are most spectacularly represented by the giant deer (*Megaceros giganteus*) which stood 180 cm (6 ft) or more at the shoulder and grew massive palmated antlers which sometimes spanned more than 300 cm (10 ft) from tip to tip. Although doubtless contemporary with man in parts of continental Europe, these almost certainly died out prior to human settlement of what are now Great Britain and Ireland, at least ten thousand years ago.

Megaceros antlers and other relics have come to light at scattered localities in Britain, rather more plentifully in the Isle of Man and in particular abundance in Ireland, where the bogs have preserved many skeletons. There seems little reason to doubt that the great size of these deer, and the immense metabolic demands of those massive antlers in particular, had much to do with their ultimate demise.

Gaelic folk memory harks back to a long-distant past when a large, dark deer roamed northern Britain. These seem most likely to have been elk (*Alces alces*), which remain plentiful to this day in Scandinavia but almost certainly died out in Britain not later than the ninth century, probably due to the desruction of the ancient forest cover which was essential to their survival.

2

THE DEER OF CENTRAL SOUTHERN ENGLAND

Hampshire

Perhaps more than any other county, Hampshire epitomises the complexities of the deer history and present-day distribution characteristic of Britain and Ireland as a whole. Less typically, especially of lowland counties, at no time in recorded history has Hampshire totally lacked wild deer, and of the six species currently present in England and Wales no fewer than five occur here.

From the time of its creation by William the Conqueror in about AD 1079, the New Forest, in south-west Hampshire, has ranked high in importance among the haunts of wild deer in Britain, and as one of the most famous of the old royal forests of England it has had a chequered history. At its beginning red deer and wild boar

A red deer stag in the New Forest, where these deer were saved from extinction by the introduction of fresh stock in 1960.

were the principal royal game. The Norman conqueror's successor, William Rufus, was apparently hunting one or the other on the August day in 1100 when an arrow ended his life instead. Roe, as an indigenous species, were almost certainly also present in the New Forest in Norman times, but documentary evidence of their occurrence here seems to be lacking. Nor is it known, in consequence, when the original roe died out, or why they did so.

There could well have been some connection between the disappearance of roe deer and the proliferation of fallow deer from the Middle Ages onward. When fallow deer first arrived, or from whence they came, is not recorded. In the woods south-east of Lyndhurst are remnant earthworks from a medieval park which could have been a point of introduction, but this is pure speculation. Roe deer initially ranked equally with the red and fallow species and wild boar as 'beasts of the forest' receiving maximum protection, and until the amelioration of Forest Law during the reign of Henry III penalties for venison trespass could include forfeiture of life or limb. At an early date, however, roe were relegated in status to 'beasts of warren' like the fox and hare, on the curious pretext that they 'drove away other deer', a trait of which they have never been accused by modern observers of deer behaviour!

The end result of this seems to have been that the other deer drove away the roe, or at any rate supplanted them in royal esteem to the extent that roe ceased to receive sufficient

A New Forest red deer stag and hind during the rut. A mixture of scrub and heathland pasture provides ideal habitat for these deer.

protection to save them from being hunted or poached to extinction, not only in the New Forest but over wide areas of England. The popularity of fallow had much to do with their being a more satisfactory quarry for hunting with hounds. Records of royal venison requisitions and of Forest Court proceedings against deer poachers suggest that by the end of the thirteenth century fallow outnumbered the local red deer, a state of affairs which appears to have persisted from that time onward.

The Civil War between Crown and Commonwealth was a time when lawless elements wreaked havoc among the deer of the New Forest and elsewhere. Red deer were particularly vulnerable. There is evidence that James I took steps earlier that century to augment their numbers by introducing fresh stock. After the Stuart Restoration Charles II set aside an area of New Park, north of Brockenhurst 'for the preservation of our red deer, newly come out of France'. There is a record of sixty French stags having arrived at Portsmouth aboard a vessel called the *Hope* for

onward transmission to the New Forest in May 1670. During that same year a 'veiw' or count of New Forest deer produced a figure of 357 for red deer and 7953 for fallow. The red deer were widely scattered over various forest bailiwicks, so are unlikely to have included the new arrivals from across the Channel, and the low numbers of red deer make it obvious why a fairly substantial infusion of fresh blood was considered necessary to boost a declining population.

Fallow deer numbers, by contrast, were far in excess of what might reasonably have been considered a suitable level of population. A hundred years later the position had changed little, and in 1787 an exceptionally severe winter resulted in the deaths of 300 fallow deer in Bolderwood Walk alone. Red deer numbers were again in decline by then. In his book *Remarks on Forest Scenery*, published in 1791, William Gilpin, vicar of Boldre, remarked that this species was mainly to be found in the north of the forest but had previously been more widespread.

Fallow deer numbers remained high well into the nineteenth century. Counts in 1828, 1829 and 1830 recorded figures for this species only, giving rise to the question as to whether any red deer remained by those dates. Any uncertainty on this matter seems to be resolved, however, by the fact that in 1836 instructions were issued for a stag – by definition, a red deer – to be harboured (located for the purpose of hunting) by one of the keepers on the forest's south side for a visit by the Royal Buckhounds from Windsor. Further evidence of the continued survival of red deer came twelve years later with the report of a supposed hybrid between a New Forest red deer and a pony, in an area where individuals of the two species had been seen consorting some time previously. Whatever may have been the true identity of the 'hybrid', there seems no reason to doubt that it was the red deer which was supposedly involved.

Meanwhile, the fallow deer population was at long last being significantly reduced. This was largely in response to complaints about agricultural damage at a time when royal interest in using the forest as a hunting ground had long lapsed, apart from infrequent visits by the Royal Buckhounds like the one mentioned.

By 1850 fallow deer numbers had been reduced to about two thousand. Moves were already afoot to take matters very much further by doing away with the deer altogether. The New Forest Deer Removal Act became law the following year. Two years were allowed for carrying out its main provision, in exchange for which the Crown was empowered to enclose additional land from the open forest for the growing of trees. By 1853 only a handful of deer remained in the forest itself, although others survived by taking refuge on neighbouring private land. It seems likely that all of these were fallow. Following the expiry of the allotted time for exterminating the deer, no further serious effort was made to accomplish this, but as the residual population slowly increased, some culling was resumed. Hunting played a part in this, and in 1883 this was placed on a properly organised footing when an official pack, the New Forest Deerhounds, came into being.

As well as fallow deer, this pack sometimes included red deer among its quarry. In 1886, for example, one of three red stags was hunted across the forest from Busketts to Linford, a 9 mile point, and a week later one of the other two stags provided a 17 mile hunt. These events are mentioned by The Hon. Gerald Lascelles in his book *Thirty-five Years in the New Forest*, published in 1915 shortly after the author's retirement as deputy surveyor or chief executive of the forest, but we are not told how the red deer came to be in the New Forest in the first place. They were clearly not supposed to be there, and in reply to an enquiry by J.G. Millais a few years after the hunts concerned, Lascelles revealingly stated, 'The modern red deer are not legitimately forest deer at all, but spurious altogether and should not be reckoned in speaking of forest deer proper.'

Wild fallow deer rarely stray far from their regular haunts, but this one turned up near Fareham, in southern Hampshire, 10 miles or more from its nearest neighbours.

Correspondence in the archives of Lord Montagu of Beaulieu's family property makes it clear that some sort of unofficial arrangement existed between Lascelles and Mr Francis Lovell, master of the newly formed pack of deerhounds, which had permitted the release of some red

A young roebuck in early spring in Hampshire's Micheldever Forest.

deer for hunting. This was on the strict understanding that the numbers of these deer were kept at a very low level. In 1892 there were said to be between fifteen and twenty.

In 1908 a red deer stag and two hinds were released on the Beaulieu estate. The stag became a nuisance and had to be shot, but not before he had fathered calves which helped establish a feral population which survived for half a century and ranged over the New Forest as far north as the main Southampton–Bournemouth railway. After the death of the second Lord Montagu in 1929 the numbers of red deer in the New Forest itself were reduced, but they continued to range the woods and heaths from Exbury west to Brockenhurst and, occasionally, north to Ashurst. They also strayed on to private property, where they made themselves unpopular and, in the course of the 1950s, came very close to being wiped out.

The red deer elsewhere in the forest fared no better. During the First World War they suffered heavily from measures taken against crop raiders, but a few remained in the north of the forest during the inter-war period, probably boosted by escapees from Broxmore Park, near Whiteparish in south-east Wiltshire, from which the entire stock broke free in about 1925. In the late 1930s a seventeen-point stag was hunted from near Fritham to a kill near Whiteparish,

which suggests that it might have been one of the fugitives from Broxmore heading back towards its ancestral acres. After the Second World War only one stag was known to remain in the north of the forest, where during its latter years it spent the rut in the company of fallow does. I last saw it in the autumn of 1955, when it was going through all the motions of the rut with some fallow deer despite having a broken foreleg, which caused it to have to be put down.

Red deer south of the main railway numbered fewer than half a dozen by 1960. I personally knew of just one survivor of the old Beaulieu-based population, a stag which was enabled to pass on its genes to a new generation by a nick-of-time introduction of fresh stock. Three hinds from Warnham Park in Sussex were released just across the railway from the wood to the south where the stag spent much of its time, the intention being to lure it across to what was considered a safer area. This worked to perfection when the rut arrived. In the meantime one of the hinds had vanished and was never seen again. Within a short time, however, the two that remained followed the stag back south of the railway, there to re-establish a small resident population.

That same year, 1960, saw the introduction of further Warnham red deer, a stag and half a dozen hinds, to a fenced enclosure on the property of Sir Dudley Forwood, Bt, near Old House, north of Burley. Two years later these deer and their progeny were released into the forest. For a time they remained near their point of release but as their numbers increased over the following years they dispersed and are now to be found in widely separated areas between the main railway on the south side and the dual carriageway A31 between Cadnam and Ringwood on the north.

Like their red deer predecessors, these sometimes stray outside the forest and on to private land within it, where they are exposed to random shooting by opportunistic trophy-hunters and others. Some of the very best stags have thus perished, whereas in the New Forest itself efforts are nowadays made to preserve a viable and well-balanced population of good-quality animals.

Imbalance between the sexes has been a particular problem for the red deer south of the railway. The pre-1960 population was short of hinds in its later years. One day in 1955 I chanced upon a herd of eight made up of seven stags and what I believe was the only hind surviving then. In the 1990s, by contrast, all the stags were shot at one juncture, with the result that no calves were born to the few hinds there the following year.

North of the A31 there are no resident red deer although occasionally some have wandered in from across the Wiltshire border, where a very small population of uncertain origin roams the woods in the south-eastern corner of the county.

Having survived the immediate aftermath of the 1851 Deer Removal Act, New Forest fallow deer were kept at a fairly low numerical level throughout the latter half of the nineteenth century and the first half of the following one. Control was mainly by drives to shotguns, at which the keepers developed an expertise hard to fault on humane grounds – a good deal more than can be said of this form of deer control in general. Hunting to hounds played a subsidiary role. The original New Forest Deerhounds eventually confined themselves to the hunting of fallow bucks, in recognition of which they changed their name to the New Forest Buckhounds. Hunting on two days a week except between April and August and during the fallow deer rut in October, they operated along very similar lines to those of the established packs of staghounds in south-west England. A suitable buck having been harboured by the New Forest keeper responsible for the area where the day's hunt was to take place, specially trained hounds called tufters would single out the buck before the main pack was laid on. After a run of varying length the buck would either escape its pursuers or be brought to bay and despatched by humane killer.

The difficulties of hunting in an increasingly confined and crowded corner of southern England segmented by ever busier roads had as much to do with the decision in 1997 to discontinue buckhunting and to disband the buckhound pack as did opposition by those who objected to the sport.

Some thirty years earlier shotgun drives gave way in the New Forest to selective control with the rifle and to a changed approach to deer management in general. No longer were deer regarded as outlaws which ought, by rights, not to be there at all, but as legitimate forest fauna fully entitled to a place in the natural scheme of things while being maintained in numbers not so great as to cause unacceptable damage to forestry, farming or other conservation needs. The fallow deer population has sometimes risen well into four figures in recent decades, but latterly the trend of management policy has been to maintain a somewhat smaller herd of prime-quality stock.

Roe deer emerging in early-morning mist in one of the many Hampshire woods which have been colonised by this species during the past half-century.

New Forest fallow are predominantly of the common variety, with dappled flanks in summer pelage and unspotted mulberry brown in winter. There are also some white deer as well as a very small number of both menil and black fallow, the latter probably having originated from escaped park stock of this colour which found its way into the forest, perhaps from over the Wiltshire border.

Fallow occur throughout the New Forest except the extreme south-east. At one time they were virtually absent south and east of the railway from Brockenhurst eastwards, where it seems likely that the 1851 Deer Removal Act was more effective than elsewhere. In 1949, however, some fallow reappeared in woods east of the line, south-east of Ashurst, where this species has been regularly present since that time, and since the early 1960s fallow have been permanently resident south of the line, between Brockenhurst and Beaulieu. There is regular movement of deer between the two sides of the line by way of cattle culverts and bridges, which they neglected to use in the past. Fallow deer all too frequently cross the A35 and A337, but the A31 dual carriageway, with its exceptionally heavy traffic, effectively cuts the New Forest fallow population into two separate entities. North of the forest fallow range several miles into Wiltshire as well as north-eastward to the Paultons estate near Ower and towards West Wellow in Hampshire itself.

The New Forest roe of modern times are mainly, if not wholly, descended from animals introduced, or reintroduced, into Dorset in or about 1800. The first recorded individual was a buck which was rescued and sent to London Zoo after being found by some fishermen stuck in the tidal mud off Hurst Castle Spit at the western end of the Solent in 1880. Others soon followed, and by the early 1890s there was a small resident population, described by Lascelles as being mainly confined to a string of timber inclosures in the forest's south-western corner. However, in 1994 a long-retired New Forest keeper, the late Mr Jack Humby, told me he clearly remembered his father, also a forest keeper, telling him that when he went to live in King's Hat Cottage, midway between Marchwood and Beaulieu on the eastern side of the forest, in 1891, roe were already present in that area and were in fact the only deer on the Beaulieu side of the railway at that date. Further evidence of the absence then of the larger deer species in that part of the forest emerges from a map of the 1890s listing meets of the various packs of hounds hunting in Hamp- shire. Those given for the then New Forest Deerhounds were all located north of the railway, which surely leaves no room for doubt that neither red nor fallow deer were to be found south of the line in the closing decade of the nineteenth century.

Not until after the First World War did the numbers of roe increase significantly. Heavy timber fellings during the two World Wars and subsequent replanting created ideal conditions for roe, of which these deer took full advantage. By the mid-twentieth century they were present in good numbers wherever the habitat was suitable and were to be seen almost as frequently as fallow in most parts. As replanted trees matured and the canopy closed, shading out ground herbage, roe numbers declined to a much more modest level, although there are still some pockets of local abundance, mainly around the forest's fringes. New Forest roe do not produce outstanding heads of antlers. There are probably more single births than twins, and fatalities from lungworm alone are sufficiently numerous to effect a significant curb on population increase.

In about 1904 the second Lord Montagu of Beaulieu received a pair of sika deer, which were placed in a pen at Old Bungalow, Thorns Beach, on the shore of the Solent. They soon escaped, and the following year a second pair were released in Ashen Wood, 2 miles south of Beaulieu, to keep them company. These original four animals, two stags and two hinds, bred successfully. They colonised the woods of Beaulieu Manor estate, west of the Beaulieu River estuary, and eventually spread into the New Forest, where they established themselves in woods south of the Southampton–Bournemouth railway, where they have been present ever since.

The origin and provenance of these sika are uncertain. They are generally assumed to be of the Japanese subspecies *Cervus nippon nippon* and were always described as 'Japanese deer' until relatively recently, although they differ in certain respects from some other sika populations which are also commonly referred to as Japanese. One of their main distinguishing features is their proneness to grow multi-pointed antlers in excess of the eight points usual to a mature Japanese sika stag. The additional tines usually grow between the normal third tine and the tip of the beam to form a crown, although this is not always the case.

Sika in the New Forest have long been a source of particular interest to biologists and others, and a special study area from which the public are excluded has been set aside for them in Frame Heath Inclosure, which is one of their main haunts. Their range extends west to Perrywood Ivy Inclosure, about a mile east of Brockenhurst, and they have colonised woods between Brockenhurst and Boldre, along the Lymington River valley. They also sometimes wander north as far as Deerleap and Churchplace Inclosures, east of the railway south-east of Ashurst, but are rarely seen east of Beaulieu although there are no physical barriers such as railways or exceptionally busy roads to hinder their movement in that direction. In recent years there has been an increasing tendency by sika deer to stray north of the railway which, for many years, they seemed very reluctant not to regard as an insurmountable obstacle, but official policy is to confine them to that part of the forest which lies south of the railway and to cull any that appear north of it.

This is mainly to minimise the possibility of sika hybridising with red deer, the great majority of which live north of the railway, as I have said. The very few red deer south of the line to the west of Beaulieu have not been seen to attract attention from sika stags, but there have been several instances of this happening at various points elsewhere in the New Forest, with the sika concerned being culled before any mischief could result.

South of the railway sika now live side by side with fallow deer without any obvious interaction. I have frequently had both species in view at the same time, each quite oblivious of the other. There was once quite a good population of roe in what is now the sika heartland, but roe are now relatively few there, possibly as a consequence of dietary competition. While sika in general are primarily grazers, those in the New Forest also browse

Two sika hinds in a New Forest ride.

extensively. They also cause damage to trees by bole-scoring with the brow tines of their antlers, a trait which appears to be peculiar to this species. Sika numbers in the New Forest and on the adjacent Beaulieu Manor and Sowley estates are maintained at a numerical level which rarely exceeds 150 in all, yearly cull targets being adjusted to meet prevailing conditions and the need to protect farm and forestry crops from damage. During the second Lord Montagu's lifetime numbers built up to a much higher level, but the sika population was substantially reduced after his death in 1929, probably reaching its lowest level during the Second World War and the late 1940s, when at one stage there were possibly fewer than fifty altogether. In the 1930s they were hunted at least once by the New Forest Buckhounds, but were found to be an unsatisfactory quarry because of their habit of running in circles. In later years, when hunting fallow bucks in areas occupied by sika, hounds were found to show little or no interest in the sika.

Isolated muntjac have been reported in the New Forest on many occasions dating back at least to 1949. Some of these reports may be the result of mistaken identity, although muntjac are so distinctive that such mistakes are not easy to understand. Certainly there have been a number of well-authenticated sightings. At least one muntjac has been shot by a New Forest keeper, and one was photographed by a Dutch visitor in Frame Heath Inclosure where she was hoping to photograph sika.

Confirmed occurrences and reported sightings have been widely separated in time and place, and up to 2000 there was no indication of colonisation by muntjac on a resident, breeding basis. This could well happen in the future, although some observers have suggested that the scarcity of browse which is not already heavily competed for by existing herbivores may discourage muntjac from high-density infiltration of the New Forest. One can see red, fallow, roe and sika deer all on the same day in this one forest without any undue difficulty, as I have done on several occasions. On the other hand, many people have spent their whole lives here, seeing deer almost daily, without ever glimpsing a muntjac.

The New Forest is by no means the only part of Hampshire with a well-established, numerous and varied deer population. Much has been said and written by stalkers and deer managers about the excellent quality of roe deer, in terms of trophies, in most parts of the county outside the New Forest. Indeed, these high-calibre roe bear little comparison to their modestly antlered New Forest counterparts, and there is little to suggest ancestral kinship with the latter. Moreover, it is a fact that the New Forest's roe population represents only a fraction of that in Hampshire as a whole.

Yet this is a very recent development. Half a century ago, when I first became seriously interested in the study of deer distribution and made fairly strenuous efforts to ascertain the situation in Hampshire as a first priority, most parts of the county outside the New Forest were virtually devoid of roe.

Paradoxically, however, some portions of three entirely separate roe populations in neighbouring counties spilled over the border into Hampshire. The New Forest ones, as I have said, had arrived in the nineteenth century from Dorset. Roe from West Sussex and Surrey were just beginning to spread into Hampshire, the

advance guard having reached Alice Holt Forest in the Wey Valley between Farnham and Alton, the Liphook area and what is now Queen Elizabeth Forest, south of Petersfield. A third roe population, entirely unconnected with these last two, had reached the Forestry Commission's plantations around Bramshill, in the county's far north, having apparently spread there from Berkshire.

The following years saw a steady expansion of range by roe in Hampshire. As far back as the Second World War, and possibly earlier, individual wandering roe had turned up from time to time in widely separated localities far removed from any regular population of the species. This seems to have been stage one in the pattern of spread, for as years went by such occurrences were more frequently reported.

The severe winter of 1962/3 may have given some kind of boost to the roe colonising process, for resident roe were first reported from a number of localities in the months immediately following. The late 1960s and early 1970s saw roe established in moderate numbers right across central and southern Hampshire. Having managed to form a single population, roe from east and west pushed north to colonise the rest of the county, mingling in turn with the hitherto isolated Bramshill area population.

Which has had the greatest influence, the heavily pearled but narrow-spanned antler configuration characteristic of Surrey and Sussex or the slightly less rugged, more lyrate-antlered roe more usual in Dorset and Wiltshire? This is difficult to answer, because what has in fact emerged is a distinctive Hampshire-type head, wider-spanned than one used to expect from counties to the east and rather more rugged than most from Wiltshire and Dorset, with many top-quality trophies among them.

Not only have roe repopulated ancient forests such as Alice Holt, Woolmer, Bere, Harewood and Pamber, which long lacked deer of any species after the earlier stock died out, but they have occupied all suitable roe habitat in the county. There are no more gaps to fill. Even such unlikely areas as a sewage farm near Winchester and a small wedge of undeveloped countryside between Lee-on-the-Solent and Gosport have received complements of roe, which in some cases have developed into flourishing populations. Other localities reached by roe where wild deer might never have been expected include Hayling Island, connected by bridge with the Hampshire mainland, and Southampton Common, which is surrounded on all sides by building development.

While nothing is known for certain about their history in pre-Norman and medieval Hampshire, we know from the examination of animal bones dug up at Portchester Castle that roe as well as red and a very few fallow deer contributed to the diet of diners there in Saxon times, and it seems likely that these were locally obtained. Of the early history of fallow deer in the county we know rather more. They were kept in numerous parks, and in the wild state in various royal forests scattered about Hampshire. They probably survived longest in the Forest of Bere and Alice Holt Forest, being killed off there around the time when these were enclosed for silviculture, in the late eighteenth or very early nineteenth century. Deer once lived on free range at Waltham Chase, near Bishop's Waltham, but these were poached to extinction by an infamous gang, called the Waltham Blacks because of their habit of disguising themselves by blacking up their faces. Bishop Hoadley of Winchester, in whose episcopal care Waltham Chase had been, refused to restock it with deer 'because they had done mischief enough already'.

Apart from those in the New Forest, no fewer than nine separate populations of fallow occur in present-day Hampshire. At the county's western extremity, fallow from Cranborne Chase, which brackets the Wiltshire-Dorset border, just trickle over into Hampshire. Another population spills over the Wiltshire-Hampshire border north of the Salisbury–Romsey railway to the west of the Test Valley, while yet another, of local park origin, is well established west and north of Hursley, between Romsey and Winchester.

Individual bucks have sometimes travelled between these last two populations, which are otherwise unconnected.

Harewood Forest in north-west Hampshire has a population of fallow thought to derive from pre-First World War escapees from Hurstbourne Park just to the east on the other side of a former railway, which then still functioned. Only a few miles, and a railway, separate Harewood Forest and its deer from fallow which overlap the borders of Hampshire, Berkshire and Wiltshire, but which are nevertheless distinct, having probably originated from Hamstead Marshall Park, near Newbury, where the Earls of Craven once kept a herd.

Moving east from here we find another group of fallow to the south of Aldermaston, in Pamber Forest and neighbouring woods. Descended from stock which escaped from Aldermaston Park at some time prior to the Second World War, nearly all of these deer are of the black type. By contrast, the fallow around Bramshill, in north-east Hampshire, include a high proportion of white individuals. The latter are fairly localised and originated as escapees from Bramshill Park, which still contains some of these deer.

Chinese water deer at Farleigh Wallop in Hampshire, where this species was formerly kept by the Earl of Portsmouth in a fenced enclosure.

Hackwood Park, south-east of Basingstoke, was the place of origin of a fallow population whose range extends from just south of Hook, in woods which bracket the M3 motorway, all the way south-west to parts of Micheldever Forest and other woods not many miles north of Winchester. The M3 south of Basingstoke on the west and the Alresford–Alton steam railway on the south appear to mark the normal limits of their range in those directions, although a few sometimes cross the railway and the parallel A31 between Four Marks and Alton and possibly elsewhere. These deer are of various colours, with the common type predominating. Many escaped over snowed-up fences during the 1963 winter, but others were at liberty a good many years before that. Hackwood Park itself still holds an enclosed herd of fallow.

Between the wars and for some years afterwards, park-escaped fallow from south-west Surrey strayed in small numbers into Hampshire. A few were at one stage resident in Alice Holt Forest, and as late as the early 1960s I remember seeing one there. However, these particular feral fallow now appear to be extinct: a rare example of this happening to a population of this species once established in the wild.

South of Petersfield, downland fallow from West Sussex extend into Hampshire as far as the railway bisecting Queen Elizabeth Forest, which they sometimes cross over Buriton Tunnel, although they normally wander no farther west than the very busy A3. These fallow are mostly of the common type, with a small proportion of black and a few menil individuals as well as occasional white deer.

Fallow in the wild have no great pioneering instinct. Once established on free range around some park from which they or their forebears have gained their liberty they tend to stay put in the same fairly clearly defined home area, large or small as this may be. Individuals, usually bucks, do occasionally wander far from their kind. I have encountered two such wanderers, one near Owslebury, south-east of Winchester, and one on the north-western outskirts of Fareham, in south-east Hampshire. The latter I helped to capture and transport to a new home with other wild fallow in north-west Hampshire.

Red deer are rather more prone to wander, although Gilbert White tells us, rather intriguingly, that those which ranged the old east Hampshire royal forest of Woolmer until the early eighteenth century were never seen in the shades of neighbouring Alice Holt Forest, which was reserved for fallow deer. White gives a charming account of how Queen Anne interrupted a journey to Portsmouth at Liphook to sit on a bank, 'smoothed for the purpose', to watch 'with great complacency' the entire herd of Woolmer red deer, at that time numbering several hundred, being driven past her by the keepers. Not long afterwards these deer were all rounded up and sent to Windsor. From that time onwards there were no wild red deer anywhere in Hampshire outside of the New Forest until well into the twentieth century.

In the mid-1960s two stags turned up from no one knows where in central Hampshire, from where they travelled in the autumn towards the southern end of the county, returning north after casting their antlers the following spring. They repeated this pattern for several seasons before one fell victim to an accident. The survivor eventually disappeared, probably into somebody's deep-freeze.

In 1977 a young red stag joined a herd of cattle on a farm at Dummer, south of Basingstoke. Much more recently another lone stag was shot near Farleigh Wallop, just east of Dummer. Escapes from deer farms, of which there are several in Hampshire including one at Ipley on the edge of the New Forest, south of Marchwood, may account for some latter-day sightings of stray red deer but not for those in the 1960s. Local geography makes the New Forest an unlikely place of origin for red deer seen east of Southampton Water or north of Winchester. A rather more likely source of such wanderers in the past was Bramshill, in north-east Hampshire as already mentioned, from which the entire stock of park red deer gained their freedom in about 1955. A few of their descendants roamed the conifer plantations thereabouts for many years, and I saw them myself on more than one occasion. By the mid-1990s only two old hinds remained. Wellington Country Park, at Stratfield Saye in northern Hampshire, includes a deer park with herds of both red and fallow deer, but I have not heard that any of these have escaped at any time.

Once having established a settled home area, sika, like fallow, wander little, at least in the south, except where continuous suitable country and pressure of numbers may tempt them to do so. As with fallow, individuals sometimes become disorientated and turn up in unusual places, though some reports of stray sika at improbable localities may stem from misidentification.

Some sika escaped from Hursley Park, near Winchester, in the 1940s but, as all were female, they did not survive for long and there are none in that area now.

Isolated reports of muntjac in Hampshire other than in the New Forest go back very many years, but their true status is still in some doubt. What is not in question is that they are certainly now resident north of Farnborough in the east and of Basingstoke, Whitchurch and Andover in the west. Areas where their presence is well known include the Stratfield Saye estate and woods near Highclere. Farther south, they have been present in Harewood Forest alongside the long-resident fallow and roe since at least the mid-1990s, and are increasing.

In woods near Farley Mount, west of Winchester, muntjac have been present in small numbers for several years. Micheldever Forest, between Winchester and Basingstoke, has been a haunt of muntjac since some time in the 1970s. How they arrived there is unknown, but assisted passage is strongly suspected since muntjac established themselves in these woods well ahead of any others locally, although now many other properties north of a line drawn between Winchester, New Alresford and Alton have resident muntjac. Farther south the occurrence of these miniature deer is still sporadic, although there have been isolated reports from many localities and full-scale colonisation is an imminent probability.

There are no known feral Chinese water deer in Hampshire now. During the middle decades of the twentieth century some were present in confinement for a time at Leckford Abbas, a property owned by the John Lewis Partnership in the Test Valley north of Stockbridge, and at Farleigh Wallop, south of Basingstoke. There were escapes from the latter, one of which I saw on a single occasion in the 1960s but none remain in the area now.

Marwell Zoological Park, at Colden Common, south of Winchester, specialises in breeding rare and threatened species for ultimate release back into the wild, and usually has a few deer among its exhibits. Recently these have included hog deer, chital and that smallest of all deer species, the pudu from South America. One of these pudu briefly escaped but was soon waiting to be let back in and so was recaptured without difficulty. Fallow and roe deer are resident in the woods around Paultons Country Park, at Ower, between Romsey and Cadnam, and the park itself usually has a few captive deer. In 1998 these included red, fallow and one very elderly muntjac.

Sparsholt College, at Sparsholt, west of Winchester, is an agricultural training college which also runs courses in rural skills such as gamekeeping and deer management, in connection with which it maintains captive herds of red and Japanese sika deer. In 1998 these numbered fifty-nine and forty-six respectively.

None of these enclosed deer populations has been a source of wild populations established through escapes.

Isle of Wight

Have roe from Hampshire crossed the Solent? They have been seen and photographed apparently trying to do so, but whether any have made landfall in the Isle of Wight is doubtful, notwithstanding the very occasional reports of sightings. Red deer remains have been found at Bonchurch, east of Ventnor, and red and fallow deer were hunted in the forests of Parkhurst and Borthwood from Norman times onward. A deer park adjacent to Parkhurst Forest had a role in supplying animals for hunting when required, which suggests that a free-living deer population, which might cause unacceptable agricultural damage within the confines of a relatively small island, may not always have been necessary to sustain the sport of hunting during the royal forest era. The last wild deer died out at some time prior to the enclosure of Parkhurst Forest for timber-growing purposes in the early nineteenth century.

Appuldurcombe House, near Godshill, at one time had a deer park from which escapes sometimes occurred, but these did not result in the re-establishment of a wild deer population. Throughout most of the latter half of the nine-teenth century and the first half of the twentieth the Isle of Wight appears to have been devoid of deer, either wild or enclosed. This situation changed when Robin Hill Country Park was opened on the slopes of the chalk downland east of Newport, with fallow deer and muntjac included among the attractions. Some or all of the muntjac escaped, and for some time afterwards there were individual sightings of what appear to have been these fugitives at a number of different places, but a feral population of muntjac does not appear to have been established.

Some of the fallow deer also escaped, and when the country park changed ownership in the early 1990s the remaining fallow gained their freedom. Efforts were made to eliminate them in the interests of maintaining the Isle of Wight as a deer-free entity so far as the open countryside was concerned, but in 1998 there were still some fallow deer at large. These included a white buck in the Parkhurst Forest area, which it was thought might have swum across from the New Forest, and a buck of the common variety seen and photographed in the Undercliff on the south side of the island in the autumn of that year.

At the same time a number of red deer were also reported to be at large. These were escapees from deer farms, of which at one stage there were three on the Isle of Wight, although in 1998 only one remained. These fugitive deer were said to range the whole of the island. A fallow buck which escaped some years ago from a rare breeds park at St Lawrence, in the Undercliff west of Ventnor, was eventually shot at Freshwater, near the island's western end. In the autumn of 1998 the rare breeds park contained twenty-five red deer, five fallow deer and one sika.

Dorset

In the story of the renaissance of roe in southern England, Dorset holds a key position. It has been noted for its roe deer for longer than any of its neighbours, which is logical enough when it is remembered that it was here that the roe population explosion over much of the south began. Dorset also boasts the largest English population of sika. There are several well-established feral fallow populations, and red deer and muntjac are not unknown.

That red deer were present in bygone centuries

A sika stag on Brownsea Island in Poole Harbour, to which this species was introduced in 1896.

is attested to by the records of the ancient royal forests. Their main haunt appears to have been the forest of Blackmoor, which also held fallow and roe deer at the time of Henry III. It was this king who, while hunting here, is said to have encountered a beautiful white hart which he ordered to be spared. A local dignitary nevertheless hunted and killed it at a spot known thereafter as Kingstag Bridge. When the angry monarch heard about this he not only heavily fined the miscreant but imposed a swingeing yearly tax called 'white hart silver' on local landowners.

Present-day Charborough Park, between Wimborne and Bere Regis, has often had one or two albinos among its herd of red deer. Apart from the odd escapee and rare wanderers from no one knows quite where, all red deer today are confined within park or deer-farm fences. Melbury Park, in west Dorset, also holds red deer in addition to fallow and sika and a few Père David's deer.

When the original roe of Dorset died out is unknown. The late Edgar N. Barclay, a mammalogist of note who was employed at the British Museum, thought that the native roe may never have quite died out but perhaps hung on in a few remote corners until reinforced by fresh stock, but there seems to be no documentary evidence to support this. What we do know is that the Earl of Dorchester, who moved the village of Milton Abbas lock, stock and barrel along with its inhabitants to a new location more suited to his personal convenience than the previous one, was also responsible for adding roe deer to the amenities of his property.

Different accounts give differing versions of where these came from. Perthshire is one suggestion, but a nineteenth-century writer, Sir Thomas Dick Lauder, in an editorial footnote to the 1834 edition of the Revd William Gilpin's classic *Remarks on Forest Scenery*, states that some came from Brooke's menagerie in London and the remainder as a gift from the Earl of Egremont.

Lord Egremont is known to have had roe on his estate at Petworth in West Sussex, to which he almost certainly introduced them in the first place. Did he, perhaps, at the same time obtain sufficient stock to be able to supply some to his fellow-enthusiast in Dorset? If so, one might have expected many Dorset roe to share the heavy pearling and narrow span characteristic of the antlers of so many Sussex roe of the present day, which is not the case.

Within fifteen years of their release, in 1800 or thereabouts, these Milton Abbas roe were sufficiently numerous to provide sport for a pack of hounds. Subsequent decades saw the progressive spread of roe throughout the county, a process aided by at least three further releases of these animals by other Dorset landowners. Several other packs of roe hounds also flourished at different periods prior to the First World War in various parts of Dorset.

By the beginning of the twentieth century roe had colonised almost all suitable localities in Dorset and begun to spread to neighbouring counties. Today they may be found in woodland virtually everywhere, quite often on farmland well away from cover, on open heathland and even on some sea cliffs which are not too steeply shelving, though they have failed to colonise Brownsea and other Poole Harbour islands.

As elsewhere, shotgun drives accounted for by far the majority of roe culled in the county until well into the twentieth century. The late Henry Tegner, a prolific writer on deer and stalking, was one of a very small number who came here to stalk between the two world wars. The great upsurge of interest in stalking which followed the Second World War helped to create a more positive attitude towards deer by the rural community and to encourage more humane methods of deer management in Dorset and in the countryside at large.

Much sought after by stalkers nowadays, typical Dorset roe heads are lyrate in shape, of good to average length and not too heavily pearled. Roe tend to produce the poorest antlers and to be thinnest on the ground in those heathland plantations of conifer which harbour so many of Dorset's sika.

Sika were introduced to Brownsea Island in 1896 and almost immediately some swam to the Dorset mainland. In 1934 a fire destroyed much of the island's timber and such deer as still remained, departed. Their descendants now occur in numbers throughout the largely afforested heathland on the south side of Poole Harbour, as far east as Littlesea, near Studland, being equally at home among harbour-edge conifers and reedbeds. The Army ranges at Lulworth have a well-established population. There they have crossed the Purbeck Hills to colonise the Tyneham valley, Tyneham Wood being one of the many places where I have seen both sika and roe. In general, however, sika distribution stops short where it meets the chalk, acid soils and boggy areas being much more to

A typical trio of sika comprising a hind, yearling and calf, photographed on Brownsea Island, to which this species returned from the Dorset mainland after several decades of absence. These deer are accomplished and ready swimmers.

the liking of these deer, which seem to need access to fresh water as an important element of their wild habitat. As I have said, sika are enterprising swimmers. When the National Trust acquired Brownsea Island in 1962 there were no known sika present, but by the early 1970s they had begun to put in an appearance. They soon increased to a level which necessitated some culling in order to minimise damage to trees, and the need for this has continued. Sika also pay occasional visits to other Poole Harbour islands, but they seldom remain for long.

Sika were also introduced to Hyde House Park, north-west of Wareham, from which some escaped in the 1920s and subsequently to populate Wareham Forest and, eventually, almost the whole of the encompassing Poole Basin north of the Wareham–Dorchester railway, extending north to Bere Wood and west to Dorchester. Individual wandering stags have also turned up in woods near Blandford, but this is well north of the regular range of these deer and seems likely to remain so, being separated from it by several miles of open chalkland with relatively little cover.

To what extent, if at all, the railway keeps these sika separate from those of Brownsea Island origin is uncertain, but the two populations together now almost certainly total at least a thousand head.

Unlike those in the New Forest, Dorset sika are grazers rather than browsers. This may be from circumstance rather than choice, being dictated by the type of feeding which is more readily available. Antler quality is good rather than exceptional, heads of more than eight points being unusual in this county. Colour abnormalities in sika are uncommon but on two or three occasions white or light-coloured animals have been reported in south-east Dorset. None is known to have been shot, so whether or not these were true albinos is not known either.

Melbury Park, between Maiden Newton and Yeovil, is the source of feral sika in the surrounding countryside. Some of these have reached the Sherborne area, and on one occasion I saw two sika stags which had taken up at least temporary residence alongside the fallow in Sherborne Castle Park, while on another occasion I saw a small group of sika stags at large not far from Melbury Park which had a black fallow buck running with them.

This buck belonged to a fallow population which has roamed wild for a fairly long time in hilly, well-wooded country to the west of Maiden Newton. Powerstock Common, Hooke Park and the Rampisham and Wraxall areas are among their main haunts. The majority are black but there are also a fair number of white individuals. I once saw three white fallow among a herd of ten of this species in a wood near Wraxall. These deer descend from a local park herd which ceased long ago to exist as such.

The deer park at Sherborne contains several hundred fallow of mixed colours, and is also a source of feral fallow which sometimes stray just over the border into Somerset but otherwise seldom wander far. Stock Gaylard Park, between Sherborne and Sturminster Newton, has an old-established herd of menil fallow which sometimes make a bid for freedom. This park is also vulnerable to break-ins by non-menil fallow bucks at the time of the rut.

Black, white and common fallow can often be seen in mixed herds in and around the woods of Cranborne Chase, in north-east Dorset. Fallow deer occurred wild here in great numbers for many centuries until the chase was finally disenfranchised in the 1820s. Whether subsequent efforts to exterminate these deer were wholly successful is uncertain and, on the face of it, seems unlikely having regard to the vast wild covers in which they could secrete themselves. The fallow that roam these covers today owe their presence at least in part to escapes from Rushmore Park, near Tollard Royal, during and since the First World War, though perhaps they only reinforced a pre-existing wild population. Nowadays, as might be expected, they share their haunts with numerous roe. For a very short time in the early nineteenth century they also had a few red deer for company when seven of these animals from a long-defunct deer park at Horton, north of Wimborne, were released there. These did not thrive, however, due in one observer's opinion to the absence of surface water, which made the habitat unsuitable.

A small wild fallow population established itself in woods near East Lulworth after escaping years ago from a former deer park in that area. In a wood which became one of their main haunts I once saw fallow, sika and roe in the course of a single visit.

Muntjac in Dorset remain elusive. In 1962 a single young buck was killed at Melbury Osmond, a few miles north of Maiden Newton, from which it found its way to the Dorset County Museum in Dorchester, and in 1997 another muntjac was shot in the same area. Elsewhere there have been a few isolated sightings, but nothing more. Roger McKinley, a staff member of Forest Enterprise at Wareham until his recent retirement, told me that neither he nor any of the local forest rangers had as yet set eyes on a muntjac, so it seems that the colonisation of Dorset by this species may hardly have begun.

Wiltshire

Wiltshire is one of those counties in which there have been deer of one kind or another throughout the centuries. Today three species are well established, two of them having dramatically increased in both range and numbers since the Second World War, while two others occur in very small numbers or intermittently.

The increase and spread of roe has been particularly dramatic. As elsewhere in the south, this species has had a very chequered history in the county. While excavating Romano-British sites in the Rushmore area of southern Wiltshire, the Victorian archaeologist General Pitt-Rivers found abundant evidence of their presence at the period he was investigating. But indications of their status in Norman and post-Norman times are sparse. In 1238 a royal instruction was given concerning the taking of eight roebucks in Savernake Forest. Although this is the only known historical record of the occurrence of roe in that forest, apparently some were still present elsewhere in the county as late as the reign of Henry VII. J. Charles Cox, in his book

The Royal Forests of England, mentions a record of venison trespass involving roe in Clarendon Forest, in south-east Wiltshire, at that time, but how long they subsequently lingered we do not know.

What is a good deal less uncertain is that Wiltshire was an early beneficiary of the reintroduction of roe to Dorset at the end of the eighteenth century. It seems likely that some of these may have reached and crossed the Wiltshire border not long after Cranborne Chase, which lies partly in Dorset and partly in Wiltshire, was disenfranchised by Act of Parliament in 1828. Although this measure terminated the legal right of Lord Rivers, last holder of the chase franchise, to keep deer not only on his own land but also elsewhere within defined geographical limits, it could even have been the case that some roe were already present in the chase when the ancient hunting right was extinguished. Whatever their actual date of arrival in Cranborne Chase, they have certainly been there ever since.

Wiltshire red deer in Tottenham Park, near Marlborough, into which these deer and fallow were driven from Savernake Forest when the Forestry Commission acquired a lease there in 1938.

The first half of the twentieth century saw their spread across much of south-west Wiltshire and their establishment in strength in many localities. By the late 1940s the Vale of Wylye, between Salisbury and Warminster, appears to have marked the northern limit of their occurrence in any great numbers, although a few were already appearing in one or two isolated coverts like Blackball Firs on Salisbury Plain. Grovely Wood and Great Ridge, two very extensive timbered expanses on the wedge of high downland between the Wylye and Nadder valleys, already had substantial roe populations, with three-figure annual culls, in those days mainly by drives to shotguns. I was walking through Grovely Wood one winter's day in 1955 when one of these drives happened to be in progress, and was dismayed, to say the least, at the number of quality bucks in velvet among the victims. That things are done differently now hardly needs to be said, and it was on the edge of Grovely Wood that I shot my own first roebuck – with a rifle, I should perhaps emphasise.

By 1950 or thereabouts roe were only just beginning to appear east of the Avon in areas like the Clarendon estate – old Clarendon Forest – where they have since become numerous, spreading south-east and east to the Hampshire border and beyond. Some of the early arrivals especially are remembered by local stalkers as bucks of truly exceptional quality.

In 1962 I saw the distinctive hoofmarks of some of the first roe to reach West Woods, south-west of Marlborough. At around that time I also saw some of the first roe to arrive in Collingbourne Wood, on the Hampshire border near Ludgershall. Since then roe have spread throughout north-east Wiltshire, recolonising Savernake Forest, where I have shared the now not uncommon experience of having had roe and fallow deer simultaneously in view on recent visits.

Visiting the Bowood estate and some other neighbouring properties in the well-wooded area bordered by Chippenham, Calne, Devizes and Lacock, north of the Plain in the early 1970s, I learned that roe were only just establishing themselves there. They have since become an everyday sight and have pushed on many miles farther to the county's northernmost limits and beyond, while on Salisbury Plain itself they occur throughout the Army ranges, where they appear to live as happily in the open as otherwise and are annually counted and culled as necessary by Ministry of Defence deer managers.

The chain of extensive woodlands along the Wiltshire-Somerset border south of Frome is another area where roe have settled in firmly since the Second World War and are now present in optimum numbers. Summarising the present status of roe in Wiltshire generally, they may be described as being distributed throughout the county, with the highest population density in the south and centre and increasing numbers farther north. As in the case of Dorset, antler quality may be said to be good to average. Being of Dorset origin, Wiltshire roe similarly produce heads that are typically lyrate in shape with modest pearling, handsome to look at as a trophy on the wall and to admire on the living animal.

Fallow were always the principal species in the county's ancient royal forests, which included Braden, just south of Cricklade; Melksham and Pewsham, between Chippenham and Devizes; Savernake and Chute in the east of the county; Clarendon and Grovely in the south; and Selwood, along the Somerset border in the south-west. Of all these, only Savernake survives as a forest in both name and fact. It still contains fallow deer descended from those of medieval times, although whether these can be considered to have remained continuously wild throughout the centuries is debatable, for there was a period between the nineteenth century and the 1930s when the entire forest was enclosed within a 16 mile deer fence, thus transforming it, in effect, into a very large deer park.

In 1938 the Forestry Commission acquired Savernake Forest on a long lease from the freehold owner and hereditary lord warden, the Marquess of Ailesbury, and announced its intention of eliminating the deer, at that time numbering some five hundred, four-fifths of which were fallow, the remainder being red deer. The plan was to drive all the deer into adjacent Tottenham Park, and boys from Marlborough College were among those lined out across the full width of the forest for this purpose. The manoeuvre was only partially successful, as some deer broke back through the beaters and remained uncaught in the forest, the encircling fence of which now ceased to be maintained.

During the war, American troops were based

in Savernake Forest, which was closed to public access. Grey squirrels were hunted for food, but the extent to which venison supplemented military rations can only be guessed at. By the late 1940s only about thirty wild deer were thought still to remain, all of them apparently fallow. These became highly elusive and it was not until after several completely blank visits that I eventually managed to see some.

Numbers slowly increased and in 1956 the Savernake Buckhounds were formed to hunt them. This pack no longer exists but sporting rights currently exercised or let by the freehold owners include stalking. Nearly all the fallow I have seen in Savernake Forest itself have been of the common variety whilst in West Woods, some 3 miles to the west, I have seen a number of black ones. Savernake Forest fallow proper also undoubtedly intermingle with descendants of fallow escapees from Littlecote Park, not far to the east, which are now numerous in many of the woods in that locality.

South of the Kennet and Avon Canal and the adjacent main-line railway, virtually bordering Savernake Forest, there appear to be no resident fallow nearer than Collingbourne Wood and the Buttermere area on the Hampshire border, where fallow from the north of the latter county overlap into Wiltshire.

Many of these latter fallow are black, as is a small herd of wild fallow in the woods of the one-time Melksham and Pewsham Forest, north-west of Devizes. These descend from escapees from Spye Park, a past owner of which made the not uncommon mistake of describing the black members of his herd as 'Japanese deer', a source of much confusion when the late Gerald Johnstone and I were trying to survey deer distribution in 1950–2. Another small herd of feral fallow is reported from the neighbourhood of Draycot Park, near Chippenham.

The fallow of Longleat Park, near Warminster, are probably descended from those that once lived wild in Selwood Forest, bordering Somerset. The forest as such no longer exists but in the extensive woods remaining there are a certain number of fallow derived from Longleat Park escapees, although roe are much more numerous. However, fallow deer numbers in the woods of the Longleat estate received a boost when hurricane-force winds flattened part of the deer-park fence a few years ago.

The Grovely Wood of today lacks fallow, but seventeenth-century Grovely Forest, according to naturalist John Aubrey, contained some of the largest fallow deer in the land. However, the same authority tells us, the fallow deer of Cranborne Chase were possibly even bigger, and their skins were certainly rated more highly by the glove-makers of Tisbury, who were prepared to pay more for them. Cranborne Chase fallow, in their heyday, are said to have numbered many thousands. Today there are possibly fewer than two hundred, ranging over very much the same extensive area as their forebears. This includes Verditch Chase, a little way east of Cranborne Chase proper and at one time part of the larger entity.

What was once Clarendon Forest, east of Salisbury, included a very big deer park with a large population of fallow. Whether the modern fallow deer of the area are in any way connected with the old forest stock is uncertain. They include a population of black individuals which, I was told by a local keeper not long after the Second World War, owed their presence to introduction in the early years of the twentieth century from Cowdray Park in West Sussex, which was certainly noted for black fallow.

The only fallow I have ever seen in the woods of the present-day Clarendon estate was a black individual. The main local stronghold of these deer, along with the common fallow which make up much of the local population, used to be Bentley Wood, a very large covert bordering Hampshire. When nearly all the trees in this wood were cut down in the late 1940s the fallow departed, many of them moving east into Hampshire. The trees with which Bentley Wood was replanted having re-established suitable cover, fallow have returned but now have to share the wood with roe.

South of the Salisbury–Southampton road are extensive woodlands which once formed part of the forest of Melchet, itself once considered as part and parcel of the old royal forest of Clarendon. These woods today hold fallow which to all intents and purposes constitute part of the New Forest population, with deer moving back and forth at will across the Hampshire-Wiltshire border.

Near the Dorset border, east of Shaftesbury, is Donhead Hall Park, which contains a small herd of fallow thought to descend from deer which once roamed Cranborne Chase and were disposed of when the chase was disenfranchised.

Since at least the mid-1960s the woods between Chippenham and Devizes have been the haunt of what once seemed to be an isolated but well-established population of muntjac. How these arrived there is unknown and one must suspect a local release. As we have seen, they are not the only deer in that area, and one early spring morning in 1980 I saw muntjac, fallow and roe there within the space of about an hour.

These muntjac have almost certainly now joined up with the incoming mainstream population, which had already reached Savernake Forest and other parts of east and north Wiltshire by the late 1980s and has continued to spread westwards. There are reports of what may already be a resident stock of muntjac as far west as the woods of old Selwood Forest, along the county border south of Frome. Muntjac are also now present in moderate numbers on Salisbury Plain as well as in the Chilmark area and elsewhere between the Wylye and Nadder valleys, south of the Plain. They are being increasingly reported from woods to the east of Salisbury, and there can be very little doubt that the whole of Wiltshire will be colonised by muntjac in the near future.

Since Norman times at least, wild red deer have never been widely distributed in Wiltshire. In times long past they were present in the forests of Braden and Chute, and as recently as 1938 there were about a hundred in Savernake Forest, but as the latter were deer-fenced in they could hardly have been called wild. Along with the fallow, as many as possible were driven into Tottenham Park when the Forestry Commission leased Savernake. There have been subsequent escapes and, from time to time, a few red deer have reappeared in the now-unfenced forest, but these seem not to be a permanent feature.

Was it a wandering red stag from Savernake that I saw in the mid-1960s consorting with cattle on one of the farms on Porton ranges? The same beast later moved south to join up with some bulls on a farm near West Dean. A short distance farther south still, where the chalk meets extensive woodlands in the south-east corner of Wiltshire, a few red deer of unknown origin have been present for many years.

Sometimes they wander into Hampshire. Sika of equally unknown origin are occasionally seen with them, giving rise to some anxiety about possible hybridisation although nothing of the kind has yet been confirmed.

During the 1980s the religious sect known as the Moonies had a small herd of Père David's deer on some property of theirs at Stratton St Margaret, just east of Swindon. At one juncture some of these escaped, but after roaming the local countryside for a short time they were recovered.

Berkshire

The last three decades of the twentieth century saw Berkshire transformed from a somewhat uninteresting county so far as its deer were concerned into one with a much greater claim to the attention of those who study or stalk these animals. Until around 1970 there were some quite extensive areas of country which were eminently suitable for deer, but which were virtually without them. More recently, however, the cervine tribe has been enriched by the arrival in strength and subsequent spread of two species of which little or nothing had previously been heard within Berkshire's borders.

Almost the whole of early medieval Berkshire was royal forest, with deer distributed accordingly. This situation changed in the thirteenth century, from which time Windsor Forest was the only area subject to the often burdensome restrictions of Forest Law. The original Windsor Forest was large, its 120 mile circumference embracing parts of several counties, but the bulk of it was in Berkshire.

Whereas fallow were the preserved deer in many, if not most, royal forests in lowland areas from the Middle Ages onwards, Windsor Forest was always noted for its red deer. At times the numbers of these ran well into four figures, but undoubtedly many fell victim to poachers during the turbulent years of the Civil War and the Commonwealth which followed. Numbers were later reinforced by the introduction of fresh stock, and throughout most of the eighteenth century there was a healthy red deer population. However, the early 1800s saw numbers dwindling dramatically, and the formal enclosure of Windsor Forest by Act of Parliament in 1813 was followed a year later by the rounding up of what deer remained.

After a number of years without deer, Windsor Great Park was restocked with red deer from Inverness-shire which have done well in their new home.

The only red deer likely to be seen at large in modern Berkshire are isolated wanderers such as are liable to turn up from time to time in almost any English county. In the recent past some of these may have stemmed from northern Hampshire, where a small and isolated feral population was present following escapes from Bramshill Park in the 1950s. Deer farms are another possible source of escaped red deer, in Berkshire as elsewhere.

Wild fallow are present in several areas as mutually discrete and fairly localised populations, all being descended from park escapees. Tracing their range from west to east, on the Wiltshire border west of Hungerford a fairly sizeable population occurs in woods near Littlecote Park, from which the original stock broke out. This is one herd which may not be quite self-contained, being close enough to Savernake Forest for some mingling with the fallow deer of that area to be likely.

The Royal Buckhounds from Windsor normally hunted carted deer and in 1889 some red deer escaped from their paddocks at Swinley, within the area of old Windsor Forest, when a fence blew down in a storm, but these did not long remain at liberty.

A remnant of Windsor Forest which still survives under that name lies to the west of Windsor Great Park, which in its early days was notable for fallow rather than red deer. Fallow remained the more numerous species even after red deer later joined them, then, with the outbreak of the Second World War, deer in the park were greatly reduced to make way for wartime food production, venison being little valued then as a meat for popular consumption.

Shortly after the war the last deer were removed, a situation which was reversed years later with the enclosure of an area to accommodate red deer caught wild in Scotland. Although these newcomers were typical Highland red deer, relatively modest in body size and antler development, within a fairly short time their offspring showed in both these respects the benefits conferred by the better feeding available in a southern English park.

Also on the Wiltshire border, not many miles north, is Ashdown Park, a National Trust property with a good population of feral fallow of local origin. Whereas most of those I have seen in the Littlecote area are of the common variety, these unenclosed Ashdown Park fallow include a number of black individuals.

Welford Park, on the south side of the Lambourn Valley, north-west of Newbury, held fallow until 1947. Some are known to have escaped, but when I explored woods in the vicinity not many years ago I saw just one roe deer and found ground signs of this species only. North of the Lambourn Valley, however, there is a thriving fallow herd on the Berkshire Downs, overlapping what since 1974 has been the Berkshire-Oxfordshire border. These apparently originate from stock once kept in Lockinge Park, north of the downs in the Vale of the White Horse, and range fairly widely through suitable country flanking the Newbury–Wantage road.

South of the Kennet Valley, just a few miles west of Newbury, is Hamstead Marshall Park, the place of origin of a wild fallow herd which extends its range well into Hampshire. The fallow I have seen in woods near the park, which no longer holds deer, have been exclusively black. Another virtually all-black fallow herd, descended from stock once kept in Aldermaston Park, overlaps the Hampshire-Berkshire border but is now mainly Hampshire-based.

Englefield Park, near Theale, west of Reading, holds a sizeable herd of fallow. For a few years it held red deer as well, but these have been disposed of due to damage they were causing to parkland trees, especially beech. Fallow deer have occasionally escaped, but this is one of those rather rare rural parks containing this species which do not have a feral population of escaped fallow in their neighbourhood. The only other herd of Berkshire wild fallow known to me occurs between Maidenhead and Wargrave, in the Ashley Hill and Bowsey Hill area, and is descended from escapees from Hall Place Park in that corner of Berkshire. All the fallow I have seen there have been of the light-spotted, menil variety, which retains its dappling all year round. Wargrave Manor, at Wargrave itself, belongs to the Sultan of Oman, and has a herd of enclosed fallow which are visible from a nearby main road but are not otherwise accessible.

In the early 1950s, when I first took a serious interest in the study of deer distribution, there were no known roe in Berkshire apart from a very small population in the south-east of the county, overlapping the border with Hampshire and Surrey. These apparently owed their presence to an introduction of stock from Petworth in West Sussex to Windsor Great Park around 1850, which in turn followed an unsuccessful release of roe from Dorset in the same park some twenty-five years earlier.

Roe, presumably from this source, were known to be at large in the 1890s in the Swinley area on the Berkshire-Surrey border, which the range of roe slightly overlapped in the 1950s. At the beginning of the Second World War all the roe in Windsor Great Park were destroyed. Those outside were not so easy to eradicate and, in any case, had already spread well beyond the Crown estate which embraced a sizeable chunk of the original Windsor Forest, a sandy wilderness of pines and rhododendrons south-west of Ascot.

The marginal nature of their main habitat did little to stimulate the growth of impressive antlers by these roe. It was a very different story with the mainstream roe from Wessex once they had spread across Wiltshire and Hampshire and begun to colonise Berkshire, a process which was well under way before the end of the 1970s. The effects of this immigration have been felt particularly in the triangle bounded by Reading, Newbury and Didcot. This is an area rich in woodlands which, apart from occasional and invariably brief escapes by fallow from Englefield Park, have almost entirely lacked deer of any species until relatively recently.

When I first explored this area in earnest some years ago, I wondered what effect, if any, the M4 motorway might have had on the northward spread of roe through central Berkshire. I was interested to discover a high roe density in woods immediately south of the M4 and signs of markedly lower density in woods just north of it. It seemed almost as if they were queueing up while summoning the requisite degree of motivation to tackle the hazardous crossing to the motorway's farther side.

Roe of West Sussex antecedents expanding their range north-west through Surrey have undoubtedly joined forces with the previously isolated roe of south-eastern Berkshire to colonise suitable areas in the eastern part of the county, where their influence is evident in the narrow-spanned antlers of many more of the bucks there than in localities farther west. As in other parts of the south colonised by pioneering roe in recent decades, the antler quality of Berkshire's best is good to excellent. Roe are now present throughout the county and their numbers are continuing to increase.

The story of muntjac in Berkshire largely duplicates that of roe, except that the swelling tide of immigrants came from the north instead of the south. When I wrote an article for *The Field* on the wild deer of southern England in 1958, I made no mention of muntjac as being present south of the Thames. A reader, Lord Remnant, wrote pointing out that some existed in east Berkshire, on the south side of the river between Maidenhead and Wargrave, where he lived.

The news surprised me because, at that time, I was unaware of muntjac, other perhaps than a few stragglers well in advance of the main population expanding its range from the East

Midlands, having reached the north side of the Thames near that point, let alone having actually crossed it. I promptly visited the area referred to by Lord Remnant, and was able to satisfy myself from evidence found in the form of slot impressions and other ground signs that muntjac existed in the woods there, although several more years were to pass before I saw them in the flesh.

Whether this pocket of muntjac stemmed from a local release or some other source I never managed to find out. But by the mid-1970s or earlier it was clear that mainstream muntjac had not only reached the Thames from the north but were crossing it in strength to colonise the area west of Reading. At the same time as roe were populating woods which were hitherto mostly deerless in the Reading-Newbury-Didcot triangle, muntjac were doing precisely the same. Nor did the M4 seem to present a serious obstacle, for in woods just to the south of it, where roe seemed to be 'queueing up' before pushing on north, I also found plentiful signs of muntjac and saw both species in the flesh.

The increase and spread of muntjac has reached the point where suitable areas more or less throughout the county hold at least a few, numbers perhaps being highest in central Berkshire south to the Kennet. The river and its parallel canal, combined with the adjacent Great West Road and main-line railway, may have slightly slowed but certainly have not stopped further spread in a southerly direction. In eastern Berkshire a population of muntjac is now thinly spread through all woodland areas.

Are muntjac and roe bad mixers? The question has been asked by people concerned for the future of roe, as it has been suggested that in the long term muntjac may flourish at their expense. Superficially it is hard to detect much evidence of this, but now that the two species co-exist in several counties, possible harm by one to the other is a matter which ought to be looked into. Berkshire would be an ideal county in which to carry out such a study.

Wild muntjac can be elusive, but one place in Berkshire where the public have been able to observe this species at close quarters in recent years is in the grounds of the Beale Centre, alongside the Thames at Lower Basildon, near Pangbourne. Owned by the Child Beale Wildlife Trust, a charitable foundation, the Beale Centre has a small deer exhibit which represented, in 1998, red, fallow and chital (axis deer) as well as muntjac. Three of the muntjac had escaped through a hole in the fence of their enclosure but it was hoped that the two remaining ones would breed and re-establish a more viable stock of these miniature deer. The deer collection was started by the British Deer Society, which had its administrative offices here before moving to its present headquarters at Fordingbridge, in Hampshire.

Three of the fallow deer on show to the public in the Thames-side grounds of the Beale Centre at Lower Basildon in Berkshire.

3
THE DEER OF GREATER LONDON AND SOUTH-EAST ENGLAND

Greater London

London may seem the least likely of places in which to find wild deer, yet they are not entirely absent and, indeed, their numbers are increasing. As might be expected, however, by far the great majority of such deer as are to be found in the metropolis live behind fences in parks and paddocks. There are a number of these deer sanctuaries, some of them several centuries old, and between them they contain several hundred deer of various species.

The best known and by far the largest of these green spaces are the royal parks. Hyde Park itself was originally a deer park, and remained so until 1831, when the deer were removed to spare them harassment by dogs. The keeper had shot a number of these dogs, to the fury of their owners, who used the park for recreational purposes, much as now.

Greenwich Park is said to date from the reign of Henry VI and was essentially a deer park until the early twentieth century. It was also a popular venue for public leisure-time enjoyment, and at weekends and on bank holidays it became necessary to protect the deer by herding them into a fenced enclosure where they were safe from disturbance. In 1918 the deer were removed, but four years later some were brought back and from that time onwards were confined within the fenced sanctuary at all times. In the autumn of 1998 there were seven red deer and sixteen fallow in this enclosure.

On the opposite side of London, Bushy Park, in what used to be Middlesex, extends to some 400 ha and in 1998 contained about 130 red deer and 200 fallow. Just across the road from here is Home Park, Hampton Court, which has complemented Hampton Court Palace since the palace was erected in the early sixteenth century

Red deer in Richmond Park, which was created by Charles I and holds both red and fallow deer. (Peter Robyns)

and has a sizeable herd of fallow. The two parks are separately administered but their keepers work together as circumstances may require for the control and management of their deer.

Larger than all these parks put together, and perhaps the best known, is Richmond Park, which was created by Charles I out of a mixture of pre-existing Crown land, cultivated private land and common land, and surrounded by a brick wall. Until well into the eighteenth century it was frequently used for hunting before the emphasis shifted to amenity. It has remained virtually unaltered in shape and size since its completion in 1637, but the numbers of deer have varied greatly at different periods. A particular low point came in the aftermath of the severe winter of 1947. A previous misfortune was a rabies epidemic in 1886–7, which caused the death of 200 fallow, although the red deer were unaffected. In the autumn of 1998 there were some 300 red deer and 400 fallow. An attempted introduction of roe in the early years of the twentieth century was unsuccessful. The deer concerned came from Dorset and were released into a fenced plantation to which the other deer did not have access, but they only survived for a fairly short time.

Several London boroughs have parks in which small numbers of deer are kept in fenced enclosures. One such is the borough of Wandsworth, which in 1998 had a quartet of axis deer (chital) in a deer enclosure in Battersea Park. These deer were managed by staff from Battersea Park Zoo, in which there were half a dozen muntjac. Clissold Park, in the borough of Hackney, had nine fallow deer in 1998, when Victoria Park, owned by the borough of Tower Hamlets, contained eight fallow in a deer pen, and Bedford's Park, in the borough of Havering, had a small group of red deer.

Formerly owned by the borough of Camden, Golders Hill Park is now administered jointly with Hampstead Heath by the Corporation of the City of London, which also owns Epping Forest. In 1998 there were twenty fallow in Golders Hill Park, one of these being a white individual. There has long been a white strain in this small herd. Epping Forest will be dealt with in chapter 7.

London Zoo in Regent's Park usually has a small number of deer among its exhibits, and these vary in species from one time to another.

Heriots Park at Stanmore, although well within the built-up north-western approaches to London proper, was visited several times during the Second World War by wild fallow bucks intent on joining the enclosed fallow does there for the rut.

Present-day Greater London has its own wild fallow deer population. Epping Forest fallow do not normally stray farther south than the vicinity of the Warren, west of Loughton, but fallow from the Brentwood area are now present on both sides of the M25 in the borough of Havering, I am informed by Mr Paul Vickers, a countryside officer employed there. These fallow are of various colours.

Increasingly in evidence in and around London's northern fringes are muntjac. They have been seen on Hampstead Heath and have penetrated to the more southerly, outlying

fragments of Epping Forest within the Greater London boundary. Muntjac are resident now in woodland on the Essex side of London and within the borough of Havering, where their presence is felt in many a private garden adjacent to the cover they use. Odd muntjac turn up from time to time in some extremely unlikely places, including the vicinity of Kew Gardens in the 1980s.

During the reign of Charles I some roe from Naworth Castle estate in Cumberland were caught up and sent down to stock one of the king's parks near what was to become Richmond Park. There is a record of some of these deer having been killed in woods near Wimbledon in 1636 after escaping, and the introduction as a whole was unsuccessful. It was not, however, the last to be heard of roe at liberty in these parts. On the south side of London they are currently pressing in ever more closely and some have made exploratory forays quite deeply into built-up areas. The time may not be far distant when they become a familiar sight on open spaces like Wimbledon Common, where very occasional escaped deer from Richmond Park have turned up in the past.

Surrey and Kent

With London as next-door neighbour, a large part of Surrey and quite a substantial slice of Kent are undeniably 'outer suburban'. While the population has grown and development has remorselessly spread, there has also been a concerted effort to retain for amenity purposes as much rurality as possible – paddocks for horses, woods for weekend walkers and, coincidentally, much more habitat for wildlife than could otherwise have remained.

Deer have benefited from this. Not only have they survived in a number of unexpected places, but one species at least has been increasing and extending its range on a truly spectacular scale during the second half of the twentieth century, and this increase seems set to continue. Astonishing though it may seem to people unacquainted with deer and their resourcefulness in adapting to changed circumstances and taking advantage of unexpected opportunities, roe have fared particularly well throughout the past hundred years and more. As a direct consequence of this,

A white fallow deer in Challock Forest, north-west of Ashford in Kent.

At that time the Hog's Back, west of Guildford, and the Tillingbourne Valley, east of it, were more or less the northern limit of roe penetration from the south. At the same time, however, there were reported to be a few roe in north-west Surrey around Bagshot, presumably descendants of animals introduced in the nineteenth century to the Crown estate at Windsor.

By the early 1970s the North Downs woods west of Dorking and Leatherhead had been colonised in strength, and I was lucky enough to enjoy some excellent stalking there as a guest. The heads of the roebucks I shot were of the narrow-spanned type common to the species in Surrey and Sussex, making up for their lack of spread by their characteristic rugged pearling.

Since then, roe have pushed on, well north and east, linking up with the Bagshot area roe, reaching woods near Esher and Chessington and even penetrating London's outer suburbs, odd ones sometimes having turned up near Richmond Park and been mistaken for escapees from there. Farther east they have crossed the Mole valley to reach areas like Ashtead Common, near Epsom, while the North Downs woods beyond provide an obvious corridor for range expansion into Kent.

Roe have already reached the western extremity of Kent, which is ripe for colonisation by this species, and are now resident in, for example, Bedgebury Forest. Some years ago a roe wanderer turned up in the Romney Marsh area, which is very many miles from the nearest known haunt of these animals.

Just as Kent is still largely bereft of roe, the same applies to wild fallow in Surrey. Before the Second World War and for some years afterwards there were feral fallow in western Surrey, from which a few strayed into Hampshire as far as Alice Holt Forest and its neighbourhood. These deer were of stock which originally escaped from Peper Harrow Park or Witley Park, or possibly both. There were also fallow in Farnham Castle Park before the Second World War, but none survive there now or in the countryside near by. As late as the early 1960s I saw a fallow in Alice Holt Forest and slots near Crooksbury Hill, in Surrey south-east of Farnham, but there seem to be none in the area now. Wild fallow populations rarely die out but this appears to be one that has done just that.

many people who live in London now have at least the possibility of seeing or even stalking wild roe deer almost on their doorsteps.

The main factor in this roe population explosion was almost certainly the escape of some from confinement in West Sussex towards the end of the nineteenth century. Petworth Park was the place, and the break-out was probably made possible by a gate being left open or a tree falling on a wall, causing a temporary breach. By 1900 or thereabouts, roe reached the Surrey border, where the extensive wealden woodlands, previously without any settled wild deer population, afforded a vacuum waiting to be filled by such cervine immigrants.

Even so, it took time for roe to establish themselves in strength, perhaps because initial numbers were relatively low and there was so much ground to colonise and through which to spread out. A further half-century was to pass before the Surrey Weald came anywhere near to being fully colonised, and then only as far east as the road and railway between Dorking and Horsham. Occasional stragglers were reported from the North Downs woods as far east as Box Hill, but when I walked almost the full length of this area in the summer of 1952 I saw not a single slot or other sign of roe.

Park Hatch Park, south-east of Godalming, still plays host to a herd of white fallow. Escapees have failed to establish a feral breeding population, however, although for several years in the 1990s a solitary buck roamed free in the neighbourhood and was seen by, among others, Michael Baxter Brown, a retired former superintendent of Richmond Park, near his home at Dunsfold. Another enclosed herd of fallow is maintained by a deer farmer at Chipstead, south of Croydon. These deer, of Swedish origin, are of exceptional quality.

Wild fallow are widespread in Kent, where I have seen them in three areas: in woods near Hildenborough; north of Tonbridge, near Mersham Hatch Park, east of Ashford; and in the large woodlands of Challock Forest, between Charing and Chilham, north of Ashford. Descendants of escapees from Godmersham Park, Eastwell Park or Surrenden Dering Park, or possibly all three, the Challock fallow are probably the most numerous herd at liberty in Kent, although heavy culling has reduced their numbers in recent years. Apart from a handful of white individuals, the ones I saw were all black, whereas those at large near Mersham Hatch were of the black and common varieties in more or less equal proportions.

Among other Kentish areas where wild fallow may be looked for are near Lullingstone Park, just off the M25 east of Orpington; between Ivy Hatch and Ide Hill, on the high ground south of Sevenoaks; near Leigh, west of Tonbridge; in the woods near Stockbury, between Maidstone and Sittingbourne; around Boughton Monchelsea; and around Bedgebury Forest, between Hawkhurst and the East Sussex border. I have also seen slots of fallow in the Cobham area, west of Rochester, where there used to be a deer park and where, incidentally, there were unconfirmed rumours of roe some years ago.

Wandering fallow are sometimes seen in woods around Orlestone, south of Ashford. There were fallow both inside and in the countryside around Waldershare Park, near Dover, in the years following the Second World War, but none had survived at the time of my visit in 1977. Nor did I find any indication at all of deer being present in the belt of extensive woodlands north and west of Canterbury, between Herne Bay and Faversham, or in woods bracketing the Ashford–Tonbridge railway, south of Pluckley.

A forest wildlife ranger with specimen antlers of Challock Forest fallow bucks culled in deer-control operations.

Boughton Park, at Boughton Monchelsea, near Maidstone, and Mersham Hatch Park, near Ashford, both contain flourishing herds of fallow, the Boughton herd having existed for four hundred years. Another old-established and flourishing herd of fallow roams the picturesque 1000 acres of Knole Park, near Sevenoaks. Of much more recent origin is an enclosed herd of fallow near Tonbridge owned by Lord Kindersley and consisting of hybrids between common and the larger Mesopotamian fallow (*Dama dama mesopotamica*).

While there are no known wild sika in Surrey, the situation in Kent is different. A post-war survey of wild deer on Forestry Commission land in England and Wales undertaken by Sir William Ling Taylor recorded both fallow and 'Japanese' deer as having been present in Challock Forest, sika being generally referred to as 'Japanese deer' at that time. Local enquiries I made about these revealed that the deer were supposed to be 'fallow with Japanese cross'. Further investigation made it clear that the deer thought to be Japanese were, in fact, the black fallow already mentioned, and that this was yet another of many examples from different locations of confusion on this subject.

Prior to the First World War, Walter Winans, a wealthy American, used Surrenden Dering Park, west of Ashford, for experimental cross-breeding of different subspecies of sika to produce bigger body size and better trophies. Sika as well as fallow survived in this park until some years later. According to the late Mr J.S.R. Chard, a Forestry Commission conservator who spent his younger days in Kent and knew the area well, at some time in the early 1930s foxhounds entered the park and chased out the remaining sika. For some time a few remained in the neighbourhood, Hoads Wood and other nearby coverts being especially favoured by them, but on my 1977 visit I found no trace of any deer there, nor were the several local people to whom I spoke aware of any.

The fallow at Mersham Hatch have shared the park there with Japanese sika. I saw only fallow during my visit and was told by the head keeper that only fallow were known for certain to be at large in the neighbourhood. In 1987 two or three sika escaped through gale-flattened fences, but it is thought unlikely that any of these or their offspring survive.

Sika as well as fallow roam Knole Park's undulating acres. Both have escaped in the past, although in recent years there have been no large-scale break-outs. One autumn some years ago, a fugitive sika stag heard whistling for non-existent hinds in a wood not many miles from Knole Park persuaded a local deer enthusiast to try to ensure that the following season such whistling would not be entirely unproductive. A small local herd of wild sika, which I was fortunate enough to be able to see on several occasions, became established in the area and I understand that they still flourish. They are the only ones known for certain to be at liberty and breeding on a self-sustaining basis in the county at the present time.

Carted red deer were hunted by local packs of staghounds in both Surrey and Kent in times past, and the quarry was not always recovered.

When the Mid-Kent Staghounds ceased operations in 1962 they left a number of deer at liberty which roamed the Kentish countryside for several years thereafter but failed to reproduce their kind. Any red deer now at large are likely to be of deer-farm origin.

Red deer were introduced to Knole Park in the hope that they would hybridise with the sika there and that the results of this cross would produce better venison. This did not work out according to plan, and trees replanted after the 1987 storms were so badly damaged by the red deer that the entire stock was disposed of.

Much of western Surrey once formed part of Windsor Forest, which was noted for its red deer in earlier times. Witley Park, south-west of Godalming, contained several hundred, as well as a few fallow, until nearly all had to be destroyed to make way for wartime food production. By the late 1950s none remained in the park itself but some were at liberty in the neighbourhood, as I discovered while investigating the status of roe in the area. The fallow seemed to have disappeared but slots of red deer told their own story. Not until 1967 did I see any of these – a stag and three hinds – in the flesh. They hung on for a few years more but were eventually shot out.

At one stage, I have been told, some red deer escaped from what used to be Chessington Zoo in Surrey and took up residence for a while in neighbouring woods, but I understand none remain there now.

Deer farms in Surrey which have had red deer include one at Newdigate, near Dorking, and another near Weybridge, which also once had wapiti but has since disposed of both in favour of black fallow from the royal herd in Sweden.

Muntjac have filtered into Surrey, much as they have into various other southern counties, with individuals sometimes turning up at some very unexpected places. North-west Surrey now almost certainly has a resident stock of muntjac, albeit still fairly thin on the ground. There are also reports of isolated pockets of local abundance well removed from other established populations, which hints strongly at local releases as their source. Most reports of muntjac in Kent relate to individual sightings of apparent wanderers, and it is likely to be a few years yet before they colonise the county.

Exotic deer of several kinds have been included, along with a variety of rare and threatened species, in Kentish zoos founded by John Aspinall at Howletts, near Canterbury, and Port Lympne, on the English Channel coast at Hythe. In 1998 the cervine tribe was represented by sambar, barasingha (swamp deer), Eld's deer, axis deer (chital) and hog deer.

Sussex

Sussex has gained an international reputation among stalkers for the exceptionally high quality of its roe in terms of trophies. It also contains two of Britain's most famous herds of park deer as well as numerous wild fallow, a few sika and an unknown but almost certainly increasing number of muntjac.

If any red deer are currently at large in Sussex, their number is certainly not significant. As elsewhere in the country, wandering red deer do mysteriously turn up from time to time and, since the advent of deer farming, the likelihood of periodic escapes has increased. Managed as a deer farm, Wadhurst Park, near the Kent border, contained not only red deer but also a number of other species including Père David's, Manchurian sika, axis (chital) and barasingha (swamp deer) when I called there a few years ago, and I understand that there are now also some Chinese water deer, but I have not heard of any of these having escaped.

Owned by successive generations of the Lucas family, Warnham Court Park, near Horsham, breeds some of the finest red deer to be found anywhere in Europe, or indeed the world. Besides supplying stock for other deer parks, farms and forests almost worldwide, Warnham Park has sometimes contributed inadvertently to the wild fauna of the neighbourhood, but never more than temporarily. At one time several other Sussex deer parks held red deer. Stagpark Farm, within the outer periphery wall of Petworth Park, is a name recalling the former presence there of a park herd of red deer, and this species was present in Arundel Great Park until a few years after the Second World War, as I personally recall. Eridge Park and Buckhurst Park, in East Sussex, both have had red deer among their occupants, while in the early twentieth century

Successive generations of the Lucas family have made Warnham Court Park, in West Sussex and its attendant deer farm world-famous for its red deer. With antlers 158 cm wide in 1998, the stag on the left in this picture achieved a new British record. (Jonathan Lucas)

A four-year-old Warnham Park red stag with a beautifully shaped head. (Jonathan Lucas)

source of some local controversy. These animals, of mixed colours, tend to secrete themselves by day in woods under various private ownerships, emerging under cover of darkness to feed on the open, unfenced forest, criss-crossed by roads on which fairly large numbers of deer are killed every year. As in so many other areas, multiple ownership contributes to the problems of achieving adequate control; some owners, at least in the past, have been reluctant to have any deer culled on their land, regardless of numbers.

Prior to the seventeenth century, Ashdown Forest was a favourite venue for royal diversion, being surrounded by a deer fence and known as Lancaster Great Park. This arrangement broke down around the time of the Civil War. Some deer survived, but the last of the original fallow is on record as having been killed in about 1808, so that throughout most of the nineteenth century there were probably no deer in the forest.

Not many miles south of Ashdown Forest is Buxted Park, near Uckfield. This still contains a herd of fallow, and there are others living wild in nearby woods on both sides of the railway which now terminates at Uckfield.

Fallow of Eridge Park origin occur in woods on the Kentish border, some of which hold substantial numbers. Farther south-east, the extensive woods around Darwell Reservoir and between Netherfield and Mountfield, near Battle, hold a good population of fallow whose forebears escaped from Ashburnham Park around the time of the First World War. These were boosted by further escapees from Brightling Park in the Second World War, and nowadays have to live alongside the complex infrastructure of a gypsum mining operation. Substantial enlargement of Darwell Reservoir also impinges upon their habitat.

several packs of hounds hunted carted red deer in the county, and did not always recover their quarry at the end of a day's sport.

While on foot in Ashdown Forest on a snowy winter's day in 1958 I was more than a little surprised to see slots of red deer as well as of fallow. Subsequent enquiry revealed the presence in that area of a small feral herd of red deer, though, to my regret, I never managed to see them in the flesh.

A local landowner later released some additional animals. Contrary to expectations, not only did these fail to boost the pre-existing stock of nine or ten red deer, but unaccountably within a short time the entire population disappeared. How long the 1950s animals had been there is uncertain, but it appears that some red deer were at large in Ashdown Forest as far back as the early 1900s, prior to which there had been escapes by the species from Buckhurst Park.

The same park was also the main and perhaps the only place of origin of the present population of wild fallow in Ashdown Forest, a flourishing herd the management of which has been a

All this land lies within the Weald, the Saxon *Andredswald* or *Anderida* which was originally one vast forest extending from Kent across central Sussex and southern Surrey into Hampshire and which is still very heavily wooded. From Ashdown Forest the Forest Ridges spread west across north-central Sussex through a region which contains several other individual forests, all first-class habitat for deer.

Just east of the London–Brighton railway, south of Three Bridges, is Worth Forest, which shares a population of fallow with other woods in the neighbourhood including the Forestry Commission's Gravetye Forest. Just where these deer originated and how long they have been at liberty I have been unable to discover. It has been suggested, however, that some of the fallow in this part of Sussex descend from animals let out of deer parks as long ago as the seventeenth century, during the time of the Civil War and the years of Cromwell's Commonwealth.

The fallow I have seen in both Ashdown and Worth Forests were a mixture of common and black individuals. In St Leonard's Forest, farther west, I have seen a number of white ones, of which I understand there are a fairly high proportion among the fallow in that area. To what extent, if any, these link up with the Worth Forest fallow has for long been hard to determine. It seems likely that there was some connection via Balcombe and Brantridge Forests, both of which lie between the two and both of which contain fallow. At least one competent observer of the overall Sussex deer scene is, however, of the opinion that nearly all of the several once disparate wild fallow populations of the county have now spread out and merged to form a single extensive area of continuous distribution.

The man concerned, Mr F.J.C. (Fred) Marshall, runs a small deer farm on the eastern outskirts of Ashdown Forest and has been involved with deer management in Sussex and elsewhere for most of his life, so his opinions on such matters are to be respected. I am, however, uncertain whether the fallow of Wiston Park origin in the woods north-west of Steyning, directly north of the South Downs, have managed to cross the fairly wide gap that has separated them from the Forest Ridges fallow to the north.

Moving west from here, the next major fallow population inhabits extensive woodlands east of the River Arun and is of the black variety as seen in Parham Park, south of Pulborough, from which the original deer escaped.

In the woods immediately west of Arundel I have found no sign of fallow, although they may have been present in the past, when the species was kept in Arundel Great Park, along with red deer, and some animals escaped. Yet not many miles north-west of Arundel fallow certainly occur in downland woods on both sides of the Chichester–Petworth road, including Charlton and Singleton Forests as well as other parts of the Goodwood estate. These fallow are of mixed colours, white individuals being quite common.

Petworth Park contains some of the finest fallow deer in Britain: big-bodied beasts with

Wild fallow in ancient woodland near Up Park on the West Sussex downs

Roadside warning sign in Ashdown Forest, East Sussex, where deer casualties from road traffic accidents have been particularly high.

broad-palmed antlers which give them particular value as breeding stock in demand for other herds. North of the deer park proper is an area of walled woodland where these deer are also sometimes present.

Woodlands north of the Rother valley and west of the Midhurst–Haslemere road were home for many years to a population of fallow which almost certainly derived from stock once kept in Cowdray Park, just east of Midhurst. These fallow were mostly black plus a proportion of white individuals, and twin births occurred among them from time to time. However, this is one of those rather rare instances when an entire fallow population appears to have been wiped out, although I hear rumours that some others may have moved into the area.

Black fallow escapees from Cowdray Park reached woodlands on the South Downs west of the Midhurst–Chichester road at some time well before the Second World War. During that war they were joined by the mainly common-coloured fallow hitherto confined in Uppark, which were set free when the park had to be ploughed up for food production. Black deer persist in this population but are now in a minority; there are also a very few menil and white individuals. These fallow now occur throughout all but the southernmost extremity of the area enclosed by the main roads and railways linking Midhurst, Chichester, Havant and Petersfield, although north of the downs they seldom make more than tentative incursions into the Rother Valley low ground.

It would be an interesting exercise to assess how many fallow in total these various populations comprise. They are certainly to be numbered in thousands rather than hundreds. Roe are probably still more numerous and are still expanding their range.

The origin of the present-day Sussex roe is still debated. The place from which the first ones gained their freedom is not disputed – Petworth Park, an enormous area of which the present deer park forms only a comparatively small part. A separate walled compartment within the perimeter wall is a woodland area long dedicated to roe – so long, indeed, that some have found it tempting to suggest that the roe there may have been a relict remnant of the indigenous roe of the south, fortuitously enclosed when Petworth Park first came into being some six centuries ago and in consequence saved from final extinction.

The facts are probably more mundane. Around the end of the eighteenth century the Earl of Egremont, the owner, is known to have had a special interest in roe deer and, according to various writers, introduced some to Petworth Park. It has also been said that he supplied some of those originally released in the Milton Abbas woods in Dorset by Lord Dorchester in or around 1800.

However roe first came to Petworth, in about 1890 their numbers appear to have dipped quite steeply from sixty or seventy to a mere seven. Precisely how this happened is not recorded. A breach in the park wall caused, perhaps, by a fallen tree seems a very likely explanation, especially in view of the fact that a decade later roe had begun to appear in numbers in woods around Shillinglee, north of Petworth, and presumably elsewhere outside the park. At any rate, fresh stock was brought down from Scotland and several internal walls were lowered to permit those within the park to range more widely.

Once roe had gained a foothold in the countryside around, colonisation proceeded at a fairly steady pace. The wealden woods and those on the downs to the south were the first to be occupied, the westerly spread along the South Downs being accomplished rather more slowly.

It was not until around 1950 that the Hampshire border began to be crossed on any really significant scale, while the lower reaches of the Arun and that river's parallel railway for quite a long time formed a barrier to any large-scale easterly spread. Farther north, however, roe pushed east through St Leonard's Forest and along the Forest Ridges generally until they met another obstacle, the London–Brighton railway. For decades this hindered any further spread, and only in fairly recent years have roe reached areas east of the line such as Gravetye between West Hoathly and East Grinstead, and Bedgebury Forest, which lies just over the border in Kent. In both of these areas I understand roe now occur regularly and odd ones have been seen in Ashdown Forest. However, wide areas of East Sussex remain to be colonised before the roe push on in real earnest into Kent.

With almost all prime habitat west of the Arun having long been colonised by roe, they have overflowed into less likely areas such as the coastal plain south of Chichester, which is almost devoid of woodland, where some farmers have greeted their new guests with something less than enthusiasm.

For all this burgeoning roe population, concern has been expressed in some quarters that pressure by trophy-hunters over-anxious to cover their walls with the famously rugged if sometimes rather narrow-spanned heads of mature Sussex roebucks may already be becoming too great for the traffic to bear. Responsible deer managers are carefully limiting the proportion of trophy bucks to be culled accordingly.

Sussex is not noted for sika, but they have been kept in one or two parks including Leonardslee, near Horsham, from which a number escaped when the 1987 storms flattened the fence. On a visit not long afterwards I enjoyed the novel experience of seeing sika at large in the surrounding countryside. Most were subsequently lured back into the park following refencing. Near Framfield, about 2 miles east of Uckfield, a number of sika escaped from a small enclosure with a fence too low to contain them. They took up residence in the countryside nearby, where some were subsequently shot to minimise damage to crops, but it seems likely that others remain in an area where there are also many wild fallow.

Muntjac were first reported in Sussex as long ago as the mid-1960s, since when a small population has become established in the wealden woods north of Rogate and elsewhere in that vicinity. Stansted Forest, on the Hampshire border, where fallow and roe are also present, is one of a number of other areas where muntjac have been seen at various times in recent years. Farther east, on the Forest Ridges south of Three Bridges and east of the London–Brighton railway, is another established muntjac population derived, as I understand, from either a local release or an escape of captive stock. Welcome or otherwise, these small deer are clearly destined to become an ever more familiar part of the countryside scene in Sussex in the future.

4

THE DEER OF
SOUTH-WEST ENGLAND

Somerset

Somerset is one of the few English counties in which wild deer have occurred continuously since very early times, with some of today's individuals directly descended, at least in part, from ancient stock. Like many other counties, it has also seen dramatic changes in its overall deer population since the early twentieth century, and in particular, as it happens, during the century's closing decades.

To deer-minded people of the past, and indeed to many of them today, Somerset's special claim to their interest has been as a haunt of red deer: the wild red deer of Exmoor, some two-thirds of which lies within the county. It is in this wild expanse of lofty moors and deep, wooded combes that the staghunting tradition has tenaciously endured in the face of threats from many quarters, and which, many have argued, is primarily responsible for the continued survival, in healthy numbers, of the deer which are its quarry.

There is strong evidence that Exmoor was a royal hunting ground as far back as the reign of Edward the Confessor, some years before the Norman Conquest. In Norman times and later it was one of five royal forests in Somerset, the others being Neroche, south of Taunton; North Petherton, between Taunton and Bridgwater; Mendip, on and around the hills of that name and originally part of a larger forest called Kingswood which extended almost to Bristol; and Selwood, on the Wiltshire border.

In spite of being too remote to be of much direct interest to the sovereign as a sporting domain, Exmoor remained a royal forest longer than any of the others. From 1508 onwards it was held on lease from the Crown by various private individuals and it was under these changed circumstances that staghunting, practised much as it is now, took firm root as a local pursuit.

The later decades of the eighteenth century

Red deer stags of various ages on the move on Exmoor, where the species has roamed wild since ancient times. (Marc Thole)

and the first quarter of the nineteenth saw the North Devon Staghounds hunting both the Devon and the Somerset portions of Exmoor. Meanwhile, Exmoor Forest was formally disafforested during the closing years of the reign of George III, the Crown's portion then being sold. The staghound pack itself was sold in 1825.

The following years brought repeated efforts from various quarters to recommence hunting, but all ended in failure until 1855 when a Mr M. Fenwick Bisset, who lived near Dulverton, formed the Devon and Somerset Staghounds.

During the years of little or no hunting, the deer had dwindled. The indications are that they had not been very numerous for several centuries, especially on the high, mainly open terrain of Exmoor Forest, where they often had to compete for grazing with very large numbers of sheep. Between 1825 and 1855 deer numbers were steadily whittled away from two or three hundred to around sixty due to indiscriminate killing, and they might have disappeared altogether if one landowner had not set aside two vital sanctuary areas for them.

Exmoor people take pride in their claim that the local red deer are the last remaining truly wild stock of the species of indigenous antecedents in the southern half of Britain. There have undoubtedly, however, been introductions or escapes of captive animals over the centuries with resultant infusions of outside blood, but the core stock almost certainly retains a significant residue of the blood of the original wild red deer of these parts.

With staghunting duly re-established, the last four decades of the nineteenth century saw red deer numbers build up to a level which had probably never been equalled since the prehistoric period. They spread well out to the west and south from the moor itself, and translocation of some to the Quantock Hills, farther east, helped the species to become firmly established there.

For a time the Devon and Somerset Staghounds hunted red deer throughout these areas but in 1896 a new pack was formed to hunt the country south of the Taunton–Barnstaple railway. This pack became a casualty of the First World War, after which it was replaced by the Tiverton Staghounds, which still operate. Another new pack, the Quantock Staghounds,

was formed in 1901 to hunt the hills of that name, which it continues to do at the time of writing. In theory, both of these latter packs hunt by leave of the senior pack, the Devon and Somerset, over what still remains part of its own country, permission for them to operate being annually renewed.

Stags are hunted from August until the middle of October, hinds from November to February and spring stags, three to four years old, from mid-March to the end of April.

Following publication in 1997 of the report of an inquiry instigated by the National Trust and headed by Professor Patrick Bateson, Provost of King's College, Cambridge, into the behavioural and physiological effects upon red deer of culling by various methods, including hunting, the National Trust banned the hunting of deer on its properties, which include substantial areas of both Exmoor and the Quantocks. The Forestry Commission has adopted similar measures in respect of land it owns. The effect of all this is to restrict fairly significantly the freedom of the staghound packs concerned to pursue their sport and to place the whole future of staghunting in doubt, quite regardless of any legislative changes that might arise in the future.

Exmoor red deer divide their time between the higher, open moorland and the surrounding woodland areas, with perhaps the majority being present in the woods at any one time. Inevitably their daily movements bring them frequently onto farmland, often in numbers which would be difficult to tolerate almost anywhere outside recognised staghunting country, or so the defenders of hunting maintain. Deer management groups have been formed to try to ensure a sensible balance between the needs of crop protection and the maintenance of satisfactory numbers of red deer not only now but in a future when staghunting may no longer have a role to play in deer management.

White red deer occur occasionally on both Exmoor and the Quantocks. A hind which was more white than otherwise ranged the Quantocks for many years but eventually came to a bad end. I was lucky enough to see it while on a brief visit in the late 1980s. Deer are readily visible here and on Exmoor at most times of the year, their relatively high density in both areas contrasting markedly with their scarcity on the intervening Brendon Hills, where their

White red deer are rare. This one lived on the Quantock Hills in Somerset with others of normal colour for many years and was all white apart from some brown markings on its hindquarters.

of during the First World War. This property is now owned by Bristol City Council and small park herds of both red and fallow deer have been re-established. At Manor Farm, Brockley, near the village of Backwell, a few miles south-west of Bristol, there is a flourishing herd of red deer maintained in confinement as farm stock. The former Cricket St Thomas Wildlife Park, near Chard, included among its exhibits small numbers of deer of several species, some of these being red deer crossed with wapiti.

Deer parks proper in Somerset include Hatch Court at Hatch Beauchamp, south-east of Taunton, and Compton Castle at Compton Pauncefoot, west of Wincanton, both with herds of fallow deer. Combe Sydenham Park, on the Brendon Hills, lost its original red and fallow deer during the Second World War, but was re-enclosed many years later and restocked with wild black fallow deer from the surrounding countryside.

Fallow were present in ancient times in the forests of Selwood, North Petherton and, particularly, Neroche, but apparently not in Exmoor Forest, where red deer always claimed pride of place. The main haunt of wild fallow deer in the county today, as I have already indicated, is the Brendon Hills, where escapes from three different deer parks have created what appear to be two distinct feral populations.

The westernmost of these originates from Dunster Deer Park, which dates from the fifteenth century if not earlier and to which, in the late 1950s, I recall watching fallow deer return after some early-morning trespassing on pastureland outside. If the deer fence was leaky then, at least there were still deer in the park, though probably rather more which had left it with no intention to return. This halfway stage from the deer here being a park herd to becoming a truly wild one belongs now to the past. The deer park area is still visited, but only

occurrence is mainly as stragglers, except on the south side of the range. On a visit there in the mid-1980s in search of fallow, of which more later, I felt I was lucky to see just one red deer in the central part of the area. The scarcity here of red deer means that the Exmoor and Quantock herds are virtually separate populations, with perhaps no more than a tenuous link by travelling stags at the time of the rut.

The Taunton–Exeter railway is about as far as red deer from Exmoor wander south in Somerset with any frequency, although one hears of venturesome wanderers turning up some miles beyond this, where the Blackdown Hills mark the county border with Devon. Elsewhere in present-day Somerset any red deer seen at liberty are likely to be even more venturesome wanderers, or possibly fugitives from some deer farm or other captive situation. Although the former Mendip Forest contained both red and fallow deer, that is a matter of ancient history.

Park herds of red, fallow and axis deer were maintained on the Ashton Court estate, on the western side of Bristol, until these were disposed as just one part of a much larger area over which a free-living population now roams. Its centre is Croydon Hill, a conifer-clad eminence where the Brendon range begins south-east of Dunster, and where on my visit in the mid-1980s I saw the largest number of fallow, most of them black but including a few lighter-coloured animals.

Later that morning, from a hilltop high above Nettlecombe, 4 miles or so south-east along the Brendons from Croydon Hill, I spied another group of fallow in a clearing far below me. A long and strenuous stalk brought me within yards of what turned out to be another bunch of mainly black deer with just a few of the white-rumped common variety. The difference was, however, that these were of stock once enclosed in nearby Nettlecombe Park and Combe Sydenham Park. Although there is no longer a deer park at Nettlecombe, it was pleasing to find at Combe Sydenham the reconstituted park already mentioned, and to see there the once wild fallow which had entered it over a deerleap.

In contrast to the fair numbers of fallow at large in the Brendons area, elsewhere in Somerset they are, for the most part, entirely absent. Apparently before the Second World War there were some in the Quantock woodlands along with the red deer, but not now. Fallow escapees from Hatch Court Park were formerly present in the neighbourhood, but recent refencing now confines the deer more securely in the park.

The chain of woods on the Wiltshire border, where once was the royal forest of Selwood, has been for many years the haunt of a few descendants of fallow escapees from Longleat Park, just inside Wiltshire. These were augmented by escapes over flattened fences after the storms of 1987, and some of this new contingent may well have strayed into Somerset.

The story of roe in Somerset has some interesting features. The species is recorded as having been present alongside red deer in medieval Exmoor Forest but, as elsewhere in southern Britain, they disappeared at an early date. The modern roe derive from Dorset stock which appears to have reached the Somerset border around the turn of the nineteenth century.

Thereafter, further spread was surprisingly slow. The woods of old Selwood Forest were colonised comparatively early and today hold a good roe population, but for a long time the main railway between Frome and Taunton was about the limit of their penetration into Somerset. Farther west, the Blackdown Hills, along the Somerset-Devon border, were another early area to be colonised, and have held good numbers of roe ever since.

The early to mid-1960s marked the beginning of a substantial outward surge, with roe being noticed for the first time in localities such as Asham Wood, west of Frome, and Forestry Commission plantations on the Mendips. From woods on the Polden Hills, farther west, the far less suitable terrain of the Somerset Levels began to be colonised. Roe eventually reached Bristol, where individuals have been seen on many occasions well within the city boundary.

In the countryside near Bristol roe have increased to the point where, to quote the city's

Roe deer were slow to colonise much of Somerset but are now widespread in the county.

Parks Manager, Mark Cox, 'they are coming out of our ears'. He was referring in particular to the parkland at Ashton Court, on Bristol's outskirts, where the enclosed red and fallow deer have had free-ranging roe as neighbours for many years now. There are also some enclosed roe, in an area of woodland where these deer happened to be present when it was deer-fenced fairly recently and where they have continued to flourish despite the loss of their liberty.

At the same time as Bristol was reached by roe, the Avon valley woods near Bath were a hitherto vacant deer habitat waiting for roe to arrive in strength and then push on north into Gloucestershire, both of which have duly happened.

In Somerset roe are now widespread and well established almost everywhere except the far west of the county. Apart from isolated occurrences of wandering individuals, Exmoor, the Brendon Hills and the Quantocks remained roeless for many decades after their arrival in strength might have been anticipated. Commenting on their continuing scarcity in the Brendons in 1976, two researchers studying the deer there, J. E. Jackson and J. Moore, predicted in an article in the British Deer Society's journal *Deer* (Vol. 3, No. 9, pp. 488–91) that within a decade roe would become established in strength, but on my visit ten years later I found the situation largely unaltered from what they had found.

Since then, however, sightings of roe have become more frequent, although colonisation as such has hardly begun. Roe have also at last reached the Quantocks on a regular, breeding basis, although not as yet in any great numbers. Penetration of Exmoor has been similarly slow, but has reached a point where the species can no longer be called rare there. Roe are now sprinkled thinly throughout most of the Exmoor area, while among the moor's southern foothills their numbers are now such as to have encouraged some local farmers to form packs of roehounds, a development which has predictably stimulated critical comment.

The colonisation of red deer country by roe has not been welcomed by people who see it as adding an unacceptable extra burden to that already borne by a farming community whose tolerance of deer damage has sometimes already been stretched to the limit. This pronounced anti-roe sentiment, and the measures taken to express it, may well have been a significant factor in holding back the immigrant tide at least for a time in earlier years, while the pre-existing presence of red or fallow in fairly high densities could, perhaps, also have played a part.

Since around the early 1980s muntjac have been reported from many widely separated localities. Although a number of these reports are based on one-off sightings there are also some places, forestry plantations on the Quantock Hills being among them, where established breeding populations are said to be present. Whether muntjac first arrived in this part of Britain by natural spread or as a result of local releases or escapes, or perhaps by a combination of both, we may never know, but with an abundance of suitable habitat not yet occupied by these newcomers, their future here seems assured.

As its name no doubt suggests, the Bristol Channel island of Steep Holm is hardly ideal muntjac habitat. Four were nevertheless released here in 1977. Thirteen years later their numbers were estimated at twenty to thirty despite more than a few having been killed by falling down the cliffs while seeking seaweed on the shoreline.

A question mark hangs over the current status of sika in Somerset. During the First World War a number escaped from Pixton Park, near Dulverton, and for several decades afterwards their descendants frequented woods in the nearby valley of the Barle, on the slopes of Haddon Hill and elsewhere, but in recent years they seem to have dropped out of notice. There have also been reports of sika escapes from the former Cricket St Thomas Wildlife Park between Crewkerne and Chard, in the south of the county, and the possibility of sika escapees from Melbury Park in west Dorset, and in particular those known to be living wild in the Sherborne area, reaching Somerset cannot be altogether discounted.

At their Shepton Mallet headquarters cider makers Showerings Limited kept a small group of captive Chinese water deer as living counterparts of their Babycham trade logo, but this firm has now ceased trading and the deer have disappeared with them. There are no known Chinese water deer at liberty in Somerset.

Devon and Cornwall

Devon shares with its neighbour Somerset England's best-known ancient herd of wild red deer, the red deer of Exmoor and its environs, and hence the distinction of having been a haunt of wild deer since early times. Whether Cornwall can lay claim to the latter distinction is open to question but, like Devon, it contains well-established populations of deer of more than one species today.

The history of Exmoor red deer is dealt with in some detail in the section on Somerset. In the Devon portion of their distribution range the fortunes of these deer have paralleled those of their Somerset brethren, with declining numbers between 1825 and 1855 followed by recovery with the resumption of staghunting. As the red deer population increased, their range expanded south and west from Exmoor proper. One consequence of this was the formation in 1896 of a new pack, Sir John Amory's Staghounds, to hunt what is known as the 'in-country' south of the Barnstaple–Taunton railway. This pack was a forerunner of the Tiverton Staghounds formed after the First World War to hunt the same area by agreement with the senior pack, the Devon and Somerset, and this arrangement still operates today.

At the beginning of the twentieth century another pack, the Barnstaple Staghounds, came into being to hunt the country west of Exmoor, but this pack had only a brief existence.

For the last hundred years and more, red deer from Exmoor and their descendants have ranged deep into mid-Devon. Their wanderings take them far and wide across the mainly agricultural country separating Exmoor from Dartmoor, with local concentrations in woods such as those along the slopes of the Exe valley and in the valley of the River Yeo, around Eggesford. Good numbers are also usually present in the region between the Rivers Taw and Torridge.

As a boy in 1937 I was on a family holiday with relatives at Lapford when, on the last day of our visit, I chanced to mention a budding interest in the deer of distant Exmoor. I was astonished to be told that one need not go so far to see them, because they were regularly found in the immediate vicinity, and, had my interest been known earlier, I could probably have been shown some. More than forty years were to pass before I saw red deer in that area, or at any rate near Chulmleigh, half a dozen miles from Lapford.

Dartmoor, like Exmoor, was at one time a royal forest with a resident stock of red deer. It seems unlikely that the bleak expanses of the open moor itself were ever much favoured by these animals, particularly in view of the abundant availability of much more attractive habitat in the form of woodlands around its fringes. On Dartmoor's western side especially, the Tamar valley woods near Tavistock offered a stronghold for red deer of which very full advantage was taken.

Eventually, however, local farmers grew tired of the crop damage these animals were causing. The Duke of Bedford, as the principal local landowner, was prevailed upon to bring his staghounds down from Woburn to help mitigate the nuisance. This was done with such effect that, according to some accounts, the deer were exterminated. Other records point to red deer having survived in the area well into the early nineteenth century. One account tells of local farmers once again rallying against them in about 1846 and somehow contriving to drive the entire herd on to the ice of a frozen River Tamar, through which they all fell and were drowned.

Despite assertions to the contrary by various nineteenth-century writers, it seems unlikely that these deer ever entirely disappeared. By the early twentieth century red deer were once again in evidence in the Tamar valley woods, and occasional efforts were made to hunt them.

It has been suggested that these were new arrivals, either as wanderers from Exmoor or escapees from captivity. The only known source of possible red deer escapees in that area is Werrington Park near Launceston in Cornwall which was stocked around 1900 with wild-caught beasts from Inverness-shire. When I visited the park in 1969 the owner, Commander A.M. Williams, told me that the last of his red deer, about a dozen hinds in all, had escaped a few years previously as a consequence of disturbance by work in progress at the time. For forty or more years previously, wild stags had been in the habit of breaking in during the rut, and this ceased a couple of seasons or so after the hinds had taken themselves off.

While park red deer from Werrington have, therefore, undoubtedly contributed to the stock

Devon red deer stags in summer velvet.

it may previously have produced heads of up to twenty-four points.

Their reputation for first-class trophies has made these red deer from the far south-west highly vulnerable to unscrupulous trophy-hunters, resulting in over-exploitation which can only impoverish the stock and perhaps endanger its long-term survival. It surely behoves all responsible stalkers to exercise maximum restraint when operating in this area.

As well as the areas so far mentioned, red deer have been present, both in the past and more recently, south of Dartmoor in the Dart valley woods near Buckfastleigh. Forestry plantations on the moor itself, at Fernworthy in particular, have also encouraged red deer to resume their ancient status as wild denizens of Dartmoor.

In a more westerly direction, Tamar valley woodland red deer occur, as might be expected, on both sides of the Cornish border. Farther west still, there is a long but perhaps not entirely unexpected history of a red deer presence deep into Cornwall. Woods along the Glyn valley west of Liskeard and around Bodmin, as well as in the Camel valley towards Wadebridge, have had a fairly small and elusive but none the less resident population of red deer for many years, and some have even turned up as far west as the Lizard Peninsula. These are generally supposed not to be of indigenous local stock but their origin, if they are alien to the area, is uncertain.

Over and above all these, wandering red deer may turn up from time to time almost anywhere in Cornwall as well as in Devon. So far as Cornwall is concerned, the only wild deer I have personally seen are fallow of a herd once enclosed in Mount Edgcumbe Park, which now range the Rame Peninsula and other surrounding areas to the west of Plymouth Sound. The deer I saw were all of the common type.

Other Cornish deer parks include Tregothnan, adjoining the Fal estuary south of Truro,

currently at large along the Devon-Cornwall border, these may well have done no more than add to a pre-existing population. The present distribution of red deer in this part of the West Country extends well north of the Tavistock area through the Lydford woods and for a good many miles beyond, to the forestry plantations around Halwill, between Okehampton and Holsworthy. It was in a dense and dim grove of sitka spruce in the latter area that I once enjoyed a close-up view of two of the largest wild red deer stags it has ever been my good fortune to see, typical products of this part of west Devon.

The exceptional quality of these red deer is exemplified by the story of the famous Endsleigh stag. Hardly ever seen in the flesh, this monster roamed the Tamar valley woods for several years, leaving tell-tale evidence of his presence in the form of massive cast antlers and slot impressions plainly indicative of a beast of quite outstanding size and weight. When it met its end in 1950 after breaking a leg when trying to join some captive hinds brought down from Woburn for the purpose of trying to lure it into captivity as breeding stock for the park there, it was acclaimed as an all-time record wild British red stag. By then a twenty-pointer and a trifle past its best, cast antler evidence suggested that

Prideaux Place, near Padstow, and Boconnoc, near Lostwithiel, all of which I have visited at one time or another. All still contain herds of fallow, plus a flourishing feral population in nearby woods in the case of Tregothnan and a smaller one in the neighbourhood of Boconnoc Park, where the deer are of the light-spotted, menil variety. Any deer that escape from Prideaux Place Park find themselves in a countryside largely devoid of woodland and thus unsuitable for the establishment of a feral population. I found the situation very different at Werrington, where a very wild herd of mainly black park fallow was complemented at the time of my visit by a small unenclosed population of escapees in the vicinity. I understand that the entire fallow population there is now feral and free-ranging. One or two other Cornish deer parks existed in the fairly recent past but their deer have disappeared with them. The Tamar Otter Park and Wild Wood at North Petherwin, near Launceston, is not a deer park as such but has included a few deer of several species among its exhibits in recent years.

Devon today has three main populations of wild fallow, all of which are of modern origin. The Haldon Hills, south-west of Exeter, are mantled by forestry plantations which are home to a fairly substantial herd. These are not, as one might imagine, in any way connected with the large and old-established herd of fallow in Powderham Park, at nearby Kenton, or at least so it has been said, but originated as escapees from Ugbrooke Park, which no longer holds deer. This is supported by the fact that, whereas the Powderham fallow are of mixed colours, those on the Haldon Hills, or at any rate all those I have personally seen, are black. Whiddon Park, near Chagford, has also been a haunt of black fallow and of escapees which have established a wild herd in the Teign valley woods, especially between Steps Bridge and Fingle Bridge. However, the fallow I have seen here have been common rather than black, albeit presumably derived from Whiddon Park stock.

Plym Forest, south-west of Dartmoor, has a flourishing population of almost exclusively common-type fallow descended from animals which escaped around the time of the Second World War from nearby Newnham Park and Blachford Park. When I first saw them I was told by the forest ranger who showed me around that

a local peculiarity was a tendency to grow a long back point from the palm of the left antler. Another was a weakness in the structure of the coronets resulting in frequent antler fracture. The River Meavy froze over during the 1963 winter, which tempted fallow to cross it for the first time, facilitating an extension of their range to the west of the river.

Other Devon areas where wild fallow have been reported include the woods north-west of Exeter, due south of Newton St Cyres, but when I visited the area in 1971 I found no trace of fallow and noted the slots of roe deer only. There have also been reports of park-escaped fallow in various parts of east Devon between Exeter and the Dorset border. Sidbury Park, near Sidmouth, has been suggested as one source, but no substantial population appears to have become established. Between the wars there were also fallow in north-west Devon near Clovelly, but these do not seem to have persisted.

If roe reached Devon from Dorset in the early years of the twentieth century they were slow to spread much further. The late Mr H.B. Salter, a Devon farmer who was also a deer enthusiast, told me how the first wandering roe had arrived

One of a herd of Formosan sika owned by John Willett at his home at Hockworthy, on the Devon-Somerset border; this stag is in summer pelage.

The position now is that roe are well established far beyond Exeter. The Haldon Hills fallow now share ground with them and they have spread north and south of Dartmoor to reach the River Tamar. On Dartmoor itself they are now sufficiently numerous in the Forestry Commission's Bellever Plantation, north-east of Princetown, to require regular culling. Halwill Forest and the whole area to the south and west of Exmoor has now been colonised by roe, and encounters with them on Exmoor itself are by no means uncommon. They are indeed present now throughout Devon wherever the habitat is suitable except, so far, in the South Hams, the most southerly part of the county, where they are still relatively rare.

As well as Formosan sika, John Willett keeps a small herd of hog deer at Hockworthy, on the Devon-Somerset border where he lives. Here he is feeding a hog deer buck in his deer enclosure.

By the early 1980s roe had gained a footing in Cornwall, through which the advance guard has since pressed on to the Bodmin area and still further. They are by no means unfamiliar as far west as Truro and near Newquay. Some have reached the Lizard Peninsula near which, in the late 1990s, a swimming roebuck was rescued from the sea by a local fisherman. Land's End is well within their reach now, and it is probably safe to say that there is not a woodland area in any part of Cornwall where they have not yet materialised as visitors, if not residents.

in the Ashclyst Forest area north-east of Exeter, where he lived, at some time in the 1920s. It was not until about 1930, he said, that they became established on a permanent basis, although within seven years the National Trust decided there was a need to instigate deer control on its property locally.

My first view of Devon roe was in woods at Offwell, near Honiton, in 1955, where by that time they were well established. A dawn foray in Ashclyst Forest sixteen years later revealed that the roe there were abundant to a degree which might surely stimulate further migration to the west.

By the early 1950s the Taunton–Exeter railway and the estuary of the Exe appeared to mark the westerly limit of penetration by roe into Devon. Once these obstacles, if such they were to some small extent, had been surmounted, a considerable surge forward soon gained momentum. In 1975 I noted the hoofprints of roe as well as red deer in woods at Lapford in mid-Devon, while some years previous to this I had identified hoofmarks of roe in Abbeyford Wood, just outside Okehampton.

Wild Japanese sika on Lundy, where they live on the eastern sidelands overlooking the Bristol Channel.

Japanese sika escapees from Pixton Park, on the Somerset border close to Dulverton, were present for some years after the First World War in the countryside around, including a corner of north-east Devon, but they do not appear to have maintained themselves as part of the local fauna. Much more recently a number of Manchurian sika escaped from an enclosure in the grounds of a hotel at Chittlehamholt, in the Taw valley south-east of Barnstaple. Efforts were made to eliminate them in order to minimise the risk of their hybridising with the local red deer, but in 1998 a few of them were still at large in the area. There have been reports of feral sika in other parts of Devon and Cornwall, and if they are accurate the deer concerned could have gained their freedom in a similar manner to those at Chittlehamholt, from captive stocks the existence of which has not been generally known. At Hockworthy, on the Somerset border west of Wellington, Mr J.A. Willett, a past chairman of the British Deer Society, maintains a small captive breeding stock of Formosan sika, thought now to be extinct in the wild in their native Taiwan, and hog deer, another Asian species, as well as a few muntjac and Chinese water deer.

A high seat used for deer control on the Cornish side of the River Tamar, where red and roe deer both now occur.

The occurrence of feral muntjac so far south-west may come as something of a surprise, but their presence has been reported from a number of places in Devon, especially in the east of the county and south of Exeter, west of the Exe. Perhaps the latter are descended from some that were said to have escaped in the Starcross area decades ago, but whose subsequent fate has not been charted. Perhaps most unexpected of all is the odd report of muntjac in Cornwall, so far-removed from any known stronghold of the species in the wild that, if correct, it must surely stem from a local release or perhaps an escape. There may indeed have been several such releases or escapes in various parts of south-west England over the last fifty years or so, so widely scattered are the localities where these deer have been reported.

There were deer, probably fallow, on the Bristol Channel island of Lundy in the eighteenth and early nineteenth centuries, after which apparently they died out. In about 1929 Mr Martin Coles Harman, the owner, introduced red deer, fallow and sika. After some initial problems the red deer flourished and increased to a pre-war population of over a hundred. Numbers later declined. The remaining deer became too tame for their own good and after two pugnacious stags attacked a girl, who was lucky to escape without serious injury or worse, red deer on Lundy were done away with.

Fallow presented no such difficulties but were never really successful. They tended to hang around the vicinity of the owner's home, Millcombe House, which is now an hotel, and the last survivor, a solitary doe, was dead by 1954.

The fallow and sika both came from Surrenden Dering Park in Kent. The sika survive, secreting themselves by day among rhododendrons and tall bracken along the eastern slopes of the island, from which they emerge to graze in the early and late hours. At one stage these deer increased to about eighty, but the policy of the Landmark Trust, the island's present owners, is to maintain a much smaller herd. They are therefore periodically culled, and at the time of my last visit had been reduced a short time previously to around seventeen from something like double that number. Not surprisingly perhaps, I found these sika by no means tame, ever ready to fluff out their white rear ends and race for cover on being disturbed.

Gloucestershire

Gloucestershire lies at the crossroads between the Midlands and the south and between England itself and south Wales, and this position is reflected in the composition of its wild deer populations. Overall it is well supplied with deer, one species being numerous and widely if discontinuously distributed, two others increasing year by year and extending their range at the same time, and a fourth present in small numbers in one locality at least.

The latter is the red deer, anciently present as royal game and therefore a beast of the first importance in many Crown forests throughout England, among them the Forest of Dean in west Gloucestershire. Dean Forest is one of a small minority which have survived with only a modest reduction in size from Norman times to the present day. There is good documentary evidence that red deer were present in

Present in ancient times along with wild boar and wolves in the Forest of Dean, wild red deer are rarely encountered in present-day Gloucestershire but have a long local history as park animals.

substantial numbers here until at least the thirteenth century, when boar and wolf were also still members of the forest's fauna.

Records suggest that a fairly rapid decline then set in, and that within a hundred years or so red deer had become extinct, their place having largely been taken by fallow. This state of affairs remained unaltered, apart from a brief attempted revival of red deer at a surprisingly late date, the 1840s, by which time the Forest of Dean's history as a royal hunting preserve, at least in name, was almost at an end. In 1842 half a dozen red deer from Woburn were released in the obvious hope that they would breed and re-establish the species locally. This was not to be, however, for a combination of premature hunting, poaching and a persistent tendency by the deer to stray outside the bounds of the forest soon brought the experiment to a close.

Midway between the cities of Gloucester and Bristol is Berkeley (Whitcliffe) Park, which dates back to the Middle Ages and is one of England's oldest deer parks. A high surrounding wall was at one stage claimed to be deer-proof, but some years ago a stalker who was involved with deer management there at the time told me that some of the red deer had found their way out and were surviving in open country within sight of their old home. I learned from the owner, Major R.J.G. Berkeley that some red deer as well as fallow still survived outside the park in 1998 and that both species also thrive within it.

Now in Gloucestershire once again, after more than two decades of exile in the now-defunct county of Avon, is the Duke of Beaufort's park at Badminton which, like the park at Berkeley, has a long history as a haunt of both red and fallow deer, in this case dating from Cromwell's time. I hear, however, that fallow are no longer kept at Badminton, although the red deer herd remains. Any red deer which may have escaped at one time or another have never managed to establish a wild population in the neighbourhood.

C1 *A mature New Forest red deer stag on his rutting stand.*

C2 *A mature New Forest red deer stag of good quality. (Peter Robyns)*

C3 *A fifteen-pointer red deer stag of Warnham Court Park descent with one of his hinds in the New Forest at the start of the annual rut. (Steve Smith)*

C4 *Photographed in September 1999, this magnificent Warnham Park red stag, a twenty-seven-pointer, with its symmetric head of antlers typifies what has made the West Sussex deer park world famous as a source of high-quality breeding stock. (Jonathan Lucas)*

C5 *Another New Forest red stag of stock introduced from Warnham Court Park in 1960. (Steve Smith)*

C6 *A red deer hind, like the one in this picture, may weigh no more than half as much as a stag of similar age. (Peter Robyns)*

C7 *A keen eye is needed to spot roe deer in thick cover before they are alerted to human proximity. This doe was photographed in north Hampshire. (Peter Robyns)*

C9 BELOW: *The dappled pelage of infancy helps to camouflage newly born roe deer kids and protect them from predation. (Peter Robyns)*

C8 ABOVE: *A roe doe photographed in September when still in summer pelage. (Peter Robyns)*

C10 *Selective breeding and prime conditions of feeding and habitat can produce fallow bucks with heavy, broad-palmed antlers like this park-bred specimen. (Peter Robyns)*

C11 *A New Forest fallow buck of the common variety in dappled summer pelage. (Steve Smith)*

C12 *A fallow buck in summer pelage with antlers in velvet. (Steve Smith)*

C13 ABOVE: *One distinguishing feature of fallow deer is a relatively long and conspicuous tail. (Peter Robyns)*

C14 RIGHT: *A New Forest fallow buck with well-developed antlers in late summer velvet. (Steve Smith)*

C15 *Fallow deer are gregarious and normally consort in sexually separated groupings of mature and maturing bucks and of does with their followers, most of these being their fawns of the year. Wild fallow like these New Forest bucks will sometimes feed well away from cover. (Peter Robyns)*

C16 LEFT: *A damaged pedicle can result in a badly deformed or absent antler on one side, as was the case with this fallow buck.*

C17 ABOVE: *A mature New Forest sika stag in typically dark winter pelage. (Steve Smith)*

C18 *Common-type fallow and sika both have dappled flanks when in summer pelage and where both occur on the same ground, as in the part of the New Forest where this picture was taken, care needs to be taken when deciding which is which! (Steve Smith)*

C19 *A New Forest sika stag in typically dark winter pelage. (Steve Smith)*

C20 *New Forest sika deer in their dappled summer pelage. (Steve Smith)*

Fallow remain the most common wild deer in Gloucestershire, although two other species are catching up and may well overtake them in the fairly near future. Most of the fallow at large today owe their existence in the wild state to escapes from deer parks during the course of the twentieth century, but the Forest of Dean and surrounding area is one of the relatively few localities where fallow may have been continuously wild since medieval times. As I have said, from about six hundred years ago fallow were the predominant, and for much of that long period the only, deer species in the forest.

It seems likely that fallow have always been subjected to a greater degree of harassment in this forest than in some others, thanks to a long-standing predilection for venison trespass by some local miners. In early Victorian times this became so bad that it was decided to do away with the deer once and for all, in 1849, and six years after the baby had thus been thrown out with the bathwater it was reported that no deer at all remained in the forest itself and only a few in the neighbouring Highmeadow Woods, at that time outside forest jurisdiction.

Flanked on three sides by the River Wye, with Monmouth just beyond this to the west and the Forest of Dean to the east, Highmeadow Woods are hilly and extensive. They hold fallow deer today which, on a visit some years ago, I was told numbered over a hundred and were thought to be descended from the original forest fallow. Whether some of their forebears had always roamed free since early times was not quite certain, an alternative possibility being that they reclaimed their old wild status after an interval in a deer park.

Wyastone Leys, the park in question, lies just north of the Wye in the county of Hereford and Worcester and, at the time of my visit locally, was said to have lost all its deer. Many of these were roaming wild in woods on both sides of the river, having undoubtedly reinforced, or perhaps initially re-established, the Highmeadow herd. These Highmeadow fallow were almost all of the common variety, although there was one black individual, which chanced to be one of the several deer I saw while being shown around by the forest ranger, the late Edgar Gwilliam.

After a century's absence, the Forest of Dean itself regained a wild fallow deer population a few years after the Second World War when a number of black deer turned up in the heart of it, apparently from nowhere. It was later decided that these had probably come from Courtfield Park, Lower Lydbrook, on the north side of the forest, which had apparently lost all its deer, some having been shot while others escaped, and which had certainly had black fallow.

Today the Forest of Dean and its immediate environs still hold two main herds of completely wild fallow. Living only a very short distance apart, as these do, there is some inter-communication. At the time of my visit the otherwise all-black central forest herd of some forty individuals included four or five common-type fallow, probably thanks to the roving spirit and enterprise of some Highmeadow buck or bucks.

Generally, however, the two herds were said not only to lead separate lives but to be distinct in other ways besides their colour. Despite a fairly high incidence of liverfluke, thought to be due to having to share much of their range with sheep turned out by commoners to graze on the open forest, the central forest black fallow were significantly heavier on average than their Highmeadow neighbours, with proportionately bigger antlers. The peak of their rut also tended to be about a week earlier than that of the Highmeadow herd.

My only view of these super-fallow was in the forest's heart not far north of the Speech House, where most of the does were concentrated, whereas the bucks wandered more widely, turning up sometimes as far east as Cinderford and even as far as Blakeney on the River Severn. I gather from Eric Pritchard, a forest ranger of long experience, however, that the Speech House fallow, as the central herd used to be called, are now more widely dispersed in general, and that the central herd and the Highmeadow one now both consist of black and common fallow in about equal proportions, suggesting a greater degree of intercommunication than formerly.

The Highmeadow deer have shown a tendency to spread south from their main haunt, exposing themselves in the process to hostility and punitive countermeasures by local farmers, and for this reason Forest Enterprise has stepped up the cull on its own ground in order to minimise crop depredations by straying animals.

South of the Forest of Dean is Lydney Park, from which fallow have sometimes escaped to create the nucleus of a third wild population in the forest and elsewhere in the park's neighbourhood, while west of the Wye, in Gwent, other fallow are at large, which must sometimes try their luck in Gloucestershire. East of the forest, beyond Cinderford, fallow turned up in the 1960s from no one knows quite where in woods near Newent. Could these have been a venturesome offshoot from the central Forest of Dean herd? It would be interesting to know.

Across the Severn, the Cotswold Hills hold several populations of fallow, some quite old-established – albeit derived from park escapees – and of considerable size. Arguably the largest is that which is thought to stem from former deer parks at Colesbourne and Rendcomb, south of Cheltenham. Road signs on the main road between Cirencester and Cheltenham warn of their presence in bordering woodlands, but Withington Woods and Chedworth Woods, a little way farther east, are probably their principal haunts.

These extensive woodlands bracket the course of the former Swindon–Cheltenham railway, the crossing of which was facilitated by a tunnel. When I first explored the area in the late 1950s fallow were plentiful on both sides of the line, and those I saw in the two woods were a mixture of the common and black varieties.

The same applies to descendants of fallow which escaped from Cirencester Park during the

First World War and which have roamed adjacent woodlands ever since, surviving persistent attempts in times past to eradicate them. When I wrote enquiring about the status of these deer in the 1950s I received a reply from the Dowager Countess Bathurst to the effect that she was perhaps their only friend. Visiting the area many years later, I found all the signs of a healthy, well-established population living on both sides of the Swindon–Gloucester railway, which they regularly crossed using one of the bridges, as slot-mark evidence there made clear. This was interesting in view of the extent to which railways in general tend to restrict the range of wild fallow and, indeed, of red and sika deer where no such easy means of crossing is discovered by the animals.

Wild fallow from these sources and others have spilt over into woodlands on the west side of the Cotswolds. Others farther south may include some which escaped in the past from Badminton Park, or their descendants, where these may not have been mopped up by appropriate measures within a short time of gaining their freedom. Dyrham Park, not far north of Bath, which is owned by the National Trust, has been a fallow deer haunt for centuries and in recent times fallow escapees have sometimes been noted in the neighbourhood.

East of Cheltenham, Leckhampton Park was one of the few in England to have had an all-white herd of fallow. Escapes from there contributed further to the wild fallow population of Gloucestershire, but the park herd has been disbanded. Farther east still, on the Oxford-shire border west of Burford, Barrington Park's fallow were able, for many years, to pass in or out of the park almost at will, with a sizeable proportion of the mainly common-coloured herd almost always at liberty in local woodlands. On a visit there some years ago I found abundant signs of these deer in the open countryside

---

Wild fallow deer occur in the Forest of Dean and in many other parts of Gloucestershire.

and I understand that there are still deer in the park as well as outside it.

At Batsford Park, near Moreton-in-Marsh, the late Lord Dulverton, during his term of office as president of the British Deer Society, established a new deer park containing both red and fallow deer. This is enclosed by a 12 ft fence and up to 1999 no deer had managed to escape.

While roe deer are fairly recent arrivals on the scene as a resident species, as far back as the early to mid-1960s there were reports of isolated individuals in the Cotswolds. This followed centuries of absence since the indigenous stock died out some time in the Middle Ages. One of their last haunts was almost certainly the Forest of Dean, where at one stage they shared ground with both red and fallow.

The last three decades of the twentieth century saw a significant expansion of range by roe pushing up from the south. They have colonised the southern Cotswolds in strength. Well before the end of the 1980s they reached the Cirencester area, where they are now well established, and the advance guard has pushed on north to link up with others already resident in the Moreton-in-Marsh area.

Having settled in well after being locally released, these north Gloucestershire roe have spread many miles from their point of enlargement, the focal point of their range being woods near Batsford, where I saw them several times when they were still an isolated population. In combination with the colonising roe mainstream from the south, they are likely to prove the forerunners of a general colonisation by roe of the west and central Midlands wherever suitable habitat presents itself, and which is already receiving support from other quarters.

There were rumours of roe in the Forest of Dean as long ago as the 1960s but these were not then substantiated. In forestry circles there was indeed a strong body of opinion that incursions by roe were not desirable; planting policy there had at least partly been determined by their absence, and they were likely to cause unacceptable damage to vulnerable tree species like western red cedar. At the century's end there was still no resident breeding population, but individual wandering roe have continued to appear from time to time before the advance of mainstream roe takes them across the lower Severn to begin a full-scale invasion of west Gloucestershire and south Wales.

At the same time as roe have gained a sure footing for further expansion, muntjac have quietly infiltrated Gloucestershire from other directions. Warwickshire seems likely to have been one source of early arrivals, while others have pushed in from the east.

As long ago as 1958 I identified muntjac slots in Withington Woods, apparently the first record of the species in this county. During subsequent years widely scattered individual sightings were increasingly reported, Chedworth Woods being one locality where they became fairly frequent from the mid-1960s onward. Twenty years later I found plentiful signs of the species while looking for roe in woods near Batsford, a little way west of Moreton-in-Marsh.

Since that time muntjac have been reported from many areas of east Gloucestershire, which they are clearly now in the process of colonising to a point where they will soon become resident in most woodlands. Isolated individuals have been reported west of the Severn, including the Forest of Dean area, and once they become established on that side of the river there will be nothing to stop them from an eventual full-scale invasion of south Wales.

There have also been isolated occurrences of wandering red deer in the Forest of Dean in recent years. Where these have come from is unknown, for there are no deer farms in the area which might have been a source of escapees, and there is no deer park containing red deer nearer than Eastnor Castle Park, near Ledbury in Herefordshire. A deer farm with red deer near Tetbury, close to the county's eastern border, can be ruled out as a possible source. A marginally more likely source, perhaps, is the small feral herd in the Berkeley area, just east of the Severn, which I have already referred to. Red deer are strong swimmers and the Severn estuary would be well within the capability of any individual that might decide to make the crossing.

If there are any wild sika in Gloucestershire their presence appears to have escaped notice. At one time some were present in Barrington Park, on the Oxfordshire border, alongside the local fallow, but on my visit to that area I failed to find any evidence that they still survived there.

5

THE DEER OF THE WEST AND NORTH MIDLANDS, CHESHIRE AND GREATER MANCHESTER

Warwickshire, the West Midlands and the Welsh Marches

Except where the Cotswolds stride across its eastern fringes, Warwickshire is mainly a rather flat west Midland county, not very well endowed with woodland or, therefore, with habitat for wild deer. By contrast, the Welsh border counties immediately to the west of it are hilly, much of their area until the late Middle Ages having been blanketed by forest, sizeable remnants of which remain in which substantial numbers of deer are still to be found even now.

Warwickshire, on closer inspection, proves to have more deer living and flourishing in freedom than the character of its countryside might suggest, mostly thanks to the number of deer parks scattered about it in times past and to a much lesser extent today, from which these animals have escaped. Leaky deer parks, past and present, are largely responsible as well for deer populations currently present in the county of Hereford and Worcester and also in Shropshire, although there is a possibility that at least some of these feral deer derive from stock which has been wild and unenclosed for a fairly long period.

The indigenous wild red deer of the Forest of Dean in Gloucestershire became extinct in the fourteenth century. Prior to that they not infrequently found their way into southern Herefordshire, where an episcopal hunting ground, Penyard Chase, sometimes gave shelter to these visitors. A dispute arose on one occasion as to whether a stag hunted in Herefordshire had been illegally chased by hounds from the royal forest and was not first found in Penyard Chase, as claimed, but the matter was settled in favour of the chase having been its actual point of origin.

As a corruption of 'Wyre-cester', the name of Worcester recalls that this was once a Roman outpost in the heart of a vast woodland tract,

Some of the red deer in Warwickshire's Charlecote Park, where Shakespeare is supposed to have been caught poaching.

Wyre Forest, the shrunken remnants of which still bracket the county's boundary with Shropshire, north-west of Bewdley. The Wyre Forest of Saxon times was split up by the Normans, who redesignated parts of it as Ombersley Forest, north of Worcester, Horewell Forest, south of the city, and Feckenham Forest to the east, extending a little way into Warwickshire. There was also, at one stage, a royal forest of Malvern, but this passed into private hands and became known as Malvern Chase. In medieval Shropshire were the forests of Clee and Clun as well as a portion of Wyre Forest, and it shared with neighbouring Staffordshire the old royal forests of Morf and Brewood.

Most, if not all, of these forests were at one time stocked with red deer, but they died out at an early date. The species survived in various parks or, in some cases, was reintroduced after a fairly lengthy absence. Some escapes have inevitably occurred, Eastnor Castle Park, near Ledbury in Hereford and Worcester, having been a source of some of these fugitives. Charlecote Park, in Warwickshire, contains both red and fallow deer, but it is better known for the legend that Shakespeare poached deer from it than for having added red deer to the wild fauna of its neighbourhood.

Deer farms in Britain mostly stock red deer and I hear that one in Warwickshire has lost some animals of this species, so any red deer found wild in the county are likely to have come from there or from some other similar source. However, another source of occasional red deer wanderers into Warwickshire has been the herd on Cannock Chase in Staffordshire, stragglers from which have been known to make their presence felt in suburban gardens close to Birmingham and even, very exceptionally, farther south still.

Fallow are by far the most numerous wild deer in these counties. Some of those in Warwickshire may descend from captive herds such as those formerly present in Stanford House Park, which all escaped during the Second World War. However most stem from stock once enclosed in Ettington Park, 5 miles or so south-east of Stratford-upon-Avon, from which escapes on a significant scale also date from the Second World War, when the park was used as a camp for prisoners of war. Although no longer maintained for deer, Ettington Park quite often plays host to fallow which happen to wander in from the countryside around. Their range extends from near Stratford to the Cotswolds east of Shipston-on-Stour, where I have seen them on Brailes Hill, a prominent feature of the local landscape.

Despite the absence of large woods on much of the ground over which they roam these deer flourish under the watchful eye of local property owners and others, who some years ago formed an Ettington Deer Group to oversee their welfare and management. Antler quality is excellent and colours are varied. Most of those I have seen in the Knavenhill area, west of Ettington, in particular, have been black, but there are also fair numbers of white individuals. A rising incidence of deer casualties persuaded the local deer group to sponsor the installation of reflective roadside mirrors to deter deer from crossing busy highways when traffic is approaching with headlights on at dawn and dusk and during the hours of darkness.

Alscot Park, near Stratford, has sometimes lost fallow which have joined up with the feral Ettington herd. Charlecote Park, near Warwick, has also lost occasional fallow which may have teamed up with their Ettington neighbours. Packington Hall Park, near Coventry, has an all-black herd which have mostly been successfully contained within park fences, and the same may be said of the menil herd at Shuckburgh Park, near Daventry. Warwick Castle Park, and Umberslade Park, at Hockley Heath, not many miles south of Birmingham, are among a number of parks in the county which have held deer in the past but do so no longer. Another is Ragley Park, near Alcester, which lost its deer between the two world wars, although some fallow remained at large thereabouts in the late 1940s and subsequently, frequenting remnants of what is still poetically known as the Forest of Arden. (No royal link has been proved, so perhaps this was never a proper forest.)

Of the two former shires which now form the county of Hereford and Worcester, Herefordshire perhaps has the edge as regards the numbers of its wild fallow. In the south, the River Wye is not infrequently crossed by deer which have their headquarters in the Highmeadow Woods, just across the border in Gloucestershire. Probably these are at least partly of ancient origin as wild

One of the long-haired fallow deer which are apparently unique to Mortimer Forest on the Shropshire-Herefordshire border.

animals, but with an admixture of blood from stock once contained in Wyastone Leys Park, on the river's Herefordshire side. Courtfield Park, near Ross-on-Wye, is thought to have links with the Forest of Dean as the place from which black fallow deer in the forest originally came.

Kentchurch Park, about 10 miles south-west of Hereford, has an old-established herd of fallow, many of which escaped in the early years of the twentieth century and whose descendants still roam widely. Moccas Park, west of Hereford, is thought to be responsible for at least some of the fallow now found wild in the Golden Valley, although Kentchurch deer seem almost as likely to have strayed in that direction. Escaped fallow from Garnstone Park, near Weobley, were the forebears of wild deer now present in the country around Wormsley, north-west of Hereford, while the Dinsmore Woods, between Hereford and Leominster, are populated by fallow from another park, Hampton Court. Both of these parks no longer hold deer, which is also the case at Ledbury Park, from which fallow sometimes escaped into the neighbouring countryside. The extensive Haugh Wood, south-east of Hereford, is another haunt of wild fallow, while still others have escaped in the past from Brampton Bryan Park, in the north-west of the county.

The forests of medieval Worcestershire must have been well populated with fallow, but as time went by these animals died out everywhere outside deer parks. Of these, Spetchley Park, near Worcester, contains red deer as well as fallow, but no large-scale escapes by either have been noted. Elmley Castle Park, near Pershore, has however lost all its fallow, with descendants of those it once contained now roaming wild over adjacent Bredon Hill.

South-east of Stourbridge, close to the West Midlands county border, is Hagley Park, which lost its entire herd of fallow quite early in the Second World War. After roaming the surrounding hills and woods for half a century, the bulk of this fallow population has been lured back into the park and a flourishing captive herd re-established, while others remain at large.

The county of Hereford and Worcester shares with Shropshire the fallow deer of modern Wyre Forest, north-west of Bewdley. These descend from fallow which escaped in 1887 from nearby Mawley Hall Park to repopulate a forest which had lost its original fallow at some unknown earlier date. When I called there in the mid-1960s, the local Forestry Commission ranger, Edwin George, BEM, informed me that, as a young man, he could remember being told by elderly local people that deer were definitely absent from Wyre Forest in their own younger days. They are now well established, not only in the forest but in suitable countryside around it. Most of the Wyre Forest fallow I saw were black, and I understand that a high proportion of the herd is of this colour. Antler quality is excellent. Bucks tend to frequent the periphery of the herd's range, exposing themselves to random culling by unscrupulous individuals, although efforts are made to curb this.

Just outside Wyre Forest, at Bewdley, is the West Midland Safari and Leisure Park, which in 1999 exhibited six deer species among a wide range of mammals on display to visitors between March and October annually. Around a dozen each of red deer, wapiti and Père David's deer are complemented by a score of fallow and Formosan sika and about thirty Japanese sika. The two types of sika are kept separate to prevent cross-breeding, and this is also the case with the wapiti and red deer.

Straddling the county border west of Ludlow is Mortimer Forest, a modern creation which takes its name from a powerful local family of times long past. This is one area where fallow may have had an unbroken history as wild animals since medieval times, although undoubtedly there has been some reinforcement by park escapees. Within this Mortimer Forest complex lies Bringewood Chase, where Henry VIII is said to have hunted. When I saw deer there in the 1970s it was pleasing to reflect that they may have been direct descendants of beasts that gave sport to the Tudor monarch and which belonged to a line whose members have, perhaps, roamed wild throughout the centuries.

A remarkable feature of these Mortimer Forest fallow is the spectacularly long hair grown by many of them. Their back and flank pelage has an unkempt, 'hearthrug' appearance, and their typically long fallow tails are made to look even longer by the hair length at their tips. The eyes of these long-haired fallow peer out from under a shaggy forelock and, perhaps most bizarrely of all, grotesquely long ear hairs dangle and quiver every time they turn their heads. Anyone who may be tempted to categorise these cervine curiosities with such candidates for total incredulity as the yeti or the Loch Ness monster are advised to visit Mortimer Forest and see for themselves at the first opportunity!

Between a quarter and one-third of the entire fallow population there is of this type, and a further proportion are intermediate between long-haired and normal fallow. Culling deals more lightly with long-haired fallow than with the others to help secure their preservation. As regards colour, in this fallow herd, the common, white-rumped variety predominates while about 40 per cent are black, and the long-haired deer seem to have no bias towards one colour type or the other. Antler quality is not outstanding, and client stalkers play a part in helping to weed out the poorest specimens.

Fallow in woods at the western extremity of the Mortimer Forest complex and to the south of Bishop's Castle are thought to stem from the Brampton Bryan Park escapees already mentioned. Elsewhere in Shropshire, Longnor Hall Park, north of Church Stretton, Loton Park, west of Shrewsbury, and Attingham Park, to the east of that town, have all contributed to the wild fallow population of the county, and all three still contain herds of these deer. Among other haunts of wild fallow in Shropshire are the wooded slopes of that well-known hill, The Wrekin, and fallow have recently shown signs of spreading south along Wenlock Edge. Chetwynd Park, near Newport, is another in Shropshire which still holds fallow, and escapees from Aqualate Park and Weston Park, which lie just over the border in Staffordshire, may sometimes wander into Shropshire. Henley Park, near Ludlow, formerly held both red and fallow deer, but these were given up in the 1960s.

A small number of fallow are included among the exhibits at Birmingham Nature Centre, at Pershore Road in Birmingham.

Until recently it was widely assumed that roe deer were absent from the Midlands and the Welsh Marches, as indeed they were until well into the second half of the twentieth century, but

Roe deer are now present in some parts of Warwickshire and the Welsh Marches.

this is no longer the case. There now appear to be three separate populations, two having originated within the region discussed in this chapter and the other having spread from just outside it.

Norman Dewhurst, a past vice-chairman of the British Deer Society who lives at Stratford-upon-Avon and who keeps a close eye on the deer of that neighbourhood, informs me that in the late 1980s or early 1990s odd roe began to appear in fallow deer country near Ettington, in south Warwickshire. A study of the map suggests that these are most likely to have spread to that area from north Gloucestershire, where a population established some years previously near Moreton-in-Marsh is in the process of extending its range in various directions.

Roe also reported from near Alcester may be from the same source or from the Henley-in-Arden area, where I understand a local release has helped to restore these deer in some numbers to parts of the so-called Forest of Arden which, like this corner of England in general, has been without roe for many centuries.

The Wigmore area of Mortimer Forest, near where Hereford and Worcester and Shropshire meet, is the focal point of another isolated roe population which, my diary reminds me, already existed in 1970 and has since consolidated its hold on a tract of country that had been roeless since at least the late Middle Ages. As with fallow in the same area, antler quality is poor, which does not discourage client stalkers from assisting with the cull carried out by local forest rangers. These roe are colonising new ground, and there are already a small number in Wyre Forest. A few roe are also present in the Hockley Heath area, a few miles south of Birmingham, but it seems most likely that these have spread there as an offshoot of the Forest of Arden population. It cannot be long before these, the Mortimer Forest roe and those from north Gloucestershire pool their resources to form a single population linked in turn with the roe of central southern and south-west England.

Muntjac were first reported in Warwickshire in 1941, when they were confirmed in woods near Kineton. This is a very long way from Woburn, where the species was first released, and the slow rate of subsequent spread makes it almost certain that a local release was

responsible for their unexpected appearance. Research undertaken by Norma Chapman into the Woburn estate archives now makes it clear that Warwickshire was one of a number of areas to which translocations of muntjac were covertly carried out at various times, mainly at the instance of the twelfth Duke of Bedford following the eleventh Duke's death in 1940.

Muntjac have now reached a stage in Warwickshire where I have heard them described as being as common as rabbits in nearly all suitable localities. I have seen them myself in the Knavenhill area and in woods south-east of Coventry, in both of which localities they are particularly plentiful. From Warwickshire they have pushed north to colonise rural nooks and crannies in the urban county of the West Midlands, embracing Birmingham, Wolverhampton and the other Black Country towns.

In Hereford and Worcester muntjac are thinner on the ground, but they have been reported from many localities and colonisation is clearly progressing. There is now a resident population in Wyre Forest and they also live alongside fallow which have spread north from that forest into woods between the roads leading from Bridgnorth to Bewdley and Stourbridge. Most of Shropshire is still in the early stages of colonisation, but in the far west of the county, on the Welsh border near Presteigne, there is one locality where muntjac have been present since at least the mid-1970s and which they share with both fallow and roe deer. This clearly points to an unrecorded local release.

Chinese water deer were introduced in about 1950 to Walcot Park, near Bishop's Castle in Shropshire, where they were confined within an area fenced against foxes. These deer increased quite rapidly and a number eventually escaped. The numbers of feral deer reached a point where, in the words of a local foxhunting farmer, it was thought necessary to 'quieten' them, but when I visited the area in 1970 I was told that numbers were again on the increase.

In 1956 the owner of Walcot Park sold the property and moved to Hope Court, at Hope Bagot on the south side of Clee Hill, east of Ludlow. He took some Chinese water deer with him and these also flourished. It seems unlikely that any now exist in either locality, for there has been no recent news of them.

Staffordshire, Cheshire and Greater Manchester

Sandwiched though they are between major industrial conurbations and with the Five Towns of the Potteries in their midst, Staffordshire and Cheshire also include some extensive areas of relatively wild country where deer are very much at home. While such deer as exist next door to the human multitudes of Greater Manchester are mostly confined more or less securely within park walls, even in this urban county it is by no means unknown for wild deer to turn up as if from nowhere, astonishing those who happen to see them and creating a major traffic hazard in the more populated areas.

The deer of today are of two main species, with a third fairly rapidly establishing itself over an ever wider area. Documentary evidence shows red deer to have occurred in all the region's old royal forests, of which Staffordshire once had five. Extending partly into Shropshire were the two now largely forgotten forests of Brewood, disafforested by King John, and Morf and Kinver, where red deer probably roamed not later than the fourteenth century. Medieval Cannock Chase was at one stage a royal forest in which red, fallow and roe deer were all to be found, but how long the indigenous red deer lingered is uncertain. Just to the east of Cannock Chase stretched Needwood Forest, which may have retained its red deer until it was formally disafforested in 1804. Even then, red deer continued to be a feature of adjacent Bagot's Park, where they remained until well into the twentieth century.

Other ancient Staffordshire deer parks which at one time numbered red deer among their occupants include Beaudesert, Ingestre and Chartley, the last-named having also once been noted for its herd of wild white cattle. In recent times ground not far from the JCB factory at Rocester, near Uttoxeter, became the setting for a beautifully landscaped deer park set up by Mr J. C. Bamford and stocked with red deer of high quality. There are also fallow deer in this park, which is located at Cote Farm, Farley, on the Wootton Lodge estate, a Bamford property.

After an absence of at least two hundred years, perhaps much longer, wild red deer are once again found among the trees of Cannock Chase, where conifers and birches mantle a sizeable tract of more or less hilly country just north of the West Midlands conurbation. Having escaped from a fenced enclosure at some time around 1970, the original deer soon took up quarters in that part of the chase which lies south of the Cannock–Rugeley main road and railway where, after several fruitless searches, I eventually had an excellent view of a number of these truly fine animals, or their progeny, while I was being shown around by the Forestry Commission's local head ranger.

Having hefted themselves for the most part to an area of the chase little frequented by the much more numerous fallow deer population, these red deer continue to flourish. A habitat of better quality than most to be found elsewhere

Belvedere, a multi-seater wildlife observation tower in the centre of Cannock Chase, in Staffordshire.

A young fallow buck of the predominant common variety in Cannock Chase.

themselves while keeping a wary eye open for human intruders.

While deerwatching in the area I have seen these deer in both situations – on farmland fields and in deep wooded cloughs – sometimes in sizeable aggregations. However, I learn from my friend Peter Davenport, who takes a close interest in these animals, that during the 1990s their numbers diminished fairly markedly due to opportunistic shooting, although it is hoped that, given time, they will build up again to a safer level.

Barely a dozen miles north of the main stronghold of these red deer, which straddles the county boundary between Staffordshire and Cheshire, is Lyme Park, close to the outer edge of the Manchester conurbation. Originally stocked in the fourteenth century with wild red deer from the old royal forest of Macclesfield, which adjoined it, this park is now National Trust property held on lease by the borough of Stockport and open to the public. It is a large park, composed of two quite different areas – the main park, at a comparatively low altitude, which contains both red and fallow deer, and the higher-altitude so-called Moor Park, which occupies some 300 ha on the fringe of the Pennines and with a much wilder herd of red deer.

Snowed-up walls and other factors have sometimes enabled red deer to escape from Lyme Park. Some of these fugitives have been known to wander into Greater Manchester, causing brief mayhem on busy roads until measures are taken to end their freedom, while others have opted for the seclusion and relative safety of the Pennines. Roughly midway between Lyme Park and the Staffordshire border the Goyt valley cleaves into the Pennines and its forested slopes have long given shelter to a small population of red deer. Whether these are of Lyme Park stock or reached the Goyt valley and its neighbourhood as a result of natural spread by some members of the more southerly population is uncertain.

What is known, however, is that in 1976–7 the North West Water Authority released a total of ten hinds to join the few stags already present on the 3000 ha or more of mainly forested land

in the area helps make for deer of matching excellence. At peril to themselves and to motorists on the intervening main road, these deer do sometimes wander north into the more central part of the chase, and I learn from leading Wildlife Ranger Peter Pursglove that others have strayed south as far as Brownhills and even farther. Indeed, some are now permanently resident in suburban green field areas near Brownhills, and the red deer in general wander more widely now than formerly. Numbers are maintained at a level sufficient to safeguard the herd's survival while minimising forestry damage and depredations on local farmland.

In the 1930s the late Captain H.C. Brocklehurst introduced four red deer – a stag and three hinds – from Warnham Court Park in West Sussex to a park on his Swythamley estate, on the Staffordshire-Cheshire border north of Leek. After war broke out these deer and their progeny escaped to establish a wild population which has persisted to the present day. Originally centred on a Pennine area called the Roches, they later began to spend much of their time at lower altitudes, making use of such woodland as is available although sometimes lying out by day close to some sheltering farmland hedgerow or dry-stone wall, sunning making up their catchment area near the Cheshire-Derbyshire border. This was done to help stabilise and maintain a wild red deer herd in what was judged to be ideal habitat with a vacant niche for a more securely established breeding population.

This modern Macclesfield Forest has thus become a more fitting successor to its medieval namesake, which was a haunt of both red and fallow deer until around the seventeenth century. The native red deer of Wirral Forest, another old royal hunting domain, died out about three hundred years earlier, but the Cheshire forests of Mara and Moudern, later combined into what has since been known as Delamere Forest, retained their deer, both red and fallow, at least as long as Macclesfield Forest.

King James I hunted red deer in Delamere Forest in 1617. Just how much longer the species survived this visitation is uncertain. There can be little doubt, however, that from the early nineteenth century to the first five decades of the twentieth the only red deer in Cheshire were confined within park walls or fences – at Lyme Park, as already mentioned, together with fallow in Tatton Park, just outside Knutsford, and formerly, though not now, at Doddington Park, near Nantwich, as well as possibly one or two others. Some of the red deer in Tatton Park escaped in the late 1990s, and by 1999 were living ferally in nearby woods, from which they emerged under cover of darkness to feed on adjacent farmland.

Cheshire is one of the very few non-metropolitan counties which appear now to have no established populations of wild fallow. Those that lived in the old Macclesfield Forest have long disappeared, while Delamere Forest lost the last of its fallow around the time when, in 1812, it was formally disafforested, if not earlier. Delamere Forest, in the heart of the agricultural Cheshire Plain, survives today as a woodland area amply large enough to justify retaining its name as a forest, but one which, from the early nineteenth century until recently, has had the rare distinction in England of being entirely without wild deer.

Beeston Castle Park, about midway between Crewe and Chester and not many miles from Delamere Forest, has long ceased to be a deer park but had the odd fallow deer at large in the early 1950s, and for a time between the wars there was a small wild fallow population in the countryside around Carden Park, a few miles south of Beeston near Broxton. In neither case, however, did fugitive fallow reach the forest; an intervening main railway line perhaps proved too much of an obstacle. None of the several other Cheshire parks which once held fallow, nor Lyme Park or Tatton Park, which still possess them, have been a source of escapees on more than a temporary basis.

The walled surrounds of Dunham Massey Park, at Altrincham in Greater Manchester, have likewise been proof against long-term escapes by fallow deer, which are obliged by the presence of public footpaths to share their home with large numbers of human visitors at all seasons. To minimise any resultant stress, sanctuary areas have been set aside where the public are not admitted.

Fallow grazing in early morning on farmland adjoining Bagot's Wood, near Needwood Forest in Staffordshire.

In contrast with Cheshire, Staffordshire has no shortage of wild fallow, thanks in particular to the survival of Cannock Chase as a deer-holding area. The history of the local fallow dates at least from the thirteenth century, when Henry III is known to have hunted them in this corner of the Midlands. Apart from kings and their courtiers, and the inevitable poachers, it appears that wolves were still a threat to the lives of deer here at that time, for there is a record of one of these predators killing a fat buck in Cannock Chase in 1281.

The recorded history of the area supplies clear evidence that fallow remained continuously at large in the chase until at least the early nineteenth century, when the Marquess of Anglesey claimed them as his personal property. Preceding centuries saw the creation of Beaudesert, Teddesley, Wolseley and other deer parks adjoining and near Cannock Chase, and it would have been natural enough for these to have been stocked mainly with wild deer from the chase. Wolseley Park, one of the most ancient, possessed a deerleap over which animals from the chase could enter it but not get out again, and this relic is still preserved although the deer park it served has long since ceased to exist.

Although records of wild deer in Cannock Chase in the later decades of the nineteenth century seem to be lacking, fallow are known to have been at large there in fairly substantial numbers in the years immediately after the First World War. Having come fairly close to

One of the red deer in Cheshire's Lyme Park.

extinction during that conflict, they slowly recovered their numbers afterwards, only to suffer another sharp reverse of fortunes in the Second World War, when their numbers were reduced by 75 per cent or more. In 1970 the Forestry Commission's local head ranger, Gerald Springthorpe, told me that at one stage Cannock Chase fallow numbers were reduced to around forty, from which they were steadily nursed back to a healthy herd of some two or three hundred by careful management coupled with selective control.

Gerald himself was one of the first members of the Forestry Commission's staff to use a rifle for deer control instead of snares and shotguns. His pioneering work in the field of practical, modern deer management along lines now universally recognised as correct for conditions in Britain in due course won recognition with the award of the BEM. He is also co-editor with Nick Myhill of the Forestry Commission's 'bible' for all those engaged in this kind of work, the *Wildlife Ranger's Handbook*.

Gerald Springthorpe's work at Cannock before his retirement in the 1980s included the creation of an impressive wildlife museum in which, of course, deer were given due prominence. Another brainchild of his was Belvedere, a multi-seater deer-watching tower made available to the public and located at a high point from which rides radiated all around to facilitate viewing as the wild deer of the chase moved about, undisturbed by humans. His public relations work included lecturing to local organisations and schools. He was also adept at establishing good liaison with farming neighbours in the matter of protecting their crops with deer-proof fencing and the like.

I toured Cannock Chase on many occasions with Gerald as my guide, viewing wild fallow at close quarters and sometimes wondering to what extent the infiltration of blood from park escapees in the neighbourhood may have been responsible for the variations of colour I observed. Whatever the importance of any such influence – and there can be very little doubt that park escapes are a factor of some importance in their history – it seems fairly certain that at least a residue of a strain which has been continuously wild since the Middle Ages persists in the fallow that roam wild over the chase at the present day. The common type, dappled on the flanks in summer and white-rumped all the year round, predominates, with perhaps one-third being black, in addition to which there are a few menil and occasional whitish individuals. They range widely over the central and northern areas of the chase and through the woods around nearby Ingestre Park, but are infrequent south of the Cannock–Rugeley road and railway.

Cannock fallow have suffered very heavy casualties on roads which lend themselves rather too readily to fast driving, and from being chased across these roads by the ill-controlled charges of dog-walkers. In recent years there has been an average of 100–120 deer deaths annually on Cannock Chase roads, in spite of warning signs and headlight-reflecting mirrors.

Only a few miles to the east a separate wild fallow population roams the woods of old Needwood Forest in which, despite a high incidence of poaching, they were still to be numbered in their thousands as late as the end of the eighteenth century. Paradoxical though it might seem, disafforestation in 1804 did not mean the end of the forest as such, simply, as in other places elsewhere, its special status as a royal hunting ground with related commoners' rights etc. Sizeable chunks of it survive as woodland owned by the Duchy of Lancaster and hence still retain royal status of a kind.

In these Duchy of Lancaster woods I have seen fallow deer whose forebears undoubtedly roamed the same area several hundreds of years ago, albeit not perhaps with an unbroken lineage as wild animals from those days to the present. Even when the royal forest was still flourishing it contained no fewer than ten deer parks. At least three of these, Bagot's Park, near Abbots Bromley, and Hoar Cross and Dunstall Parks, near Yoxall, retained their fallow well into the twentieth century, until the effects of the Second World War helped restore them to their ancient liberty.

The television presenter and countryside writer Phil Drabble re-enclosed a few fallow so that he could watch them through the drawing-room window of his home near Abbots Bromley a few years ago. I have happy memories of watching local wild fallow in his company in the early light of a fine spring morning, grazing on fields between his home and the Forestry Commission's Bagot's Wood. Black deer probably predominate among these Needwood fallow, and their body weights tend to be greater than those of their neighbours on Cannock Chase.

A folk custom of unknown origin still enacted in this area is the Abbots Bromley horn dance, a team performance in which each member holds aloft a pair of antlers which, for reasons which are lost in the mists of time, originated not from the local fallow but from reindeer.

Elsewhere in Staffordshire, Aqualate Park, on the Shropshire border near Newport, dates from soon after the Norman Conquest and is still a haunt of fallow, some of which have escaped in the past to establish a local feral population. There is also a small herd of red deer in Aqualate Park. A few miles to the east, at Weston-under-Lizard, is Weston Park, with its own small herd of fallow. A few of these have also escaped to live ferally in the area. Whiston Eaves Park, at Froghall, north of Cheadle, no longer has fallow, and past escapees from it apparently failed to survive for long in the surrounding countryside. The fallow of Ashcombe Park, near Cheddleton, south of Leek, seem to have suffered a similar fate.

A survey of deer near Stoke-on-Trent carried out by local members of the British Deer Society a few years ago revealed the presence of four apparently quite separate populations of wild fallow in countryside bracketing the M6 motorway in north Staffordshire. All derive from former park herds, two of the most important being Swynnerton Park, which lost all of its fallow through escapes in 1936, and Trentham Park, once a seat of the Dukes of Sutherland and now a popular recreational area for people who live in the Potteries, which ceased to be a deer park proper around the start of the Second World War. These various populations were identified as the Swynnerton, the Whitmore, the Trentham and the Tittensor herds or groups, depending on which locality was the focal point of each. The different groups have different colour compositions. The only ones I have seen belonged to the Trentham group and were black. Also near Swynnerton is Clouds Park, from which red deer escaped before the Second World War but did not long survive.

Muntjac have been unobtrusively colonising suitable areas in Staffordshire for a considerable number of years now. In Needwood Forest muntjac and fallow slots are about equally in evidence, and I have seen muntjac in the flesh in

Fallow deer are present in a number of Cheshire deer parks.

woods close to Phil Drabble's home while being shown around by him.

Gerald Springthorpe used to keep muntjac in an enclosure by his cottage at Moors Gorse on Cannock Chase. After his departure I photographed one of several then living in freedom thereabouts but still coming regularly for food put out for their benefit. I learn that muntjac are now independently resident, not only in Needwood Forest and Cannock Chase – which is not particularly well-suited to this species – but throughout Staffordshire wherever the habitat meets their needs, being most plentiful in the south while still quite thin on the ground in the north. They have also penetrated Cheshire, where a few years ago there were reports of one or two having reached Delamere Forest. If these reports were correct it appears that muntjac have not settled there, for in 1999 Forest Enterprise told me there were still no known deer of any species in that forest.

Attempts have been made to introduce both roe and sika to south Staffordshire and at one stage Phil Drabble and Gerald Springthorpe both possessed small captive breeding stocks of roe, but so far as I have been able to discover neither species is currently present in the wild state in either Staffordshire or Cheshire. The indigenous roe of Cannock Chase were probably extinct well before the end of the seventeenth century. Between the two world wars a small herd of Japanese sika was kept in Weston Park, on the Shropshire border. One of the stags escaped and was possibly the one that turned up in 1936 in Hoar Cross Park, near Needwood Forest on the opposite side of Staffordshire. With fallow deer as its companions, this stag remained at its new home until the Second World War, when all the deer in the park escaped.

Chester Zoo, at Upton-by-Chester, includes deer among its exhibits, barasingha, Burmese brow-antlered deer, chital (axis deer), Père David's deer and reindeer, all being present there in 1999.

6

THE DEER OF THE SOUTH
AND EAST MIDLANDS

Oxfordshire and Buckinghamshire

A century ago there were probably no wild deer in either Oxfordshire or Buckinghamshire except, it seems, for a few fallow in the woods on the Chiltern Hills, where the two counties meet. Today, free-living deer in both of these counties are to be numbered in their hundreds – I was tempted to say 'thousands' – representing four or more species, and stocks are steadily increasing.

If modern Oxfordshire is mainly a county of broad agricultural acres, with relatively few woodlands except near its southern and eastern borders, in medieval times it contained no fewer than four royal forests. Of these, Wychwood, north-west of Oxford, was perhaps the most important, and in those early days, in common with other Oxfordshire forests, was well supplied with red deer. As elsewhere, these dwindled over the centuries, although it appears that some remained until about two hundred years ago.

Long before that, fallow became established as the principal deer of this forest and the others in Oxfordshire – Bernwood, Shotover and Stowood, towards the eastern side of the county – as well as in Woodstock Chase, adjacent to Wychwood and, no doubt, at least partly reliant for stock on overspill animals from that forest.

Wychwood Forest fallow were reckoned to number at least a thousand until well into the nineteenth century. Forest officials were accused of neglecting their duties of ensuring a sufficiency of supplementary food for these deer in winter, causing the animals to wreak havoc on neighbouring farmland. All this was ended after the forest was enclosed by Act of Parliament in 1862. Residual woodland passed into private ownership, what remained of the former open forest being converted into farmland.

There seems little doubt that the wild deer were wiped out. In nearby Cornbury Park, however, there already existed a herd of fallow which were almost certainly at least partly of common origin with the wild herd of the neighbourhood. These continued to flourish. After the Second World War it transpired that deer were again to be found in what remained of old Wychwood Forest. When I enquired about these in the early 1950s I was told by the owner, Mr Oliver Vernon Watney, that they were the result of wartime escapes from the deer park, that they had no business to be there, and that no effort would be spared to bring their freedom to an end.

Mr Watney further assured me that there were definitely no wild deer in Wychwood Forest before the war. Their renewed presence, however, was not to be terminated so easily. In 1958 I found them still there in modest numbers, as well as being extremely shy, ready to flee at the slightest hint of disturbance. On visits in the late 1970s and again in the late 1980s and early 1990s I found them just as much in evidence, if not more so, and no less shy. In fact they have increased in recent years to something approaching their numbers in the closing decades of the royal forest era, and are now systematically managed as re-established permanent residents.

The modern Wychwood Forest fallow have produced antlers of very high quality which are much in demand by client stalkers from Britain and abroad. Current deer management is in the hands of a syndicate of stalkers headed by Mr Jim Brannan, who leases the stalking from the Cornbury Park estate at Charlbury. All the fallow I have seen here have been of the common variety, but menil and black deer are also present as well as occasional white ones, although the latter are not encouraged.

Fallow of mixed colours also occur north-west

of Woodstock, in woods around Ditchley Park and Glympton Park, from which their forebears escaped during the Second World War or earlier, but which are now no longer deer parks. Glympton Park retains an ancient deerleap as indisputable evidence of the presence of free-ranging deer in the surrounding countryside in previous years. A few deer, presumably from one or the other or possibly both of these two parks, must certainly have been at large before the war, for it was in the late 1930s that the first wild fallow deer of modern times was reported from woods near Tackley, between the A423 and the Cherwell, where they have been more or less regularly present ever since and where I have seen them several times.

South of the Thames, in what was part of Berkshire until the local government boundary changes of 1974, Wytham Woods are the haunt of another herd of very wild fallow, mainly, so far as my own observations go, of the common variety. These descend from stock once confined in Wytham Park. When I first enquired about these in the late 1950s I was told that it was intended to shoot them out because of their impact on an area where a variety of important research projects were being undertaken by

Oxford University, who now own the Wytham estate. As has been so often the case elsewhere in similar situations, however, the deer survived and were still very much a feature of Wytham Woods on my visits in the 1980s, since when the entire woodland complex has been deer-fenced to prevent the animals from straying onto farmland.

In Oxford itself, Magdalen College has long maintained a small herd of fallow in an enclosure near the Cherwell. In the mid-1980s five deer escaped into the city but were speedily recaptured.

The Aynho area, south of Banbury on the border with Northamptonshire, is another locality where park-escaped fallow have been reported, although on fairly recent visits I have found no sign of them there. Nuneham Courteney Park, south of Oxford, had fallow and also, apparently, Japanese sika before the Second World War, when all the surviving deer escaped, but none of either species now remain thereabouts.

East of Oxford, however, park-escaped fallow have repopulated woods which once were royal forest but which for a very long time had been deerless until the fortunes, or misfortunes, of two world wars and their aftermath helped restore the *status quo ante*. The present range of these deer overlaps the Buckinghamshire border.

Waterperry Wood, a nature reserve, and Shabbington Wood, both of which form part of the Forestry Commission's Bernwood Forest, are among their main haunts. It was in Shabbington Wood that I once watched a triple rutting combat, with three well-matched fallow bucks noisily tangling their antlers.

The other main fallow deer haunt in Oxfordshire also extends into Buckinghamshire and occupies a fairly wide area of the southern Chiltern beechwoods. Stonor Park, north of Henley-on-Thames, has been a source of local escapees, and Crowsley Park, between Henley and Reading, has been reported as another.

Formosan sika deer in Oxfordshire's Charlbury Park. Some of this subspecies also occur wild in Wychwood Forest.

Investigating this area in the early 1950s, I found no sign of deer in the woods near Crowsley Park but numerous fallow of both the common and black varieties in woods around Stonor on both sides of the county boundary. At one stage before the Second World War black fallow were allowed to become the dominant type in Stonor Park but were later largely eliminated in favour of the common variety. Conspicuous among these in 1950 was a solitary white individual which had made its way into the park from the surrounding countryside.

While acknowledging that park escapees had boosted the numbers of deer at large locally, the then owner, the Hon. Sherman Stonor, told me he believed fallow had 'always' occurred wild in the woods of the southern Chilterns. Another informant assured me that there had been fallow in and around Bledlow Great Wood, on the Chilterns a little way south of Princes Risborough, since at least 1870. Further confirmation of the long-standing presence of wild fallow came in a letter in 1950 from 84-year-old Mr Francis L. Fane of Wormsley, just north of Watlington, who said they had occurred in his woods there for at least 70 years to his personal knowledge.

Fallow I have seen in the Wormsley woods have been of the common variety which originally found most favour in Stonor Park and later regained their old predominance there. The foundation stock at Stonor came from Watlington Park, quite close to Wormsley, in about 1830, and is said to have been herded on foot from one park to the other. Apparently, hurdles and other obstacles were erected along the roadsides at the time of the forced migration to prevent any deer from escaping, but one cannot help wondering whether some may have gained their liberty all the same to initiate a wild population which has been present ever since.

Some of these southern Chiltern fallow are of truly excellent quality, the bucks growing heavy, broad-palmed antlers equal to any to be seen anywhere in the wild state in Britain. A number of them lost their liberty in the early 1980s when a new deer park was created at Fawley Hill, near Henley-on-Thames. Originally stocked with wild fallow deer which entered it over deerleaps, the park now also contains small herds of chital (axis deer), sika and hog deer.

Medieval Bernwood Forest extended some way into Buckinghamshire and was well stocked with fallow, as was adjacent Brill Forest, which was sometimes reckoned as part of its neighbour rather than as a separate entity. Whaddon Chase, towards the north-east end of Buckinghamshire, was another ancient haunt of fallow, but there is little news of the species in these areas today. For a time after the First World War, I understand there was a feral herd of fallow in woods south of Beaconsfield, but these have not survived.

At Weston Underwood, near Olney, Flamingo Gardens and Zoological Park exhibits a small number of white fallow, but the chital and Chinese water deer formerly kept were no longer present here in 1999.

On Oxfordshire's western border, Barrington Park, just inside Gloucestershire, at one time held both fallow and sika, but when I visited the area some years ago only fallow remained, leading a semi-wild existence wandering in and out of the park more or less at will. I believe the park is now fenced more securely, but any fallow still at large may sometimes stray into Oxfordshire. Fawley Court Park and Crowsley Park, both near Henley, also held sika at one time as well as fallow. The former occurrence of sika, and the fairly common error of mistaking black fallow for what used to be universally called 'Japanese deer' once led to a widespread supposition that park-escaped sika as well as fallow were to be found in the southern Chilterns. If any wild sika did briefly exist there, they have long since ceased to do so.

Fawley Court Park also held red deer. In 1950, nine years after the last of them had been disposed of, I was told that the odd red deer was still at large in the area. It was generally supposed, however, that any such animal was likely to be an ageing fugitive from the pre-war activities of the Berkshire and Buckinghamshire Staghounds, a pack which hunted carted deer and was known to have been responsible for a number of unrecovered outliers. Any red deer at liberty today in these two counties is almost certain to be an escapee from a deer farm.

Other former deer parks include Langley Park and Black Park, both in Buckinghamshire near Slough. Both at one time held sika and Langley Park was noted for its herd of all-white red deer. Neither species has been reported as occurring wild in that area. Nor are any feral sika known to exist near Waddesdon Park, in central

Buckinghamshire, where the species has also been kept. There were also chital here at one time. Waddesdon Manor is a National Trust property and does not now include a deer park.

Where Buckinghamshire meets Hertfordshire and Bedfordshire, Ashridge Park, on the Chilterns above Berkhamsted and now also a National Trust property, once held sika in addition to red and fallow deer. Only fallow, in fairly large numbers and of mixed colours, survive today, together with immigrant muntjac. Completely wild and unenclosed, these fallow range the former deer park and the woods of Berkhamsted Common and are also often to be seen in neighbouring fields. This is a localised population, separated by a motorway, several railways and a dozen miles of well-wooded hill country from the southern Chiltern fallow.

Probably the only place today where unenclosed sika are present in the two counties is the Wychwood Forest area. Formosan sika have found their way there from adjacent Cornbury Park, where they live alongside the old-established herd of fallow. Since wild Formosan sika are almost certainly extinct in their native Taiwan, it is to be hoped that the small feral herd in Wychwood Forest will endure.

Only a few decades ago roe were virtually unknown in this part of England. For a long time the Thames seemed to mark the very northernmost limit of spread by roe from the southern counties. As far back as the 1940s, however, there were rumours of odd animals turning up in the southern Chilterns, although confirmation was not forthcoming until 1976, when one was photographed on the Stonor estate by Mr Roy Worsfold of Reading, the result being published in the British Deer Society's journal *Deer*.

Eleven years later I was astonished to learn that a roebuck had been shot in the Tackley area, about 10 miles north of Oxford. This was intended by the owner of the property in question to be the first and last roe on his land, where he already played host to what he regarded as more than adequate numbers of fallow and muntjac. On a visit the following spring, however, the very first deer I saw was a roe doe, and over the following four years, on further visits, I grew accustomed to seeing roe almost as often as I saw muntjac.

From whence did this roe invasion stem? At first I supposed that it was part of the onward march of roe from the south. I now believe it is more likely, however, that roe have spread east into central Oxfordshire from just over the Gloucestershire border, where the species was covertly introduced at some unknown date well after the Second World War, and from where it has since spread a good many miles in several directions.

Roe remain rare east of Oxford, where they are actively discouraged from colonising forestry plantations which are especially vulnerable to damage, and where the M40 motorway now presents a substantial obstacle to spread in that direction. West of the city roe reached Wytham Woods before that area was deer-fenced. Since the mid- to late 1980s they have been present in the Wychwood Forest area, mostly around the fringes rather than in the forest itself, where the high numbers of fallow are thought to be an inhibiting factor.

Near the Wiltshire border north-west of Faringdon, in the spring of 1992, I saw a number of roe as well as muntjac and found both species to be well established, as was the case in suitable habitat throughout the slice of what used to be Berkshire, north of the Ridgeway, which was gained by Oxfordshire in 1974. These roe have undoubtedly reached Oxfordshire from the south, and if they have not already joined forces with the ex-Gloucestershire contingent, as I suppose the others to be, this is bound to happen soon.

In the early years of the twentieth century Siberian roe deer (*Capreolus capreolus pygargus*) were released into the Woburn woods by the eleventh Duke of Bedford. It was thought that all had succumbed to poaching during the Second World War, but three or four survivors were found as late as the early 1950s when I made several attempts to observe them – unsuccessfully, I regret to say – in woods on both sides of the Bedfordshire-Buckinghamshire border, west of Woburn. These fascinating animals have, unfortunately, long since died out.

The story of muntjac and their introduction to Britain really belongs to Bedfordshire and is dealt with in the next section. Suffice it to say here that Buckinghamshire was colonised very early and that muntjac are now to be found throughout the county, wherever the habitat is suitable and sometimes where it is less so. I have seen a muntjac in my car headlights on the outskirts of urban Aylesbury.

Waterperry Wood and Shabbington Wood, on the Buckinghamshire border east of Oxford, are among areas where I have seen numerous muntjac as well as fallow, as are both Wytham Woods and Wychwood Forest. Muntjac in the latter area have produced antlers of trophy quality much in demand by visiting Continental sportsmen. By contrast, in the late 1990s those in Wytham Woods were systematically reduced in number to the lowest level possible as part of a large-scale cull designed to limit damage to the woodland environment. Within a short space of time no fewer than ninety muntjac were shot and three hundred fallow. The end plan here is to stabilise fallow at around twenty-five head all told while encouraging roe to establish themselves more strongly.

Apparently muntjac first appeared in strength on the west side of the Cherwell when that river was frozen over during the 1963 winter, since when they have spread to all parts of Oxfordshire. Many muntjac have died under the wheels of motor traffic on the A34 where it passes through wooded country north of Woodstock.

Chinese water deer, like muntjac, first gained their liberty in Bedfordshire, but their spread into neighbouring counties has been a good deal less spectacular. They have certainly reached Buckinghamshire, not only from the Woburn area but also probably, to a lesser extent, after escaping from Whipsnade Zoo (now renamed Whipsnade Wild Animal Park). Their range as wild animals extends little farther west than the A5 (Watling Street) or farther north than Milton Keynes, so far as is known at the present time. Since they are often confused with muntjac, however, they may have spread further than is generally realised. A few years ago a deerstalker friend of mine reported finding some in a localised wetland area near Banbury in north Oxfordshire, although these have since disappeared.

Bedfordshire and Hertfordshire

Bedfordshire's chief claim to fame as a deer county centres on Woburn Park and its collection of cervine exotics, representing at different times almost a quarter of the world's species, while Whipsnade Wild Animal Park, as it is now known, is only marginally less famous for the same reason. Neighbouring Hertfordshire's name recalls the past occurrence of red deer. While these have not been entirely absent in recent times, the smaller Chinese water deer is better established in the wild in several areas, and the still smaller muntjac is numerous and widespread in both counties.

Until quite late in the nineteenth century Woburn was just another deer park owned by an ancient noble family, occupying a thousand or so acres and containing both red and fallow deer. Then, in 1893, the eleventh Duke of Bedford took the first steps in establishing a collection of alien herbivores, among which deer from all parts of the world claimed pride of place.

Père David's deer were saved from extinction by being bred successfully in Bedfordshire's Woburn Park.

Many of these introductions proved short-lived, the animals involved finding the climate or other conditions at their new home unsatisfactory. A notable exception was Père David's deer from China, first known to Western science only some thirty years before the Woburn herbivore collection was initiated. It was discovered by the French missionary Père Armand David when he looked over the wall of the Imperial Hunting Park at Peking (Beijing), where the entire world population of the species was then confined. Around the end of the nineteenth century a succession of natural and other disasters caused the whole herd to be wiped out. Luckily, by then a few had been smuggled out of China or otherwise obtained for various parks and zoos in Europe. Realising how grave was the danger of total extinction, the Duke of Bedford purchased as many of these deer as he could lay hands on and brought them to Woburn, where by great good fortune they rallied and slowly built up a viable herd which has been the basis of breeding nuclei elsewhere and, in due time, has provided stock to be shipped back to their native China.

Thus it was that one man's wealth and timely enterprise saved the day for one of the world's most curious cervids. Varying degrees of success were achieved with other imports of Asian origin, including rusa deer from what is now Indonesia, and barasingha or swamp deer and chital (axis deer) from the Indian subcontinent, although these never increased substantially. On my first visit to Woburn as a guest of the twelfth duke, in 1950, I learned that chital, which produce calves at any season, depended for their survival at least in part upon the provision of sheltered accommodation where they could seek some protection from the elements and from the food-purloining habits of some of their

Another exotic deer species with a lengthy history at Woburn is the swamp deer or barasingha.

neighbours, especially fallow deer.

Hog deer were also then present, segregated from other species within a small wooded enclosure where there was also some long grass in which they could hide. These deer died out, although hog deer survive and seem to do reasonably well at other locations, including a deer paddock owned by Mr John Willett at Hockworthy in east Devon.

John also breeds Formosan sika, whose former sub-enclosure in Woburn Park no longer contains these animals, which are believed to be extinct in the wild state in their native Taiwan. Manchurian sika flourish at Woburn, which has supplied stocks of these for parks and deer farms elsewhere. They have to be kept separate from other subspecies of sika to prevent interbreeding.

Père David's deer apart, the Asian immigrants which have done well most conspicuously at Woburn are the muntjac and Chinese water deer. Indian muntjac were introduced in 1893. After being confined at first in a restricted space, where they failed to flourish, some were set free in the park itself and others in the woods outside. An oft-repeated tale tells that these animals proved pugnacious, and that after one had attacked a park-keeper's dog it was decided to eliminate Indian muntjac and replace them by the smaller Reeves's muntjac from China. According to the twelfth Duke, who succeeded his father in 1940 and died in 1953, this substitution was most likely to have been made because of the greater rarity and interest of the Reeves's muntjac rather than on account of the bellicosity of the Indian.

However, recent investigations of the Woburn archives by Norma Chapman, Kathy and Mick Claydon and Stephen Harris indicate that Reeves's muntjac arrived at almost the same time as the Indian ones, and that both species were released both inside and outside the park in 1901. How this squares with the better-known version of what is supposed to have happened is unclear, as is precisely how and when the Indian muntjac disappeared. A common assumption has been that at least a few of the larger species must have survived to mingle with their Chinese relatives and, in all probability, to interbreed with them. It has been determined, however, that Indian and Reeves's muntjac have different chromosome counts and cannot produce fertile hybrid offspring. All available evidence seems to indicate that the entire population of wild muntjac in Britain today is of the Reeves's species, so that one way or another the Indian did indeed die out.

Having been released outside Woburn Park as well as within it, Reeves's muntjac enjoyed a charmed life on the estate as a whole throughout the lifetimes of the eleventh and twelfth dukes. While spending a week there shortly after the twelfth duke's death I found these animals, unmolested as they had been up to that point, easier to approach and to observe at very close quarters than any others I have seen elsewhere, or indeed at Woburn in later years when control was routinely undertaken.

At an early date muntjac began to spread beyond the bounds of the Woburn estate, progressively colonising woodland areas elsewhere in Bedfordshire, in adjacent parts of Buckinghamshire and, later, in Hertfordshire. Extension into Northamptonshire and other counties was stimulated by local releases. Although they are well able to survive normal English winters, those of exceptional severity have been apt to cause high mortality. The Arctic conditions of early 1947 were estimated to have brought about the deaths of up to three-quarters of the entire muntjac population. Similar conditions in 1962–3 caused many muntjac deaths in some localities and markedly fewer in others.

On the latter occasion muntjac at Woburn suffered rather badly. Exploring the woods there during the weekend of the British Deer Society's inauguration, we saw no live muntjac at all but found several dead ones, including a buck and a doe lying side by side in a woodman's hut, where they had presumably gone in search of at least some degree of warmth and shelter from the elements.

These deer showed no sign of malnutrition and so probably succumbed to hypothermia, to which these natives of sub-tropical climes presumably would have less natural resistance

Chital (axis deer) have been kept in Woburn Park for many years.

than species evolved in more northerly latitudes.

Concern has lately been expressed about the impact of these small deer on the natural environment in Britain, and in particular the possible impoverishment their feeding habits may cause to woodland flora and thus to dependent butterflies and other indigenous wildlife. As is also the case with roe, it has been found that high-density muntjac populations and attempts to re-establish coppicing regimes do not go well together, and the knock-on effects of this are a ripe subject for further study.

Here, in their oldest-established haunts as British wild animals, muntjac numbers have long since reached saturation point in many areas. Densities are controlled by a number of factors, culling by rifle and, regrettably, by shotgun perhaps accounting for no more than road fatalities. Food availability and mutual intolerance by what, after all, is a highly territorial species also help to regulate numbers to a significant degree.

Muntjac in these two counties, as elsewhere, are more essentially woodland animals than any other of Britain's six wild deer species. Deciduous woodland is preferred, especially that with a dense understorey of bramble, although conifer plantations – the thicker the better – are not by any means neglected. Shrubberies and wild gardens also attract their quota, while market gardens with their

Manchurian sika deer in Woburn Park.

brassicas, carrots, soft fruits and kindred temptations, where they are not too far from cover, afford welcome dietary variation.

Whereas muntjac favour woodland above all other types of habitat, Chinese water deer, in the absence of their preferred wetland, are as much at home among farm crops as in tree cover, if not more so. In Woburn Park itself, as well as at Whipsnade – to which these small deer, tusked but antlerless, were introduced many years ago from Woburn – they like nothing better than to lie couched on open grassland, well away from cover.

According to the twelfth Duke of Bedford, Chinese water deer first gained their liberty through park gates carelessly left open during the war. Although the population at large has been reinforced by later escapes, its subsequent history has not matched the quite spectacular success achieved by muntjac in the wild. Partly this is due, perhaps, to the greater vulnerability of this mainly farmland-dwelling species to human control, though another factor almost certainly is their lesser ability to withstand the worst of our winter weather. Overall, these deer show signs of a lack of hardihood in general, with a very limited resilience in stressful situations.

Even so, the numbers of Chinese water deer at large are probably greater than most people realise. Being small, they are often mistaken for muntjac. The distinguishing characteristics of these two species are described in chapter 1, but in view of the frequency with which the two are confused it is worth repeating the key points of distinction here. Chinese water deer are somewhat larger – about midway in size between muntjac and roe deer. And apart from being antlerless, Chinese water deer have only very short tails, whereas the tail of a muntjac is quite long, being conspicuously raised to reveal its white underside when its owner takes off at speed after being disturbed.

The main area of Chinese water deer distribution in Bedfordshire and adjacent east Buckinghamshire appears to be bounded by the A5 (Watling Street) in the west and the M1 in the east, although with some overlapping of both highways, and to extend from Milton Keynes in the north to Dunstable in the south. Clive Harris, a professional deer manager in whose company I saw a number of these animals in local fields of young oilseed rape a few years ago, estimates their total number within this area to be somewhat in excess of a hundred.

'Slot' of a Chinese water deer on farmland in Bedfordshire where this species occurs in the wild state as well as in Woburn and Whipsnade Parks.

Both Chinese water deer and muntjac were reported years ago to have escaped from Whipsnade Zoo, which had obtained its original stocks from Woburn. Muntjac are numerous there-abouts, the woods in the Ashridge area being one place where I have seen them, but Chinese water deer in the wild seem to have dropped out of local knowledge.

Caucasian and Siberian roe were both introduced at Woburn by the eleventh Duke of Bedford. The former survived only very briefly but the large Siberian roe appeared to do rather better until the Second World War, when they were thought to have died out or succumbed to poaching. Shortly

Feeding time for a muntjac in a back garden enclosure in Hertfordshire.

afterwards, however, a few survivors were found, three being known for certain to be present in 1950 in the woods west of Woburn village. I searched for them in vain, and after the middle 1950s nothing more was heard of them.

Lying midway between the distributional areas of the European roe of southern England and those of East Anglia, Bedfordshire and Hertfordshire might still be expected to register a blank so far as records of these animals are concerned. Undoubtedly they were present in times long past, but how long they lingered is not known. It was a cause of some local astonishment and more than a little mystification when in 1959 the skeleton of a roebuck, including its antlers, was discovered in Northaw Great Wood, near Cuffley in east Hertfordshire, close to the Greater London boundary.

In 1981 a roebuck was killed in the Woburn area. Its head is now in the possession of Clive Harris, who tells me there have been recent reports of other roe in Bedfordshire. It is thought to be more likely that these come from the north or north-east than elsewhere. If they are the forerunners of a spread into these parts by roe from East Anglia, they are well ahead of the mainstream, which so far appears to have reached no farther than near Duxford, south of Cambridge, where the M11 presents something of an obstacle to further large-scale expansion.

Roe are being increasingly reported from Northamptonshire, but while these could have come from East Anglia they seem likely to have arrived there from a westerly direction.

Unlikely denizens of modern Hertfordshire though wild red deer might be thought to be, there have been several occurrences of them in the fairly recent past. In 1965 two stags turned up in Dowdells Wood, just outside Welwyn. A few months later one of these, a ten-pointer, was seen to have an antler hanging and to be in obvious pain from the broken pedicle which had caused this. It was culled in time for the carcass to be inspected by those of us who attended a muntjac live-catching operation in the area in March, 1966.

The surviving stag moved away, but may well have been the selfsame animal as the twelve-pointer which spent the 1968 rut with a herd of cattle at Bramfield, a few miles east of Welwyn. At around the same time another red stag turned up with cattle on a farm near Luton. Although railways and a motorway intervene to impede such movement, Woburn Park is always suspected as a local source of wandering red deer, which have certainly escaped at various times to roam in freedom for a while, as also have Manchurian sika, although I gather that none of either species is permanently at liberty.

The situation is different with fallow, which are now to be found in woodlands all around Woburn, I am informed. In the twelfth Duke's day it was rare for the larger deer species to escape or, at least, to remain at large for long, although I recall that at the time of the British Deer Society's inauguration, in the snowy February of 1963, some fallow had found a way of negotiating at least one of the cattle grids to graze at leisure outside the park, to which they returned in their own good time.

Wild fallow, descended from park escapees, are nowadays fairly widely distributed in both Bedfordshire and Hertfordshire. From near Royston in the north to beyond Knebworth in the south and the King's Walden Bury area in the west, among other localities, pockets or larger groupings of fallow are to be found almost wherever suitable cover is available. Where these two counties meet Buckinghamshire, north of Berkhamsted, numerous fallow of Ashridge Park origin roam the surrounding Chiltern woodlands.

In 1951 I saw in a wood not far south of Hatfield some black fallow descendants of a herd which escaped from Hatfield Park in the course of the First World War. These deer had subsequently vanished, only to reappear, as if from nowhere, many years later, Lord Salisbury told me. Hatfield Park remained deerless until quite recently, when a small enclosed herd of fallow was re-established there after a lapse of some eighty years.

In recent years sika as well as red deer have been kept in Knebworth Park, north of Hatfield. Broken-down fences have sometimes resulted in sika escaping into woodland outside the park, but efforts have always been made to recover or cull all such animals. I understand that the sika are a cross between the Japanese and Kerama subspecies, the latter being the residue of stock once kept at Whipsnade. I well recall the woods at Knebworth as a haunt of numerous muntjac when I explored them in the early 1950s, and I understand that this is still the case.

Yet another acclimatisation venture by the eleventh Duke of Bedford involved white-tailed deer from North America. These were released into the woods but failed to prosper in the long run, due, it was thought, to a scarcity of young hardwoods on which to browse. They have been kept in the past at Whipsnade.

The deer species present at Whipsnade in 1999 were red, fallow, chital (axis deer), hog deer, Père David's deer, barasingha (swamp deer), Formosan sika and reindeer, as well as muntjac and Chinese water deer. In what is now called Woburn Safari Park, the 1999 stock of deer included red, fallow, chital, Père David's deer, Manchurian sika, barasingha and rusa in addition to muntjac and Chinese water deer.

No attempt is made in this book to deal comprehensively with deer farms, more than a few of which have proved to be short-lived. One that has flourished since the mid-1980s, however, is at Furneaux Pelham Hall, near Buntingford in Hertfordshire, to which red deer of prime quality from both Germany and Denmark have been imported in the past. And a recent addition to the deer parks of these counties is at Picts Hill, near Turvey, which contains a flourishing herd of red deer.

Northamptonshire, Leicestershire and Rutland

These east Midland counties, with their gentle undulations mainly devoted to agriculture interspersed with no more than a modest amount of woodland, are in many ways characteristic of middle England as a whole. The same applies to their deer populations. Two species predominate, one of which, fallow deer, is of ancient origin while the other, muntjac, is a very recent arrival on the scene, and roe and red deer occur in very small numbers outside deer parks.

Red deer are not known to have survived as an indigenous wild animal in Northamptonshire, Leicestershire or Rutland later than the thirteenth century. Up to that time they were present in the royal forest of Rockingham, in the north-east of Northamptonshire, which to this day is the most extensively wooded area of this county. Medieval Rockingham Forest was one of the few in which records of presentments for venison trespass at the forest courts indicate red, fallow and roe all to have been present. It was also one of many where the disappearance of red deer at an early date was very markedly in contrast with the fate of fallow on the same ground, another being the Forest of Rutland, which lost the larger species at much the same time.

In our own time, red deer have roamed at large in varying numbers at various places as a result of escapes from deer parks or deer farms. Bradgate Park, on the outskirts of Leicester, dates from about 1230 and has both red and fallow deer, both of which have occasionally found their way out of the park to roam the countryside around. The sight of such animals had been more familiar in this area many centuries earlier when Leicester Forest was still in being, and not just the name of a service station on the M1 motorway.

Donington Park, on the Leicestershire-Derbyshire border, was securely walled and fenced until it was occupied by the Army during the Second World War, when its defences were breached, enabling both red and fallow to gain their liberty. Deerleaps embodied in the restored fences later lured many deer back in, but most of the red deer had to be culled because of the damage they were causing to local market gardens and otherwise.

Not all were accounted for, however. For quite a long time after this damage-limitation exercise, red deer continued to be seen by the park's owner, Mr J. Gillies Shields, and others while hunting in the neighbourhood, but it is unlikely that any still survive. In the early 1980s red deer were reintroduced to Donington Park, where a flourishing herd is now present.

At around the same time, a new deer park, Mill Park, was created at Arnesby, near Leicester and stocked with red deer from various sources, as well as a few fallow.

Adjoining and partly bisected by the M1 south-east of Northampton is Salcey Forest, one of Northamptonshire's three main royal hunting grounds of old. On a fairly recent visit there I was surprised to see the undoubted slots of red deer, in an area I had never associated with this species. Subsequent enquiries revealed that one or more red deer had apparently escaped from a local deer farm, a situation one may imagine to be likely to be repeated nowadays in many areas, for all that such farms are as securely fenced as commercial considerations make possible.

About 6 miles south-east of Salcey Forest is Whittlewood Forest, another ancient royal domain adjacent to which is Whittlebury Lodge Park. This formerly held both red and fallow deer, and in the early twentieth century some

Slots of fallow deer and muntjac mingle in Salcey Forest and a number of other woodlands in Northamptonshire.

wapiti were introduced, presumably with the aim of enhancing the quality of the former, although any obvious signs of their influence were short-lived. Nowadays red deer are the favoured species in this park, which I understand is managed largely along deer-farm lines. Not long after the Second World War a number of red deer escaped, but they did not long remain at liberty.

Fallow deer were widely distributed in these counties in the Middle Ages and in some places much later. Salcey Forest's original fallow had disappeared by the end of the eighteenth century, but in Whittlewood Forest this species remained numerous until well into the nineteenth century. Records tell of them lying out in their hundreds on Wakefield Lawn, an open space in the forest, and as late as the 1820s fallow deer numbers still ran well into four figures. Disafforestation in 1850 resulted in much of the forest land being given over to agriculture, but substantial areas of woodland remained to preserve something of the area's character.

Fallow deer survived too, albeit mainly within park fences at Whittlebury Lodge. A few remained at liberty, either because they escaped extermination after Whittlewood lost its royal forest status or after subsequently escaping from the deer park. In 1949 all the bucks broke out of

This muntjac from Salcey Forest, Northamptonshire, was a regular visitor to a local gamekeeper's garden, where it shared food put out for pheasants.

the park and, on visiting the area in 1953, I saw slots of fallow in the forest. Ten years later the park's owner urged the newly formed British Deer Society to concentrate some of its attention on eliminating escaped park deer, and since that time this seems to have happened in the Whittlewood Forest area. I understand, however, that a few fallow which may be a remnant of the Whittlewood population may still be found in the Forestry Commission's Hazelborough plantations, which originally formed part of Whittlewood Forest. Enclosed fallow are now present in a park of recent origin at Wakefield Lawn, within the old forest, where wild fallow used to graze in numbers during the royal forest era.

Of Northamptonshire's numerous deer parks of a century ago, only a very few remain. One of these, at Yardley, on the Marquess of Northampton's Castle Ashby estate east of Northampton, is said to date from around the time of the Norman Conquest and may thus be England's oldest non-royal deer park. It lies adjacent to Yardley Chase, an ancient unenclosed hunting ground which probably benefited from being next door to Salcey Forest, just to the west.

The woods of modern Yardley Chase are populated by fallow whose forebears escaped from the nearby park, and those I have seen there have all been black. I have also seen black fallow, undoubtedly from the same source, in present-day Salcey Forest, indicating that history has repeated itself, with Yardley Chase and Salcey Forest once again sharing the same wild fallow population. Movement of deer between the two areas has undoubtedly been made easier by the closure and dismantling of an intervening railway.

Also near Northampton is Earl Spencer's park at Althorp, which dates from the seventeenth century, though whether black fallow escapees from here have contributed significantly to the local wild fallow population I have not been able to discover.

The deer of Fawsley Park, south of Daventry, have long since disappeared, unless a few still remain in nearby Badby Wood, in which park fugitives sought refuge decades ago when they gained their freedom. Feral fallow have also been reported from the Aynho area, on the Oxfordshire border south-east of Banbury, but I failed to find any signs of them there when I made a brief search a few years ago.

Between Kettering and the Lincolnshire border near Stamford extends what remains of Rockingham Forest: no longer a homogenous whole but a sizeable sprawl of disparate woodlands like so many islands in an agricultural sea. Fallow deer here remained abundant until as late as the 1830s, when an estimate by the forest's master keeper, Lord Winchelsea, put their number at around twelve hundred. As the nineteenth century advanced, however, numbers were whittled away. In 1890 the owner of Rockingham Castle thought that only about a dozen still remained. The continued survival of a few around the end of the nineteenth century was also referred to in the writings of J.G. Millais and one or two others. Largely as a result of this the accepted wisdom is that the original wild fallow of this forest never quite died out.

Since then, the local deer situation has changed beyond all recognition. Fallow are present once more in strength throughout the old forest, mostly as a result of break-outs from various parks within and outside it. Boughton Park, near Kettering, Deene Park and others leaked almost their entire stocks of fallow into the countryside during the Second World War or before, since when wild deer have held their own in numbers not greatly inferior to those of the royal forest era. Those I have seen include representatives of the common, white-rumped variety and of the black type allegedly imported to these islands by James I – a mixture which probably reflects their assorted ancestry.

A local deer management society was formed some years ago to co-ordinate deer control on different properties between which these animals move in the forest area.

Between Rockingham Forest and Peter-borough, at the north-eastern end of North-amptonshire, is Castor Hanglands National Nature Reserve, in an extensively wooded area where Naseborough Forest once was, which was disafforested by King John. This has its own wild fallow population, the descendants of a herd once enclosed in Milton Park in this area.

The Donington Park area is where fallow are now most likely to be found in Leicestershire. Those of purely local origin have been reinforced by fugitives from Calke Abbey and Staunton Harold Parks in nearby Derbyshire, some of which have re-enclosed themselves by jumping over deerleaps to join the deer in Donington Park.

Charnwood Forest, west of Leicester, is notable nowadays more for its scenery than for its deer, although fallow were present in ancient times, and a few are still sometimes to be seen there. The Former royal forest of Leicester had the Forest of Rutland as its neighbour, and the two were often referred to as if they were a single entity. The original wild fallow probably vanished before the end of the seventeenth century, but woods in the recently reinstated county of Rutland are once again a haunt of these animals. This is largely as a result of escapes from Exton Park, near Oakham, which is no longer a deer park, although farther east, near the Lincolnshire border, there are fallow which may well be of common origin with some of those in Kesteven.

After the last war there were strong rumours of roe in Rutland, especially in the Pickworth area. These rumours were never substantiated, having almost certainly arisen through misidentification of fallow at a time when many people were still unable to tell one species from another. This may not be the end of the story, for roe from the north are already present in neighbouring Lincolnshire and Nottinghamshire and are steadily spreading farther south.

At various times between 1982 and 1987 roe were seen by the late Kenneth Morrison, a roe stalker of long experience, near his home at Byfield, about halfway between Banbury and Daventry, in west Northamptonshire – possibly a first record for the county in modern times. He was greatly puzzled as to their origin, being unaware of the presence of any other roe within at least a 20 mile radius of that area. In the late 1980s, however, I saw roe myself in the Cherwell Valley, not far south of Banbury in neighbouring Oxfordshire. This is an area which the species has since colonised in some strength, having arrived there, I am now convinced, from a westerly direction, where a roe population is well established near Moreton-in-Marsh in north Gloucestershire. A study of the map suggests that roe from the same source could just as easily have reached Byfield. Whatever may be the true explanation, it is fascinating to know that roe are reappearing in Northamptonshire after so many centuries' absence. They are constantly turning up in new areas. In the early months of 2000 David Muttock, a local professional deer manager, was called out to deal with a roebuck road casualty at Roade, 6 miles south of Northampton. This was a beast of excellent quality which Mr Muttock believes most likely to have been of stock which has reached Northamptonshire from the west.

Shortly before the Second World War, and again soon afterwards, there were reports of Siberian roe in some of the Forestry Commission properties in south Northamptonshire. As with the rumoured roe of Rutland, confirmation of these reports proved elusive, and expert opinion is now at one in disregarding them entirely.

Muntjac arrived early in south North-amptonshire, to which their spread from the Woburn area was assisted by local releases. I shot my own first muntjac in a wood not far from Northampton and have many times seen the species in various other parts of the county, including Salcey Forest, Whittlewood Forest and the Hazelborough woods near Silverstone. On a visit to Rockingham Forest in 1980 I found abundant signs of muntjac and understand that they are now well established throughout that corner of the county and, indeed, in all parts of Northamptonshire wherever suitable habitat occurs. Much the same applies in Rutland and over the greater part of Leicestershire as colonisation extends ever farther north and west, although I understand that their occurrence in the Leicestershire-Derbyshire border area is still sporadic.

Neither Chinese water deer nor sika appear so far to be present in the wild state in these three counties, although it would not be wholly surprising if the former species should prove to have infiltrated south Northamptonshire after spreading there from Woburn. If this has happened, however, their numbers are probably very small. I understand they are present in a woodland enclosure at an undisclosed location near Uppingham, in Rutland. There are also reports of some unenclosed sika in the Stamford area, just inside Lincolnshire, and if the reports are correct some of these might be expected to stray into Northamptonshire.

Red deer in Chatsworth Park, Derbyshire.

Derbyshire and Nottinghamshire

The Midlands, in the main, is not a region of dramatic scenic contrasts, but few topographical extremes are more pronounced than those to be found in Derbyshire and Nottinghamshire between, for example, the bleak Pennine uplands around Buxton and the fertile Trent valley farmlands north-east of Nottingham. Contrast is also apparent when the deer populations of these two north-east Midland counties are subjected to detailed scrutiny, revealing some areas with a relatively high density and variety of species and other extensive tracts of country which are virtually without deer.

Historically, both counties had substantial deer populations. The Pennine uplands were an important red deer stronghold dating back to Saxon times or earlier. In Norman times this region was known as the Forest of the High Peak, a royal domain and a classic example of a forest which, for the most part, was without trees.

At this forest's centre was Castleton, where the castle which gave the village its name served as a prison for many people found guilty of venison trespass. If poaching was always a serious problem, accounting in one short period for upwards of two hundred head of deer, it appears that, in early days at least, the numbers of these animals were such as could safely withstand a sizeable cull. Towards the end of the twelfth century Giraldus Cambrensis, a travelling man with an eye for the local wildlife wherever he went, remarked of this forest that 'the number of deer was so great that they trampled both dogs and men to death in the impetuosity of their flight'.

The deer may have been officially sacrosanct, but during the reign of Henry II permission was granted to certain landholders to hunt hares, foxes and wolves in this part of Derbyshire. Hounds must have been essential for this purpose and it is hard to believe that these animals and their owners were not sometimes tempted by larger, cloven-hoofed quarry encountered by chance along the way. Indeed, if Giraldus is to be credited, it must have been difficult for these hunters to locate their legitimate quarry among such a multitude of deer.

Forest records make it clear that, apart from the odd stray fallow at lower altitudes where there was, it seems, a small amount of woodland, and perhaps the odd roe in similar habitat, red deer were the only species present in the High Peak. As in other royal forests, grazing rights were enjoyed by commoners, and as time went by it became increasingly evident that the numbers of sheep, in particular, had become so great as to leave little pasture for the deer. An Elizabethan record tells of 'the game of redd deare in this forest' being 'much decayed'. In the following century, on top of all his other problems, Charles I had to face a petition from local people to destroy such deer as still remained. This he agreed, under pressure, to have done on his behalf, and during the reign of his successor the High Peak was formally disafforested.

If deer are ever seen today within the bounds of this ancient forest, they are likely to be stray red deer from the resident population just across the border in Cheshire and north Staffordshire, where the species has been at large in varying numbers following the escape of captive stock in the Second World War.

Not far east of the erstwhile forest the Duke of Devonshire's park at Chatsworth dates from at least the mid-sixteenth century and retained a herd of red deer until the middle of the twentieth century. In 1947 a number escaped over snowed-up fences and a few remained at large in the estate woodlands and elsewhere for several years afterwards. Red deer were later reintroduced and when I visited the park in the early 1980s a flourishing herd had been built up. Nowadays there are no resident wild deer on the Chatsworth estate; any which get out of the park are accounted for as quickly as possible. A few miles south, in woods near Matlock, a few wild red deer have been reported which, like others on the high moorland to the north, may be of Chatsworth antecedents, although they seem just as likely to stem from the Cheshire and north Staffordshire population.

Black fallow deer like these predominate in the Clipstone area of Sherwood Forest.

There are also fallow deer in Chatsworth Park. A quite separate population of wild black fallow occurs in woods on the west side of the Derwent valley, near Rowsley, about 4 miles south of Chatsworth. These descend from animals once enclosed in Stanton-in-Peak Park, which ceased to be a deer park not many years after the Second World War. Stray deer from this population sometimes turn up on the Chatsworth estate.

Much of the countryside between this area and Derby was within the medieval forest of Duffield Frith. As well as being much lower-lying than the Forest of the High Peak, this second Derbyshire royal forest was extensively wooded, providing ideal habitat for the fallow deer which were its speciality. Whereas the deer of the High Peak were almost exclusively red, with just the occasional stray fallow, the exact reverse was true of Duffield Frith, where any red deer which materialised were itinerants from the uplands.

Duffield Frith was paled around its perimeter, but this was to prevent commoners' stock from straying rather than to contain the deer. Within the bounds of the forest there were also a number of deer parks whose occupants were more or less free to jump in or out at will. As the centuries went by the amount of woodland in this forest was progressively reduced, and deer were last recorded in it in the early seventeenth

ABOVE: *A deerleap constructed to enable feral fallow deer to rejoin their captive brethren in a reconstructed deer enclosure in Welbeck Park, Nottinghamshire.*

BELOW: *Bark-stripping damage to a young conifer by red deer in Sherwood Forest.*

century. From the time of the Commonwealth onwards Derbyshire's deer were confined to deer parks. There were a number of these well into the twentieth century, especially in the south of the county where, along the Leicestershire border, fallow of stock once enclosed in parks like those at Calke Abbey, Donington (both of which still contain deer), Locko and Staunton Harold still roam wild in nearby woodlands.

Some of the fallow bucks in Donington Park, which straddles the Derbyshire-Leicestershire border, exhibit antler abnormalities such as sometimes failing to cast and retaining bulbous, spike-like vestigial antlers for two or more years in succession. The cause of this awaits investigation.

A deer-farming development involving red deer was started in 1979 by the owner of Scotland Farm, at Ockbrook, a few miles east of Derby. Riber Wildlife Park at Matlock exhibits a small number of fallow deer as well as a few muntjac.

Nottinghamshire boasts no such giddy altitudes as its neighbour, but its one ancient royal forest is better known, at least in name, than either of those in Derbyshire. Whether or not an outlaw named Robin Hood ever helped himself to the King's deer in the glades of Sherwood, his legendary exploits have been the substance of rhyme and fable since at least the fourteenth century.

What records do indicate is that Mansfield was an important royal manor with which Sherwood Forest was closely associated in earlier times. Fallow deer were present here from the Middle Ages onwards, and in the first half of the thirteenth century they were sufficiently plentiful for Henry III to make numerous gifts of them, in many cases for stocking local deer parks. There were several of these, Clipstone Park and Bestwood Park being among the most important. Neither now exists, but parks of one sort or another have been a particular feature of Sherwood Forest throughout its history and have made important contributions to the continued survival of deer here.

Extending from Worksop in the north of the county, all the way to Nottingham in the south, Sherwood Forest was long and, although relatively narrow, had space enough in its heyday for a relatively large population of red deer. Indeed, it was primarily as a red deer forest that Sherwood was long noted. Estimates at various dates in the sixteenth and seventeenth centuries put their numbers at around a thousand. Their subsequent decline as wild animals was largely due to progressive habitat reduction, with large chunks of the hitherto open forest being enclosed behind park fences from the 1680s onwards.

By the early nineteenth century not much unfenced forest remained. When Sherwood was formally disafforested in 1827, the last of its free-ranging red deer had already joined the fallow behind park fences. Records suggest that as early as the sixteenth century most if not all of the local fallow were already confined in parks, leaving only red deer free to roam the open forest.

The three northernmost parks, which were carved out of the forest at various dates, lay in what became known as The Dukeries. Welbeck Park can trace its history back to the early fourteenth century and became the seat of the Dukes of Portland. A Duke of Kingston created Thoresby Park in the late seventeenth century, and a Duke of Newcastle was responsible in the early eighteenth century for the creation of what he called New Park, later known as Clumber Park. Each of these parks was very extensive and contained large numbers of deer. Farther south was Annesley Park, first stocked with deer in the seventeenth century, while on the east side of the forest there was a deer park in the grounds of what had once been Rufford Abbey. On Nottingham's outskirts was Wollaton Park, dating at least from the seventeenth century and with herds of both red and fallow deer.

After Sherwood's royal forest era ended, the nineteenth century saw few changes. At some stage, Clumber Park ceased to be a deer enclosure, and in the early twentieth century Thoresby Park, which once held a thousand deer,

ceased to contain red deer, although it retained its herd of fallow. Welbeck was subdivided into smaller parks before the Second World War. One of these was for red deer, another for fallow of various colours and yet another for white fallow only. Once there were a few white red deer as well, not to mention a small herd of Japanese sika deer, the latter having been supplied by Joseph Whitaker, author of that late-nineteenth-century work of reference *A Descriptive List of the Deer Parks and Paddocks of England*, from a herd he owned at Rainworth Lodge, another Nottinghamshire deer park.

The outbreak of the Second World War turned this situation upside down. Welbeck Park became a military training area, and when the Army moved in, the deer, or nearly all of them, moved out. The park at Rufford Abbey lost all its deer. As for the fallow in Annesley Park, many escaped and the rest were shot. Thoresby Park's fallow were joined by some of these fugitives, while other deer from the same park joined in the general exodus, which effectively turned the clock back to the time when Sherwood Forest had a resident wild deer population.

The white deer alone remained behind park fences at Welbeck, at least for a time, but when I visited Sherwood Forest in the early 1970s I found that they, too, were at liberty. The many I saw in the Welbeck Park area had no deer fence

Deer fencing had to be temporarily lowered to enable a trapped red deer to be driven back into Sherwood Forest by the estate staff in the background of this picture.

A red deer wallow in Sherwood Forest.

broke out of Welbeck Park during the course of the Second World War. A dozen or so of these animals still survived, thanks to careful protection, it being agreed between the two or three major estates over which they wandered not to shoot red deer except in the case of sick or badly injured individuals. As an additional safeguard, some were later caught up and placed in a special enclosure, from which they were subsequently removed to join the fallow deer still behind park fences at Thoresby.

There are still a few wild red deer in the Sherwood Forest area, as are a moderate number of fallow. Wild white fallow are rarely seen now, almost certainly because of their high vulnerability to poaching. By contrast, the deer enclosure at Welbeck now holds an all-white herd of fallow, no deer of any other colour having been born there since 1983.

Although wild fallow are now less plentiful than they were in the early 1970s, they still occur throughout Sherwood Forest except in the vicinity of one or two villages like Blidworth, where disturbance by dog-walkers is particularly pronounced. There are, in effect, three separate populations: the main one, of mixed origin, in the northern part of the forest; the mainly black fallow in the Clipstone plantations, which are of Rufford Abbey origin; and descendants of the Annesley Park deer. Many of the last-named live on the west side of the M1 motorway and are more or less isolated by it from the other fallow in Sherwood.

Thoresby Park and Wollaton Park both retain their herds of fallow. Wollaton Park, which also has red deer, is nowadays owned by the City of Nottingham, which maintains it as a public open space. The Rainworth Lodge sika ceased to be kept there several years before the Second World War. Sika did not long remain at Welbeck, and no deer of this species are currently known to be at large in either Nottinghamshire or Derbyshire.

One interesting development in the later decades of the twentieth century has been the arrival of roe in Nottinghamshire, where they now occur in small numbers in Sherwood Forest and possibly elsewhere after an absence of many

to restrain them by then, and a large proportion of the fallow I saw in Sherwood Forest proper were also white. Two years later, however, I found that a radical change had occurred. Some of the deer had been lured into a brand new deer enclosure, while most of those that escaped recapture on the Welbeck estate had been shot. This had been done ostensibly in response to complaints of damage from farmers, although perhaps an additional reason was to help discourage foxhounds from pursuing the wrong quarry. This I thought rather sad, in view of the fact that on my earlier visit I was told that the then Duke of Portland had been happy to have a reasonable number of wild deer on his property.

On this second visit I saw far fewer fallow than previously in Sherwood Forest itself. However, the high point of my brief sojourn was a sighting of wild red deer on the Thoresby side of Sherwood: three prime stags, with antlers in early velvet, which had emerged on a fine spring evening from bordering beeches and rhododendrons to graze in a secluded pasture. With meadow grass dangling from their mouths, they paused periodically and stared towards my wife and myself, but otherwise paid us little attention as we watched from 200 yards distance.

These red deer were descendants of those that

centuries. Surprisingly, they are thought to have arrived, not from the north but from across the Trent to the east. Even so, they must have filtered down to these parts from the north of England by way of Yorkshire, and their future progress will be worth watching. Several have already met their deaths on the roads of Sherwood. The forest itself is not thought to offer much in the way of good roe habitat and so any future increase of the species here may be limited. Roe have also reached Derbyshire, and are reported by the National Trust to be present in the vicinity of Hardwick Hall near Chesterfield.

Another recent arrival in Sherwood Forest is the muntjac, again in fairly small numbers so far and with limited potential, it is thought, for future increase in the forest itself. This incursion into Nottinghamshire is, however, part of a general pattern of spread which has already brought these deer to virtually all parts of the Sherwood and Lincolnshire Forest District of Forest Enterprise. Reports of muntjac in Derbyshire are as yet few and far between, though this situation could soon change. There are no known wild Chinese water deer in either county.

Japanese sika deer like these were formerly kept in two Nottinghamshire deer parks.

7

THE DEER OF
EAST ANGLIA AND
LINCOLNSHIRE

Essex

Deer are among the last things most people associate with Essex, yet the county has strong historical links with these animals, and within the last half-century the number of species known to be breeding in the wild within its borders has increased from one to no fewer than four. It was not until the nineteenth century that the last of the indigenous wild red deer of Essex died out, and within the last few decades they have unexpectedly reappeared as regular local residents.

Non-black fallow deer have infiltrated the ancient Epping Forest population, noted for once having been all black.

The agricultural character of so much of Essex is at odds with the status of almost the whole of the county in times past, as a royal forest. At quite an early date the area subject to Forest Law was substantially reduced, but the Forest of Essex, later more generally known as the Forest of Waltham, remained of significant size and importance as a royal hunting ground, although there are relatively few records of kings having hunted there in person.

The core of the somewhat shrunken forest was in the south-west of the county, centred upon the tract of woodland which, at a very much later date still, was called Epping Forest. This evolved from the local practice of naming different parts of the larger forest after places in their individual areas as if, indeed, they were separate entities. It was in this fashion that Hatfield Forest and Hainault Forest, along with others now largely forgotten, came to acquire separate identities.

The early disafforestation of much of Essex, as well as concentrating most of what was left in the south-west, left a number of isolated fragments of Crown land widely scattered about the rest of the county, and these remained subject to Forest Law for a time at least.

It was in the main forest, however, that most, if not all, of the red deer had their stronghold from the Middle Ages onwards. They were the fairly frequent subjects of various grants issued under the royal warrant and of presentments at the courts for venison trespass. They were also hunted by various packs of hounds at different periods. Not all such hunting was of wild stags. For many years there was an Easter Monday hunt which the citizens of London were invited to attend, and at which a carted stag with gaily beribboned antlers was released. These ribbons apparently aided followers in locating the hunted stag, which was often reluctant to enter into the sporting spirit of the occasion and was eventually caught unharmed to repeat the process another day.

Red deer numbers slowly declined and in 1820 orders were given for those that remained to be caught and transferred to Windsor Great Park. Not quite all were captured and the very last, a stag, was hunted and killed at West Ham, probably in the 1830s. Under a different administration, in about 1883, an attempt was made to reintroduce them to Epping Forest. Within a short time, however, the stag and two hinds involved caused so many problems in the neighbourhood that the experiment had to be ended.

A few years after this, there were reported to be five red deer at large in the Hatfield Broad Oak area, near Bishop's Stortford, close to the county's western border. These were said to have been the result of a pregnant hind being left out by a pack of hounds hunting carted deer; the hind eventually produced a stag calf which fathered subsequent calves on its mother. Carted deer continued to be hunted in Essex up to the time of the First World War.

The story of red deer in Essex thus came to an undramatic end – or so it seemed for half a century. Then, in the mid-1960s, at almost exactly the same time as red deer occasionally turned up in neighbouring Hertfordshire, others materialised in Essex, at first in the north-west of the county, then, in the following years, at many widely separated localities.

As was pointed out by the late Dr Donald Chapman, following an Essex Field Club survey of deer in the county up to 1970 it was clear that in north-west Essex, at any rate, wild red deer were resident and breeding in small numbers. This state of affairs, I am reliably informed, continues but it is emphasised that numbers so far do not justify any intervention by visiting stalkers.

Nearly all reports of red deer elsewhere in Essex relate to isolated wanderers, mostly stags or, in some cases, pairs of stags, sometimes in company with fallow deer or cattle in the case of single individuals. As well as sightings of some of the numerous local fallow, in April 1976 I saw the undoubted slots of a red deer in a wood within 2 miles of Great Dunmow, quite close, as it happens, to Easton Park, which contained both red and fallow deer until about half a century earlier. Occasional red deer have been seen much farther south, including such unlikely places as near Southend-on-Sea and near Tilbury – remarkable testimony indeed to the nomadic tendencies of some of these animals.

From where have these red deer come? Dr Chapman's survey leaves us wondering. A glance at the map, however, reminds us that a mere 25 miles of quiet East Anglian countryside separates Essex from the Newmarket area and its approaches to the Thetford Forest complex, where red deer have been present for many decades. Having regard to their very obvious propensity for fairly long-distance explorations within Essex itself and elsewhere, such a journey as that between their Thetford Forest stronghold and where they have lately occurred in breeding strength in Essex would be in no way out of the ordinary. Journeys of similar length in a westerly direction are known to have taken Thetford red deer deep into Cambridgeshire in the past.

In 1960 a new deer park was created at St Osyth's Priory, about 3 miles west of Clacton-on-Sea. Both red deer and fallow were introduced. Within a few years some of the fallow deer escaped to found what became a locally flourishing wild population, but there are no reports of any red deer having followed their example.

Fallow deer are known to have been present on Crown forest land in Essex since at least the late Middle Ages, and probably earlier. The fallow of present-day Epping Forest are among the very few herds in England which are known for certain to have had an unbroken history as wild animals since the heyday of royal forests. This is not to say that there have been no later infusions of fresh blood. According to the nineteenth-century naturalist and writer J.E. Harting, King James I diverted to Epping Forest and Enfield Chase a consignment of black fallow deer from Norway which were sent originally to Scotland.

This was possibly done after a particularly bad outbreak of 'the murrain', as nearly all epidemic diseases affecting deer were at one time called, had devastated the previous fallow population locally. Whether those earlier fallow were black is not recorded. Subsequent ones certainly have been, Epping Forest's fallow having gained some degree of fame from their all-black colour. Strenuous efforts to preserve this have not been helped by post-war escapes of other park fallow of mixed colours. These fugitives have infiltrated the Epping herd to such an extent that a significant proportion of the deer there are now non-black.

When Epping Forest fallow lived alongside the native red deer, they often outnumbered the larger species by as much as six to one. After the red deer disappeared, fallow also dwindled. Halfway through the nineteenth century what remained of the once great Forest of Essex was fast being eaten away by enclosures and conversion to agriculture.

After Hainault Forest suffered this fate in the 1850s there began a swing of public opinion towards preserving at least something of what was left in other areas. This at last found expression in the 1870s in a series of measures designed to perpetuate Epping Forest, not as a

royal hunting preserve but as an open space and recreational area for Londoners. Queen Victoria herself attended a ceremony to mark the handing over of the forest to the care of the Corporation of the City of London, which remains its guardian to this day.

If the forest was saved, the deer very nearly were not. By 1860 their numbers were down to about ten. They just about hung on until the life-saving change of regime, and as the 1880s progressed they increased again quite quickly. By the end of the century numbers were up to about two hundred, with others known to be present on neighbouring private ground. The First World War saw a drop in numbers to about a half of their previous peak, but the Second World War and the years immediately following produced annual counts of well above a hundred. One day in the late 1940s my wife and I saw a herd of seventeen fallow within yards of the busy crossroads by the Wake Arms public house in the heart of Epping Forest.

Since then the trend has been markedly downward. A combination of such factors as increased disturbance by the public, with many fawns being killed by uncontrolled dogs, and a remorselessly rising toll of fatalities on the roads has made any sightings of deer among the hornbeams and other picturesque old timber of Epping Forest proper a rare event. Nearly all of those that remain have gravitated to the relative peace and quiet of private property north of the forest, where concern for the herd's survival helped bring about the provision, some years ago, of a fenced fallow deer sanctuary from which the public are excluded.

Any control of fallow deer numbers in Epping Forest has been carried out by the keepers. Elsewhere in Essex it is very largely in private hands. There has been plenty of scope for such activity since the Second World War, when most of the deer parks still remaining disgorged most, if not all, of their deer into the countryside around.

Wild fallow deer distribution is now so complex that it is difficult, in some areas, to be sure which deer originated from which park or parks. The general picture is of fallow being present in most of the major woodlands, and in more than a few of the minor ones, north of the London–Colchester railway. As I have said, I have seen them in woods near the former Easton Park, west of Great Dunmow and near Marks

A small population of wild red deer has been resident in Essex in recent years, and isolated wanderers have turned up in some areas, sometimes associating with cattle in the absence of their own kind.

Hall Park, south-east of Halstead, both of which lost all their deer before or during the Second World War.

I had a memorably unexpected sighting of an assemblage of sixty wild fallow on a grassy slope overlooking Brentwood bypass, from which my attempts at camera-stalking were critically scrutinised by the occupants of a police car while traffic streamed past in both directions. These deer, of mixed colours, mostly live on publicly owned open space preserved as a local amenity and lead a reasonably charmed life. They provided much of the source material for Donald and Norma Chapman's monograph on fallow deer, first published in 1975 and reprinted in 1997. They descend from Second World War escapees from nearby Weald Park and are primarily responsible for introducing a non-black element to the Epping Forest herd.

Hatfield Forest, near Bishop's Stortford, was a fenced deer park from the mid-nineteenth century until the First World War and contained a few red deer as well as several hundred fallow. Deer are no longer enclosed on what is now a National Trust property where open pasture is mixed with woodland and where I have seen abundant signs of fallow on three separate visits.

Other Essex areas with good numbers of fallow include the Rodings, woods to the north and south-west of Chelmsford, and woods in the countryside around Quendon Hall Park in the north-west of the county, which still has its own park herd of fallow. Occasional wanderers do sometimes appear south of the railway from London to Colchester and Ipswich, but the only established wild population of recent times appears to be that in the vicinity of St Osyth.

Other Essex parks which lost their deer at various times in the twentieth century include Thorndon Park near Brentwood, Wivenhoe Park south-east of Colchester, and Langleys Park at Great Waltham.

It was while making my third unsuccessful attempt to see the now free-ranging fallow in Hatfield Forest that I enquired of a local cottager about muntjac in that area. I was told that very occasionally they were seen, which struck me as strange, having regard to the fairly plentiful muntjac slots I had noted mixed up with those of fallow, and I had hardly left the cottage when a muntjac doe pottered out into full view from a nearby thicket.

Muntjac were first reported in Essex around the time of the Second World War. The earlier ones were isolated wanderers, the very first having apparently been shot just outside Colchester in 1941. The skull of another, killed on the road near Gosfield north of Braintree, was reported in the Chapmans' survey as being in Colchester Museum.

Not until 1958 was the first breeding population noted, in woods near Margaretting, about 3 miles south-west of Chelmsford. From the mid-1960s onwards reports of muntjac became more frequent. Isolated wanderers continued to appear at unpredictable locations, but regular sightings of one or more individuals began to be noted in some localities, such as Debden and Radwinter in north-west Essex, the Marks Hall area south of Halstead, and woods just north of Tiptree, south of the London –Colchester railway. Odd ones turned up in built-up areas such as Chelmsford and even in the heart of West Ham. Some found their way into Epping Forest, a few by being released there following rescue from a variety of predicaments elsewhere, but most by their own unaided efforts. A proportion of these latter were recognised for what they were after coming to grief on forest roads.

Since the mid-1970s muntjac have continued to increase and to spread across the county, where they are likely now to be found in wooded areas almost anywhere, with high-density populations in many places.

Sika have sometimes been reported but never confirmed in the wild in Essex, although a hundred years ago there were a few in Weald Park near Brentwood, where there were also, at that time, a couple of roe deer. Roe were reintroduced into Essex when, in about 1884, two bucks and four does from the Milton Abbas area of Dorset were caught up and released in Epping Forest. At first these increased in number quite quickly, although by the turn of the century most had drifted out of the forest itself into neighbouring private woodlands. Having peaked at just over forty head, this population sharply declined, perhaps mainly due to the unwillingness of property owners to tolerate them, and by the mid-1920s, at the latest, they had disappeared entirely.

Roe, then, seem to have been absent from Essex for almost forty years. It was not until the mid-1960s that they were noticed once more in the county, not as Epping Forest fugitives returned at long last from limbo but as unexpected arrivals in one or two woods near the Suffolk border. Having spread south from the Thetford area, they are now resident in small numbers to the east of Saffron Walden and in the Colne valley between Halstead and Haverhill, but have yet to start full-scale colonisation of the county farther south.

In 1999 Colchester Zoo included reindeer among its exhibits and Mole Hill Wildlife Park at Waddington, near Saffron Walden, had red deer, fallow, sika and some muntjac.

Norfolk and Suffolk

Mention of Norfolk and Suffolk brings to the mind of many a stalker an instant vision of the large Thetford forest complex, with its coniferous expanses well-stocked with deer affording sport of which full advantage has been taken by enthusiasts for many decades. There the vision, in general, ends, wholly failing to take into account the widespread occurrence elsewhere in these two shires of no fewer than five wild deer species dispersed in interlocking patterns of distribution.

The presence of deer in this corner of England in ancient times is attested to by the antler picks and similar prehistoric artefacts discovered at Grime's Graves, not far from Thetford. Thetford Chase, as its name makes clear, has a history as a hunting ground, albeit of lesser status than a royal forest, although King James I is on record as having visited the area.

The modern history of Thetford Chase as a deer area dates from about 1884, when a gentleman named William Dalziel Mackenzie apparently imported some roe from Wurtemberg in south-west Germany. These were released on one of the local landed estates, which remained more famous for producing prodigious bags of pheasants than for any deer-stalking potential

which might at that stage have been envisaged, and for years little more was heard of the deer.

The situation began to alter after the First World War, when the newly formed Forestry Commission acquired substantial acreages of rather bare and desolate ground for planting trees in what is now known as the Breckland. Having survived up to that point by securing at least a toehold in such plantations and game coverts with tolerant owners as was available, the roe were not slow to take advantage of this radical transformation of their hitherto less than ideal adopted homeland in East Anglia. Within a few years they were well established and becoming increasingly unwelcome to a generation of foresters unused to coping with such animals in highly damage-prone young plantations.

Red deer in early morning in a clearing in Thetford Chase.

The middle decades of the twentieth century saw the replacement of shotgun drives by rifle control and related modern management techniques. Coupled with this was the lease of stalking rights over a substantial area of this wholly man-made forest to a sporting organisation, the St Hubert Club of Great Britain, for the benefit of its members.

Under this new regime, overall deer management in the Thetford group of forests, which overlap the Norfolk-Suffolk border, was placed in the hands of a team of rangers headed by Mr Rex Whitta, as dedicated a deer man as has ever been so employed. Rex's lifelong work in promoting the proper treatment of deer and harmonising their presence with the demands of commercial forestry were recognised with an MBE and the award in 1992 of a prestigious trophy for outstanding services to wild deer conservation.

Roe have continued to flourish at Thetford and yet, despite endeavours to improve their quality by long-term selective culling of poor specimens, antler development in general is mediocre. Whether this reflects a fundamental genetic inferiority or merely poor feeding has been much debated and the true explanation could well be a combination of both.

If roe were initially slow to expand their range beyond their Thetford Forest stronghold this process has lately accelerated to the point where they have appeared with increasing frequency in various other parts of Norfolk, have pushed west into Cambridgeshire and have spread south across Suffolk to the Essex border and just beyond. A recent *Provisional Atlas of Suffolk Mammals*, published by the Suffolk Naturalists' Society, shows roe as having been recorded in almost all parts of the county, although in the east they do not yet appear to have gained a firm foothold. The forester in charge of the forests of Rendlesham, Tunstall and Dunwich, near the coast to the east of Woodbridge and south of Southwold, reports that roe were still not resident there in 1999, and the warden of the bird reserve owned by the Royal Society for the Protection of Birds at Minsmere, south of Dunwich, tells me that roe have not been observed there since an isolated report of one in about 1991.

Up to the late 1990s the East Anglian roe have remained geographically isolated from those elsewhere in England, but as the range of the latter, as well as of the Thetford roe, inexorably spreads to fill vacant areas, the time cannot be far distant when all the roe of England, and indeed of mainland Britain as a whole, are united as a single population.

Although it was as a roe haunt that the Thetford forests first came to the notice of deer-minded people in general, great excitement was caused when, in the 1950s, it became clear that red deer of truly exceptional quality were present as well. In 1956 a magnificent twenty-

A typically modest-sized cast roe antler from Thetford Chase.

one-point stag was shot by a visiting stalker. Two years later another twenty-one-pointer yielded its trophy, and in 1959 a twenty-pointer was secured.

Blood from prime stock obtained from Warnham Court Park in West Sussex was, without doubt, largely responsible for the antler size of these stags and others of scarcely lesser quality, which were acknowledged to have been the progeny of animals left out by the Norwich Staghounds, which hunted carted deer and continued to operate until 1963. Hinds were the normal quarry of this pack, which from 1947 maintained a small stock of deer for this purpose in a park at Diss.

Good breeding apart, the continuing high quality of the now purely wild red deer of Thetford contrasts so strikingly with that of the roe in the area that it can only be explained by high-quality feeding – not in the forest itself but outside it, on agricultural land where their wandering habits readily take them and where their wellbeing crucially depends upon a degree of toleration by local farmers. These people work in close co-operation with Forest Enterprise in ensuring the survival of a healthy stock of red deer while also maintaining the population at a level where the damage they cause is not excessive.

Although giant stags have eluded me, dawn and dusk forays into the forest with head ranger Rex Whitta and his associates have given me memorable sightings of some of the finest wild red deer in Britain, grazing placidly in clearings among the all-embracing conifers which cover so much of western East Anglia in the neighbourhood of Thetford, where the counties of Norfolk and Suffolk meet.

A rather more unexpected sighting was of three red deer on a frosty dawn in a field near the Suffolk coast, with the North Sea sparkling in the early morning sunlight in the background. These belonged to what was then a small but healthy wild population which now numbers two hundred or more and has maintained itself for years in the countryside around Minsmere bird reserve, extending west as far as Framlingham. One of their haunts is Dunwich Forest where, surprisingly as some may think, until recently they were found to cause little damage

Rex Whitta, MBE and one of his wildlife rangers examine a newly found cast roe antler before setting off to track down a radio-collared deer.

and so were tolerated at a level of population which might not otherwise have been acceptable. Latterly, however, the damage has increased and the management policy has had to be adjusted accordingly.

More than twenty years ago, when I first enquired about these red deer, I was given to understand that their place of origin was Henham Park, midway between Halesworth and Southwold. As this had ceased to be a deer park by the middle of the twentieth century, if the red deer did in fact stem from there they must have been at liberty for about as long as those at Thetford.

Are they perhaps connected with a group of up to thirty red deer reported in 1970 in the Haveringham-Huntingfield-Walpole area, a few miles west of Halesworth? These were thought to have been descended from a single pregnant hind left out by the Norwich Staghounds some twelve years earlier, which was later joined by a stag of unknown origin. At the same time another small group of red deer were reported from woods in the Bradfield St George area, south-east of Bury St Edmunds, while not long previously some others, supposedly also descended from hunt outliers, were said to exist in the Palgrave area near Bungay, just south of the Norfolk border. The Suffolk mammals atlas suggests that red deer are to be seen sometimes in a number of other areas, and there seems to be very little doubt that red deer recently reported as resident in Essex first arrived there from across the border in Suffolk.

The wandering habits of red deer in Suffolk appear to be matched by their neighbours in Norfolk, where they occasionally break in to join the resident fallow in Holkham Park, near Wells-next-the-Sea. Isolated individuals have turned up from time to time in the vicinity of Norfolk Wildlife Park near Great Witchingham, north-west of Norwich, where red deer have also been known to be killed on the roads.

Norfolk Wildlife Park exhibits red deer as well as fallow and muntjac. Melton Constable Park, at Melton Constable between Fakenham and Holt in the north of Norfolk, has had red deer since the thirteenth century, as well as fallow for an unknown period and Japanese sika since about 1900. In Suffolk, Helmingham Park, near Stowmarket, has both red and fallow deer, while Ickworth Park, near Bury St Edmunds, now has fallow deer only.

If the distributional pattern of red deer in Norfolk and Suffolk is a trifle complex, that of fallow is infinitely more so. All the fallow deer at large in these two counties derive from stock which originally escaped from one of the once numerous local deer parks. In Norfolk these still include Holkham Park, which dates from the eighteenth century, and Houghton Hall Park, near King's Lynn, which nowadays contains Père David's deer, barasingha (swamp deer) and chital (axis deer), as well as its famous large herd of white fallow. There are also wild fallow in its neighbourhood. As well as the fallow, red and Japanese sika deer inside it, Melton Constable Park has a few wild fallow and roe and occasional muntjac in the countryside around it.

Blickling Park and Dudwick Paddock once contained fallow but do so no longer, and at Sandringham, before the Second World War, there were red deer as well as fallow. The north and north-west of the county in general, where all these parks are or were located, is where wild fallow are now most likely to be found. Populations are small and discontinuous, one of the best-known being in the Stratton Strawless area, a well-wooded locality a few miles north-west of Norwich.

Suffolk parks, past and present, which have held fallow include Flixton Hall Park near Bungay, Ickworth and Livermere Parks near Bury St Edmunds, Orwell and Woolverstone Parks near Ipswich, and Somerleyton, Polstead and Campsea Ash Parks in other areas, as well as Henham Park, already mentioned, and Helmingham Park east of Stowmarket which, like Ickworth Park, has also played host to red deer.

At various times nearly all of these parks have leaked fallow deer into the countryside around them, so that today there are wild fallow populations, mutually isolated except where their parks of origin were close enough together to make it easy for escaped animals to mingle, over wide areas of the county.

In Thetford Chase the only fallow are apparently a few which have found their way into the area of forest between Thetford itself and Brandon. However, King's Forest, to the south of the main Thetford forest block, is a haunt not only of numerous roe and muntjac and itinerant red deer but of a resident herd of fallow, almost certainly descended from stock once enclosed in nearby Livermere Park.

Significant fallow populations are also present in the Frostenden-Henham-Byford area, a few miles east of Halesworth and extending south to Dunwich Forest; in Rendlesham and Tunstall Forests, east of Woodbridge; between the Deben and Orwell estuaries; between the Orwell and Stour estuaries in woods south of Ipswich; and in the area between Ashbocking and Helmingham, a few miles north-north-east of Ipswich. Among other Suffolk fallow haunts are the woods around Ickworth Park, some 3 miles south-west of Bury St Edmunds; around Stansfield, Cavendish and Boxted, north-west of Sudbury; in woods between Stansfield and Bridge Street, close to Sudbury; and in the Hawstead-Lawshall-Stanningfield area, some 9 miles north of the same small town, as well as the Milden-Chalesworth-Whatfield area, east-north-east of Sudbury.

Such Suffolk fallow as I have seen, in one of the woods between the Orwell and Stour estuaries and in Rendlesham Forest, have been almost all of the common variety. However, the Tunstall and Rendlesham fallow of today, totalling around 150, include animals of various colours from white to black, while the Henham group also includes some white individuals, which the owner of Henham Park regarded as a disincentive to poaching because their tell-tale colour made their place of origin all too obvious.

The most dramatic local deer development of the last few decades of the twentieth century has been the increase and spread of muntjac. Up to the late 1960s and early 1970s most reports of the species were of isolated individuals observed by chance in widely separated localities. Since then these miniature Asian cervids have become well-established residents in suitable areas over much of Norfolk and almost the whole of Suffolk, including such places as the Minsmere bird reserve, on the North Sea coast. Revisiting Thetford Chase in the 1980s after many years'

A Thetford high seat, designed locally for wildlife observation.

absence, I saw muntjac almost as readily as roe – and at one point had both muntjac and roe in view at the same time.

The numerous muntjac of nearby King's Forest have been the subjects of detailed study by Norma Chapman and others, one purpose being to identify possible interaction with roe. One still somewhat tentative conclusion is that roe now find it necessary to forage farther afield for food, on agricultural land in particular, as a result of competition for woodland browse with the smaller species. Should such behaviour be proved beyond all doubt, and found to apply in other areas, a significant anti-muntjac backlash by roe enthusiasts may be expected.

Whereas roe have yet to colonise the eastern Suffolk forests or to establish more than what seems a tenuous toehold east of the Ipswich–Great Yarmouth railway, in the forests of Rendlesham, Tunstall and Dunwich the muntjac population now runs well into three figures, while in Minsmere bird reserve their browsing habits are hampering efforts to maintain a sound coppicing regime.

It now appears that muntjac did not originally reach these counties by their own unaided efforts, but at least partly as a result of covert releases in the Thetford area in the middle of the twentieth century. Others may well have escaped from private ownership or been set free when their owners tired of keeping them.

An interesting recent development is the arrival at Minsmere and neighbouring wetlands of Chinese water deer. So far no more than a few isolated individuals have been identified, but in so suitable a habitat they may be expected to increase and flourish. Where these have come from is not known, but they seem quite likely to be the advance guard of range expansion from farther north where, almost unnoticed by the world at large, Chinese water deer have established themselves in many wetland areas.

Many years ago now, I recall Philip Wayre of Norfolk Wildlife Park, at Great Witchingham, telling us at a British Deer Society symposium that some Chinese water deer had escaped from there and were thought to have survived, perhaps to found a feral colony. Whether from this or some other source, this secretive species is now at home among the reedbeds of the Norfolk Broads and in such places as Rainworth Marshes nature reserve, midway between Norwich and Caister.

Farther south, Strumpshaw Fen RSPB reserve, in the Yare valley east of Norwich, wetlands near Loddon and wetlands in the valley of the Waveney near both Bungay and Beccles have also been reached by Chinese water deer, which might easily have pushed farther south still to arrive in the Minsmere area.

Another known source of Chinese water deer is the former Kilverstone Wildlife Park, near Thetford. These have made their home, not alongside red, roe and muntjac in the forest but among wetland vegetation along the banks of the River Thet which, no doubt, they find much more suitable.

In the December 1994 issue of *Stalking Magazine*, Mr Arthur Cadman, a former Deputy Surveyor (chief executive) of the New Forest, reported that when cycling to work in Thetford Forest in 1935, he saw a solitary sika stag almost every morning. Where this stag may have come from is uncertain. The likeliest place of origin appears to be Melton Constable Park, some 25 miles distant, from which sika have sometimes escaped, although they do not appear to have established a feral breeding population. An isolated stag might well have become disorientated and thus ended up in Thetford Forest after wandering haphazardly across country.

If any wild sika are present today in Norfolk or Suffolk they have so far not been recorded. They could have occurred as recent escapees from the park at Melton Constable or from one of the wildlife parks which have stocked them in small numbers, as well as various other deer species, in recent times.

As well as the various parks and wildlife collections already mentioned, Banham Zoo at Banham, between Diss and Attleborough in Norfolk, exhibited Formosan sika and Chilean pudu in 1999, while the Otter Trust at Eastham, near Bungay, included fallow deer and muntjac among its exhibits. Suffolk Wildlife Park at Kessingland formerly exhibited deer but does so no longer, and Kilverstone Wildlife Park, as noted above, is now closed.

New deer parks run along traditional lines are comparatively rare. One such in Norfolk is Gunton Park at Suffield, about 5 miles south of Cromer, which contains Formosan sika as well as red deer, fallow and barasingha. There are also a number of deer farms in various parts of East Anglia, most of which are stocked with red deer.

Chinese water deer habitat in Woodwalton Fen, Cambridgeshire.

Cambridgeshire and Lincolnshire

The combination of wide, treeless expanses and highly intensive agriculture characteristic of so much of these two counties adds up to a countryside which, on the face of it, leaves little spare space for deer. While to a large extent this superficial impression accords with the facts, as in so many other unlikely seeming shires as haunts of deer, there are considerably more of these animals, and in a wider range of species, than many a stranger might think even remotely possible.

The fact that modern Cambridgeshire includes the ancient county of Huntingdonshire may, in view of the latter's highly suggestive name, allow, on due reflection, second thoughts to prevail about the probable lack of deer, at least historically. It turns out to be the case, indeed, that medieval Huntingdonshire was, in part at least, royal forest and thus subjected, at least for a time, to the Draconian penalties for venison trespass embodied in Forest Law. There seems to be clear evidence that red, fallow and roe deer were all present in varying numbers, the last-named being perhaps the most numerous while the red deer were especially fond of the wet and woody wastes of the fens.

Wild deer of all three species probably vanished in the late Middle Ages and for centuries thereafter were almost exclusively confined within deer-park fences. Cambridgeshire, as originally defined, had few such parks. Lincolnshire had not many more and, in common with other counties, has latterly lost some of those which it once possessed. Again, as has been the case elsewhere, the disappearance of deer parks has coincided with the reappearance of deer as wild animals in a number of localities. The fact that most of these are close to the parks is no coincidence. There has also been some immigration by unenclosed deer from outside these counties.

A total absence of wild red deer would not be altogether surprising, but this is not quite the way things have been in recent years. Cambridgeshire lies close enough to the Thetford group of forests on the Norfolk-Suffolk border for some of the red deer from that quarter sometimes to wander that far west. Odd red deer and even small groups have turned up from time to time. A stag and two hinds which were seen a few years ago at Wicken Fen National Nature Reserve, just inside Cambridgeshire a few miles north-west of Newmarket, were thought at the time to be escapees from a deer farm not many miles away across the fens. Since then, however, wild red deer have become quite frequent visitors to Wicken Fen, and there is now thought to be little doubt that they are of Thetford Forest stock.

There have been red deer in south Lincolnshire for an unknown period of time. Their territorial stronghold has been Grimsthorpe Park, near Bourne, where until the Second World War red and fallow deer enjoyed

Chinese water deer droppings in Woodwalton Fen.

the free run of some 450 ha of pasture and old woodland, the latter being a preserved remnant of the ancient Kesteven Forest – or so it was described to me when I visited the park, although Lincolnshire has no royal forest history as such.

In 1941 all the deer escaped. Some of the local people saw this as a golden opportunity to augment their meagre wartime meat ration. So many red deer in particular were converted into venison that within a fairly short time only one hind remained. She was given special protection, and as she happened to be pregnant, hopes for the future of Grimsthorpe red deer were pinned on her producing a stag calf. This she duly did, and once this matured other calves resulted from the bond between mother and son. The small herd which was thus re-established was given a subsequent boost by fresh blood introduced from Scotland.

In post-war conditions the deer at Grimsthorpe recovered their numbers while adapting to changed circumstances. No longer restrained by deer-park fences, they turned to using the park as a base from which they forayed at will, and at some risk to themselves, in the countryside all around.

This Kesteven countryside, west of the fens, differs from much of the rest of Lincolnshire in being comparatively well wooded, an important factor in enabling park-escaped deer to survive in numbers. Red deer recovered to a point where, by 1973, there were reckoned to be nearly forty hinds and calves, which tended to remain fairly localised to the park and its immediate vicinity, where they enjoyed a degree of sanctuary as part of Grimsthorpe estate policy. An unknown number of stags wandered more widely, in peril of their lives when they crossed property boundaries onto land where they were not welcomed.

On a visit that year, my wife and I toured the park in company with the Grimsthorpe agent, the late Philip Grimes, who did much to conserve the deer of southern Lincolnshire and to ensure their proper management through the medium of the Kesteven Deer Society, which he helped found. He showed us a fine group of eighteen hinds and followers, which watched us warily through the gnarled trees of old Kesteven Forest as the Land-Rover in which we were driven came to a halt not many yards from them.

Twelve years later I timed a further visit to coincide with the rut. By then the hinds were ranging more widely and were not so easy to find. After scouring the park and seeing only one fallow buck, I called on the estate forester, from whose house on the edge of the park he had heard a stag roaring a short while previously. After our chat I waited and listened nearby as dusk merged into darkness. It was well after dark when I heard the first roar, from a direction I carefully noted for following up at dawn next day.

Daylight revealed an autumn countryside densely blanketed by fog. Locating a wild Lincolnshire stag in that murk would have been impossible without auditory assistance. I was about to give up when I heard the long-awaited roar which turned my steps towards a field of winter wheat in which two hinds loomed momentarily from the mist just feet away. The stag then fleetingly materialised alongside them before all three took off at speed.

Earlier that year, in Philip Grimes's company I was able to see a fair number of the local wild fallow. At one time the intention had been to cull selectively in favour of the light-spotted, menil variety, but this idea was later abandoned. I did see menil fallow as well as some black and some white individuals, but all the rest were of the common variety – unspotted chestnut brown on the flanks in winter, changing to dappled fawn in summer.

Most of these fallow were undoubtedly of Grimsthorpe Park ancestry, although Irnham Park, not many miles to the north-west, has also contributed its quota of escapees to the neighbourhood, resulting at that time in an estimated population of a thousand wild fallow in southern Lincolnshire. This number was later reduced in the interests of farm and forest crop protection, but still amounts to several hundred, while the red deer, although somewhat reduced in numbers in the late 1990s, continue to be maintained at a suitable level to safeguard the herd's survival. Other sources of escaped fallow deer at this end of the county include Burghley Park, near Stamford, and the National Trust's Belton Park, just north of Grantham, both of which still contain park herds of this species, while feral fallow from just over the border in Rutland have almost certainly mingled their blood with that of the local strains in Kesteven.

The deer parks in central Lincolnshire – Scrivelsby and Revesby – have been the source of feral fallow in some of the woods south of Horncastle. The Revesby Abbey deer came originally from Syston Park, near Grantham, a bygone haunt of both red and fallow deer, and are of the light-spotted, menil variety. As happened at Stonor Park in Oxfordshire, the first deer at Revesby Abbey were herded there by dogs and horses. How such a method of moving deer could ever have been successful – over many miles in this case – without all the animals escaping defies modern imagination. Both Revesby Park and Scrivelsby Park still hold fallow, those at Scrivelsby being of the black variety.

Brocklesby Park, near Brigg in the north of Lincolnshire, lost all its deer as a result of military activity during the Second World War. Although many fallow deer escaped, their early demise was predicted. They continue to flourish, however, in woods between Brigg and Caistor, as I was reminded by deer warning signs when I drove that way a few years ago.

Normanby Park, north of Scunthorpe, lost its deer many years ago when it was still in private hands, but has been restored as a deer park under local government ownership. Red and fallow deer are both present, and when the fence was cut some years ago a number of deer escaped. There are still wild fallow deer in the neighbourhood as well, apparently, as some red deer, because males of both species sometimes break in to join the park deer during the rut.

North Lincolnshire's other chief claim to our notice centres on the fallow deer of Read's Island. Introduced to the low-lying Humber island in the early 1970s to replace conventional farm livestock, these deer had increased to around 180 at the time of my visit in 1989, when it was planned to live-capture and dispose of the entire stock to purchasers on the mainland.

In the event, I later learned, this proved impracticable. After a series of unforeseen problems, such as deer getting stuck in the tidal mud surrounding the island while trying to evade their would-be captors, the decision was reluctantly taken to cull them instead. When this operation had been completed as far as practical, two or three deer remained unshot. Four or five years later the population on Read's Island had increased to about a dozen. The island, with its large winter wildfowl population, is now a bird

Wild fallow deer in the Grimsthorpe area of south Lincolnshire.

highly vulnerable areas of Hayley Wood have been deer-fenced.

The fallow deer I saw hereabouts were predominantly black, with a minority of common-coloured animals and a few white individuals. They seemed as much at home on the wide open spaces well outside Hayley Wood as in the nature reserve itself.

Even if some doubt still lingers as to whether red deer from the Thetford forests have travelled west into Cambridgeshire, there can be no uncertainty regarding roe from the same area – the only feasible place of origin of the modest roe population which now lives on Wicken Fen. From another source I learn that the Duxford area, about 8 miles south of Cambridge, represents the approximate westerly limit of spread by roe in that direction, a situation which has not noticeably changed for several years. The unwooded nature of much of Cambridgeshire seems much more likely to slow than to halt further range expansion by roe in years to come, a process which will bring them into much more suitable country once they reach Northamptonshire and are able to join the roe already there in small numbers.

reserve in the care of Lincolnshire Trust for Nature Conservation. I understand that in 1999 the number of fallow had increased further to around thirty, completely wild and self-sustaining. As also happened in earlier years, Read's Island deer sometimes swim to the mainland and are at least in part responsible for the present widespread occurrence of wild deer in northern Lincolnshire. On Crowle Moor, west of the Trent, there are red and roe deer as well as fallow.

Cambridgeshire's wild fallow derive from immigrants from across the county border in Bedfordshire, where fair numbers frequent woods in the Royston area. In Cambridgeshire itself I have seen them in and around Hayley Wood, an important nature reserve towards the south-western end of the county, where their presence has caused concern to botanists because of their possible impact on the oxlips and other rare flowers for which this wood is especially noted. Such fears, I believe, have proved largely groundless, to the relief of local mammalogists who take pleasure from seeing these deer in the otherwise prairie-like, sparsely wooded Cambridgeshire countryside. As an extra precaution, I understand that the most

South Lincolnshire also lies within colonising reach of roe from East Anglia once they have surmounted the hazards and obstacles of the intervening fens. The gap might then be closed quite quickly between these invaders from the south and others which have already spread into Lincolnshire from the north. Having rounded the Humber from what was briefly North Humberside and found their way across inhospitable terrain in South Yorkshire, roe have crossed the Trent to colonise much of north and central Lincolnshire, in parts of which I understand they are now well established. The Bardney and Wragby areas east of Lincoln have been mentioned by one informant as among the local haunts of roe, and I learn from another source that roe and muntjac as well as fallow are to be found in the countryside surrounding Scrivelsby Park, near Horncastle.

Muntjac are widely reported in Lincolnshire, especially in the south, where until the mid-1980s there were only sporadic occurrences. They are now resident on the Grimsthorpe estate, in the Stamford area and elsewhere. Studies by Norma Chapman and others indicate that many of the muntjac now present in areas remote from Woburn in Bedfordshire, their original point of enlargement, were deliberately released much nearer to where they now occur. In the case of Lincolnshire it seems likeliest that natural spread from Northamptonshire brought them into the south of the county. On the other hand I understand that there have been muntjac in central Lincolnshire since the early 1970s, although apparently they have not yet crossed the intensively farmed Lincolnshire Wolds to colonise country farther east.

In Cambridgeshire muntjac have been present in the Hayley Wood area since at least the mid-1970s. They were first noted in the nature reserve at Wicken Fen ten years later and have since become well established to the point of causing problems for local gardeners by feeding off carrot tops and the like. Spring bulbs have also attracted unwelcome attention from these animals, and bluebells and fritillaries have been browsed down to the ground.

Monks Wood National Nature Reserve, which lies 5 miles north of Huntingdon, has had muntjac since the early 1970s, and numbers here later built up to saturation level. This was allowed in order to facilitate studies of their impact at high densities upon a woodland ecosystem. At Holme Fen, which is relatively dry and wooded and lies 5 miles farther north, I saw a muntjac in 1980.

Chinese water deer were also present, and I subsequently learned that, as the muntjac increased in numbers, Chinese water deer in Holme Fen decreased more or less in proportion.

Woodwalton Fen, about 3 miles north-east of Monks Wood, has a resident population of both muntjac and Chinese water deer. Here the two seem to co-exist fairly happily, perhaps by virtue of the fact that muntjac keep mostly to the dryer parts while most of the water deer live in the wet fen, where the water level is carefully regulated to maintain a predetermined amount of aquatic habitat. Two of us spent a short spring holiday watching and trying to photograph Chinese water deer in Woodwalton Fen, where this species is well established and has been present for several decades, having been locally introduced, as it now turns out. When first seen they were mistaken for muntjac, an error not corrected until a knowledgeable observer pointed out their true identity.

Chinese water deer have also been seen in Monks Wood, which has no obvious attractions for this species. Indeed, if competition for habitat is an underlying cause of the decline of these deer in Holme Fen, Monks Wood, with its teeming muntjac, might be considered anything but attractive.

At Wicken Fen, some 20 miles south-east of Woodwalton Fen, Chinese water deer were reported in the early 1980s. Judging by the frequency with which they are now seen there, it seems likely that a resident population is now established in this wetland. The distribution of these secretive Asian immigrants is a subject about which much remains to be learned.

8

THE DEER OF
NORTHERN ENGLAND
AND THE ISLE OF MAN

Lancashire and Yorkshire

To couple Lancashire with Yorkshire may seem like mixing oil and water, at least in the eyes of many who hail from these two northern English shires. For the present purpose, however, joint treatment makes very good sense, not least because county boundary changes, with the appearance of new counties and their subsequent dismantling into multiple unitary authorities, has given rise to widespread confusion as to where these historic shires begin and end. To make matters infinitely worse, land has been transferred from one to the other, a fact which must be a source of agonising irritation and regret to many a native.

One could go on to complain about the disappearance, in 1974, of Yorkshire's Ridings and their replacement by the separate counties of North, West and South Yorkshire – East Yorkshire having somehow become as mythical as the South Riding once was, and insult being added to injury by the detachment of part of Yorkshire to form half of the new county of Humberside. What was so briefly North Humberside has now been reincarnated as East Yorkshire, to the considerable satisfaction of all who live there and call themselves Yorkshiremen and women. However, lamentation about such changes would clearly be fruitless. For practical purposes I shall deal with Yorkshire as one unit, treat Merseyside as part of the geographical county of Lancashire, and deal with that part of modern Lancashire which was transferred in the 1970s to what then became Cumbria in the section on that county.

When the Bowland area was taken from Yorkshire and added to Lancashire, a whole

A sika stag in early velvet in the Ribblesdale area of Lancashire.

population of deer went with it, thus substantially enriching the cervine fauna of a county which, having lost the Furness Fells, would otherwise have had little to boast about.

Modern Yorkshire has more wild deer, with a greater variety of species, than one might at first suppose and, contrary to what superficial impressions might suggest, neither Merseyside nor the former North Humberside are entirely devoid of deer.

Historically, the deer of Lancashire and Yorkshire have a number of features in common. Much of the high Pennine moorland which the two shires share, as well as the North York Moors abutting the North Sea coast, was Crown forest land reserved for deer in the Middle Ages and, in some cases, for a fairly long time afterwards. As might be expected from the amount of treeless ground at higher altitudes, a high proportion of the deer in these upland hunting preserves were red deer, the species best suited to such an environment, then as now.

It has often been said that red deer are, by nature, woodland animals which only choose to live in the open where no more suitable habitat is available, but this is surely a misunderstanding. On Exmoor, for example, a high proportion of the red deer live in the open at any one time, despite an abundance of lower-ground woodland where plenty of deer are also present. On the Continent too, in mountainous areas such as the Swiss National Park, many red deer live in the open from choice, in the summer at least, despite there being no shortage of woodland on adjacent lower ground. A shrewd and experienced observer once suggested that red deer are beasts of the forest border rather than forest animals proper, and I think this is nearer the truth.

In many mainly high-ground forests, records indicate that there were also fallow and roe deer, although these were likely to have lived for most of the year at lower altitudes. There were also several sizeable low-ground forests where red deer as well as fallow were present, but most of these were disafforested at a fairly early date.

West of the Pennies, the Forest of Blackburnshire was one of the most extensive, and appears, to some degree, to have been used as an umbrella title for a number of smaller forests or chases south of the Ribble. These bore the names of localities such as Rossendale, Accrington, Pendle and Trawden, and were to a large extent separate entities. Red and fallow deer both occurred, but the red deer probably lasted no longer than the seventeenth century at the latest.

North of the Ribble were the Lancashire forests of Wyresdale and Quernmore, where red deer probably died out at much the same time as they did in Blackburnshire Forest. In this area, too, was the Chase of Myerscough which once had both red and fallow, as did Fulwood and Bleasdale Forests in their heyday, names now virtually forgotten.

Not quite so unfamiliar to modern ears is the name of the Forest of Bowland, which retained its special status until the early nineteenth century and its indigenous wild red deer almost as long – longer, almost certainly, than any nearby forest either in Lancashire or Yorkshire, to which latter county it originally belonged. Bowland's relative remoteness undoubtedly helped to give the red deer a longer lease of life here than elsewhere, and as long as they survived here they are likely to have strayed, at times, into neighbouring forests, where they had formerly also been present as a resident wild species.

Whereas all these forests were in more or less hilly country, marginal from an agricultural standpoint, the more southerly Lancashire Forest of West Derby was essentially a low-ground one. Extending well into modern Merseyside, its name finds an echo in the title borne by the heads of the Stanley family, whose ancestors have had Knowsley Park as their seat since the Middle Ages.

Enclosed in 1348 and still with a 9 mile wall around it, this park held both red and fallow deer until well into the twentieth century. A number of both species escaped in the course of the 1940s. Latterly the deer park proper was home to red deer only, which came to lead a completely wild existence, wandering in and out of the park entirely at will. Eventually, the depredations of these Merseyside red deer became too much for neighbouring farmers. Some had to be shot, but most were live-captured after being lured by handouts of feed into a small enclosure where they could be narcotic-darted before being sent to a deer farm in Scotland. Since the late 1980s the resident deer at Knowsley have been some fallow and Père David's in the safari park which now occupies a section of the larger park.

In the late 1980s or early 1990s a roebuck was killed on a main road at Croxteth, next door to the Knowsley estate and only a little way

The Ribblesdale sika of east Lancashire live largely on farmland.

outside Liverpool. This was one of several isolated occurrences of roe deer noted around that time and more recently in various parts of south Lancashire, including Merseyside, in what can only be described as less than hospitable roe habitat.

Such reports reflect the southerly spread of roe from the border counties, which continued throughout most of the twentieth century. Just before the First World War some Austrian roe were introduced to the Belle Isle estate alongside Windermere, but to what extent this speeded up the arrival of roe in Lancashire is debatable. G. Kenneth Whitehead tells us, in his book *The Deer of Great Britain and Ireland*, which was published in 1964, that by the early 1960s Carnforth, in the far north of modern Lancashire, was about as far south as roe had then reached.

Since then, the push south has proceeded at a slow but steady pace. Around the mid-1970s forestry plantations in the Gisburn area of Bowland began to be colonised in earnest. Roe have since become resident in suitable habitat, and sometimes in less suitable locations, throughout Lancashire north of the Ribble. South of that river they are thinner on the ground but are none the less present in increasing numbers wherever conditions make this possible. Their farthest spread has now just about reached the industrial heartland of south Lancashire and the approaches to Greater Manchester. Whether they can manage to penetrate this zone and thus reach Cheshire, we should find out in the fairly near future.

In the Gisburn plantations and around Bolton-by-Bowland in Ribblesdale, roe now live alongside the descendants of sika deer introduced around 1907 to provide a quarry for hunting. Already, some two years earlier, black fallow deer from Littlecote Park in Wiltshire had been brought up to these parts and released for the same purpose. The man behind this, Lord Ribblesdale, had been Master of Buckhounds to Queen Victoria, and he now proceeded to form his own pack of buckhounds in his home area.

The Ribblesdale Buckhounds have long departed, and if the black fallow have not followed suit they keep a very low profile nowadays. Not so the sika, however, which I have seen on several occasions on the Ribblesdale hill farms over which they still range fairly widely, thanks to a measure of protection without which they might well not long survive. Away from the Gisburn plantations woodland is scarce. The deer use such of it as there is but at any one time a good proportion seem to live more or less in the open, using such shelter from the elements as they can find in the lee of drystone walls, in scrubby hollows and elsewhere.

The precise identity of these sika seems uncertain. They were always assumed to be Japanese until Kenneth Whitehead pointed out that their average weight was considerably greater than that recorded for most Japanese sika elsewhere, and he believed that they might be of the larger Manchurian subspecies, *Cervus sika mantchuricus*.

Odd red deer have occasionally strayed south from the Middleton Fell area of Cumbria into the heart of sika country, but their presence here is not welcomed because of the risk of hybridisation. Red deer have also sometimes turned up near where Lancashire borders Cumbria, close to the shore of Morecambe Bay, as have fallow deer escapees from either Dallam Tower or Holker Hall Park, just inside what is now Cumbria but what used to be the far north of Lancashire.

Deer ground in bygone centuries on the Yorkshire side of the Pennines included Skipton and Craven Forests, where red deer flourished until Stuart times, and Wensdale or Wensley Dale Forest, which a deer count in forests north of the Trent in 1538 revealed to have within its boundaries sixty red and ten times as many fallow deer at that time. Wharncliffe Chase, north-west of Sheffield, dates from 1252 and was once partly forest and partly enclosed park. In later centuries it was more park than forest with enclosed populations of both red and fallow deer. Eventually it lost its fallow and the 1947 winter almost put paid to the red deer also, which nowadays lead a wild existence, ranging the woods along the slopes of a steep-sided valley through which runs the road linking Sheffield with Huddersfield.

The numbers of these feral Wharncliffe Chase red deer built up to a level where they were causing serious damage to trees around a reservoir. The water authority responsible decided to end this problem by having the deer eliminated. Local stalkers declined to do this, but eventually help was obtained from another quarter. Some thirty red deer were shot, but enough survived to save the herd from immediate extinction.

Near Otley, north of Leeds, was an ancient hunting ground called the Chevin, next door to which was the Forest of Knaresborough, both at one time well stocked with deer. Across the Plain of York once spread the royal forest of Galtres, in early days stocked with both red and fallow and still with 800 fallow at the time of the 1538 census.

The fens and other flat lands south of Goole and west of the Trent formed another large and well-stocked hunting ground up to the early seventeenth century. Hatfield Chase, as this was called, covered some 28,000 ha, over which roamed several hundred red deer. One day in 1609, to entertain a visiting prince, a special hunt was arranged in the course of which a large number of stags were driven to the Trent. Hunt followers took to boats to pursue and kill such deer as they could before they reached dry land again.

There were also some fallow in Hatfield Chase, although whether these were free ranging or enclosed within a park – or possibly both – the records do not make quite clear. In this area today, on the Lincolnshire border near Crowle I understand that three species of deer – red, fallow and roe – are all to be found roaming wild.

A Yorkshire park of ancient origin which may well have obtained its original stock from the wild deer of the neighbourhood is Studley Royal, near Ripon, which is now a National Trust property. Both red and fallow deer have long been kept here, and at various times dating back to the First World War some of both have escaped. I once had a brief view of a red deer in one of the nearby wooded valleys where this species has re-established a small wild population based on some of the larger local estates between Wensleydale and Nidderdale. Like wild red deer everywhere, individual animals sometimes travel quite long distances and their survival largely depends upon tolerant treatment on ground they visit.

Red deer on farmland near Hellifield, North Yorkshire.

Swinton Park, near Masham, has an old-established herd of fallow, a number of which escaped some years ago to set up home in local woodlands which were also sometimes visited by red deer. At one stage these increased to such an extent that a substantial cull was necessary to appease the local farming community. Since then the deer-park fence has been strengthened and strenuous efforts have been made to eliminate fallow deer outside the park, this being deemed necessary to protect vulnerable young plantations as well as to minimise damage to agricultural crops. A further break-out more recently was responded to with vigour, and in 1999 only a very few fallow remained at liberty in the area.

A number of other Yorkshire deer parks, of which there were many more before the Second World War than now, have at various times lost stock over crumbling walls, through broken fences or simply through gates which have been carelessly left open. For example, Ripley Castle Park, which lies south of Ripon, has been another source of fallow roaming wild in the nearby countryside. Baldersby Park at Topcliffe, north-east of Ripon, lost all its fallow during the

Red deer in Yorkshire's Studley Royal Park at the time of shedding their winter coats, when they look decidedly tatty.

war, shortly after which Wentworth Park, near Rotherham, lost deer through fences damaged by open-cast mining operations. The latter deer park has since been restored and today has a herd of red deer. Of the deer which escaped in the 1940s and their descendants, none are known to survive in the countryside around Wentworth Park.

Cawthorne Park, north of Barnsley, and Nostell Priory Park, east of Wakefield, both lost fallow through wartime escapes. For many years after the war a number of deer remained at large in the Nostell area in particular and some may still survive in the woods there, while the same applies to fallow which took refuge in nearby Black Fen after breaking out of Parlington Park, near Leeds. Next door to this Park, at Aberford, the local authority at Leeds now owns a park at Lotherton Hall, to which red and fallow deer were originally introduced. The two did not get on well together, fallow fawns sometimes being killed by the red deer, and in 1999 it was decided to dispose of all the fallow and concentrate on red deer only. In the 1980s a deerleap was constructed to enable any deer that escaped to re-enter the park, but up to 1999 this had never been used. Muntjac were formerly kept in a separate enclosure, but these have now died out.

East Park, in Hull, is another municipally owned deer park, and the deer here are fallow. At Holywell Green, Halifax, a privately owned deer park created fairly recently was stocked with red, fallow and Manchurian sika deer, which were intended mainly as breeding stock for sale to other establishments.

A few miles south-east of York wild fallow have made themselves at home in the Wheldrake and Skipwith Common areas as well as near Strensall and Sand Hutton to the north-east of the city. These are thought to have originated as wartime escapees from Escrick Park and Aldby Park, neither of which now holds deer.

Perhaps most interesting of all Yorkshire's deer areas, both historically and today, is the region which flanks the Vale of Pickering on its north side, inland from Scarborough. The medieval Forest of Pickering was one of England's most important, with good stocks of three deer species and wild boar. By the sixteenth century fallow outnumbered red deer, which were probably extinct here as wild animals by the early eighteenth century. When fallow died out in the wild is uncertain, but red and fallow both survived until recent times in Duncoombe Park, near Helmsley on the southern fringe of the North York Moors.

Fallow deer in Yorkshire's Studley Royal Park.

Wartime escapes led to both species becoming wild once more. The numbers of red deer at liberty from this source are thought never to have been large. The local Chief Ranger for Forest Enterprise, Charles Critchley, told me in 1995 that he believed that none then remained. Occasional isolated red deer still turned up, but these were thought to be deer-farm fugitives rather than remnants of the Duncoombe Park stock. Red deer have reappeared, not as mere isolated wanderers but as a small but coherent population – not so small, however, as not to require some modest culling in the interests of forestry protection. To what extent this resurgence is attributable to the unsuspected survival of Duncoombe Park stock on the one hand and to deer-farm escapes or releases of stock on the other, Mr Critchley is hesitant to hazard an opinion.

The fallow deer have never been in serious danger of extinction. They continued to use Duncoombe Park as their headquarters long after they were free to wander at will, but nowadays they roam more widely, their regular range covering an area some 5 or 6 miles in diameter.

The southern foothills of the North York Moors are mantled nowadays by forestry plantations which clearly offer ideal deer habitat.

So obvious was this that when I made enquiries locally in the early 1950s I was astonished to be told that, apart from small and isolated populations of red and fallow, these extensive forests were deerless.

The roe I had hoped to learn about had seemingly not been heard of in these parts since the Middle Ages. Indeed, a late 1940s survey by Sir William Ling Taylor of the Forestry Commission had pinpointed Arkengarthdale, in Yorkshire's far north-west, as being the county's only known haunt of roe deer at that time, so perhaps I should not have been surprised that forests in the Pickering area should apparently have had none of the species a few years later. Chief Ranger Charles Critchley tells me that a report on local fauna published in 1951 by Scarborough Natural History Society mentioned roe as being present then in all the local forests, but in view of the contrary indications from Sir William Ling Taylor's survey as well as what I was told shortly afterwards, the accuracy of this report seems open to question.

The position since then has undergone a very dramatic transformation. During the 1970s I learned that a few roe had begun to filter through, and on a very brief visit I was lucky enough to see some in the Dalby Forest area at a time when numbers were still very low. On my next visit, in the mid-1980s, I not only saw more roe, this time on a large estate in the Vale of Pickering, but learned that energetic steps were having to be taken to initiate systematic management of the burgeoning population.

Mr Critchley and others have drawn attention to the exceptionally high performance of these Pickering roe, more especially in the excellent feeding conditions associated with the

Manchurian sika deer in Studley Royal Park.

Jurassic limestone at lower altitudes. A study over a four-year period in the early 1980s produced the remarkable finding that more than 50 per cent of roe doe kids became pregnant in their first year, most having single foetuses, although a small proportion had twins. An exceptionally high proportion of triplet births have also been noted here, more especially when a low roe density coincided with the optimum conditions mentioned above. As the numbers of roe have increased, their excellent quality and breeding performance have moderated in proportion, although both remain well above average. Recent research has cast some doubt upon whether roe kids can carry pregnancy to full term, and even whether they are actually capable of conceiving in the first place, but people involved with deer

management in the North York Moors Forest District of Forest Enterprise remain convinced that what they have reported is well founded.

Where did these Pickering roe originate? A recent study involving the comparison of blood types found that the roe which compared most closely with those in the Pickering area were those at Thetford Chase in East Anglia, which are descended from animals introduced in the nineteenth century from Germany. Just what conclusions might be drawn from this similarity are uncertain, unless perhaps there was a covert introduction of Thetford roe at some time after the Second World War, when an interest in woodland stalking for trophies became more general.

A rather more credible explanation is that they spread there from farther north in the course of progressive range expansion. The last twenty-five years or so have seen a steady expansion of range by roe in a southerly direction right across Yorkshire.

In the woods around Ripon and Masham roe are now common. In summer a few take to the high ground, where the still fairly unfamiliar sight of these red-pelaged beasts on the grouse moors sometimes causes brief consternation to breeding birds and to grouse-moor keepers used to associating red with an entirely different and decidedly unwelcome mammal.

Their push south across the Plain of York has brought roe into the outskirts of Leeds and well beyond to the Doncaster area, where many have been drowned while trying to cross deep drainage channels in some of the least suitable countryside for roe anywhere in England. Indeed, they have colonised almost the whole of Yorkshire where conditions make life possible for them and they have already pushed on into Lincolnshire and Nottinghamshire, although not yet, it seems, into Derbyshire to any significant extent. The limit of their range in that direction is the countryside around Sheffield, where they are still very thin on the ground.

South of the Vale of Pickering, roe have crossed the gentle-contoured Yorkshire Wolds into East Yorkshire, where the Humber itself is their limit. In Hull they have been seen well within the city itself and sometimes even in the docks.

Japanese, Manchurian and Formosan sika have all been introduced at various times to deer and wildlife parks in Yorkshire. Twenty-five years or so ago a number of Japanese sika escaped from Allerton Park, near Knaresborough, which they shared with a herd of fallow, but they are not thought to have survived. Manchurian sika do well alongside red and fallow deer in Studley Royal Park, near Ripon, from which one or two have escaped in the past but have not established a wild population. It is interesting to note that there have been no recorded instances of hybridisation between these sika and the red deer. In East Yorkshire, Formosan sika are among the exhibits at Sewerby Hall Park and Zoo at Sewerby, near Bridlington, which is owned by the local authority.

A sika stag of unknown origin was killed some years ago on a main road near Helmsley, west of Pickering, and identified beyond all doubt as a sika by Charles Critchley.

Local releases or escapes are clearly responsible for a number of sightings of muntjac in recent years in various parts of Yorkshire, including the outskirts of Leeds. Many years ago a muntjac caused a local flutter of excitement by turning up from no one knew where on Flamborough Head, just north of Bridlington.

In the early 1950s two attempts were made to introduce Chinese water deer to Studley Royal Park. At least two were killed by visitors' dogs and the remainder all escaped but did not long survive in freedom.

No account of deer in Yorkshire would be complete without a few words about the red deer kept by the late Mr Eric Foster at Little Newton, a hill farm at Long Preston between Hellifield and Settle, not many miles from the Lancashire border. A stag and four hinds from Warnham Court Park in West Sussex were acquired in 1956 as foundation stock for a herd which flourished for over thirty years. These deer were free to roam at will, the drystone walls dividing Eric Foster's fields being no barrier to their movement. A few did sometimes wander off on to the nearby Pennine high ground, but most remained for most of the time on the farm, where they ran to be hand-fed by Eric when the called them, as I once saw for myself.

I am told that when Eric had to give up the farm, not long before he died, most of the deer were successfully live-captured and sold. A few eluded capture, and it would be interesting to know whether any still survive.

Cumbria

Cumbria shares with the far west of Somerset and adjacent north Devon, but with no other part of England, the claim to have had wild deer of the same indigenous strain among its fauna ever since prehistoric times, without any interruption. But unlike the West Country, Cumbria can probably also claim to have been a haunt of roe deer since before recorded history. The only other English counties which may also be able to make this claim are neighbouring Northumberland and Durham, which will be dealt with in the next section.

Another important point of difference with Somerset and Devon is that Cumbria has never seen its red deer population shrink to such a low level as to necessitate the importation of fresh stock to stave off possible extinction. There have been some infiltrations of new blood, but not, in the main, into areas where the indigenous genetic strain could have been significantly affected. A far greater threat, which has materialised during the course of the twentieth century, is that of hybridisation with an alien species which has established itself in some strength not many miles from red deer country.

Before discussing this in detail and taking a look at other aspects of the contemporary deer scene, a few words about Cumbria's deer history should throw some light upon how the present-day situation has come about. Because of the wild and rugged nature of much of this region, substantial areas were devoted to deer and to hunting in ancient times. The names of bygone deer forests such as Mallerstang and Furness convey little or nothing to those of our own generation who know their way reasonably well around the English countryside, although the Furness Fells area of what used to be north Lancashire and is now part of Cumbria is known to more than a few of us as the twentieth century haunt of some particularly fine red deer.

Almost equally unfamiliar is the name of Inglewood Forest. This appears on modern maps as a mere area designation, yet once it identified a hunting ground of considerable extent to the west of the Eden valley, stretching from Penrith to Carlisle and containing wild boar as well as red and fallow deer. The mountainous character of many old Cumbrian forests limited tree growth, but Inglewood, being comparatively low-lying, was able to justify its name by including at least some woodland. This would have been an important factor in making it suitable for fallow deer. When these ceased to roam wild here is uncertain, but the last of Inglewood's red deer died some three hundred years ago and the forest passed from the Crown into private hands a short time afterwards.

East of Carlisle was Walton Forest, where red deer and timber were plundered freely by intruders from across the border when England and Scotland were still separate kingdoms.

Of the several Lakeland deer forests which still appear as names on the map, though without much modern justification, Coupland or Copeland Forest was among the most important. With Ennerdale and Wasdale Forests, which were more or less parts of it, it covered a large area near Wast Water and Ennerdale Water, on the west side of the Cumbrian Mountains, where red deer were

The head of a woodland stag from the Furness Fells, south Lakeland, showing the wide span and multiplicity of points characteristic of red deer in this area.

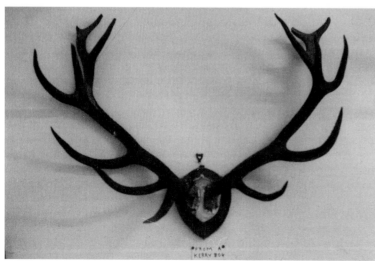

present in strength for many centuries. At one time there were also fallow, presumably at lower altitudes and possibly in parks rather than living as free-ranging animals. The eighteenth century saw a substantial reduction in the ground dedicated to deer, and resident red deer were extinct well before the end of the following century.

Other deer forests of the past included Skiddaw, east of Bassenthwaite Lake, and Thornthwaite, west of it. Any red deer to be seen in either area today will be wanderers from one of the few remaining Lake District strongholds of the species. In northern Lakeland the chief of these is Martindale. This lies to the east of Ullswater, and its survival as a deer forest stocked with red deer whose forebears have roamed wild here since time immemorial owes much to one landowning family, the Hasells of Dalemain.

Successive generations of Hasells have preserved the deer of Martindale either for their own enjoyment or for that of a sporting tenant. In earlier times the deer were hunted with hounds, but nowadays they are managed and stalked along similar lines to those employed on a typical Scottish deer forest. Indeed, Martindale has been described as the only true deer forest still remaining in England, although due to recent range expansion by red deer originating from here this is no longer strictly the case.

As in so many parts of Scotland, Martindale red deer live almost wholly in the open, on hilly terrain which culminates in a ridge, the highest point of which is over 600 m in altitude and is known as High Street. Despite what this may seem to suggest, limited road access and semi-isolation between Ullswater and Haweswater have helped to preserve for Martindale some measure of seclusion from the motor-borne holiday multitudes which swarm throughout most of Lakeland. However, human intrusions on foot have come to cause a degree of disturbance which may well have been a contributory cause of at least some red deer moving out in recent years to seek quieter quarters.

My first view of Martindale red deer was through a telescope thrown down from an upper storey of the Haweswater Hotel by the late Major H.A. ('Herbie') Fooks, who as the Forestry Commission's first game warden was one of the principal pioneers of modern deer management techniques in woodland conditions in Great Britain. The occasion was the first ever field meet of the original Deer Group, the embryonic organisation from which the British Deer Society was later to emerge. Among those present were such other stalwarts of the developing deer interest in Great Britain as the late Henry Tegner, author of numerous countryside books including some on deer, Baron Adam Konopka, who helped found the St Hubert Club of Great Britain, and four people who became vice-presidents of the British Deer Society – Dr Peter Delap, John Willett, the late Jim Taylor Page, MBE, and the leading world authority on deer, G. Kenneth Whitehead. We were all enjoying deer and talking about them in each other's company for the first time ever, in several cases, on that memorable weekend in August, 1956.

Kenneth Whitehead led us in convoy in his single-seater sports car at what I recall as a hair-raising speed along twisty byways into Martindale where, on a fine and brilliantly sunny day between two very wet ones, we were able to watch a good number of the two hundred or so red deer on the forest at that time, a focal point of our attention being a sanctuary area where they were never shot.

On another sunny day, a good many years later, I sat enjoying a lunchtime sandwich with Lakeland deer expert Peter Delap on a steep timbered slope overlooking Thirlmere from the west, watching red deer among the trees only yards below us. Like Haweswater, Thirlmere is now a reservoir helping to supply the needs of faraway Manchester, and conifers planted extensively within its catchment area have

A woodland red stag in Grizedale Forest, south Lakeland. (Peter Delap)

attracted a small resident stock of red deer, numbers being kept at a fairly low level to minimise tree damage.

Between Martindale and Thirlmere, Gowbarrow Park, west of Ullswater, dates back to the Middle Ages and has been a haunt of both red and fallow deer for most of the intervening time, with wild red deer sometimes jumping in to join the resident stock. Some Warnham hinds were once introduced here, and at one period there were also a few white red deer. It is no longer a deer park.

In the same area is Glencoyne, another ancient park haunt of red deer, while the Helvellyn area, east of Thirlmere, is visited by the local wild red deer. The Hasell family home, Dalemain Park, at Pooley Bridge near the north-eastern end of Ullswater, has long held a small herd of fallow, and at one time appear to have been a few wild fallow on Martindale, probably mostly confined to the low ground along the east side of the lake.

East of Haweswater, Naddle Forest had a resident stock of red deer until Manchester Corporation's waterworks department, which had enlarged the lake and acquired adjoining land, decided between the wars to have them killed off. This was unfortunate, because the woodland which clothes Naddle's lower altitudes afforded excellent habitat for the production of quality antlers.

In the mid-1950s resident deer had still to re-establish themselves. Since then, however, red deer have pushed well east of Naddle Forest to repopulate ancient deer ground on Shap Fells, where I have seen them within a mile or so of the Kendal–Penrith road. Sometimes they wander farther east towards the M6 motorway, on which I understand one or two of these venturesome animals have been killed.

The Shap Fells form part of the Earl of Lonsdale's Lowther estate, where red deer from Lowther Park, now a public leisure centre, have sometimes escaped to the hills to join their wild brethren, and vice-versa. In the past, both fallow and sika have also been kept in Lowther Park, from which the fallow in particular sometimes managed to escape, but these only remained at liberty for short periods.

As one would expect from their mainly mountainous, open-ground habitat, the red deer of Martindale and elsewhere in the northern Lakes area do not normally attain heavy body weights or outstanding antler development. The reverse is true of their mainly woodland-dwelling neighbours farther south, which appear at first sight to have no connection at all with their more northerly relations, though this is probably deceptive because the two populations live only 10 miles or so apart – far too short a distance to deter a travelling stag in the rut.

One of the main haunts of these woodland red deer is the Graythwaite estate, where the Sandys family have, for many years, given them a

A young red deer stag on the open hill in north Lakeland's Martindale area. (Peter Delap)

substantial degree of protection. My first view of red deer in this region was on the Claife Heights, west of Windermere, and a particularly memorable encounter some years later occurred at dawn in the Forestry Commission's Grizedale Forest, where a long string of hinds and calves made their way uphill from where they had been grazing on neighbouring pastures to filter back into the forest within stone-throwing distance of where I sat. Equally unforgettable was an October dawn in the 1980s, when stags were roaring all around the rim of the valley which cradles Satterthwaite, although the deer I saw most clearly on that foray was a roe bounding off into cover as I was heading back for breakfast.

Red deer on Shap Fells in Cumbria.

The bulk of this red deer population lives between Windermere and Coniston Water. East of Windermere there are others which, in the mid-1950s and later, were contaminated in some degree by hybridisation with sika. Peter Delap's wide-ranging deerwatching forays had made him aware of the existence of a small pocket of sika, both stags and hinds, in one area of the valley of the Lune, east of Lakeland proper, in the immediate post-war period.

From the colour of their antler velvet, the shape of their antlers and various other characteristics, Dr Delap believed these sika to be of the Manchurian subspecies. The assumption that these found their way into Lunesdale after wandering north from the Ribblesdale area, near the Lancashire-Yorkshire border, presupposes that the sika which remain quite common in Ribblesdale are therefore of the Manchurian and not the Japanese subspecies, as had generally been assumed. G. Kenneth Whitehead, who knows the Ribblesdale sika better than almost anyone else, now believes that they are indeed Manchurian, so a link with those in Lunesdale seems very likely.

By the early 1960s only two of these Lunesdale sika were known to remain, and both were stags. Meanwhile, in 1955 Peter Delap had been startled to see a sika stag keeping company with a red stag on Cartmel Fell, which lies many miles west

of Lunesdale. The 1960s brought clear evidence of hybridisation; the main culprit was thought to be one particular sika stag which was only in the Furness Fells area for a comparatively short time. In August 1967, in Chapel House Plantation near the southern end of Windermere, my wife and I had a clear view of what might have been taken for a typical red hind had it not been for dappling on its flanks, such as one might expect on a sika in summer pelage – a typical hybrid we were assured by Peter Delap, with whom we were staying at the time.

Opinions differ on the extent to which the Furness red deer population has been affected by hybridisation. Some of those who are closely in touch with the local situation suggest that the long-term effects have been slight, with none of the red deer having shown any outwardly visible sign of sika influence for many years prior to the millennium. Others believe, however, that almost the entire red deer stock is affected to some degree by the cross-breeding which has occurred. Obvious hybrids were rigorously culled whenever they were identified.

There has also probably been some infusion of park red deer blood as a consequence of the Oxenholme Hunt having decided in the late nineteenth century to turn its attention to hunting deer. Park deer were obtained for the

Roe deer are common at lower altitudes in Cumbria. (Peter Delap).

purpose, and although carted deer were the main quarry of what became known as the Lunesdale and Oxenholme Staghounds, some were inevitably not recovered, enough being left out not only to infiltrate and interbreed with the wild deer farther west but also to establish a wild breeding population among themselves.

Some of these red deer found their way to Middleton Fell, which lies immediately east of Lunesdale, south of Sedbergh. Here they settled, sometimes ranging south onto the adjacent Barbon Fells as well, and have built up their numbers to a level recently estimated at around sixty. On at least one occasion a stag supposedly from this area has strayed south into sika country near Bolton-by-Bowland. The reverse has also happened, and in the early 1990s a sika stag was shot after seeking the company of red deer in the Middleton Fell area. Forest Enterprise do their best to keep the red deer of south Cumbria and the Ribblesdale sika apart.

Rigmaden Park, in Lunesdale, is a former haunt of red deer which once had wapiti for company, with the inevitable result that any

escapees were liable to introduce an element of wapiti blood into the local wild deer population. There is a story to the effect that over a century ago some wapiti hinds were introduced to the Belle Isle estate, bordering Windermere. Since wapiti hybridise readily with red deer, this could also have happened here, though there are now no signs of it.

In addition to the parks already mentioned there have been several others in Cumbria which have held red deer in the past, and which may have contributed, in some degree, to the wild deer population as a result of escapes. Among these were two near Wigton and another, Muncaster Castle Park near Ravenglass on the Cumbrian coast, which also had fallow until the earlier years of the twentieth century. Armathwaite Hall Park, at the northern end of Bassenthwaite Lake, formerly held a small herd of fallow. At one stage some escaped into nearby woodland, but none now survive, in the woods or otherwise, the only wild deer in that neighbourhood being roe, which are fairly numerous. However, a small herd of red deer and some muntjac are kept on Trotters and Friends Animal Farm, in grounds close to Armathwaite Hall, which is now an hotel.

South Cumbria still has three old-established deer parks with herds of fallow. Holker Hall Park, at Cark-in-Cartmel near the north side of Morecambe Bay, is noted for its herd of menil fallow, one characteristic of which, as I observed for myself on a visit there, is that apart from a generally pale appearance with dappled flanks in both summer and winter, the white rump is surmounted by a horseshoe-shaped stripe of brown rather than black as in common-type fallow.

Dallam Tower Park, at Milnthorpe, also has an all-menil herd of fallow, while at Levens Hall Park, a few miles farther north, the fallow are all black. Fallow now at large in these areas can thus be traced to local escapes, as can any that may still linger near Burrow Hall Park close to Kirkby Lonsdale, which held fallow until the fairly recent past. No escapees have been reported from Park Farm at Dalton-in-Furness, a deer farm stocked in the 1980s with both red and fallow deer but containing fallow only by the end of the 1990s. However, red, fallow and roe have all been reported from the Forestry Commission's Dalton Forest as well as from the Silverdale area, directly south-east of the River Kent's estuary. At High Hay Bridge, Bouth-by-Ulverston, is a small enclosed herd of fallow, while nearby Low Hay Bridge is the focal point of a nature reserve where wild red and roe deer can be viewed from observation hides.

Deer farms tend to come and go, but one which has lasted longer than many and holds several hundred deer is in Matterdale, near Greystoke, on the Lake District's northern boundary. Species present in 1999 included Père David's and Formosan sika as well as red and fallow deer.

Whether roe deer survived in Cumbria after becoming extinct almost everywhere else in England is a question which may never be answered to everyone's satisfaction. In the first half of the seventeenth century they were still present on the Naworth Castle estate near Brampton, east of Carlisle, as is apparent from records of some being live-captured and sent south to London on at least two occasions during that time.

Around the end of the eighteenth century and in the early nineteenth century several writers agreed that roe no longer existed anywhere in England. In the middle decades of the nineteenth century there were, however, one or two isolated reports of individual roe being seen, and in 1868 one such individual was shot at Crookdyke, about 3 miles north-west of Carlisle, an event which excited comment as being unique in the experience of local people.

The 1890s brought recognition that roe might not be extinct as residents of Cumbria after all. In his book *A Vertebrate Fauna of Lakeland*, published in 1892, the Revd H.A. Macpherson reported the occurrence of a few roe near Naworth as well as a few more near Longtown, within 3 miles of the Scottish border. Five years later, in his classic work *British Deer and Their Horns*, J.G. Millais said that in England there were still a few roe in Cumberland and Northumberland, but that they appeared to be decreasing.

Whatever their true status towards the end of the nineteenth century, the story of roe in the twentieth century, in Cumbria as elsewhere, has been one of increasing numbers and progressive range expansion. This process may have been accelerated by the release of half a dozen pairs of Austrian roe on the Belle Isle estate, Windermere, shortly before the First World War, as a result of which the roe now so widespread and plentiful in south Lakeland may be mainly – some suggest wholly – of Austrian ancestry.

These Austrian roe are described as having been conspicuously lighter in colour than their native British brethren and to have been distinguishable in the field. Many south Lakeland roe of the present day are, indeed, paler grey-brown in winter and of a brighter shade of red in their summer pelage than the roe from the north and the east of the Cumbrian Mountains. Most of the latter which I have seen have been in winter pelage of a fairly dark chocolate-brown, which appears to be typical of northern English roe of indigenous stock. The mountainous nature of central Lakeland makes it less attractive to roe than lower-lying peripheral areas, which may help to keep the roe of south Lakeland, with their distinctive colour characteristics, more or less separate from those farther north. All in all, it can be said that roe today are present in Cumbria wherever the habitat is suitable, and in many areas are numerous.

At High Hay Bridge lived the late Herbie and Tissie Fooks, who maintained a small private deer menagerie. One of its members was a roe doe which wandered in and out of the house more or less at will. It was house-trained to the extent of using one particular corner of the main downstairs room for sanitary purposes. While Tissie scarcely approved of this, she shared her husband's enthusiasm for the deer which they kept in enclosures outdoors – not only roe but also red and muntjac as well as the fallow deer which are still kept there by her granddaughter.

After Herbie's death Tissie created the formal nature reserve now centred on Low Hay Bridge and under different ownership. This included a deer museum, to which the public were admitted.

Muntjac sometimes escaped from their enclosure at High Hay Bridge and were sometimes seen in the neighbourhood. Odd muntjac have also been reported from farther east in the Furness area and from the countryside near Carlisle, undoubtedly as a result of local releases or escapes. However, in 1999 no muntjac were known to be at liberty in any part of Cumbria. There were, though, some in confinement at South Lakes Wild Animal Park, which is located at Dalton-in-Furness.

At Satterthwaite, near Grizedale Forest, the excellent quality of red and roe deer antlers from the area may be judged from those exhibited in the wildlife museum there, which is run by Forest Enterprise.

Northumbria

In the late nineteenth century such deer as existed in the north-easternmost counties of England were nearly all confined in parks. Escapes undoubtedly occurred, but in those labour-intensive days, with a far higher proportion of the working population employed on the land than is now the case, there was plenty of manpower available to ensure that any unwanted wild deer were either driven back into the parks or converted promptly into venison.

As for deer naturally occurring in the wild state, so far as Northumberland and Durham were concerned this could only mean roe. There has been much head-scratching over the past status of roe in these two counties, and whether or not the roe that occur there today are direct descendants of native stock which never quite died out in Northumbria. One fact about which

The Forest Wildlife Ranger, the late Tommy Rogerson, and the author's wife, Gladys Carne, with two roe heads from the Redesdale area of Northumberland.

there can be no shadow of a doubt, however, is that at the start of the twentieth century extensive areas of the north-east, where roe are commonplace today, were entirely devoid of these deer, and had been without them for a very long time.

Fossil evidence points to roe having been plentiful in Northumberland and Durham in early times. Their bones have been found in association with those of red deer and wolf in a cave near Stanhope in County Durham, and kitchen refuse unearthed at Roman sites has included the bones and antlers of roe, suggesting the ready availability of a plentiful source of supply.

Writing in 1769, J. Wallis, a local natural historian, quotes a record of there having been nearly six hundred head of red, fallow and roe deer in the various forests and parks of the Earl of Northumberland in 1512, the fourth year of the reign of Henry VIII. Twenty-five years later, according to that much-quoted itinerant J. Leland, there was no forest then remaining in Northumberland except that of the Cheviot Hills, which had 'plenty redde-deere and roo-bukkes', or so he had heard.

In the 1760s the Northumbrian writer T. Percy referred to roe as having been present on waste areas near Hexham some forty years earlier, when George I was on the throne. By the closing years of the eighteenth century encounters with roe in much of Northumbria must have become a rare event, for Thomas Bewick, writing in 1790 about a wild roe killed around that time in Northumberland, supposed it to be a wanderer from either Cumberland or Scotland.

Early nineteenth-century writers were almost at one in stating more or less categorically that roe were extinct as indigenous animals in England. Not until that century's end did there begin to creep into print a grudging admission, by John Guille Millais and one or two others, that native roe in the north of England might not all be dead after all. The twentieth-century roe resurgence which has been so marked a feature of both Northumberland and Durham did not begin in earnest until after the First World War. Its foundation stock had to come from somewhere, and just where might that have been in Northumberland itself?

In the early 1960s three distinguished Northumbrian naturalists, Viscount Ridley, G.A. Cowen and the late Henry Tegner, undertook a comprehensive survey aimed not only at determining the contemporary status of roe in Northumberland and Durham, but also their recent, and indeed not-so-recent, history in the various parts of their then still expanding range.

Cowen had previously brought to light the fact that in 1847 a pack of hounds was formed expressly to hunt roe in an extensive area of woodland known as the Lord Bruce's Plantation, near Consett in County Durham. Founded by a Mr Richardson of Consett, and known as the Castleside Hounds, this pack concentrated on roe for several years before transferring its attention to foxes because these gave a better run.

Estate records scrutinised for the purposes of the 1960s survey revealed the presence of roe in the late nineteenth and early twentieth centuries in at least three other locations as well as the

Castleside area, all three being in Northumberland.

No great distance north-west of the Castleside woodlands is the Slaley Forest area, south of Hexham. Well wooded in Victorian times, as now, this is another locality where roe are now known to have been present at a time when the species had been generally written off as extinct in Northumbria. Woods near Haltwhistle in the South Tyne valley and others in the Wark area of the North Tyne valley south of Bellingham were also discovered to have held roe when most people thought they had long vanished. Was it, perhaps, from the latter quarter that a roebuck strayed in 1854 to be shot by one of the Duke of Northumberland's keepers near Kielder Castle, the Duke's Scottish border shooting-box? The killing evoked a ducal instruction not to slay harmless rare wild creatures on his sporting estate in the Cheviots, itself a clear indication of how scarce roe were at that time.

The First World War was the precursor of a new era for roe in Northumbria. In a report on their survey, published in 1965 by the Natural History Society of Northumberland, Durham and Newcastle-upon-Tyne as part of that society's *Transactions*, Ridley, Cowen and Tegner note that wholesale timber fellings undertaken during that war would have deprived the few surviving pockets of roe of much of their habitat, causing them to disperse.

The return of peace and the inauguration in 1919 of the Forestry Commission brought about the beginnings of re-afforestation on an unprecedented scale. New forests provided cover, food and shelter for deer where previously much ground now planted with trees had been bleak and open, unattractive to a woodland-loving species like the roe. At the very time when widespread woodland devastation had just forced Northumbrian roe, few as they then were, to seek new quarters, these were becoming available on a scale hitherto unimagined, and with the advantage of vacant possession, albeit that those who planted and created such ideal homes had no intention of providing accommodation for such guests.

Yet perhaps this is not the whole story. There is evidence that some degree of revival of the fortunes of roe in Northumberland may have begun before the First World War, and may therefore have been influenced by other factors than that conflict's consequences for forestry policy in Britain.

By far the most extensive area of new roe habitat afforded by re-afforestation after the First World War was the 24,000 ha of the Kielder forest complex, comprising not only Kielder Forest itself but the adjacent forests of Wark, Redesdale, Kershope, Spadeadam and now also Rothbury, while just across the Scottish border is the contiguous Newcastleton Forest.

On a visit to Kielder in 1970 I had the privilege of meeting and being shown around by the Head Forester, 'Mac' McCavish, who was also directly responsible for deer management. Then on the point of retirement, Mac had worked at Kielder, on and off, for thirty-two years. When he first came there in 1938, he recalled, there were just a few roe beginning to colonise the then very young plantations, mainly of sitka spruce at higher levels and Norway spruce lower down. Numbers steadily increased, with snares and shotguns being employed to try to keep the burgeoning population in check. Selective control with the rifle began in 1958 under the auspices of the Forestry Commission's newly appointed Game Warden, Herbie Fooks.

By 1970 six rangers were employed more or less full time on deer control, culling up to four hundred roe a year from a population then estimated at around three times that number. I learned, twenty-five years later, that the Kielder Head Ranger, Peter Eccles, and his staff of nine rangers were responsible between them for an annual cull of around twelve hundred out of a population which could be as high as seven thousand, and still rising. As well as the deer they cull themselves, the rangers supervise fee-paying client stalkers, many of whom return year after year, not only to shoot bucks on a fee-paying basis but to help with the all-important roe doe cull.

I learned in 1999 that particular emphasis was being given to reducing roe deer density to a significantly lower level of no more than four or five deer per hundred hectares, implying a total roe population limited to around 2,500 for the entire Kielder group of forests. More attention was also being given to fencing those plantations most vulnerable to deer damage – deemed of particular importance at a time of extensive clear-felling and replanting.

Roe I have seen on visits to Kielder have been of the relatively dark-coated type which are supposed to represent the indigenous northern English strain as opposed to the typically lighter-pelaged south Lakeland type, which is purportedly a legacy of the Austrian antecedents of at least a proportion of them. Touring Redesdale Forest years ago with the local ranger, the late Tommy Rogerson – a dedicated deer man if ever there was one – I learned that some of the roe on his beat were markedly darker-faced than others. He showed me living examples to prove the point, as well as the best buck then in that forest, with a handsomely lyrate six-point head of antlers which must have been at least 9 in in length. Feeding conditions in these Scottish border forests are not such as to produce exceptional antler development other than in a small minority of cases, but Peter Eccles tells me that there have been instances of bucks growing six-point heads in their first year.

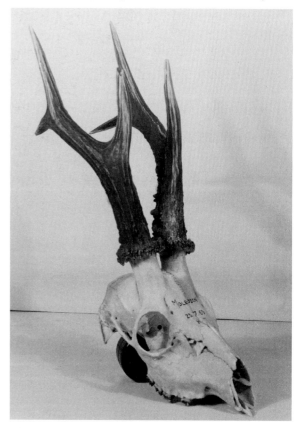

The head of a good-quality roebuck obtained in Northumberland in 1969 by the late Henry Tegner, a noted author and roe enthusiast. (Veronica Heath)

C21 ABOVE: *Wild sika deer are sociable and sometimes highly inquisitive. (Steve Smith)*

C22 LEFT: *Fallow deer are also present in Richmond Park. (John K. Fawcett)*

C23 BELOW: *A red stag and some of his hinds at rutting time in Richmond Park, on London's outskirts. (Michael Baxter Brown)*

C24 *Red deer on Exmoor, with Dunkery Hill in the background. (Jochen Langbein)*

C25 *Red deer stags on Exmoor, where this species has roamed wild since ancient times. (Marc Thole)*

C26 ABOVE: *A red deer stag and hinds amid typical Exmoor scenery. (Marc Thole)*

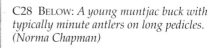

C27 LEFT: *A muntjac buck with antlers in velvet. (Norma Chapman)*

C28 BELOW: *A young muntjac buck with typically minute antlers on long pedicles. (Norma Chapman)*

C29 *Summer herbage affords good concealment for a recumbent muntjac. (Norma Chapman)*

C30 *An adult Chinese water deer buck with typically prominent upper canines and very short tail. (R. P. Lawrence)*

C31 *A Chinese water deer doe in autumn. (R. P. Lawrence)*

C32 *Thick seasonal pelage helps Chinese water deer weather an average English winter. (R. P. Lawrence)*

C33 *A Northumbrian roebuck in winter. (Veronica Heath)*

C34 *Relaxing in summer sunshine, a Northumbrian roe doe. (Veronica Heath)*

C35 LEFT: *A very young Northumbrian roe kid in late spring. (Veronica Heath)*

C36 RIGHT: *Twin roe kids in Northumbrian spruce woodland. (Veronica Heath)*

C37 BELOW: *Reindeer are now well established and accessible to the public at Glenmore, Inverness-shire.*

C38 *A wild red stag of indigenous Irish stock in Killarney National Park, County Kerry. (Sean Ryan)*

C39 *A Japanese sika stag in Killarney National Park, where these deer have lived alongside the native Irish red deer since the nineteenth century. (Sean Ryan)*

Another feature of Kielder roe heads is a tendency towards being narrow-spanned and upright rather than lyrate and wide at the tips. As to their alleged old English pelage as true-blue Northumbrians, I have heard it suggested that the original Kielder roe arrived from across the Scottish border as immigrants from Roxburghshire!

Whatever may be the truth of this, from around 1925 onwards roe began to appear in many places for the first time within living memory, and by the time the Second World War broke out they were present in most parts of Northumberland. The war

Typical roe deer country in Northumberland. (Veronica Heath)

years and immediate post-war period saw a further progressive increase to the point where almost every suitable corner of the county had been colonised, with high-density populations becoming established in many areas. Within the county of Tyne and Wear, roe penetrated to the outer fringes of Newcastle-upon-Tyne.

Progress in County Durham was slower, with roe still turning up for the first time in some areas in the 1950s. Since then, as in Northumberland, practically every hitherto vacant habitat niche has been occupied, and they have pushed on into Cleveland and south across almost the whole of Yorkshire. Among the more notable roe strongholds are forestry plantations at Hammersley, in County Durham, where studies have been conducted on roe population dynamics and interactions with their habitat, and Harwood Forest, near Rothbury in Northumberland, now part of the Kielder forest complex.

The harvesting of mature timber in the new forests began in earnest in the 1970s, allowing the redesign of plantations to include a proportion of hardwood species and open spaces in the form of deer lawns to facilitate roe control. Venison sales produce significant revenue, and fees from client stalkers now make a useful contribution towards the basic costs of deer management. Stalking clients are mainly catered for in May and June before summer vegetation affords the bucks increased concealment.

As I have said, red deer appear to have been fairly plentiful in remoter parts of Northumberland at least as late as the sixteenth century, though perhaps not for very much longer. One of their haunts was Rothbury Forest, in the unenclosed parts of which, according to the estate records of the Earls of Northumberland, there were 153 in 1512. They seem to have died out there not long afterwards, and probably ceased to roam the Cheviots at some time in the seventeenth century.

Their later history is as park deer. For a time in the nineteenth century the Duke of Northumberland's Hulne Park, at Alnwick, included some white deer of German origin among its herd of normal-coloured red deer. The First World War brought an end to Hulne Park's red deer, while at Chillingham, where the resident fallow deer and the famous Chillingham herd of wild white cattle had been joined in the nineteenth century by red deer, the latter existed for an even shorter time. At Hulne Park, however, they were given a second lease of life in the late 1990s with the arrival there of two stags and nine hinds as foundation stock for a future herd.

In County Durham, Teesdale Forest contained both red and fallow deer at least as late as the sixteenth century, though perhaps not for much longer. During the Second World War, escapees from Lord Barnard's Raby Castle Park at

Staindrop, near Darlington, were, however, sometimes seen in upper Teesdale. There has been a deer park at Raby Castle for eight hundred years or more. Both red and fallow deer are still kept there, the fallow being mainly of the black variety but also including a few white deer. Fallow also escaped during the last war, but in 1999 the head keeper told me that the only deer then at liberty in the area were roe, and two red stags which had recently broken out.

Beamish and Wynyard Parks, also in Durham, no longer hold deer, but Whitworth Park, near Spennymoor, which dates from the fifteenth century, has survived as a haunt of fallow. A few feral fallow may persist near Beamish Park and elsewhere, but their numbers are not significant. Several other former deer parks ceased to contain deer as long ago as the First World War or even earlier.

Former deer parks in Northumberland which once held fallow include Eslington Park at Whittingham, north of Alnwick, and Billsmoor Park, north of Otterburn, which lost its deer through escapes in the Second World War, although a few still remained in the area in the early 1950s.

Hulne Park, at Alnwick, once embraced several smaller sub-parks and there was a large herd of fallow here in the sixteenth century. For a time between the seventeenth and the early nineteenth centuries there appear to have been no deer here, but when red deer were reintroduced in 1824 fallow also returned to the scene. At one stage there were also some sika, but the First World War spelt the temporary end of Hulne as a deer park proper and of most of the deer within its walled expanse of 1200 ha.

Some fallow, however, survived, leading a completely wild existence, and for many years they were left very much to their own devices, largely free to wander where they pleased, including in and out of the park through open gates should they so wish. This situation continued until quite recently, but with the difference that the herd, currently numbering some three hundred, was once again carefully managed with a view to maintaining high quality. In this guest stalkers play a part, and fresh blood has been introduced in the form of prime quality bucks from Petworth Park in West Sussex. These have included a black buck, and the influence of this beast upon a herd which,

until his arrival, had been almost entirely of the common variety, is already plainly apparent. Meanwhile, with red deer once again present, and forestry and agriculture needing additional protection, steps have been taken to contain the deer more securely within the park and to fence them out of plantations inside it.

The presence of roe deer in the park dates from the times when gates were frequently left open, but they are not encouraged because of their tendency to damage fences which then allow fallow deer to enter where they are not wanted.

Chillingham Park fallow deer were also free until quite recently to make excursions over a wall which was by no means deer-proof into the countryside around. I saw one in Chillingham Wood while exploring the area years ago, but noted that roe hoofmarks outnumbered those of fallow by something like three to one. At that time no culling was done within the park itself, but leakage to the outside world was sufficient to ensure that culling done there kept the herd as a whole from increasing out of hand. Now, however, new fencing again confines these deer to the park.

Muntjac were reported in the Embleton area, near the coast not many miles north-east of Alnwick, a few years ago. Clearly, these must have either escaped or been released locally, but whether any still survive I have been unable to discover. One would have thought the Northumbrian winters and the scarcity of suitable habitat were hardly favourable to this species.

There have been odd rumours of sika, apart from those known to have existed in Hulne Park many years ago. These reports include mention of some that are supposed to have escaped from a wildlife park somewhere in Roxburghshire and strayed towards Northumberland's border, but none have so far been confirmed as occurring anywhere in Northumbria. However, this situation could alter. Sika at large for many years past from a park in Peeblesshire have been expanding their range progressively and could well reach the Borders forests before long – as also, indeed, could red deer from the Galloway population which are doing their best to spread east through Dumfriesshire despite efforts to prevent them doing so. Any future link-up of these two species might not be good news for either.

Isle of Man

The Isle of Man has so many links with northern England that it seems appropriate to deal with it in this chapter.

Its prime claim to our attention is as a one-time haunt of the long-extinct giant deer (*Megaceros giganteus*), commonly known as the Irish elk from the quantity of its remains which has come to light in bogs in Ireland – far greater than from archaeological sites in England or Scotland. Complete *Megaceros* skeletons have been dug up in the Isle of Man, the first having been discovered in 1819. Another, found in 1897 at Close-e-Garry, alongside the old railway between Peel and St John's, is on display at the Manx Museum in Douglas.

This latter skeleton has recently been carbon-dated and found to be nearly twelve thousand years old (the actual age arrived at is 11,495 years ± 95). This suggests that the giant deer must have reached here soon after the end of the

The skeleton of a giant deer (Megaceros giganteus) *unearthed from peat on the Isle of Man and now on display in the Manx Museum in Douglas.*

last glaciation, when there was still a land-bridge between what is now the Isle of Man and the land-mass of continental Europe, of which Britain and Ireland then formed part.

This raises the question whether other deer species may have reached the Isle of Man in the same manner. Red deer in particular have been the subject of speculation on this score. There is good evidence of their occurrence in bygone centuries, when the Earls of Derby had a sporting interest in the island and prescribed penalties for the illegal taking of 'hart or hind' there, and it appears that as late as the eighteenth century there was an attempt to establish deer on the Calf of Man.

It has been pointed out by at least one writer, a Mr D.E. Allen in an article in the journal *Peregrine* in 1952, that bones thought to be those of red deer have been found in post-glacial deposits on the island. He suggests that the

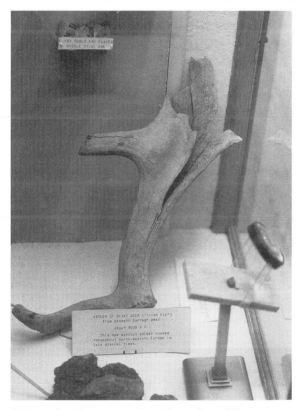

The antler fragment of a giant deer (Megaceros giganteus) *found in peat on the Isle of Man and estimated to date from 9000 BC.*

The Curragh's Wildlife Park at Ballaugh, owned by the Isle of Man government, held red and Japanese sika deer in 1999.

better, and much larger domestic livestock have been conveyed by sea to island communities since time immemorial, and across oceans for hundreds of years. There is some suggestion that the bones of fallow deer may also have been found in the Isle of Man, and if fallow did indeed ever occur here, in the Middle Ages or at any other time, they must clearly have been introduced, as they undoubtedly were to Ireland and, at some stage, to Great Britain.

After a lengthy total absence, deer returned to the Isle of Man in the second half of the twentieth century as live exhibits in the government-owned The Curragh's Wildlife Park at Ballaugh, near Ramsey, towards the northern end of the island. On a visit in 1979 I saw there red, Japanese sika and Père David's deer. In 1999 there were no longer any Père David's deer, but red and sika deer were still there as well as a solitary male muntjac. The sika were in a walk-through enclosure while the red deer were separated from the viewing public by a moat. There were plans to replace red deer with fallow, also in a walk-through enclosure, and the sika with chital (axis deer) if suitable stock could be obtained.

hazardous conditions of navigation in the Middle Ages would have made it unlikely that animals the size of red deer would have been shipped to the Isle of Man, so it is likely that indigenous deer were present at that time.

However, deer must have reached the Calf of Man by sea at a time when conditions were little

Père David's deer were present in the Isle of Man's The Curragh's Wildlife Park in the late 1970s.

9
THE DEER OF
WALES

If deer in Wales are not quite such creatures of myth and legend as the proverbial snakes in Ireland, the parallel has until recent decades been rather too close for comfort from any deer enthusiast's standpoint. Even now, there are many people who may not realise that there are any wild deer in Wales at all, still less that in some parts they are sufficiently numerous to require systematic control.

Historically, red and roe deer were to be found in suitable areas throughout the principality. Remains of red deer in particular have come to light around the coast as well as at Roman sites and elsewhere well inland. As late as the sixteenth century the species was preserved as royal game in the Snowdon area. The indigenous wild red deer of Wales seem to have been in steady decline thereafter, almost certainly disappearing from their last stronghold, probably in the old county of Merioneth, at some time in the eighteenth century.

A short-lived attempt in the 1840s to reintroduce red deer to the Forest of Dean in Gloucestershire led to these animals sometimes straying in a westerly direction, across the River Wye into neighbouring Monmouthshire, which Wales now claims once more for its own, but their survival there was brief. From time to time in the nineteenth century and later red deer have turned up in south Wales, allegedly having swum the Bristol Channel from Exmoor to escape pursuing staghounds or perhaps for some other reason, but such instances have been rare and the animals' origin hard to prove. Any other unenclosed red deer seen in the countryside of Wales during the last 200 years have been captive animals which somehow have managed to gain their freedom, mostly for very short periods only.

One source of temporarily wild red deer has been Powis Castle Park near Welshpool, in what in 1974 became the county of Powys. This park has held deer for many centuries. One break-out occurred in 1947, when red and fallow deer both escaped, but the red deer at least did not remain at liberty for long. During the early 1990s fallen trees on the park's boundary created a temporary gap of which some red deer took advantage, but their spell of freedom was equally brief. There have been some subsequent escapes, but any red deer which have not speedily returned of their own accord have been culled to prevent serious forestry damage. In the spring of 1999 there were about a hundred red deer in the park and some thirty fallow.

Margam Country Park near Port Talbot, in West Glamorgan, now contains red deer, Père David's deer and some chital (axis deer) as well as the fallow which have long roamed its grassy

Fallow deer in Margam Country Park, near Port Talbot, which is now owned by the local authority.

A black fallow deer and a white one in Margam Country Park, near Port Talbot in West Glamorgan, where most of the fallow are of the common variety.

acres. Red deer have sometimes broken out and in the spring of 1999 three pregnant hinds were at liberty, although up to that time there was not thought to be any established wild population of this species in the neighbourhood. On the other hand, a Père David's deer which 'went walkabout' in the early 1990s took up residence in the adjacent Coed-y-Morgannwg – the Forestry Commission's Forest of Glamorgan – where it was seen fairly frequently for several years and never recovered. Attempts to live-capture and return it to the park were unsuccessful.

Dynevor Park, between Llandeilo and Carmarthen in what emerged from the 1974 local government boundary changes as the south-west Welsh county of Dyfed, had a few red deer until fairly recently, but these have not been persevered with by the park's present owners, the National Trust, who have chosen to concentrate their attention upon the fallow which have a more ancient lineage there.

In 1998 I was informed by Forest Enterprise's acting Chief Ranger, John Westlake, that some red deer escapees from a deer farm were present in the Abergavenny area, in Gwent.

As the species preferred by most deer farmers, red deer have also undoubtedly sometimes escaped from other such farms in Wales, as elsewhere in Britain. In 1979 one deer farmer, Mr Robin Pratt, introduced red deer to Ramsey Island, separated by a mile-wide channel from Dyfed's westernmost extremity. With the co-operation of the RAF, these deer, of stock from the famous Warnham Court herd in West Sussex, were narcotic-darted and spared a rough sea crossing by being conveyed by helicopter to their new home. Eventually, Robin decided to move his stock to the mainland. All but a very few were successfully caught and airlifted across the water *en route* to a more prosaic location near Fishguard.

The surviving remnant took up a completely wild existence on Ramsey Island, breeding and building up their numbers until they totalled about two score, subsisting on the island's abundant heather. This state of affairs was brought to an end in 1993 when, following the introduction of sheep by a new farming tenant, heather began to be heavily browsed and became much scarcer. The deer took to browsing even scarcer birch scrub in the absence of any other available food source. As the island clearly could not support both deer and sheep, the deer had to go.

Towards the end of the 1990s red deer presumed to be escaped farm stock were reported from near Sennybridge and elsewhere in the Brecon Beacons area of Powys, in east Wales. These may well be linked with the red deer in the Abergavenny area mentioned above. It will be interesting to discover whether they will become established as a breeding population.

The common wild deer of Wales, if any species may be truthfully so described, are fallow. These are present in widely scattered, mostly mutually isolated, pockets, almost all of which owe their existence to escapes from deer parks near where the wild herds now occur.

In what we used to know as Monmouthshire (now Gwent) fallow are numerous in woods around Monmouth itself, along the Wye Valley to the south and on high ground between the rivers Wye and Usk, especially around Trelleck.

Veteran British Deer Society member Frederick Hingston, who lived locally, told me that the quality of these deer, at higher altitudes especially, reflects the quality of their habitat, much of it poor hill-farming country. One source of fallow deer in Gwent is a former deer park on the Hendre estate, descendants of whose one-time occupants now roam wild in the vicinity. Others probably originated from Wyastone Leys Park, just inside Herefordshire, while mixed with these may be an element of the old wild stock of the Forest of Dean in neighbouring Gloucestershire, which strayed west across the Wye from the Highmeadow Woods, where this strain probably survived after dying out in the forest itself. North of Monmouth some of the numerous fallow escapees from Kentchurch Park, in Herefordshire, have wandered into Wales from the east, while less than 5 miles north-east of Newport there are fallow deer in Wentwood, a large covert directly east of the River Usk.

The exceptionally good head of a wild Welsh fallow, from the forest of Coed-y-Morgannwg, near Margam Park in West Glamorgan.

What is probably the largest population of wild fallow deer in Wales is to be found in Coed-y-Morgannwg, which nowadays clothes in trees the once bare hills overlooking Port Talbot. These fallow, numbering several hundred, originated as escapees from adjacent Margam Park, once privately owned but now a public amenity area belonging to the local authority.

When I first visited Coed-y-Morgannwg in the late 1960s I learned that two-thirds of the fallow were reckoned to be of the common variety, the remaining one-third being black, a ratio reflected by those I saw myself while touring the forest. There was a theory that common-type fallow produced better body weights and antlers, and partly because of this the black ones were more heavily culled in relation to their total numbers. I was told in 1995 that this notion no longer held sway, but that common fallow still pre-dominated in about the same proportion.

Despite having been wild since at least the Second World War and now being present in relatively high numbers, these fallow have only spread to a fairly limited extent. The Port Talbot–Maesteg road on the north and the Maesteg–Bridgend road on the east are the normal limits of their range in those directions, although a few venturesome individuals do stray farther, while to the south and west the M4 motorway and the main railway from Cardiff to Swansea bar the way to significant movement towards the coast.

Now being transformed from what was originally a sitka spruce monoculture plantation to a mixture of tree species including hardwoods where appropriate, this Forest of Glamorgan is intensively used by the public. For administrative purposes it forms part of a much larger forest unit, Coed-y-Cymoedd, which extends east to the English border.

The other main fallow deer haunt in south Wales extends along the Vale of Towy between Llandeilo and Carmarthen, where Dynevor Castle Park on one side of the vale and Golden Grove Park on the other have leaked many of their deer into the countryside around. Golden Grove was a deer park in Cromwell's time but when I called there in the 1960s the deer had ceased to be enclosed and were ranging through woods all along the valley. Those I saw among the bluebells on a delightful evening in May were a mixture of common and black. There is now once again a small enclosed herd of fallow at Golden Grove and about a hundred in Dynevor Park where, as well as the predominant common variety, there are also some black and some menil individuals. This latter park has been in existence since around 1500 if not earlier, I am informed.

The 10,000 ha of mainly coniferous Coed-y-Brenin, in the old county of Merioneth (was part of Gwynedd) in the heart of mid-Wales, are home to a small population of wild fallow derived from stock once enclosed in Nannau Park, a little way north of Dolgellau. When I called there in the late 1970s I learned that these tended to be widely scattered, owing it was thought, to a combination of poor habitat and frequent disturbance by fox-shooting clubs.

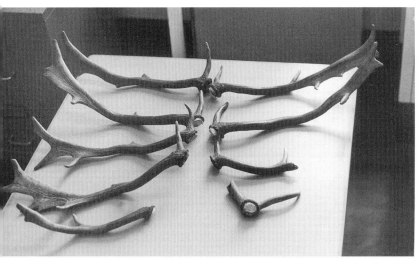

Specimen cast fallow antlers from the mid-Wales forest of Coed-y-Brenin.

An interesting management feature was an annual get-together organised by the Forestry Commission for local farmers who might need advice about controlling deer which stray on to their land, and this had been found to be a very useful public-relations exercise.

I have a vivid recollection of watching some of these mid-Welsh wild fallow deer from a car as I drove around on a snowy morning in early May, of all times of the year for such weather. All but one was of the common, white-rumped variety, of which the bulk of this herd is comprised, the remainder being black. As a free-ranging population, they date mainly from the snowy

winter of 1962/3, when the extreme weather conditions enabled park deer in many parts of Britain to liberate themselves.

The former north Wales counties of Denbigh and Flint which, with Caernarvonshire and Anglesey, were combined in 1974 to form Clwyd, contained a scattering of deer parks, of which several have been the focal points of subsequent wild fallow populations. One of these was Kinmel Park, near Abergele between Colwyn Bay and Rhyl, where some years ago I spent an afternoon hour or two watching the predominant common-type fallow of that area among forestry plantations not very far from the Irish Sea coast.

Woods in the vicinity of Trefnant, near St Asaph, are another haunt of feral fallow. Llanerch Park in that area lost all its deer through escapes years ago, but the deer park was later restored and opened to the public. South-east of here, near the English border, descendants of fallow once enclosed in Wynnstay Park have been reported from woods near Chirk, between Wrexham and Oswestry.

Fallow escapees from Loton Park in Shropshire have crossed the Welsh border to establish a wild population in woodland on Breidden Hill, north-east of Welshpool. On the other side of Welshpool, woods on the Powis Castle estate harbour fallow whose forebears were confined in the deer park there. Unlike park red deer in the same area, some of the fallow which have broken out have maintained themselves in freedom, and are not infrequently reinforced by further escapees. Most of these fallow at large in this eastern corner of Wales are black.

Bodorgan Park, on the isle of Anglesey, lost all of its deer through broken fences in the Second World War. When I called there in 1979 a post-cull population of some sixty to seventy fallow was at large on the estate. In accordance with the estate policy of maintaining an all-black herd of fallow, an off-white individual had been shot the previous year. All the fallow I saw while being driven around in late evening by the head keeper in his Land-Rover were not only black

Conservation forester Fred Curtis points out bark-stripping damage by fallow deer in the forest of Coed-y-Brenin.

extinct before the end of the seventeenth century. Roe venison featured on dining tables at various Roman stations in Wales and there is archaeological evidence of the once widespread occurrence of this species. A sixteenth-century writer and traveller, Leland, described roe as being present, along with red deer, in Clun Forest, on the English border, as late as the reign of Henry VIII. Roe seem likely to have lingered a little while longer among the rugged fastnesses of Caernarvonshire and perhaps also in Merioneth, but woodland destruction has been blamed for their eventual disappearance.

In about 1874 G. Assheton Smith introduced some roe to Vaynol Park, in north Caernarvonshire opposite Anglesey. Despite the fact that some of them reportedly suffered fatal consequences from browsing yew, they flourished within the confines of the fairly extensive park for several decades, but by the First World War they had disappeared.

By 1970, however, a local release had led to their presence in the Wigmore area, close to where Herefordshire and Shropshire border Wales, south-west of Ludlow. By the end of the twentieth century this population had for many years been sufficiently well established to sustain a significant annual cull and had crossed the border to begin recolonising Wales in earnest.

There is more than a slight suspicion that roe have also been released in Wales itself, where after many decades of extensive reafforestation there is still a very great deal of suitable habitat unoccupied by deer of any species. Roe immigrants from England first reached the old Welsh county of Radnor, but by 1999 they had apparently spread much farther. Some were reported as having reached Penllyn Forest, south-east of Bala Lake, as well as Dyfi Forest, near Dolgellau, and Machynlleth Forest, not many miles north-east of Aberystwyth, all in mid-Wales. Another mid-Welsh area specifically named as having been reached by roe is Hafren Forest, on the slopes of Plynlimon Fawr, about 15 miles east of Aberystwyth.

There have also been isolated reports of roe in Gwent which, if correct, can be explained in no

but extremely wild and unapproachable. Most of the wholly feral deer lived not far from the old deer park, although a few sometimes strayed into the Forestry Commission's nearby Newborough plantations.

Individual deer had sometimes wandered from Bodorgan, in the south-west of Anglesey, right across the island to the north coast, near Amlwch. Deer still sometimes turned up in the north in the mid-1990s, but I gathered that there was some doubt as to whether the animals concerned were Bodorgan deer or escapees from elsewhere on the island. In any case, the head keeper told me, the deer park had been restored and held well over a hundred fallow. Two bucks from Burghley Park, near Stamford in Lincolnshire, had recently been added to the herd to introduce new blood, and it was intended that two or three does would follow suit. In 1999 I learned that the herd had been reduced to a pre-fawning strength of thirty, and that further new blood was being sought to improve the stock. In the interests of crop protection wild deer had been reduced to very low numbers, probably not more than five all told.

At Colwyn Bay Welsh Mountain Zoo a small herd of fallow deer is one of the exhibits.

Indigenous Welsh roe were almost certainly

Fallow deer country near Dolgellau, in mid-Wales.

many parts of Wales where their appearance has so far been only sporadic. Assessing the general situation, acting Chief Ranger John Westlake confirmed in 1998 that reported sightings had been widespread, in south and mid-Wales in particular.

The mid-Welsh county of Powys, especially that southern portion of it that used to be the county of Brecknock, has produced more reports of muntjac than most other parts of the principality, and may already have a small resident population in some areas. Odd muntjac have also been reported from places as widely separated as Snowdonia and the Conwy Valley in north Wales and the old county of Pembrokeshire, including the offshore island of Skokholm, in the south-west. Local releases or escapes are a far more likely explanation of the occurrence of this species in Wales than natural immigration from England.

other way than that they arrived by human agency. The same must apply to roe reported as being present on at least one of the Ministry of Defence training areas in south-west Wales, and at Coed-y-Morgannwg in West Glamorgan where, although the forest's head ranger tells me he has yet to see them himself, reliable observers claim to have been more successful.

The reappearance of roe in Wales is not welcomed, it has to be said, by the Forestry Authority, as planting policy in hitherto deer-free areas has concentrated to at least some extent on three species especially vulnerable to damage by deer from browsing and bark-stripping. A shoot-on-sight policy is in force against roe on Forestry Commission ground throughout the Principality.

Muntjac are likely to prove unwelcome for much the same reason if and when they establish a firm foothold in the

Wild red deer are rare in Wales. These were photographed on a deer farm near Fishguard.

A few muntjac have been kept in a small enclosure with much ground cover in Margam Country Park, near Port Talbot, but so far as is known none have escaped. When Penscynor Wildlife Park at Cilfrew, near Neath, closed a few years ago, all the deer, which included Formosan sika as well as muntjac, were disposed of as captive stock, none being allowed to escape. As for the future of muntjac in Wales, it seems likely that they will lag well behind roe in establishing a resident population widely distributed through the country.

Another species which has been added to the collection in Margam Park is Chinese water deer. Several of these have escaped and have been killed by motor traffic on the M4 motorway, apparently while trying to reach some coastal marshland not far beyond.

I had not suspected that sika might be at large anywhere in Wales until I heard, in the mid-1990s, of some which had taken up residence in marshland bordering the River Teifi, near where it flows into Cardigan Bay quite close to the town of Cardigan. The original stock were apparently released from a wildlife park when it became bankrupt, and I was informed in 1998 that the herd was well established.

10
THE DEER OF SOUTHERN SCOTLAND

South of the central Scottish lowlands, between the Firths of Clyde and Forth, is a region largely disdained by holiday visitors heading for the Highlands, intent on enjoying what they mostly regard as richer pickings there. Yet southern Scotland also has highlands, or at any rate uplands, some of which are not very much lower than their grander counterparts farther north. Insofar as deer are concerned, some of these uplands are the haunt of red deer second to none elsewhere in Scotland in the matter of size and antler quality.

Nor is this by any means the sole claim of southern Scotland to our serious attention. Roe, fallow and sika are present in significant numbers; roe occur wherever the habitat is suitable, while sika have been increasing and extending their range in recent decades at a rate which is a considerable cause for concern for various reasons. As well as these four well-established species, muntjac have been reliably

Red deer stags on high ground in the heart of the Galloway wilderness in south-west Scotland.

reported from one or two places and may well turn up at others in the future.

Indigenous red deer, as one might expect, were widespread in the well-wooded southern Scotland of early times, falling prey to Neolithic hunters and leaving their bones in the kitchen middens of that period. Robert the Bruce and later kings preserved them in royal forests such as Ettrick in Selkirkshire, Ference in Renfrewshire and Cumbernauld, north-east of Glasgow. In a great sixteenth-century hunt attended by several thousand people, James V is said to have accounted for some 'eighteen score of harts', which must have made a substantial impression on a deer population probably declining even then.

Late Stuart times brought an edict forbidding trafficking in venison, but by that time it was probably too late to reverse a process of decline accentuated by habitat destruction through the wholesale felling of woodland as much as the killing of too many deer, by authorised persons and otherwise.

Tradition has it that the last southern Scottish red stag was killed in the forest of Buchan, Kirkcudbrightshire, in 1747. How, then, has it come about that red deer are not only present today, but are more than sufficiently numerous to present quite serious problems to foresters and others in some parts of the region now known as Dumfries and Galloway? Some people have suggested that they never in fact completely died out, and that it is likely, even probable, that a few survived, unnoticed by the world at large, in remote parts of such places as Glen Trool and the Merrick hills to repopulate a very much wider area when conditions

became more congenial, as happened during the twentieth century. On the other hand, the apparent absence of firm evidence that any wild red deer were present in southern Scotland in the late eighteenth century and throughout most of the nineteenth rather undermines the theory, based perhaps on hope rather than conviction, that the indigenous strain endures among the red deer of today.

As Chairman of the Galloway Deer Control Group, a consortium of organisations and property owners concerned with keeping red deer numbers within acceptable limits, Mr H.A. (Tony) Waterson, has an intimate knowledge of the area and its deer of the different species. He inclines to the view, he has told me, that the modern wild red deer are all descended from a combination of park escapees and introduced stock.

Cumloden Park, near Newton Stewart, is a wild and rugged area, nearly 1000 ha in extent, which has had red deer since the early nineteenth century. If its retaining walls were ever entirely deerproof they are certainly not so now, and red deer have been able to get out for quite a long time, though precisely how long is hard to say. At the end of the nineteenth century the same Duke of Bedford who was responsible for adding muntjac and Chinese water deer to Britain's fauna is also known to have introduced red deer to property he owned at Cairnsmore of Fleet, an upland area to the east of Newton Stewart.

Whether these Cairnsmore deer were intended to augment a pre-existing stock or to found a new one was never made entirely clear. Initially, at least, the new arrivals were enclosed. As also happened, it seems, in Cumloden Park, where at one stage some wapiti blood was added to the herd, and a few chital (axis deer), presumably from Woburn, kept them company for a time.

Red deer were soon at liberty on the hill and being stalked. Whether because of the wapiti influence or the prime conditions of climate and feeding offered by south-west Scotland, some fairly spectacular heads were produced in the earlier decades of the twentieth century. Visiting Cairnsmore of Fleet in the 1960s, I had some excellent views of its red deer but saw a great many more wild goats, these being very much a feature not only of this corner of Galloway but of some other parts farther north.

A young red deer stag on the open hill in south-west Scotland.

I saw more red deer a few days later as a guest of Ken MacArthur, who was awarded the BEM for his pioneering work on modern methods of deer management in southern Scotland during the post-war period. He took my wife and me into the heart of the Galloway wilderness where he had converted a former shepherd's cottage, 6 miles from its nearest neighbouring habitation, into a leisure-time base for deerstalking forays in the area. On the surrounding hills we were taken within easy photographic range of some of the local red deer, in an area where open high ground, which had been sheep range for several centuries, was in the early stages of being transformed into conifer forest.

State forestry came to south-west Scotland in earnest between the two world wars, at a time when red deer numbers were insignificant. Deer fencing was therefore dispensed with, but as the forests became established the deer responded to this coincidental provision of better habitat by moving in among the trees, where they secreted themselves with ease and began to increase.

In the mid-1960s Galloway red deer were still reckoned to number no more than some four hundred all told. During the following ten years, however, the population burgeoned, rising well into four figures, while at the same time serious damage from bark-stripping began to be noticed. A substantial cull was undertaken. The numbers initially shot were not many fewer than the supposed total population, making it clear that there must have been many more than some early censuses suggested. Counting methods were revised to give a more accurate picture of numbers, and cull targets were increased, with forest wildlife rangers working in the challenging conditions imposed by blanket forestry, the original planning of which had taken little account of deer and the need to control them. It is not to be wondered at, perhaps, that night-shooting under licence was resorted to as an additional means of achieving an adequate cull.

Carefully supervised sporting shooting by client stalkers has played a not insignificant role in curbing the increase of Galloway red deer while also yielding a useful revenue to help fund important conservation work by Forest Enterprise. This aspect of deer management has, however, always been secondary to that of professional rangers and the work of control-group stalkers on private land outside the state forests.

For many years past a primary management aim has been to contain red deer within a predetermined area, mainly among the forested hills of what used to be Kirkcudbrightshire, and thus prevent them from extending the problems to which their presence gives rise to other forests in southern Scotland and over the border in northern England. To a large extent this has so far been successful, thanks to unremitting efforts to eliminate interlopers into such areas as the Forest of Ae and upper Nithsdale, north of Dumfries. Over recent decades the general picture has been one of red deer consolidating their hold on forest areas where previously they occurred in smaller numbers rather than colonising new ones.

Near Clatteringshaws, on the road between Newton Stewart and New Galloway, an enclosed Red Deer Range occupying more than 200 ha caters for visitors anxious to see these otherwise elusive animals. There is a separate Wild Goat Range as well as a Galloway Deer Museum here in the heartland of southern Scotland's red deer country.

In contrast with their relative local abundance here in Galloway, red deer remain absent from much of the rest of Scotland south of the Highlands. Roe, on the other hand, are

At Black Loch, west of New Galloway, is an enclosed red deer range where visitors can view these animals.

wide spread throughout the region, although this was not always so. In his classic *British Deer and their Horns*, J.G. Millais relates how, in the early nineteenth century, the first Marquess of Ailsa introduced roe deer to his Culzean Castle estate, near Maybole in Ayrshire. That any such introduction should have been necessary may be taken to imply that roe were previously absent from that part of southern Scotland, as also seems to have been the case with the south of the country generally at that time. Millais goes on to say that all the roe present in various southern Scottish counties in the 1890s were said to be descended from the Culzean introduction, as a result of which they were numerous in Peeblesshire, Dumfriesshire and Wigtownshire by the end of the nineteenth century. Apparently, however, they had not yet reached Roxburghshire or Berwickshire.

However, this may not be the whole story, for Drumlanrig, in Kirkcudbrightshire, was the scene of another roe introduction in or about 1860, while others were said to have been introduced to the Duke of Buccleuch's property in Selkirkshire. The latter were later allegedly banished in the interests of foxhunting, but clearly some could have survived to boost the further spread of the species.

It does not seem to be known when the native roe disappeared from most of these counties, though the eighteenth century has been suggested as the very last time when any were present in Dumfriesshire.

The woods which once covered so much of southern Scotland had largely disappeared by the end of the eighteenth century, if not earlier, and this must have been a major cause of the virtual disappearance of roe. I say 'virtual' because evidence which eluded J.G. Millais suggests that they did not vanish entirely but that some lingered in Lanarkshire, where *The New Statistical Account of Scotland*, compiled between 1834 and 1844, notes their presence at that time in some localities. These, as well as the reintroduced roe farther south, were able to establish themselves more widely and securely as fresh habitat was provided by nineteenth-century tree planting by a number of large landowners.

As has happened with red deer in Galloway, extensive reafforestation in the years since the First World War has vastly increased the amount of country suitable for roe in southern Scotland. Nowhere are the effects of this more apparent than in the large area of Economic Forestry Group plantings around Eskdalemuir in Dumfriesshire, where on once bare sheep ground which was almost without roe their numbers now run well into four figures. Touring these forests with the Wildlife Manager, Ronnie Rose, MBE, a few years ago, I saw many roe and heard how careful forest planning with deer as well as timber in mind had proved highly beneficial to both.

The roe I have seen farther west in Dumfriesshire, in the Forest of Ae for example, and near Newton Stewart in Kirkcudbrightshire, have been of a type once described to me by Ken MacArthur as characteristically growing fairly short but well-pearled antlers. By contrast, the roe at Eskdalemuir have produced some excellent heads whose quality stalking clients travel far to appreciate. Some very passable heads have also been obtained in Berwickshire

which, like the rest of the Borders region as well as Strathclyde and the Lothians, now has roe in good numbers wherever the country is suitable. Where Scotland borders England roe pass freely from one to the other in what is now densely forested country over a great part of the area.

Scotland is not well off for wild fallow deer but has several long-established populations. One of these is centered on the Raehills estate, south of Moffat in Dumfriesshire, where the species was introduced as long ago as 1780.

Most of the fallow I saw here on a brief visit some years ago were of the common variety but there are also a good number of the black type. Antler quality is relatively good and stalking clients of Forest Enterprise sometimes have the chance to shoot fallow from this source in the Forest of Ae, west of Raehills, where a few are usually present, although roe are a far more numerous and more predictable quarry. The sheer tenacity of wild fallow once established in an area where they may not be widely welcomed is apparent in many localities, and Raehills is one of these, for over the past two centuries there have been many attempts to shoot them out at times when damage has been complained of.

The public can watch red deer at close quarters in the Forestry Commission's red deer range.

As well as red deer, Cumloden Park near Newton Stewart has also had fallow for quite a long period. The state of the wall is such that either species can leave or enter the park at will, but many of the fallow, I am told, are still to be found within the park, even though it is no longer strictly a deer park. Their antler quality is inferior to that of the fallow at Raehills, where better feeding is available.

In the 1970s an attempt was made to establish a small wild fallow population in another part of Galloway, the precise location of which was not disclosed. Whether this was successful in the long run I have not heard. There have been one or two other attempts to introduce fallow to southern Scotland, including one about 1860 from the Duke of Buccleuch's Boughton Park in Northamptonshire, but this was fairly short-lived.

The original Raehills fallow came from Hopetoun Park, South Queensferry, which continues to hold this species as well as red deer, which are separately emparked. Any fallow at large in the Lothians are likely to be escapees from here.

A few captive fallow are kept in Millgreen Park, Dumfries, and on the Belleisle estate in Ayr, both of which are local authority owned and open to the public. Also owned by the local authority is Palacerigg Country Park at Cumbernauld, 10 miles or so north-east of Glasgow, which in 1999 had a small number of red deer and reindeer as well as fallow. At one stage this latter park kept up to half a dozen roe in an enclosure of less than half a hectare, but persistent fighting between the bucks and other problems persuaded the management to dispose of them and they went to Auchingarrith Wildlife Centre at Comrie, in Perthshire.

Now in the care of the National Trust for Scotland, Culzean Country Park, near Maybole, has an enclosed herd of red deer and a population of wild roe which have the free run

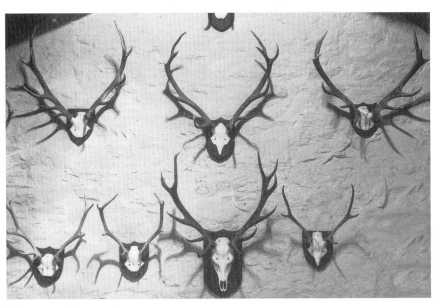

Specimen heads of Galloway red deer, of higher average quality than those of less well-favoured areas.

of the park. This of course is the property where roe were reintroduced to southern Scotland in the early nineteenth century. It is ironic to recall that where these deer are now given sanctuary efforts were made to eradicate them not long after their release because of the damage they were causing to young plantations on the estate. This failed largely because the roe had already spread to neighbouring properties outwith the Marquess of Ailsa's jurisdiction.

Edinburgh Zoo has a fairly large collection of antelope and a smaller one of deer, with Père David's, pudu and muntjac being present in 1999.

The Dawyck estate in Peeblesshire is notable as the place of origin of deer-park escapees which have given rise to a good deal of controversy. Eight sika deer imported direct from Japan were placed in a small park here in 1908. Four years later some broke loose to found a free-living population which has flourished ever since. It has been reinforced more than once by further fugitives from the residual captive herd which still existed up to the 1960s and possibly later.

When first I called there, in 1966, I was urged to 'take a rifle and shoot every deer you see, both sika and roe'. The deer, I gathered, had fallen from grace after causing some serious crop damage which had resulted in a tenant farmer having to be paid several hundred pounds in compensation. I had a walk around anyway and saw a number of very wild sika, perhaps not surprisingly so in the circumstances. Walking around once more four years later, I was again struck by the extremely wild and wary character of all the sika my wife and I saw.

Notwithstanding their unpopularity three decades and more ago, these Dawyck sika, and also those on the neighbouring Stobo estate, have long been considered a sporting resource, albeit one that needs culling fairly heavily to minimise farm and forest damage. Stalking takes place not only in woodland but also on adjacent grouse moors, where the deer emerge to feed in the open during the first and last hours of daylight, and the stags are said to produce better trophies than sika elsewhere in Scotland.

At the time of my two visits the sika were concentrated mainly on and around the Dawyck and Stobo estates, with no more than a few wanderers elsewhere. Heavy shooting in this core area may have encouraged some dispersal, however, accelerating their subsequent spread, mainly to the south and west – a process aided, without much doubt, by on-going reafforestation of the sheep ground which formerly blanketed almost the whole of the Southern Uplands. This

has brought the advance guard of colonising sika, mostly stags, within a short distance of Galloway red deer country. There have, indeed, already been instances of individual sika turning up on the west side of the Carlisle–Glasgow motorway, which one might have hoped would have proved an obstacle to their movement in that direction, and of odd red deer crossing it to reach country to the east where this species had been absent. Possible future hybridisation should the two populations be allowed to merge is one of several reasons for strenuous efforts being made by stalker members of the Borders Sika Deer Management Group to keep them apart. This group, like its Galloway red deer counterpart, has been chaired for a number of years by Tony Waterson, a past Scottish Area Chairman and Honorary Secretary of the British Deer Society.

Muntjac are not known to have established themselves in a wild state so far in any part of Scotland, and their arrival by natural spread from the south seems very unlikely indeed – for the foreseeable future at least. However, odd ones have been reported from one or two southern Scottish localities, almost certainly as a result of individual captive specimens either escaping or being released. On the whole it is fair to say that Scotland has little to offer this species and can perhaps very well do without it.

Senior Wildlife Ranger Ronnie Rose, MBE, has seen roe deer numbers grow from almost none to many hundreds following reafforestation of the once bare hills around Eskdalemuir in southern Scotland.

145

11
THE DEER OF CENTRAL AND NORTHERN SCOTLAND

With the possible exception of Spain, no other European country can boast more than a fairly small fraction of the numbers of red deer to be found in the Scottish Highlands. At first this may seem surprising when it is remembered how long a tradition there has been in many countries to conserve red deer as a highly regarded sporting quarry protected by law over many centuries. By comparison, red deer conservation in Scotland has been haphazard to say the least, and very much at the mercy of changing patterns of land use as well as of attitudes by sportsmen.

The key to this contrast is the very wide difference between the conditions in which the animals live in the different countries. Wild red deer on the Continent are almost exclusively forest-dwellers, occupying a habitat where high-density populations of the species are incompatible with sound forestry practice and with adjacent farming interests, not to mention any aim of producing optimum quality trophies. Most of today's Scottish red deer, on the other hand, are almost uniquely beasts of the open hill, where they can flourish in quite high densities without impinging upon competing human interests to a degree which most of those whose concerns are affected by their presence would regard as unacceptable. Largely as a consequence of a combination of climate and topography, it so happens too that red deer country, a high proportion of which is contiguous rather than scattered in mutually isolated 'islands' of suitable habitat as in much of continental Europe, comprises a higher percentage of the total land surface of Scotland than of other countries in Europe.

Fossil evidence shows red deer to have been widespread throughout the Scottish mainland, though perhaps with greater numbers in the Lowlands than in the Highlands during the prehistoric period. Forest clearance for cultivation banished them at a fairly early date from fertile areas such as the central Scottish plain, except where they were preserved for the sport of kings and other privileged individuals.

Much of the land which now constitutes Scotland's Highland, Grampian, Strathclyde, Central and Tayside Regions remained extensively wooded until as late as the seventeenth century. Destruction of the native Caledonian pine forest was brought about not just by factors common to forest clearance everywhere but also by some of more local significance, the extirpation of wolves being one of them. Deprived of tree cover, except in some relict pockets of forest such as Rothiemurchus in the Spey Valley, red deer had no alternative but to adapt to life in the open to survive in the changed conditions.

The fact that they did so with such success underlines what is often not fully realised, that red deer are, by nature, not so much forest animals *per se* as beasts of the forest border – in other words, beasts that prefer at least some woodland as part of their habitat, but which like open ground as well and can flourish exclusively in the open where woodland is totally unavailable. Clear evidence of this partiality may be found in areas such as Exmoor and the New Forest, where there is plenty of woodland cover but where a fairly high proportion of these deer are to be found living in the open at any one time.

Three Highland red stags photographed against a wintry background. (Lea MacNally, BEM)

It is almost impossible now to say to what extent the presence of red deer in what may have been too high a density may have contributed to the ultimate disappearance of nearly all the original forest cover in the Highlands. It can only be assumed that, when Scots pine and other trees spread back to these latitudes after the end of the last Ice Age and red deer followed in their wake, predation by wolves as well as by early human settlers kept their numbers at a level which the forest could sustain. Otherwise, would not the native forest have been laid waste by invading herbivores? This is a question one would like addressed by those who advocate virtually eliminating the present red deer populations as the only way of restoring something akin to the primeval woodland. Such woodland can in any case only

have clothed the lower and middle altitudes: those very 'wintering grounds' so many of which are now blanketed by commercial conifer forestry where incursions by deer are decidedly unwelcome.

In bygone centuries Highland chieftains gathered their clansmen and others together to organise deer drives on a truly heroic scale to entertain distinguished guests and to augment meat supplies when other sources of protein were scarce. These drives were known as *tainchels*, and one of the most famous was held in 1563 when Mary, Queen of Scots, was a guest of the Duke of Atholl. Mass execution was wrought when a total of some two thousand red deer were driven in for the occasion, and the bag included roe and fallow deer as well as a few wolves.

Wolves continued to prey on deer until the last of these feared carnivores was killed in the eighteenth century. Radical changes to life in the Highlands quickly followed the defeat of Bonnie

Prince Charlie in the Jacobite rising of 1745–6, which virtually ended the old clan system. The ensuing Highland Clearances coincided with the beginning of the depasturing of sheep in very large numbers where cattle had once been the principal livestock, and this adversely affected red deer. From around 1750 onwards deer numbers steadily declined. Some contraction of range occurred, especially around the Highland fringes, and by 1811 only six of the old deer forests still had fairly good stocks of red deer.

During and after the 1820s, the species' fortunes began to change for the better, with the development of stalking as a recognised Highland field sport, a process encouraged by William Scrope when, in 1839, he published *The Art of Deer-stalking*. The new sport was further stimulated by the greater ease of access to remoter Highland areas made possible by better transport as steamship services proliferated and railways penetrated farther. An additional fillip was given by Queen Victoria's

ABOVE: *Red deer are part and parcel of the Scottish Highland scene. (Lea MacNally, BEM)*

BELOW: *Red deer stags photographed against a typical Highland background. (Lea MacNally, BEM)*

acquisition of Balmoral, where Prince Albert became an enthusiastic stalker.

With an ever-increasing demand for stalking, often impoverished Highland proprietors rented deer forests to the industrial *nouveaux riches* from farther south, a breed made prosperous when Britain became 'the workshop of the world'. As the nineteenth century advanced, more and more land was cleared of sheep and given over entirely to deer, while wealthy incomers boosted employment by building estate roads and sumptuous shooting-lodges as well as by engaging professional stalkers and other staff.

The last two decades of the nineteenth century and the years leading up to the First World War saw a doubling of the amount of land devoted to deer forests and officially registered as such. The term 'forest' in this sense, of course, had nothing to do with trees as such, many deer forests indeed being virtually treeless. It was used with the ancient meaning of a more or less wild area mainly devoted to deer and to hunting.

Deer stocks were replenished in part by the natural increase of residual pre-existing populations where numbers had sunk to a low level during the decades of neglect, and by natural spread from neighbouring ground. As might be expected of a time when the upper echelons of society were awash with money as never before or since, Nature did not go entirely unaided in this rehabilitation process. Numerous red deer from English deer parks and from some Scottish ones were sent north in repeated efforts to give a kick-start to the improvement of Highland deer quality, famously modest as this was in terms of antler development, with body weights to match. It cannot be claimed that these importations have had any very lasting effect, except to dilute the genetic integrity of indigenous Highland deer, which were well adjusted in size and in other respects to life in a fairly harsh environment, with a climate close to the limits of their tolerance. Even wapiti blood has been introduced at various times and in various places, in the course of unavailing efforts to breed a 'super' race of red deer inappropriate to this region.

Some lasting effects, apart from the highly elusive bigger and 'better' beasts (as some would judge them), have manifested themselves in one or two places, such as Glenlyon, in Perthshire, where a white-faced or 'bald-faced' strain persists as a result of some deer of this

A Highland red deer hind with her newly born calf. (Lea MacNally, BEM)

type having been released towards the end of the nineteenth century by a Marquess of Breadalbane at nearby Drummond Hill. Other 'bald-faced' deer were turned out on Blackmount Forest, Argyllshire, from which the strain spread to surrounding forests.

Red deer once ranged as far east as the Aberdeenshire coast and north to the forests of Nairnshire and Morayshire, close to the Firth of Moray coast. In the early 1940s some red deer from Warnham Court Park in West Sussex were released at Pitgaveny, north of Elgin, well outside the normal contemporary range of these deer in what is now the Grampian Region, but persistent poaching kept this isolated population at a low level. In the far north, much of Caithness is hardly suitable for red deer,

A native roe doe on her ancestral Highland acres. (Lea MacNally, BEM)

Roe have survived in the Scottish Highlands since early times. (Lea MacNally, BEM)

exceptions being the southern and western deer forests of Langwell, Braemore and Dunbeath and some other areas along the Sutherland border. It was in the wilds of Sutherland that I shot my first red deer in a small deer forest south of Tongue many years ago.

A line drawn between the Firths of Clyde and Forth marks the absolute southernmost limit of spread by red deer from the Highlands, but their regular range stops some miles farther north. Apart from the agricultural lower ground of east and north-east Scotland, and parts of Caithness as I have indicated, almost the whole of the rest of the Highland zone is red deer country. Look to the high ground almost anywhere and there is a good chance of seeing a few. I saw my first in the late 1940s high in the Inverness-shire deer forest of Ardverikie while on my first-ever Highland holiday, an encounter as clearly etched in my memory now, more than half a century later, as if it had happened only yesterday.

From an estimated 100,000 in 1950, Scotland's total red deer population had increased threefold within a few decades as a result of mild winters and dryer than average summers coupled with problems, in some areas, in achieving an adequate cull. Under the terms of the Deer (Scotland) Act of 1959 the Red Deer

Commission was set up to monitor deer populations and to intervene where problems of management arise. The scope of this body is now extended to cover species other than red deer and its powers enlarged accordingly, changes which are reflected in a change of name to the Deer Commission for Scotland. One of the Commission's aims has been to encourage neighbouring deer forest owners and others to combine for deer-management purposes, and this has been achieved with good results in some vital areas.

Stepped-up hind culls in particular have also helped in the last few years in trimming back numbers to a level where winter mortality is reduced, and other problems caused by overabundant deer are mitigated.

As well as the recognised deer forests, numbering 445 at a recent count, Highland red deer occur on many grouse moors and marginal areas of various kinds where their presence is tolerated to a varying extent. They are least welcome in those areas to which they tend to be most attracted – commercial forestry plantations. Nearly all of these are initially protected by deer fencing, despite which almost all are vulnerable to deer breaking in sooner or later.

With their instinctive attraction to woodland, alike for shelter, food and concealment, it is inevitable that red deer should invade these timbered fastnesses, so many of which are located on ground to which deer once had free access to escape the worst rigours of winter at higher altitudes nearby. It is inevitable, too, that they should cause quite serious damage and present problems of some magnitude to those who try to control their numbers in the difficult conditions presented by the dense cover which is afforded by blanket forestry over very extensive areas.

Wildlife rangers do their best to control deer according to the basic principles of sound deer management, but tend to be too thin on the ground to avoid having recourse to additional measures, such as night shooting under licence from the Deer Commission for Scotland and some shooting out of season, to accomplish essential culls. With some fifty thousand red deer currently reckoned to live in these plantations, effective deer management has become a major challenge for those responsible for such matters. Research in the west Highland

forest of Glenbranter and elsewhere has yielded interesting data on such aspects as estimating red deer numbers from sample dung counts and thus the culls required, and forest planning nowadays gives increased emphasis to the need to retain open spaces to facilitate deer control.

On the other side of the coin, red deer in commercial forests have responded to the more congenial habitat thus afforded by producing bigger antlers and better body weights than their neighbours on the open hill. Reduced winter mortality and higher than average fecundity are other by-products of life for these deer in a sheltered woodland environment. Another marked difference from life in the open is that stags tend to be less vocal during the rut and harems smaller.

A Japanese sika stag photographed in the Great Glen, Inverness-shire, where these deer are well established and spreading. (Lea MacNally, BEM)

How many roe are there in Scotland? Estimating numbers of this species is notoriously difficult and can rarely amount to more than 'guesstimates', probably erring on the low side to a very marked degree in most cases. One such estimate at the end of the 1950s produced a figure of 100,000 for the whole of Scotland, including the south, while it was reckoned that the immediate pre-war total was twice that number.

Recently, however, a careful analysis of cull totals based on numbers of carcases known to have passed through the hands of venison dealers in one year (30,000–40,000) – plus others privately disposed of as indicated by a survey among a cross-section of stalkers, and making a reasonable allowance for roe mortality from other causes – has produced some surprising conclusions. Another factor in the equation is the apparent fact, which emerges from research carried out by the Forestry Authority, that an annual cull of one-third to keep a roe population level is too high, and that a more realistic proportion is from 15 to 25 per cent. In other words, culls estimated as one-third which have not caused an overall reduction of the residual stock from one year to another imply that the actual stock, before culling commenced, must have been higher than was supposed.

The basic conclusion of this study, as spelled out in a recent British Association for Shooting and Conservation two-part paper on *Deer Management in Scotland*, is that only 10 per cent of roe carcases are ever sent to venison dealers. On this assumption, the present roe population of Scotland is reckoned to be somewhere between 300,000 and 400,000.

A Japanese sika hind and calf in Inverness-shire. These deer have proved themselves well able to withstand the Scottish Highland winter climate. (Lea MacNally, BEM)

It is fairly safe to say that more than half of this staggering total occur in central and northern Scotland, that is to say, north of the central lowlands. It is also an undisputed fact that, at this northern end of Great Britain, indigenous roe have never died out, although they went through a fairly bleak period in the early eighteenth century due to habitat reduction when the Caledonian pine forest was very nearly destroyed. Recovery began around two hundred years ago when tree-planting began to make some amends for the damage done.

Having possibly lost all their roe for a time, Stirlingshire, Clackmannanshire, Kinross and Fifeshire, and perhaps one or two other counties, were repopulated by natural spread in the course of the nineteenth century. Strongholds of roe survival, when the species was at its lowest ebb elsewhere, include Deeside in Aberdeenshire, Rothiemurchus in Inverness-shire and, in particular, well-wooded Morayshire and Nairnshire directly south of the Moray Firth. From these and other areas, such as the woods along the south side of Loch Rannoch in Perthshire, where roe had persisted in lesser numbers, depleted populations elsewhere were in the course of time replenished as numbers built up the in core habitats and outward spread began in earnest.

This roe recovery took place with little or no encouragement from nineteenth-century lairds and has continued throughout the twentieth century, largely of its own volition, although on a few estates under the watchful eye of sympathetic owners intent on practising sound roe management in accordance with modern ideas. The genetic purity of these native Scottish roe appears to be almost entirely unsullied by introductions, although there has been at least one instance of roe from West Sussex being translocated to Speyside in recent times in an effort to improve antler quality.

The booming demand from client stalkers, especially from continental Europe, has done a great deal in recent decades to give Highland roe a more secure place among the valued game species of the region. Quality naturally varies according to local circumstances of both habitat and climate, but roe from many parts of what used to be Perthshire probably rank among the best in terms of antler shape and dimensions.

To sum up, the present-day picture is that roe are established in varying densities throughout central and northern Scotland wherever the habitat is suitable, except at the higher altitudes. I saw my first ones near Kingussie way back in 1949, and the Spey valley woods have afforded some of my best views of roe in Scotland.

Fallow deer, of course, are not indigenous, but their history in this region dates from medieval times, some being known to have been present in Stirling Park in the thirteenth century, and there are several wild populations which have a respectably ancient lineage.

Fallow deer have had associations with the Loch Lomond area since at least the sixteenth century and probably for well over six hundred years. At the time of Robert the Bruce the largest and most southerly of the loch's islands, Inchmurrin, as well as Inchcailloch, close to the eastern shore, are known to have been deer parks, and although the species involved is not recorded it seems likely to have been fallow, which are known to have been present on Inchmurrin two hundred years later. Fallow remained on Inchmurrin, at times in substantial numbers partly sustained by supplementary feeding in winter but latterly in much reduced strength, until about 1930, when the island was sold, after which they ceased to be resident. For at least three centuries, however, there have been fallow deer on Inchlonaig, the most north-easterly of the cluster of islands between Luss on the western mainland and Balmaha on the east. Inchlonaig was used as a deer park by successive generations of the Colquhoun family of Luss until one of them, Sir James Colquhoun, and four of his keepers were drowned in 1873 while shipping deer carcases to the mainland in stormy weather after a day's shooting.

Around the turn of the nineteenth century a deer park was formed on the western mainland at Rossdhu, the Colquhoun family home, and it seems likely that this took the place of

Inchlonaig as the estate's main source of venison. Meanwhile, fallow remained on Inchlonaig, leading a purely wild existence, and after a tree breached the deer park wall at Rossdhu in 1917 fallow broke out from there to form a wild herd of their own in surrounding woods and on a number of loch islands within easy swimming distance.

Although black or brownish-black fallow predominate, about one-third of these deer are white, as were all those I saw in the Rossdhu policies and on the island of Inchconnachan when I went there in the late 1970s. On Inchlonaig, however, all but one of the fallow I saw were black, and the Rossdhu keeper told me that his prime concern when culling deer on the islands was to weed out white ones because they showed up more clearly and became a magnet for poachers.

Unlike Inchmurrin, Inchcailloch retains a few fallow and is probably the source of those that range the Balmaha woods on the eastern mainland in small numbers.

James V and Mary of Guise are reckoned to have hunted fallow from the royal residence at Falkland in Fifeshire in 1539 but, occasional wanderers apart, any deer larger than roe to be seen in that corner of Scotland today are most likely to be either farm stock or denizens of the Scottish Deer Centre at Bow of Fife, near Cupar, where red deer, roe, sika, fallow, muntjac, chital (axis deer), hog deer, Père David's deer and wapiti were all present in 1999 as well as reindeer during the winter months.

Fallow were also among the quarry at the great sixteenth century *tainchel* organised by a Duke of Atholl when Mary Queen of Scots was his guest. A later duke was responsible for introducing to the Dunkeld area of Perthshire a herd of wild fallow which still flourishes and is almost certainly the largest individual fallow population at large in Scotland today. The range of these deer has changed little since John Guille Millais wrote about them in 1897, describing them as being present in woods within an area of about ten square miles (26 sq km) centred upon Dunkeld and extending north to Ballinluig, east to the Loch of Clunie, the Loch of Lowes and Rohallion and south to Murthly, where he and his father resided in the autumn and winter for many years. All the fallow I have seen in the Dunkeld area have been black, but

Millais made reference to some having been of the light spotted variety. He described them as being exceptionally cunning and shy, an assessment that does not seem to have been disputed by later observers.

Drummond Castle Park, near Crieff, was the source of fallow which became established on Forestry Commission land at Drummond Hill, and fallow have also been reported from the nearby Bolfracks estate, between Loch Tay and Aberlady. In what used to be Argyllshire, woods in the Inverary area, and near Carradale in Kintyre, have also held fallow in recent times. Aberdeenshire has had fallow deer in the past and there may be a few in this part of the Grampian Region now, while Kincardineshire is another past haunt. Farther north, the same applies to Morayshire, and perhaps also to Banffshire, though some may still be present near Craigellachie in the Spey Valley.

Reindeer are at home again in Scotland.

Fallow once present in woods near Arisaig, on the west coast of Inverness-shire south of Mallaig, are apparently now extinct, although the Balmacaan area on the north side of Loch Ness is believed still to hold a few, and there are also some in parts of Ross-shire. In the latter county fallow were reported as having been present in the eighteenth century, and Millais wrote of their later occurrence at Achnashellach, Inchbae and Kinlochluichart, also in Ross-shire. I saw a single fallow deer while walking near Loch Luichart in 1952 but failed to find any sign of them in a large wood called Dubh Choille, alongside the road from Garve to Ullapool, where the writer Alex I. McConnochie had described them as being present decades earlier. However, I understand there are still a few fallow in the Strathgarve area, not far from Loch Luichart, today.

In Sutherland, fallow were introduced to the Dornoch woods about 1890, and they flourished for a time but have since died out. Rosehall Park, in Strath Oykell, was the scene in the 1870s of

another fallow introduction, but these deer failed to survive the Second World War. In the east coast woods around Dunrobin the species seems to have done better, a small herd of white fallow having lived there for many years.

In Caithness in 1970, I saw white fallow at Berriedale, to which a Duke of Portland had introduced some from Welbeck Park in Nottinghamshire in about 1900. At the time of my visit, when I watched several of these fallow placidly grazing in a paddock within full view of Langwell House, they numbered about a dozen, but I am told they no longer survive. As well as the fallow and some red deer I also saw a few sika, the latter species having been introduced on two separate occasions from Welbeck. There were about twenty sika all told, and these, like the fallow, rarely strayed beyond the woods around Langwell House, which they shared with the red deer which winter there.

Sika were first brought to Scotland in about 1870 and placed in a park at Tullieallan, in western Fifeshire. In due course they escaped and set up home in nearby woodland where, after fluctuating fortunes including reduction at one stage to barely more than single figures, they are still to be found today and from which they have spread into other woods in neighbouring Clackmannanshire.

In about 1990 sika from Powerscourt in Ireland were introduced by Sir Arthur Bignold to Achanalt in Ross-shire where, like the Tullieallan sika, they were at first kept in confinement. Wartime difficulties led to their being released in 1915, since when they have spread along Strathbran to populate neighbouring deer forests, though when I first visited the area and made extensive enquiries about them the railway from Dingwall to Kyle of Lochalsh apparently restricted their range to the south. The Achanalt woods remained their head-quarters, and there I watched them in the evening as they emerged to feed in the open on higher ground above the timber.

Alladale in Easter Ross is another haunt of sika, which I spent an early October morning watching a good many years ago. There was some doubt as to whether these represented an easterly offshoot of the Achanalt population or a southerly one from those introduced to Rosehall Park in Strath Oykell at the end of the nineteenth century.

A broken fence gave these their liberty to spread along Strath Oykell and establish themselves in Glencasserley, Glenlossit and other areas where they have access to large forestry plantations, to which they have caused significant damage requiring enhanced measures of control. Indications are that these Rosehall sika and their Achanalt near neighbours have now linked up to form a single population whose range is likely to expand further.

Only a narrow gap separates the sika of Ross-shire and Sutherland from those in Inverness-shire, which are now equally wide-ranging. These stem from at least three separate introductions: to Glenmazaran and Glenkyllachy at some time around the turn of the nineteenth century and at another date to Aldourie Castle estate, near Inverness. For a time the Glenmazaran sika remained largely separate from those at the two other locations, but inevitably all three eventually merged and began to spread along the Great Glen, almost the whole length of which they now occupy, numbers being greatest on the south side. My sole encounter with these sika was with four grazing near Loch Ness in a field along with some red deer, raising anew in my mind the question of the extent to which hybridisation was likely to happen in such situations.

Cross-breeding between the two species has indisputably occurred on a fairly significant scale in Kintyre, where the story of sika began with the introduction in 1893 of two stags and nine hinds from Fawley Court Park in Buckinghamshire. These were initially enclosed behind a fence on the Carradale peninsula, or at any rate this was the intention, but since the fence was confined to the landward side the deer soon escaped by swimming around it. At first they had no contact with red deer, but as they steadily increased and spread, the gap between the two progressively narrowed. By the 1960s, if not earlier, the range of the two species already overlapped and hybrids began to be suspected. In 1964 I spent a day with the late Captain Ian Coats on his Carse estate in Knapdale, where sika were by that time well established after swimming north across West Loch Tarbert or crossing the isthmus at its head. He was of the opinion that hybrids usually resulted from a cross between a red stag and a sika hind, contrary to the common belief that it is physically more feasible for a lighter-weight sika stag and a red hind to effect such a union.

During our tour of this corner of Knapdale we saw a number of all three deer species present: sika, red and roe deer. One group of red hinds was accompanied by a stag which looked suspiciously like a hybrid. However, my host's suspicions were greater concerning a very large sika-like stag which suddenly moved in to join a sizeable assemblage of sika hinds we were watching. He later told me that when he subsequently shot this stag it proved to be twice as heavy as any previously culled there, albeit that in other respects it looked like a pure-blooded sika.

Now, more than three decades later, red deer from farther north in Argyll have colonised almost the whole of the Kintyre peninsula, while sika, in their turn, have pushed in the opposite direction, some having penetrated north well beyond the Crinan Canal to reach the seaward end of Loch Linnhe, at the south-westernmost extremity of the Great Glen.

The gap is thus greatly narrowed between these sika and those which are now spread along the Great Glen proper as is that between the latter and the sika of Ross-shire and Sutherland. The day may not be far off, it is now obvious, when the range of sika deer will extend, without a break, all the way from the Mull of Kintyre to Sutherland, with consequences for the future of pure-bred red deer which are hard to predict and not to be lightly disregarded when management strategies for these immigrants from east Asia are considered.

There have been other releases of sika with less dramatic implications, including a short-lived attempt to introduce the species to the Black Isle, Inverness-shire, before the last war. Sika introduced years ago to Kinnaird Castle Park in Angus succeeded in escaping into neighbouring woodland. They no longer survive but the park's long-established herd of fallow were joined by red deer in the 1980s.

The sika menace – as some regard it, where this species is on the increase – is so serious that a shoot-on-sight policy is being urged in some quarters, coupled even with the suspension of close seasons, a trend of thinking with very worrying implications of its own for the possible future of good deer management in general.

A native species which died out at least eight hundred years ago, the reindeer (*Rangifer tarandus*) has staged a comeback to Scotland since the Second World War after a Swedish reindeer owner, Mikel Utsi, pointed out that plenty of natural food for these deer, in the form of lichens in particular, was available on and around the Cairngorm Mountains. After some early trial and error, a herd was successfully established under the auspices of the Reindeer Council of the United Kingdom, a body especially set up for the purpose.

Camera-stalking some of these reindeer high in the Cairngorms some years ago, I abandoned any subterfuge when I realised fairly quickly that these animals were hand-tame, as the tinkling bells around some of their necks clearly proclaimed. Now owned by the Reindeer Company Limited, based at Reindeer House, the Cairngorm Reindeer Centre, Glenmore, Aviemore, in 1999 the herd numbered well over a hundred. Most of them live on free range at high altitude, but between May and October a proportion are kept in a large enclosure on lower ground, where they are accessible to visitors. A few years ago, as the herd increased it was decided to establish a subsidiary herd at Glenlivet, near Tomintoul, some miles north-east of Glenmore, where suitable high ground is also available.

In addition to the enclosed deer already mentioned, others are kept in a number of country parks and the like as well as in various private collections. Auchengarrith Wildlife Centre at Comrie, in Perthshire, exhibited red,

roe, fallow, sika, muntjac, chital (axis deer) and hog deer in 1999. The Highland Wildlife Park at Kincraig in Inverness-shire concentrates on British species. Its herd of red deer, numbering seventy in 1999, are descended from local wild stock which were fed into the park in the first place, and roe are kept in two separate enclosures. As a native species reintroduced after earlier extinction, reindeer are also represented, although there were just two in 1999. The European elk (*Alces alces*) would likewise qualify for inclusion if suitable wetland habitat could be made available.

Located just outside Stirling is Blair Drummond Safari and Leisure Park, which in 1999 had Père David's, fallow and Japanese sika deer, while at Camperdown, Dundee, is the Scottish Wildlife Centre, owned by the City of Dundee and exhibiting red deer, roe, fallow and muntjac as well as Manchurian sika.

Private collections include a few red deer in a small enclosure at Blair Castle, ancestral seat of the Dukes of Atholl at Blair Atholl in Perthshire, a herd of red deer in Kinmonth Deer Park, the home of the Moncrieff family at Bridge of Earn, also in Perthshire, and another enclosed herd of red deer at Rothiemurchus in Inverness-shire, owned by the Grants of Rothiemurchus.

Deer farming looms large in parts of this region, notably at Auchtermuchty in Fifeshire, where Dr John Fletcher and his wife, Nichola, were pioneers of the industry. In 1999 John had a stock of some four hundred red deer plus a few fallow at Reediehill Farm, where Nichola looks after venison sales to national supermarkets and other retail outlets as well as a mail-order business with a range of private customers. John and Nichola were involved in setting up and equipping the nearby Scottish Deer Centre, which is now run independently.

Other deer farms in the region include Cluanie Tennassie and Culligran, both near Beauly in Inverness-shire and specialising in red deer, as well as Strathgarve at Garve in Ross-shire, which in 1999 had a sizeable herd of red deer and a few fallow.

The commercial viability of deer farming in the Highlands was examined in detail in the first instance by the Rowett Research Institute of Aberdeen, and it was following this study and recommendations ensuing from it that deer farming fairly quickly took off as a major rural enterprise.

12
THE DEER OF THE
SCOTTISH ISLANDS

By their very nature, islands tend to have fewer land mammals than continental areas, smaller islands being worse off in this respect than larger ones. Scotland's many islands are no exception, yet all of the larger Western Isles, as well as some that are not so large, have well-established populations of deer, which in more than one instance considerably outnumber the human population.

As might be expected, red deer are the predominating species. Most of the islands where these now occur have been their haunt since ancient times, with at least a nucleus of the original island strain still represented among the deer of the present day. In no case, however, can it be confidently asserted that island blood has not been diluted by importations. The deer forest proprietors of the past saw no merit in preserving the genetic integrity of local deer populations, whether on islands or otherwise, their prime aim mostly being to produce the biggest and best deer, with the biggest possible trophies, by whatever means might be available. Thus a great many English park stags and some hinds found themselves being translocated to what, by comparison, are the brutally harsh conditions of the Scottish Highlands and islands, there to pass on their sterling qualities to the far less impressive local stock – or so it was hoped.

This treatment of deer as domestic bloodstock may have something to be said for it in a farming situation, but where wild animals are concerned it has had little lasting effect apart from irrevocably polluting the indigenous local bloodline, which was best adapted to the habitat available.

Artificial importations apart, island bloodlines have in a number of cases received infusions of outside blood by natural means. Red deer are strong swimmers, stags in particular crossing quite wide stretches of water from one island to another or between island and mainland,

Relaxing in summer sunshine, a red stag on the Isle of Rhum with Loch Scresort in the background.

especially when food is locally scarce or during the rut.

The history of deer on the different islands is complex and varied, hardly any two islands having precisely parallel links between past and present, although there are some factors common to nearly all. Arran is one of those with a discontinuous deer history. According to one chronicler, this Firth of Clyde island was considered to have some of the best hunting in either Ireland or Scotland in ancient times, its red deer being the focus of this activity. 'Arran of the many stags' is how another early writer summed it up, while according to Martin Martin, whose book *A Description of the Western Islands of Scotland*, published in 1703, contains much interesting detail about deer populations; some four hundred deer were then preserved by the island's owner, the Duke of Hamilton.

However, by 1840 the *New Statistical Account of Scotland* noted that only a few dozen red deer remained in each of Arran's two parishes. Within a few years they were extinct, the late Duke of Montrose having had in his possession the head of the last stag. In 1859 a new era began with the importation of five stags and fourteen hinds from Lord Derby's Knowsley Park in Lancashire. This was followed some time later by a wapiti hind (*Cervus canadensis*). Within a few years stalking was possible and has continued ever since, with the northern half of Arran devoted to deer and the much more gently contoured south to stock-raising, farming and forestry.

Since the early twentieth century a deer fence has had some effect in containing Arran's deer in the mountainous north, but some have managed to get round it into the agricultural south. Red deer from Welbeck Park and Windsor Great Park have reinforced the Knowsley strain, and the island's relatively mild climate has undoubtedly been a factor, combined with a congenial habitat, in producing some heavy body weights and creditable trophies. On a visit in 1949 I saw many red deer at low altitudes, some of them quite close to the road which circles the north of Arran and to the String Road which cuts across its centre and is paralleled by the deer fence. Arran's red deer population is something in excess of a thousand and has occasionally included the odd white individual.

Arran stags have been known to swim the 4-mile width of Kilbrannan Sound to reach the coast of Kintyre. If a stag which turned up in 1950 on the Ayrshire island of Little Cumbrae originated from Arran, a swim of at least 12 miles was involved. The Island of Bute, farther north, is less than a mile from the Scottish mainland at its nearest point, so it is not surprising to learn that red deer sometimes swim to it, and before the First World War a few

were apparently resident.

Mountainous Jura, off the Argyllshire coast, is a red deer haunt *par excellence*. Its name is thought to derive from the Gaelic *deira*, meaning 'deer island', which is essentially what it has been since early times, and still remains. In his *Description of the Western Islands of Scotland*, of 1549, Dean Monro referred to 'a fyne forest for deire' as being a principal feature of Jura, where the deer at that time were hunted by means of drives, many being slain as they tried to pass through a half-mile gap between Loch Tarbert and Jura's east coast halfway along the island's length.

A red deer heavyweight on Rhum, in the Inner Hebrides.

Later writers, ranging from Thomas Pennant in 1772 and William Scrope in 1839 to H. Evans in 1890, confirm the consistently high population of red deer on this island, which at one point between the two world wars was reckoned at over 7000. When I visited Jura in the early 1960s the deer were thought to total a rather more modest 3000, but even at that level there were some fifteen deer to every human resident on the island, a ratio which has remained largely unaltered since that time. I saw many red deer alongside the single-track road which follows the island's east coast. Among the stags I looked in vain for individuals of the 'cromie' type which, apart from rare examples elsewhere, is peculiar to Jura, being characterised by back-curving antlers not unlike the horns of a goat. Perhaps three or four in every hundred are of this type. Half-cromies also occur, with one normal antler and one of the 'cromie' variety.

The 9-knot tides which sweep through the intervening Sound of Islay are no deterrent to stags determined on crossing from Jura to Islay, as I was reminded during my visit. A far kindlier island than Jura, Islay has had red deer of its own at least as long as its neighbour, and some of these run to quite remarkably heavy body weights. Antler quality too is good, and the many Islay red deer I saw included ten- and eleven-point specimens.

Prior to the First World War, all but a few Islay red deer were confined in the 1600 ha Kildalton Park, a hilly moorland area in the south-east of the island. After the war the deer fence fell into neglect and the deer have since been free to roam the surrounding countryside. The hilly eastern side of Islay is now recognised red deer country, with a population of the species estimated when I was there as totalling some 1300. As well as immigrants from Jura, red deer from Warnham Court Park in West Sussex have been imported in the past.

Just north of Jura and well within swimming distance for red deer across the Sound of Corryvrecken is the small and semi-mountainous island of Scarba which, even more than Jura, is a place for deer rather than for people and probably has always been so. Deer sometimes swim between here and the still-smaller island of Lunga, still farther north, and perhaps occasionally to the Argyllshire coastal islands of Seil and Luing, both of which are visited by these deer from time to time.

The Inner Hebridean islands of Colonsay and Oronsay have no red deer today, but bones of the species have been found as evidence of past occurrence. The same applies to Lismore at the entrance to Loch Linnhe, which is said to have been a great hunting forest in times long past.

Mull is another of the larger Inner Hebridean islands which have had deer since time immemorial, often in substantial numbers. Monro writes of 'maney deire with verey fair hunting games' in the sixteenth century, while Martin in 1703 brackets deer with cattle, sheep and goats as among Mull's most important features. Towards the end of the eighteenth century the *New Statistical Account of Scotland* lists red deer, foxes, eagles, hawks, blackgame, ptarmigan and woodcock as being members of Mull's fauna. It is worth noting that foxes no longer occur on this island.

The mid-nineteenth century was a low point for Mull's red deer. After a period of decline, when extinction seemed a very real danger, the species was saved by a combination of measures to conserve such stocks as remained and to reinforce them by introductions from English parks and mainland deer forests. Numbers steadily increased until a healthy population was re-established on the island. Stepped-up culling during and after the Second World War reduced them from a pre-war total of almost 6000 to less than half that number, and the Deer Commission for Scotland nowadays assists, here as elsewhere, in ensuring the maintenance of an acceptable balance between preserving adequate stocks of deer and protecting farming and forestry interests.

The well-wooded eastern side of Mull attracts a certain number of red deer, not just in winter but all the year round, and it was here, in Salen Forest, that I saw my first ones on a visit in 1964. In the mountainous centre of Mull, around Ben More, I saw many others from the road while touring the island, while farther south I saw some on the coastal cliffs. Nearly all were in small groups, the largest number I had in view at any one time being some ninety on the high ground of Laggan Deer Forest, the proprietor of which told me that the best trophy ever shot there was a fourteen-pointer a few years previously. At one stage deer from Warnham Court Park in West Sussex had been introduced in an effort to counter the tendency of Mull stags to produce short, thick antlers of no great merit. In this forest, which occupies a remote area in the extreme south of Mull, I also saw a number of wild goats.

Just off the north-west corner of Mull is the island of Ulva, the small size of which has not discouraged red deer from trying to make themselves at home there. At the time of my visit

Red deer on high ground on the Island of Mull, where agricultural and forestry interests require deer numbers to be carefully controlled.

I learned that a dozen or so of these animals were usually present in the woods around Ulva House. Farther west is another small island, Gometra, which I understand has been the setting for a deer farming enterprise involving red deer.

The Sound of Mull is no barrier to enterprising red deer, and has often been crossed between Mull and the mainland, especially by stags at the time of the rut.

Since the isle of Rhum was acquired by the then Nature Conservancy in 1957 its main use has been as an outdoor laboratory for research into all aspects of red deer, primarily with the aim of developing optimum methods of management. When I went there I learned how every theory was being subjected to critical tests. The effects of such treatment as deliberately distorting the sex ratio so as to create a gross imbalance of stags to hinds and vice-versa, and of completely suspending control of deer numbers in selected areas for limited periods, upon deer fertility, body weights and antler development were being monitored with a view to arriving at conclusions of practical value to deer managers.

A red deer population of some 1500 animals is distributed throughout all of this bleakly rugged and rainy island except for a few deer-fenced plantations around Loch Scresort, on the east side. Notwithstanding Monro's description of sixteenth-century Rhum as 'ane forest of high mountains with abundance of little deire on it', this island seems unlikely ever to have been more than sparsely wooded. Towards the end of the eighteenth century, however, it was lamented by one observer, the Revd Donald Maclean, that the destruction of such woods as were formerly present had led to the extirpation of the deer that had once been so plentiful that island people had built some dykes between which to drive and corral them for slaughter without making any lasting impression on total deer numbers.

Whether Rhum's original red deer were in fact exterminated is uncertain but it is likely that today's population is mainly, if not wholly, descended from fresh stock introduced at some time after the human population of over four hundred was shipped out to Newfoundland in 1828 and replaced by several thousand sheep, a flockmaster and a few shepherds. The deer-forest era in its modern sense dawned later, but not until after 1957 were the last of the sheep removed and some cattle brought in.

Rhum's nineteenth-century shooting-lodge, Kinloch Castle, is nowadays used in part as a self-catering hostel for visitors, and it was this that my wife and I used as our base for a series of field excursions. As well as the many deer we saw in remote parts of the island, two magnificent stags, a seventeen-pointer and a ten-pointer, spent much of their time loafing about in the miniature village of Kinloch, one of their favourite places for an afternoon siesta being some greensward just in front of the post office. Such superlative stags are hardly what one expects to find on Rhum, although Sir George Burrough, the last private owner, imported stags and hinds of high quality from Warnham Court Park in West Sussex and had recourse to supplementary winter feeding in his efforts to produce bigger and better deer.

In proportion to its size, Skye has fewer red deer than almost any other Hebridean island where this species is present, although this was not always so. Monro described Skye as having many deer, although his sixteenth-century contemporaries apparently killed large numbers. Three hundred years later, Scrope reckoned that in the whole of Skye there were not many more than 200. Just prior to the Second World War there may have been around a thousand, but two decades later there were scarcely more than a hundred. The only area where I personally have seen them is among the hills of the island's eastern extremity south of Kyleakin, which in recent times has been the principal haunt of those that remain, although they have also been reported from other localities widely scattered throughout the island.

From near Broadford, on the east coast of Skye, on one of my last visits I watched red deer through binoculars on the nearby island of Scalpay, an ancient haunt of the species, although the modern population probably stems from introductions at various times since 1927, when some Warnham stock was brought there. In recent times the island has been managed as a combination of deer forest and deer farm, its isolation and hilly character making it ideal for both purposes.

Hand-reared deer, like this red hind on Mull, become almost fearless of humans, and stags thus reared can be dangerous during the rut.

Deer sometimes swim between Skye and the mainland and between Skye, Scalpay and Raasay, in essence a miniature replica of Skye which lies close to Skye's eastern shore. Monro confirms the presence of red deer on Raasay in the sixteenth century, but Dr Johnson on his Hebridean tour 200 years later noted that there were then none.

Fresh stock was introduced to Raasay in the late nineteenth century, since when numbers have fluctuated according to prevailing circumstances. The Second World War saw a marked reduction and in 1950 there were reckoned to be only four stags and twelve hinds. Afforestation since that time has afforded alternative habitat to the open hill conditions to which they were previously exposed. The deer have benefited accordingly, although when I visited the island twice in the late 1970s I was told that there was quite serious damage from bark-stripping, so that culling had to be stepped up. There were then thought to be not many fewer than fifty deer altogether, and I saw several in the open near a plantation on Raasay's east coast which was one of their favourite lying-up places.

North of Raasay, the now uninhabited island of Rona was at one time a haunt of red deer, but any that ever occur there now will be visitors from elsewhere.

In the Outer Hebrides, Harris and Lewis – all one island – have since ancient times had red deer which, compared with their mainland counterparts, were described a century ago by a visiting sportsman, Lieutenant-General H.H. Crealock, as being as the pony is to the horse: small but well proportioned, heads of ten, eleven or even twelve points being by no means out of the ordinary. This small size, a clear adaptation to harsh conditions of climate and habitat, has been little affected in the long run by importations of mainland stock intended to bring about 'improvements'.

Deer are normally confined to the various deer forests in the mountainous south of Lewis and in North Harris, where I saw them in good numbers on the heights above Hushinish. Their range in Lewis is restricted by a deer fence across the island which protects the crofting lands to the north. There is no official deer forest now in South Harris but red deer do sometimes still turn up there.

North Uist's red deer tend to be larger and they live at lower altitudes, mainly on remote hills on the eastern side of the island where, on a memorable visit, my wife and I had excellent views not only of deer but of golden eagles and a peregrine falcon at close quarters.

In the late nineteenth century, and again in the 1930s, park deer and Scottish mainland beasts were shipped across to North Uist to supplement an island strain which until then had almost wholly escaped dilution by non-native blood. Four hundred years ago the deer here were numbered in their hundreds, a situation largely unaltered when we went there in the 1970s. Although free to wander throughout the island and to cross to the bridge-linked neighbouring islands of Benbecula and South Uist, we were told that they were normally restricted to North Uist. Later, however, I learned that there are once again resident red deer on South Uist after an absence of well over a hundred years.

In 1975 seventeen red deer were brought to South Uist from Dr John Fletcher's Reediehill Deer Farm at Auchtermuchty, in Fifeshire. These and their descendants were joined ten years later by six hinds from Glencoe. In 1999 I learned from Mr Alastair Scott, Factor of South Uist estate, that a stock of some two hundred red deer were ranging all over the island. They have linked up with the North Uist population and have produced some very good weights, including stags of 125 kg and more. As is the case with many other island-dwelling red deer, seaweed forms an important part of their diet.

Between North Uist and South Harris lies the 80-ha island of Pabbay, to which red deer were introduced in the late nineteenth century. The stock has sometimes numbered a hundred or more, and on at least one occasion deer from here have swum the Sound of Pabbay to reach North Uist.

Roe deer are resident on only a very few Scottish islands today. The most southerly is Bute, where on a visit in the 1960s I was told that a hundred or so were normally present. In 1996,

however, I learned from the Bute estate's Head Gamekeeper, Mr Ian Alexander, that some eight hundred roe were then present on the island. These are thought not to be indigenous, for records suggest that the species was absent throughout most if not all of the eighteenth century and the early nineteenth century, reappearing at some date before about 1865, when they were described as being most plentiful in the southern part of the island. Whether these deer were reintroduced or arrived of their own accord after swimming the narrow Kyles between Bute and the mainland is uncertain, but they are clearly now well established in a congenial habitat mixture of farmland and woodland. Roe from Bute are also reported to have turned up on occasion on the small island of Inchmarnock, a mile or so to the west.

Any roe once native to Arran died out a very long time ago, but in the mid-nineteenth century some were briefly introduced. The new arrivals proved destructive and were accordingly disposed of. A similar fate appears to have been dealt out to roe introduced to Jura in the early twentieth century, although records suggest that the species was present here several centuries ago.

They have fared better on neighbouring Islay, where they have been present for so long that their origin is shrouded in mystery, although it seems certain that they must have been introduced in the first place. On a visit in 1962 I saw some in woods around Loch Ballygrant, in the centre of the island, and among plantations on the Island House estate, just outside Bridgend. Small woods are widely scattered throughout Islay, and almost wherever there is woodland there are likely to be roe.

Linked by a road bridge with the mainland, the Argyllshire coastal island of Seil is home to a dozen or so roe which are free to come and go at will. On neighbouring Luing I was told, on a visit in 1964, that roe were also present. The channel between Seil and Luing is so narrow that transit from one to the other on a regular basis is quite possible. A few years ago I was informed that the island of Shuna, east of Luing, contains what are almost certainly roe deer, although I have been unable to confirm this.

Kerrera and Lismore, farther north, are two other coastal islands where roe have left bone deposits as evidence of past occurrence although they are not present now.

Roe introduced to Mull in 1865 were described by John Guille Millais as having established a flourishing population on that island. This situation did not last. I made extensive enquiries on a visit in 1964, and it was clear that roe no longer existed in the woods they had formerly frequented, having become extinct on the island at least twenty years before that time. Other accounts of their decline on Mull suggest that they died out as long ago as the 1920s.

On his eighteenth-century travels, Dr Johnson noted that Skye had 'stags and roebucks, but no hares'. When roe disappeared from that island is not known, but later recorders of the Hebridean scene were at one as late as the 1960s in reporting their absence from Skye. A decade later I was intrigued to learn that, if roe had indeed been absent in the recent past, they were so no longer. How and when they reappeared is as much a mystery as the time and manner of their earlier extinction locally. As in the case of Bute, natural immigration across the narrow waters between island and mainland is quite feasible but covert assisted passage seems likelier, quite possibly by someone who thought the forestry plantations established on Skye in the twentieth century lacked at least one important ingredient. A British Deer Society survey in 1993 revealed the presence of roe in localities widely scattered throughout Skye.

Now that Skye is a mere bridge-island it might be thought to be easier than hitherto for mainland mammals to find their way onto the island, but so far as deer at least are concerned the new road link, with its toll barriers, seems an unlikely means of ingress.

Raasay's name is said to derive from the Scandinavian *raas-a*, signifying 'place of the roe deer'. Any that may have been indigenous must have vanished by the eighteenth century, however, for Johnson mentions a reintroduction in 1771 which was thought to have failed because of severe winter weather shortly afterwards. However, about ten years prior to my visits in the 1970s a solitary roebuck appeared on Raasay and remained there for some time before being shot after harassing domestic livestock with which it presumably sought to keep company in the absence of its own kind.

Fallow deer have possibly been present even longer than roe on Islay. Tradition has it that some monks brought them there in AD 900, while another version credits a certain John the Good of Islay with having introduced the species in the fourteenth century. Whatever the truth about their origin, it is generally agreed that fallow are old-established residents, probably uninfluenced by blood from outside for several centuries.

Scattered scrub woodland and rough pasture in the south-east corner of the island are the main haunts of these fallow, which I saw feeding in close proximity to the road at Kildalton on several occasions during my visit in the 1960s. All the Islay fallow I saw were of the common variety, dappled-flanked in summer pelage. The antlers of the bucks were of poor quality, with little palmation. Just off south-east Islay is the small island of Imersay, which in times past has been a wintering ground for some of the Islay fallow, which may still visit it occasionally.

Fallow deer also occur on Mull, to which they were introduced in 1868 by Colonel Greenhill Gardyne, and they were allowed to roam free on Glenforsa estate. Their main haunt nowadays is in woodland bordering Loch Ba, from which they emerge towards dusk to graze on neighbouring pastures. It was here that I saw them on my visit. All were of the light-spotted menil variety and the total population was thought to number about forty.

Scarba, north of Jura, has had a few fallow deer since the early years of the twentieth century, when some were introduced, I gather, to provide an alternative and more accessible quarry than red deer for more elderly and less robust stalking guests. Twenty or so of these fallow have been present in recent years, mostly in woodland around the lodge.

Other islands to which fallow have been introduced in the past include Hermetray, north-east of North Uist in the Outer Hebrides, and Cara, west of Kintyre, where they were present for short periods in the nineteenth century. Fallow from Cara sometimes swam to neighbouring Gigha. Apparently Rhum also had a few fallow at one stage in the mid-nineteenth century, when it seems they made their home on the sheltered low ground around Kinloch.

Gigha has been visited at least once by sika swimming across from Kintyre. Sika are resident on none of the Western Isles, but a few years ago a correspondent who lives on Skye and has stalked deer there for many years, told me he had definitely seen a sika stag there once. If it was correctly identified, it must have swum across the Sound of Sleat from the woods around Loch Morar, just south of Mallaig, where a few of the species are now reportedly present.

Bones of red deer have been discovered in both the Orkney and Shetland Islands, but an attempt in the nineteenth century to reintroduce them to the island of Hoy in Orkney was short-lived. Orkney was also the scene, last century, of a failed attempt to introduce reindeer, the former

occurrence of which is evident from the discovery of antlers buried in peat on the island of Rousay. One would have thought it most improbable that roe ever occurred on Shetland, but bones of the species have apparently been found there in the past.

It will be seen that the Scottish islands offer very fertile ground indeed for researches into deer history and on-going changes of distribution.

Wild fallow deer are present on three Hebridean islands.

13
THE DEER OF
IRELAND

Ireland and Great Britain being the very near neighbours they are, the deer of the two islands might be expected to have many features in common, and historically there are a number of close parallels. Patterns of present-day distribution in Ireland, with wild deer occurring in greater or lesser numbers in almost every county, north and south, and the reasons behind them, also mirror those in Britain to a significant extent.

There are, however, important differences. Whereas Britain today has no fewer than six different species of deer living wild in different parts, Ireland has only half that number. One of Britain's two indigenous species, roe, moreover, is absent from the Emerald Isle despite attempts in the not too distant past to remedy this deficiency by introducing stock from its sister island.

While modern Ireland boasts only three species of deer as members of its wild fauna, this is three times as many as hunters in that country could

hope to find two millennia ago. So although introduction failed in the case of roe, it was successful with sika and fallow.

Prehistoric Ireland famously had more than one deer species. Reindeer were once present, and may have lingered in some places until 3000 years ago. Of far greater note, however was the so-called Irish elk, the *Megaceros* or giant deer which stood 180 cm (6 ft) at the shoulder and whose broad-palmed antlers sometimes spanned an almost incredible 300 cm (10 ft). Human hunters in Ireland probably never came face

LEFT: *An antlered skeleton of the giant deer* (Megaceros giganteus).

BELOW: *Three sets of mature* Megaceros *antlers from Ireland. The upper set are viewed from below, the middle set from above and the lower set from in front with the head held in the display posture.*

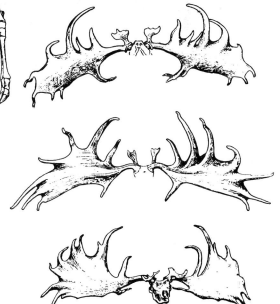

A red stag in Killarney National Park, the last remaining haunt of truly wild red deer of indigenous Irish stock. (Sean Ryan)

Remains found in association with the lake dwellings of early man in Ireland show red deer to have been hunted probably from the very beginning of human settlement. The twelfth-century chronicler, Giraldus Cambrensis, in his *Topographia Hibernica*, recorded deer as having been present along with wild hares and martens, and he might well have added wolves, which lingered until the second half of the eighteenth century, some decades after their final extinction in Great Britain.

Various later writers confirm the continued presence of red deer in many parts of Ireland from the Middle Ages onwards, although these animals may have become locally rare or extinct at an early date. There is an interesting record of an importation of red deer from the forest of Chester, in England, in the thirteenth century, the purpose being to stock the royal forest of Glencree in County Wicklow, not far from Dublin, so this may have been one area where deer numbers had declined. Or it may have been merely the intention to bring in fresh blood to improve stock quality, in anticipation of the day when the sovereign might decide to hunt there.

In the latter half of the sixteenth century, when Lord Mountjoy was Lord Deputy of Ireland, his secretary, Fynes Moryson, described red deer as being widely scattered through Munster and Leinster, in the south and south-east of Ireland, and a hundred years later another writer mentioned their presence in the westerly province of Connacht.

The seventeenth century marked a transitional point in the fortunes of deer and of much else in Ireland. Civil war and the disruptions of the plantation period coincided with the widespread clearance of woodland, greatly reducing the suitable habitat available for wild deer. During times of disturbance broken park fences liberated many, but the trend overall was for such deer as remained to become denizens of deer parks rather than free-ranging wild animals.

Peripheral wilderness areas, mostly in west and south-west Ireland, afforded some degree of

to face with these cervine colossi, which are thought to have died out here some ten thousand years ago, a few millennia before man first arrived in this corner of Europe.

Megaceros was not confined to Ireland. As we saw in chapter 9, remains of these giant deer have also been found in the Isle of Man, where I have seen them in the museum at Douglas, and in various parts of Great Britain. They have also been found, as one might expect, in continental Europe, in parts of which it was almost certainly contemporanious with man. Its special association with Ireland derives from the very large quantity of fossil remains entombed and preserved in Irish bogs. The extinction of these deer may have been due to climatic change, to the immense metabolic strain imposed by the growth of such massive antlers and their annual renewal, or perhaps to a combination of both.

Fossil evidence points to red deer having reached Ireland over the land-bridge which once linked it with Britain, and Britain with Europe, before the melting polar ice-cap after the end of the last glaciation made such migration no longer possible. Indeed, it seems almost certain that *Megaceros* and red deer enjoyed a spell of common occurrence before the larger species vanished.

sanctuary to residual populations of wild deer, but by the early nineteenth century even these were under threat. Writing in the 1840s in his book *The Natural History of Ireland*, William Thompson recorded that in 1834 only thirteen wild red deer remained in County Galway and a mere dozen in the Erris area in County Mayo. None survived the potato famine of the following decade, when starving peasants roamed the countryside seeking any and every edible morsel, although the deer may have succumbed during a period of exceptionally heavy snow a few years earlier.

Only in County Kerry, on the mountains and moors south-west of Killarney, did the native red deer survive, thanks to some protection by two landowners, Lord Kenmare and Mr Herbert of Muckross, whose properties were adjacent. The red deer country was managed along traditional deer-forest lines. In common with those in Scotland it was deemed to need fresh blood from time to time. It is a matter of regret that the indigenous Irish strain was thus diluted by importations from at least one English deer park as well as from Scotland, although these were perhaps not on such a scale as to have introduced more than a fairly minor modifying influence.

Sufficient indigenous blood persists to make it a matter of national pride to ensure the survival of red deer in Kerry in as pure a form as may now be possible. Numbers have fluctuated considerably, sometimes dipping to a level which has excited concern for the future of ancestrally wild red deer in Ireland with an uninterrupted history dating back to early times.

From being a purely sporting property in private ownership, an important part of the red deer country near Killarney at length became a national monument as the Bourn Vincent Memorial Park. Protective measures were reinforced, and at the time of my visit in 1973, when red deer were estimated to number about two hundred, all shooting had been suspended until 1975, when the situation was due to be reviewed.

The year 1976 was a red-letter one for conservation in the Republic of Ireland for it was then that a Wildlife Act became law, affording protection in

various forms to a range of species. For the first time deer were given close seasons, with the red deer of Killarney going one better than those elsewhere by being totally protected except in individual cases where ministerial authorisation may be given for culling for crop protection or some other special reason. In what is now Killarney National Park, a mountainous area which in many respects may be likened to the Scottish Highlands in miniature, and in adjacent woodlands as well as on private land nearby, the total red deer population peaked in 1990 at around six hundred. Since then there has been a decline in numbers to around four hundred, partly attributable, it seems, to higher than average winter mortality. Competition for grazing with sheep, the reduction of cover in woodlands by the clearance of rhododendron and greater than ever visitor pressure, with the disturbance and stress this causes are other factors impinging upon the wellbeing of the red deer.

There are two more or less distinct populations in this area: a mountain herd and a low-ground herd. Better grazing at lower altitudes and the better conditions of life there in general are reflected in heavier body weights, bigger antlers and all-round better performance by the red deer there than those on the high ground.

A deer fence encloses what used to be Glenveagh deer forest, now Glenveagh National Park, in County Donegal.

Red deer in Caledon Park, County Tyrone, Northern Ireland. A wapiti hind was introduced to the herd in the late nineteenth century and wapiti influence is thought still to persist.

In 1891 some 9000 ha of mountain wilderness at Glenveagh, in County Donegal, were surrounded by a 28-mile fence and transformed into a Scottish-type deer forest. Donegal's native red deer having died out some while previously, fresh stock was obtained from various quarters: Glenartney deer forest in Perthshire and deer parks in England and Ireland. Numbers built up in a fairly short time to a satisfactory level, peaking at around 1800 at one stage during the Second World War.

In 1921, during the Troubles of that time, the deer fence was broken and for thirteen years the deer were no longer confined. Most remained within the deer forest but inevitably a few found their way outside to establish a free-ranging population which has persisted to this day. One of the haunts of these wild red deer is the nearby Dunlewey estate, where after a lengthy climb on a very damp day in 1978 my wife and I were lucky enough to see some at fairly close quarters: a hind with a yearling and calf which made off at speed through the mountain drizzle when they became aware of our presence.

Six years previously I had spent a day on the hill with a stalking party at Glenveagh at a time when this property was owned by Mr Henry P. McIlhenny, from whom it later passed to the Irish state as Glenveagh National Park. At the time of my visit the recent Northern Ireland Troubles were at their height, with repercussions in the Republic which resulted in a ban on the use by private individuals of rifles of more than .22 calibre. Deer still needed to be culled at Glenveagh as in many other localities, but after a long climb over extremely rugged ground a misplaced shot at the only stag we saw, which was accompanied by some thirty hinds and followers, brought the day's proceedings to an end. It transpired that an unfamiliar rifle with hair-trigger action was to blame.

Whereas Killarney stags, especially those on the low ground, tend to be heavy, I learned that those on the bleak hills of Donegal sometimes scale as little as 70 kg when mature, with antlers of modest size in proportion. In 1972 Glenveagh red deer numbered around six hundred. In 1994 there were reckoned to be 520, with a further hundred roaming free outside the deer-fenced area, and five years later the figure was 530 within the deer fence plus an unknown number outside.

Red deer of Glenveagh antecedents are widely scattered through Donegal. There are thought to be some fifty along the border with Northern Ireland, including a few already resident just inside County Tyrone and perhaps in County Fermanagh as well. Wandering stags sometimes turn up many miles from others of their species.

Woods and marshes near Seaforde, between Newcastle and Downpatrick in County Down, are the haunt of fifty or sixty red deer descended from animals left out by the County Down Staghounds, a pack which hunts carted deer and keeps its main stock at Montalto Deer Park, Ballynahinch. These deer are of stock originally supplied from Warnham Court Park in West Sussex, having been replenished from this English park by the pack over many years.

At various times in the nineteenth century, red deer from England were introduced to parks at

Baronscourt, County Tyrone, and at Colebrooke, County Fermanagh, but neither retains these deer today. Another nineteenth-century introduction was to Caledon Park, where Counties Tyrone and Armagh border County Monaghan in the Republic. This herd was reinforced at one stage by wapiti blood from Canada, the enduring influence of which, in terms of larger than usual body size and bifurcating back tines to some of the antlers, was pointed out to me by the late Earl of Caledon on a visit in 1972. Also evident at that time was the incidence among some members of the herd of enzootic ataxia or swayback, a disease of the central nervous system which has some affinity with multiple sclerosis in man and results in poor co-ordination of movement between the forequarters and hindquarters and is seemingly peculiar to park red deer. These Caledon red deer have sometimes escaped but have usually found their way back into the park after only a brief absence.

Gosford Forest Park in County Armagh is another Northern Ireland locality with a captive herd of red deer, which were introduced as a public amenity. At one stage there were also a few red deer in confinement at Randalstown Forest, County Antrim, but I understand that these are no longer present.

Moving back into the Republic, Doneraile Court Park in County Cork has an old-established herd of red deer. Slane Castle Park, County Meath, has been maintained as a source of carted deer for the local Ward Union Staghounds and seems most likely to be the source of feral red deer in the same county and perhaps also in County Louth, just to the north.

Glenstal Park in County Limerick once contained red, fallow and sika deer, and among those that escaped when stock was dispersed in the 1930s were apparently some red deer, descendants of which may still occur in hilly country in the neighbourhood. Liam Nolan, who has made a lifetime's study of all aspects of deer in the Emerald Isle and whose book *Wild Deer in Ireland* is soon to be published, tells me he has stalked feral red deer in the Comeragh Mountains in County Waterford, a wild, remote and little-visited area which is possibly one of several places where these deer occur in small numbers, little known to the world at large.

Reference is made in the literature to the presence of red deer in Counties Wicklow and Dublin at various places from the Middle Ages onwards. Of by far the greatest significance, in the light of subsequent developments, was the introduction of this species in the mid-nineteenth century to Powerscourt Park, at Enniskerry, County Wicklow, on the north-eastern fringe of the Wicklow Mountains.

In 1860 Viscount Powerscourt obtained a sika stag, which cost him £10, plus three hinds at £8 apiece, from a well-known London animal dealer, named Jamrach. Wapiti, sambar and chital (axis deer) and even eland antelope were experimentally added to a collection which previously consisted only of red and fallow deer. All but one exotic species soon succumbed to the Irish climate or to other unfavourable conditions but the sika proved the hardy beasts that we now know them to be.

They increased with surprising rapidity. As early as 1865 sika were deemed to be sufficiently well established for a stag and two hinds to be supplied from Powerscourt as foundation stock for a new population alongside the red deer on the Muckross estate near Killarney, something which was later to become the source of a good deal of controversy. Five years later a sika stag and five hinds were sent to Colebrooke Park,

Wild sika deer on the move on the Colebrooke estate in County Fermanagh.

A hybrid sika/red deer stag bred experimentally at the Irish School of Forestry, Avondale, County Wicklow.

County Fermanagh, which in turn supplied a stag and some hinds for the deer park at Baronscourt, County Tyrone, in 1891–2. Other deer parks, not only in Ireland but also in Scotland, England and Wales, received sika deer from Powerscourt over the following decades, and for a while, at least, other Asian immigrants were widely welcomed as a seemingly benign and altogether pleasing addition to the decorative fauna of many a country estate in the British Isles and elsewhere in the west.

The first small straws in the wind concerning the wisdom of importing sika were seen as early as the 1870s with the birth of the first undoubted hybrids, reportedly sired on each occasion by sika stags on red deer hinds at Powerscourt. In 1885 and again in 1887 hybridisation between the two species was noted at Colebrooke. During the following years other such mismatches

occurred. While these caused some mild disquiet, for a long time they were regarded as sufficiently infrequent to be of no great consequence.

Disturbances arising from the Troubles of the early 1920s enabled a number of deer to escape from Powerscourt Park. A study by Peter Delap during the first half of the following decade revealed the presence of at least fifty red deer at large on the Wicklow Mountains as well as a smaller number of sika. After the Second World War the range of both species considerably expanded and numbers increased in proportion. As time went on it became clear that as well as what were apparently pure red and sika deer, there were also substantial numbers of what were unmistakably hybrids.

During my visits in the 1970s I was shown a film taken from a helicopter of deer on open ground high on the Wicklow Mountains and was startled at the number showing obvious hybrid characteristics, representing almost every possible degree of variation between almost pure red deer and almost pure sika. Most of the deer I saw on the open hill on each occasion looked like pure red deer, and most of those in the lower-ground forestry plantations were to my eye indistinguishable from pure sika, but in the opinion of Dr Rory Harington, a biologist who has made a detailed study of the subject, all deer apparently of these two species on and around the Wicklow Mountains, amounting now to several thousand, are tainted by hybridisation to a greater or lesser degree.

The fruits of experimental cross-breeding shown to me at Avondale, once the home of Charles Stuart Parnell and now headquarters of the Irish School of Forestry, included a two-year-old hybrid stag, red deer in size but with sika dappling and with the latter's typical short muzzle – as obvious a cross between the two species as one might hope never to encounter in the wild, in Ireland or elsewhere.

So what has happened in County Kerry? From the original three animals, sika had increased by the 1930s to a level estimated by one writer at from three to five thousand. Later estimates are more modest, generally hovering around the thousand mark, at which figure they have indisputably outnumbered the local red deer, which are highly regarded as representing the native strain.

A critical watch has been kept for signs of possible hybridisation. Apart possibly from some isolated instances, the general impression is that, by great good fortune, the Wicklow experience has not so far been replicated in Kerry. It is an article of faith that this should never be permitted. Just as a safeguard for the future, some years ago a number of wild Killarney red deer were caught up and translocated to a special enclosure at Letterfrack, County Galway, where a small but healthy herd is now kept.

Others were given sanctuary on Inishvicillaun, one of the Blasket Islands 8 miles off the coast of County Kerry. Owned by Charles Haughey, a former Taoiseach (Irish prime minister) and his family, this 80-ha cliff-girt island received its first consignment of red deer from Killarney in 1980 followed by others in subsequent years, eleven animals in total up to 1991. A total of forty deer were counted by Liam Nolan on a visit in the early 1990s, so early indications are that the introduction has been a success, but much depends upon the island's long-term ability to sustain a healthy and viable herd.

Visiting the Killarney area, I saw numbers of both red deer and sika well out on the open hill, including members of both species grazing within yards of each other. In circumstances such as these, and knowing what has happened elsewhere, it is difficult not to believe that hybridisation on a significant scale cannot be delayed indefinitely.

Whereas protection has allowed the Killarney red deer to increase to safer numbers, reckoned in 1999 to be at least four hundred and perhaps as high as seven hundred if one includes those living outside the national park, sika are now more rigorously culled. Their numbers within the national park had been reduced to an estimated five hundred by 1999. A relatively small proportion of these live on the open hill. The majority favour low ground, where they find cover in ancient woodland and in forestry plantations where they cause a certain amount of damage by browsing. The recent clearance of rhododendron from much of the local native woodland has helped to make sika more accessible for culling. They sometimes swim to a small island in Lough Leane, west of the town of

A sika stag in early velvet in Killarney National Park, where these deer live alongside red deer without apparent interbreeding. (Sean Ryan)

Wild fallow deer in Portumna Forest, County Galway.

Killarney – as, indeed, also do red deer – while to the south their range extends to the Glengarriff area of County Cork.

In County Fermanagh there is no longer a deer park at Colebrooke, where in any case red deer ceased to be kept many years ago. However, sika survive in numbers, and on a visit in 1978 I saw groups of up to fifteen at a time grazing at dusk on open pastures, onto which they emerged from adjacent plantations. The estate owner, Viscount Brookeborough, told me that these deer, now completely wild, were still largely confined to his family's property, as short shrift was given to any that strayed very far outside it. He personally disliked shooting sika although he accepted client stalkers, including many from abroad.

Although no longer resident locally, red deer were not unknown in the area. In 1971 a red stag, presumably of the Donegal stock, paid a visit to Colebrooke during the rut, and in the rut of 1973 two red stags arrived. One was fairly promptly shot, but the other sired on a sika hind a hybrid stag calf which was not itself shot until it was three years old. Lord Brookeborough's belief was that pure sika in Northern Ireland were ultimately doomed to hybridisation with incoming red deer from Donegal, which were turning up with increasing frequency.

At some time in the early to mid-1920s the entire stock of sika and fallow deer escaped from the deer park at Baronscourt, in County Tyrone. The fallow survived for a time but were extinct before the 1950s, whilst sika survived and continued to flourish in the estate forestry plantations which were mainly established after the First World War. In the mid-1950s deer drives to shotguns ceased and gave way to control by the rifle. Client stalkers, mainly from Belgium and Germany, helped transform the deer from a financial liability into a modest source of revenue, and in 1972 I enjoyed a delightful week's stalking there, seeing fair numbers of the two hundred or so sika at that time resident there, quite enough for the habitat available in the view of the late Duke of Abercorn, whose family own the property. Some fifty sika of Baronscourt origin had colonised nearby Gortin Forest, but there was not thought to be any link between the feral sika of Baronscourt and those of roughly equal numbers living at liberty at Colebrooke.

However, I gather that this situation has since changed, with sika now more widely distributed through Counties Tyrone and Fermanagh and the Colebrooke and Baronscourt populations now almost certainly united.

Fallow deer reached Ireland not later than the thirteenth century, Glencree royal park or forest in County Wicklow being one of the earlier recipients of this species. Within a fairly short time this forest was supplying fallow deer for introduction elsewhere. At the end of the sixteenth century Fynes Moryson, in his book *Description of Ireland*, referred to 'parks of fallow deer' and also mentioned the presence of fallow in the woods of Counties Offaly and Waterford, a clear indication of their occurrence in the wild state as well as in parks.

In 1638 Lord Deputy Stratford was in communication with the Archbishop of Canterbury about the hunting of wild fallow. In his book *The Experienced Huntsman*, first published in 1714 and reissued in 1977 by the Blackstaff Press of Belfast, Arthur Stringer wrote of the widespread distribution, especially in the north of Ireland, of both red and fallow deer as park escapees in the years immediately following the war of 1688 which climaxed with the Battle of the Boyne between the forces of James II and William of Orange. He added, however, that within twenty-five years few deer remained outside the parks, where they were preserved primarily for hunting.

Deer parks are a long-established feature of the rural scene in Ireland. Research by Liam Nolan for his book *Wild Deer in Ireland*, from which he has generously allowed me to quote, reveals that there are some 118 Irish placenames which indicate the presence of a deer park at some period. A 'new wave' of deer parks, intended mainly for amenity, came with those who settled in Ireland and acquired landed estates there during the plantation period.

The widespread occurrence

of fallow outside parks in the nineteenth century attracted the notice of various writers, including J.E. Harting in the 1880s and John Guille Millais during the following decade. Many more park fallow were liberated as a by-product of the 1920–2 Troubles, and extensive reafforestation, in both the Republic and Northern Ireland, from the 1920s onwards helped provide additional habitat on a fairly generous scale. Many of these new feral populations have survived. Only four of the thirty-two counties have no wild fallow, among those in which they are most numerous being Wicklow, Offaly, Laois, Tipperary, Waterford and Galway.

The east-coast island of Lambay, north of Dublin, has a flourishing herd of fallow, all apparently descended from a single buck and two does introduced in 1889. Although the original deer are described as having been of the dappled variety, many of those now present are said to be black, with unspotted flanks.

Dublin's Phoenix Park has had fallow deer since 1669, having originally been stocked at the behest of Charles II and now owned by the Irish state. Other noteworthy park herds include

Fallow deer in Dublin's Phoenix Park, where these deer were introduced in 1668.

Mallow Castle's white deer, in County Cork, some of which were sent not long ago to Northern Ireland to start a new captive herd at Parkanaur, near Dungannon in County Tyrone. Unlike the red deer at Caledon, County Tyrone, which live in a fenced enclosure within the original walled deer park, the fallow deer there are no longer enclosed but also range freely over the surrounding countryside, some of them having crossed the border to reach Glaslough in County Monaghan. All the fallow I saw on my visit to Caledon were of the black variety.

As I also saw for myself, the dark confines of Randalstown Forest on Lough Neagh's northern shore, in County Antrim, are matched by a predominantly black herd of wild fallow, descended from stock once enclosed in Lord O'Neill's Shanes Castle Park nearby. Two or three decades ago a new herd of wild fallow was established in Tollymore Forest Park, on the slopes of the Mourne Mountains in County Down, and these now flourish to the extent that a sizeable cull is annually taken by the Northern Ireland Forest Service.

Menil fallow released in the 1970s on a private estate at Lissanour, County Antrim, only survived for a very short time in a part of Ireland which had seen no wild deer for several hundred years.

Red and fallow deer in an enclosure adjoining Randalstown Forest, County Antrim.

Rockingham Park, near Boyle in County Roscommon, was the source of a sizeable herd of wild fallow now present in Lough Key Forest Park. Most of the deer I saw there during a visit in the 1970s were of the common variety but with dark brown, unspotted flanks in summer pelage. The forestry plantations near Lough Gill, on the border of Counties Leitrim and Sligo, is another haunt of wild fallow which I visited where deer numbers are fairly substantial.

One of the largest single populations of wild fallow deer in Ireland is to be found in Portumna Forest, at the northern end of Lough Derg in County Galway. Here, according to recent estimates, some 500 ha of conifers shelter up to four hundred or more fallow, a very high density indeed by any standard. On a visit in 1973 I learned that the population then was in the region of 150. Even at that level damage to crops on neighbouring farmland was deemed unacceptably high, and steps were in hand to mitigate this by fencing much of the forest perimeter. Around three-quarters of the fallow here were of the common type, we were told, the remainder being black, and among the many deer my wife and I saw were specimens of both. Portumna Forest fallow are not averse to entering water and sometimes swim to nearby lough islands.

Elsewhere in County Galway there are four or five other entirely separate populations of wild fallow, all of course of deer park origin although no such parks have existed for quite a long time. Well north of Portumna, close to the border with County Roscommon, we visited two other fallow deer areas: forestry plantations at Mount Bellew, near Ballinasloe, and around Aughrane Castle, near Ballygar. The former, we were told, consisted of some 306 ha holding seventy or eighty deer, while about 150 fallow roamed 800 ha of woodland at Aughrane. We saw a number of the Aughrane deer, all of the common variety, and were lucky enough to find a cast antler.

Liam Nolan estimates that the total wild deer population of Ireland, both north and south, is in the region of 20,000. Some 8000 of these are fallow, and a similar number are sika, the bulk of them in County Wicklow. Red deer and obvious red/sika hybrids make up the balance of about 4000, a sizeable proportion of these also being resident in County Wicklow.

Despite suggestions to the contrary by some medieval writers and by one or two others of more recent vintage, there is no evidence that roe deer ever reached Ireland before access was denied them by the melting polar ice-cap after the end of the last Ice Age. In the early 1870s, however, some roe kids were caught up in Perthshire and sent to Sir Henry Gore-Booth's property at Lissadell, County Sligo. Here they were penned and bottle-fed until they were old enough for release, the pen door at first being left open to allow free movement out and in.

Once established in the wild, the roe found sanctuary by day in hydrangea shrubberies and other appropriate cover. When there were sufficient of them, the practice was to stalk them in the evening with a .300 calibre rook rifle. For a time they not only flourished, sometimes wandering into neighbouring County Mayo and turning up as far as 30 miles from their original point of enlargement, but also produced some of the most massive roe antlers ever seen anywhere, before or since, in any part of the British Isles.

In the early part of the twentieth century the continued existence of these roe was thought to be incompatible with the establishment of some conifer nurseries, with the result that they were shot out. Subsequent rumours of the survival of some of them have never been substantiated. The present climate of opinion being strongly against any repetition in Ireland of the Lissadell experiment, the history of roe in that country appears to be finally closed.

While many former deer parks holding one or more of the three deer species resident in Ireland have disappeared, due to the break-up of landed estates or other factors, a number are still frequented by the descendants of deer once enclosed within them. The difference is that they now wander in and out at will, treating their ancestral home as part of their self-selected range as completely wild animals.

Other parks have been transformed from amenity areas into deer farms, rearing deer for sale as breeding stock or for the venison market. On the other side of the coin, some deer farms are presented as deer parks, ostensibly combining amenity with an overriding commercial purpose. In 1999 the number of deer farms in Ireland was estimated by Liam Nolan at 550, holding an overall basic breeding stock in the region of 20,000 – in other words, roughly comparable with the wild deer population. Most farm deer are red deer.

Although security arrangements are necessarily tight, deer do sometimes escape from deer farms. Most are quickly recovered, but there is always the possibility, in Ireland as in Great Britain, of new feral deer populations being established by deer-farm escapes.

Zoos and wildlife parks are few in Ireland. Belfast Zoo had no deer in 1999, having sent some chital (axis deer) which were previously held there to a private purchaser who owns a deer park near Waterford, where he also keeps red and sika deer. Fota Wildlife Park, near Cork, formerly had a herd of chital but these too have been disposed of. The only deer held by Dublin Zoo in 1999 were muntjac.

Menil fallow deer awaiting release at a new location in County Antrim.

APPENDIX 1
DEER FARMING

Although we do not know for certain, it seems highly likely that prehistoric European man may have caught up live deer and kept them in confinement for greater ease of access as a meat source than relying solely on hunting wild deer.

From very early times deer parks in one form or another served a broadly similar purpose and were also used for sport. From around the seventeenth century onwards there was a decided shift of emphasis from utility to amenity, a trend which reached its peak in the nineteenth century when a well-stocked deer park became an almost universal feature of country estates in England especially, and to a lesser extent in Wales, Scotland and Ireland.

Almost without exception, the deer were purely ornamental. Any venison procured as a by-product of essential culling to keep numbers within the carrying capacity of the park were likely to be retained for domestic consumption or given away to friends rather than sold for profit.

Social changes and two world wars in the twentieth century saw the end of many deer parks. A few were later revived and some new ones set up, while during the last few decades of the century many wildlife parks were opened, mostly with deer among their exhibits, to cater commercially for an increasingly mobile public.

The lack of any commercial incentive to keep all but a very few deer parks in being through difficult times undoubtedly hastened their decline. In the 1970s, however, a new and compelling reason for keeping and breeding deer in confinement came with the advent of deer farming, an entirely new form of livestock husbandry largely inspired by a growing market in Britain and elsewhere for lean red meat, low in cholesterol and rich in protein.

The economic viability of deer farming in the Scottish hills was put to the test by the Rowett Research Institute of Aberdeen, and their recommendations formed the basis of what developed as a flourishing rural industry by no means confined to hill-farming areas. Among the commercial pioneers were Dr John Fletcher and his wife, Nichola, whose deer farm at Auchtermuchty in Fifeshire has served as a model of its kind which many have chosen to emulate.

Deer farming boomed in its early years, when a ready market for breeding stock earned good revenues for those who were first in the field. The number of enterprises soon reached a point where a national organisation to promote standards and to represent the interests of the industry became desirable and in 1978 The British Deer Farmers' Association was formed to meet this need.

Deer farms are strictly regulated to ensure healthy, good-quality stock which is hygienically handled at every stage of being converted into venison. Every deer intended for slaughter must be subjected to veterinary inspection and given a clean bill of health not more than seventy-two hours before being either shot on the farm or dealt with at an abattoir. Tightly controlled conditions at every stage of rearing and handling have enabled deer farmers to obtain a better price for their product than is payable for wild deer venison, and several supermarket chains offer farm venison to customers.

In the late 1990s there were more than three hundred deer farms in Great Britain and Northern Ireland, with a total breeding stock of more than 30,000. Deer farms in the Republic of Ireland also numbered several hundreds and held some 20,000 deer.

Deer farming in Britain and Ireland is mainly focused on red deer, although a few stock fallow and a range of exotic species including sika, chital (axis deer), barasingha and Père David's deer. To help produce bigger and better red deer, stock has been imported from Hungary. Wapiti have been crossed with red deer and Persian fallow with the common fallow for essentially the same purpose.

Some deer farmers call their farms deer parks and manage them accordingly, while conversely some deer parks have been upgraded into deer farms. Whereas park deer are governed by the same close-season restrictions as wild deer, deer farm stock can be legally slaughtered regardless of season.

Although they are not normally open to the public, deer farms, and for that matter deer parks in private ownership, may sometimes be visited by prior arrangement with the owner. New deer farms are frequently opened and others closed down, and no attempt has been made in this book to identify more than a few of the more important ones.

Deer farming is not confined to Britain and Ireland. It flourishes in France, and in Germany where fallow deer are a favoured species, which is also true of Australia. The industry has been developed with particular vigour in New Zealand, which exports antler velvet in large quantities to Korea for the Oriental medicine market. Deer-farm stock in New Zealand numbers something like 1½ million, mostly descended from wild red deer which were caught up for the purpose.

APPENDIX 2
CLOSE SEASONS

The following are the statutory close seasons for deer in Britain and Ireland. All dates are inclusive.

Species	Sex	England and Wales	Scotland	Northern Ireland	Republic of Ireland*
Red (*Cervus elaphus*)	Stags	1 May – 31 July	21 October – 30 June	1 May – 31 July	1 March – 31 August
	Hinds	1 March – 31 October	16 February – 20 October	1 March – 31 October	1 February – 31 October
Sika (*Cervus nippon*)	Stags	1 May – 31 July	21 October – 30 June	1 May – 31 July	1 March – 31 August
	Hinds	1 March – 31 October	16 February – 20 October	1 March – 31 October	1 February – 31 October
Red/Sika hybrids	Stags	1 May – 31 July	21 October – 30 June	1 May – 31 July	1 March – 31 August
	Hinds	1 March – 31 October	16 February – 20 October	1 March – 31 October	1 February – 31 October
Fallow (*Dama dama*)	Bucks	1 May – 31 July	1 May – 31 July	1 May – 31 July	1 March – 31 August
	Does	1 March – 31 October	16 February – 20 October	1 March – 31 October	1 February – 31 October
Roe (*Capreolus capreolus*)	Bucks	1 November – 31 March	21 October – 31 March		
	Does	1 March – 31 October	1 April – 20 October		

*Close seasons for deer in the Republic of Ireland are reviewed annually by the relevant government minister, who is responsible for the arts, heritage matters and the offshore islands as well as wildlife. Close seasons indicated in this table were those applicable in 1999–2000 when there was a temporary extension of the open season for sika hinds and red/sika hybrid hinds to 28 February in the Wicklow Mountains area. The open season for all male deer ends on 28 February, regardless of whether it is a leap year. There is no open season for red deer in Co. Kerry.

Roe deer are absent from Ireland and there is no legal close season for muntjac or Chinese water deer in the UK.

GLOSSARY

The royal forest era, when the sovereign claimed exclusive rights for himself and his guests to hunt deer on land designated for the purpose, saw the development and use of a rich and diverse terminology relating in one way or another to deer and to hunting. Much of this special language has long since fallen into disuse, but a sizeable remnant survives and has been absorbed into everyday language or is otherwise in current use. Outright archaisms have for the most part been omitted from this glossary, but some terms, which may be worth reviving or which crop up in the literature of the past, have been included along with a selection of other terms in more general use.

Albino. An organism lacking the pigmentation which produces normal external body colour, resulting in white hair and pink eyes among other characteristics in deer and other animals thus affected.

Anal tush. A common misnomer for the tail-like tuft of white or whitish hair below the vaginal orifice of female roe deer, which is prominently visible when these deer are in winter pelage and readily distinguishes them from male roe which have cast their antlers.

Antlers. Bony appendages regrown annually on the heads of male deer of nearly all species, those of female reindeer and caribou and sometimes, abnormally, those of female deer of other species, especially roe. The deciduous character of antlers is what primarily distinguishes them from horns such as those grown by antelopes, cattle, goats and sheep, which are retained throughout life.

Bare buck. A four-year-old male fallow deer.

Bark. The alarm or challenge call uttered in mutually distinctive forms by deer of many species.

Bay tine. See *Bez tine*.

Beam. The stem or trunk of an antler.

Beat. An area of ground for which an individual gamekeeper, forest wildlife ranger or forester is responsible.

Bell. Poetic term for the rutting call of a male red deer.

Bez (bay) tine. Branch of a red deer's antler between the first (brow) tine and the third (trez or tray) tine; bez tines are sometimes absent.

Bifurcation. Abnormal dividing of a branch or tine of an antler, producing one or more subsidiary tines.

Black fallow deer. A colour variety of fallow in which the pelage is predominantly black or very dark, especially in summer but also to a slightly lesser extent in winter. Black fallow have no white rump patch.

Bole-scoring. Forestry damage sometimes caused by male sika deer gouging the boles of trees with the brow tines of their antlers, usually as part of their rutting activity.

Brocket. A one-year-old male red or sika deer, sometimes also called a pricket.

Brow tine. The first branch of a deer's antler, immediately above the coronet.

Browsing. The action by a herbivorous animal of eating buds, leaves or other parts of a tree or shrub, as distinct from grazing (feeding on ground herbage); where deer are numerous a distinct 'browse line' at deer's head height is often visible in plantations.

Buck. Among British wild deer, the male of Chinese water deer, fallow deer, muntjac or roe deer. In ancient royal forest nomenclature the term was applied more specifically to a five-year-old fallow buck.

Burnishing. The action by a male deer of cleaning velvet from newly grown antlers.

Burr. The base of an antler beneath the coronet.

Calf. Among British wild deer, a young red or sika deer in its first year.

Call. An implement for simulating vocal emissions by a deer for the purpose of luring it to a human observer.

Cast. To shed an antler prior to growing a replacement; a cast antler.

Catch-up. The live capture of deer, usually by narcotic-darting or by driving them into nets.

Cleaning. See *Burnishing*.

Close season. A designated period during which deer of a specified species and/or sex may not legally be shot except in special circumstances.

Close time. The nocturnal period (in the UK between one hour after sunset and one hour before sunrise) when deer may not legally be shot except in special circumstances.

Common fallow deer. One of the two living subspecies of fallow, *Dama dama dama*, native to the Mediterranean region but now much more widely distributed as a result of introductions by man. The other subspecies is the much rarer Persian fallow, *D. d. mesopotamica*, characterised by larger body size and differently shaped antlers. Not to be confused with the common subspecies is the so-called common colour variety, dappled on the upper flanks in summer changing to dark brown on the back and upper flanks in winter with lighter-coloured flank spots only faintly visible. The common colour variety has a white rump throughout the year.

Conservation. The management of habitat and wildlife on a sustained, on-going basis by means of human intervention.

Coronet. The raised rim of an antler immediately above the base.

Couch. An area of flattened herbage or bare ground where a deer has rested.

Cover. Trees, shrubs or other growth providing concealment, shelter and seclusion for wildlife.

Covert. An area of woodland or other cover providing harbourage for game or, sometimes, foxes.

Creep. A worn area where deer have passed under a fence or other obstacle.

Crotties. Heaps of fewmets (deer droppings).

Crown. The cluster of points around the tip of a fully developed red deer antler, also called a cup.

Cull. The killing of deer or other animals in order to reduce numbers, to eliminate undesirable elements or to achieve some other predetermined objective.

Cup. See *Crown*.

Deer drive. The unselective mass destruction of deer by being driven by beaters to individuals armed with shotguns, often resulting in many animals being wounded but not recovered; an inhumane and largely outmoded method of deer control once almost universally practised in the UK in woodland areas.

Deer farming. The breeding of deer in confined conditions as a meat source and for other commercial purposes.

Deer forest. A term applied, particularly in Scotland, to an area of what is normally unenclosed ground, usually hilly or mountainous and very sparsely wooded or even treeless, set aside primarily for deer and for deer-stalking 'open hill' style.

Deer larder. Enclosed accommodation for the storage and butchering of deer carcases.

Deer lawn. An open area, usually in woodland, where deer are encouraged to graze and where they are thus made more accessible for observation and culling.

Dew claws. The two rear cleaves or 'toes' of the hoof of a deer or other cloven-hoofed mammal, often the only part imprinted on soft ground by a deer in motion.

Doe. Among British wild deer, the female of Chinese water deer, fallow deer, muntjac or roe deer.

Entry. A gap made by deer when passing through close cover or when circumventing an obstacle.

Fawn. Among British wild deer, the young of a Chinese water deer, fallow deer or muntjac under one year old.

Fewmets. Individual deer droppings.

Foil. The track of a deer through grass or other herbage.

Fraying. The damage resulting from a deer using a tree to rub off the dead velvet from its newly grown antlers.

Fraying-stock. Sapling, branch or other object against which a male deer rubs its newly matured antlers to remove dead velvet and set scent.

Gait. A mammal's style of locomotion, e.g. walking, cantering, running or galloping.

Going back. Used to describe a male deer past its prime, with antlers of declining quality.

Gorget. An area of pale coloration around the throat, apparent in some roe deer in winter pelage.

Gralloch. To eviscerate a deer; the viscera of a deer once removed.

Grass. To 'render a deer into possession' by shooting it; the term is mainly used in connection with red deer stalking in Scotland.

Grazing. Feeding on grass or other ground herbage, as opposed to browsing, which is feeding on the buds, foliage or other parts of trees or shrubs.

Great buck. In ancient forest terminology, a male fallow deer six years old or older and at its pinnacle of development.

Groan. The characteristic, belch-like call uttered by a male fallow deer during the rut.

Gutters. Linear indentations in the main beam of an antler.

Harbouring. The traditional method by which a 'harbourer' locates and identifies a suitable deer for hunting with hounds prior to a meet of the pack concerned.

Hart. Alternative term for a red deer stag, now little used except on the Atholl estates in the Scottish Highlands. As employed in ancient times, the term usually applied to a stag of particularly high quality.

Havier. A castrated male deer.

Head. An alternative name for a deer trophy, e.g. 'a head of antlers'.

Heel trail. The trail of a deer followed in a reverse direction from that in which it moved.

High seat. An elevated seat from which to observe or shoot deer, a development of the *hochsitz* and *hochstand* which originated in Germany for shooting deer and boar in woodland.

Hind. Among British wild deer, the female of red deer or sika deer.

Home range. The area within which an individual deer normally lives and travels but which it does not defend, often coinciding with or overlapping the home range of other deer of the same species.

Horn. A bony outgrowth from the skull of e.g. a cow, goat, sheep or antelope, not deciduous like an antler but lasting a lifetime; not an acceptable alternative term for 'antler' although frequently misused as such, most notably by John Guille Millais as the title of his book *British Deer and their Horns*.

Hummel. A male red deer which fails to grow antlers but is otherwise normal; half-hummels with an antler on one side only also occur.

Kid. Young roe deer under one year old.

Knobber. Young male deer with short, single-spike antlers; usually a yearling with its first head.

Lair. Where a deer lies down (ligging). (A red deer 'harbours' and is 'unharboured', a fallow deer 'lodges' and is 'roused', and a roe deer 'beds' and is 'dislodged' according to the traditional terms for describing these activities.)

Ligging. See *Lair*.

Management. The control and care of deer and their habitat along systematic lines.

Melanistic. Predominantly black or very dark in coloration as in the black variety of fallow deer. Black roe also occur, notably as a local variety in parts of Germany and the Netherlands, but are extremely rare in Britain.

Menil. A colour variety of fallow deer characterised by light overall coloration, with white dappling on the flanks especially prominent in summer but also a feature of the winter pelage.

Misprint. Hoofprints of a deer in which the imprints of a hind hoof fail to be superimposed precisely on the imprints of the fore hoof on the same side of the animal; a hind hoof consistently misprinting to the rear of the corresponding fore hoof when the deer is moving at walking pace is characteristic of an ageing animal.

Moving deer to rifles. A co-ordinated means of enhancing a cull, especially of female deer in winter, wherein one, two or possibly more rifles (participating stalkers) wait in ambush while a similarly small number of individuals quietly walk through cover where deer are likely to be present, with a view to disturbing them sufficiently to move them past the rifles, who are thus presented with opportunities for selective shooting. This type of operation is in no way comparable to the indiscriminate slaughter and wounding so often inflicted by the drives to shotguns so generally practised in woodland areas in particular in the past.

Nott. A traditional term used in south-west England for what in Scotland is called a hummel – an otherwise normal male red deer which fails to grow antlers.

Offer. A bony projection from the beam of an antler which is too small to rate as a tine; traditionally, if binoculars could not be hung by their strap from such a projection, it was not a tine.

Outlier. Quarry animal of a pack of hounds which hunts carted deer (i.e. deer released for the purpose of the chase) which is later intended to be caught alive and returned to captivity, but which has failed to be recaptured. Carted deer are no longer hunted in Great Britain but two packs of this nature were still operating in Ireland in 1999. The term also sometimes applies to escaped park deer.

Pace. The speed of movement by a deer as indicated by the length of step or stride as the trail of the unseen animal is followed.

Paint. A local term for blood splashed from a wounded deer on the ground or vegetation.

Palm. The broad, flattened upper portion of a mature male fallow deer's antler.

Parcel. A Scottish Highland term for a group of red deer, e.g. 'a parcel of hinds'.

Pass. A point where deer regularly cross a river or surmount some other obstacle.

Pattern. The relative placement of hoofprints in a trail, indicative of a change of gait.

Pearling. Knobbly excrescences along the antlers of a male roe or other deer, on the main beam in particular; heavy pearling is characteristic of the antlers of a mature, top-quality male.

Pedicle. The stem erupting from the skull on which an antler develops and grows.

Pelage. The coat of a deer, which varies seasonally in colour and texture.

Perruque. The grotesquely abnormal development of antlers into a semblance of the type of wig of the same name, usually as a consequence of injury to the reproductive organs.

Pizzle. The penis of a deer; one of a number of deer by-products used in Oriental medicine.

Point. The distal end of an individual antler beam or tine, expressed in the plural as so many points for a specific 'head' of antlers, e.g. 'an eight-pointer' or 'a twelve-pointer'.

Pollarding. A local term for antler casting.

Pricket. A one-year-old male fallow deer, usually with short, single-spike antlers. See also *Brocket*.

Rack. A track made by deer when passing through vegetation. The term is also used in some English-speaking countries to denote a head – e.g. a rack of antlers.

Register. The action of a moving deer in placing a hind hoof precisely on the spot vacated by the fore hoof on the same side, thus leaving a single imprint.

Rifle. A gun with a rifled bore designed to fire a single projectile to which the spiral nature of the rifling gives a spin for the purpose of stabilising its flight. In stalking parlance the term is also used to denote an appropriately armed participant, as in 'two rifles will be on the ground today'.

Ring. A circular track in woodland vegetation, field crops or other herbage made by roe deer during the rut, when a male commonly circles in the wake of a female in oestrus (in season) prior to mating; these rings sometimes develop into figures of eight. 'Play rings' also occur, especially where fallow deer congregate and fawns may be present in the group.

Roar. The characteristic call of a rutting red deer male. In New Zealand the red deer rutting season is commonly known as 'the roar'.

Roe ring. See *Ring*.

Royal. A male red deer with a total of twelve points on its antlers, preferably six on each antler. Subsidiary tines within the crown or cup of such antlers are traditionally known as 'sur-royals'.

Rubbing. The action of a deer in marking its territory by rubbing its antler and the scent glands on its forehead against a sapling or other vegetation. The term is also applied to the action of shedding its winter coat by rubbing it off against a tree or other object.

Rut. The mating season of deer, varying in time and duration between individual species.

Rutting stand. The location where a male deer takes up its stand for rutting purposes.

Sanctuary. Designated area(s) within deer-populated ground where no shooting ever takes place and the deer are left undisturbed.

Scrape. A patch of ground scraped bare by deer for territorial marking purposes by setting scent from interdigital glands and sometimes, additionally, by urinating. Scrapes are also made by deer preparatory to couching (bedding down) on some patch of ground selected for the purpose.

Selective shooting. A policy of culling specific deer or categories of deer to the exclusion of others in pursuance of a predetermined plan.

Signs. Ground evidence and other visual indications in general as to the identities and activities of deer as they have moved around their habitat.

Single. A traditional term for the tail of a deer.

Slot. The hoofmark of a deer in soft ground; also sometimes applied to the foot of a deer.

Snag. A minuscule bony projection from the beam of an antler, smaller than an offer.

Sore. A three-year-old male fallow deer.

Sorel. A two-year-old male fallow deer.

Speculum. The white or light-coloured rump patch of a deer, also called a target.

Spellers. Spiky projections along the rear edge of the palm of a fallow deer's antler.

Splay. The spread of the cleaves of a slot, especially apparent in very soft ground and where deer have been moving at speed.

Stag. Among British wild deer, a male red or sika deer.

Stalk. To track a deer stealthily, moving on foot; an outing for this purpose. By common consent the term 'stalking' also applies to still-hunting (shooting from a predetermined location), especially in woodland situations.

Step. The distance between one hoofprint and the next imprinted by hooves on opposite sides.

Stride. The distance between successive imprints of the same hoof.

Sway. A conspicuous lateral deviation between the imprints of left and right hooves in the trail of a deer, usually indicative of an ageing beast or a heavily pregnant female.

Target. See *Speculum.*

Territory. An area of ground dominated by one mature male deer and defended by that male against incursions by rival males, as commonly happens with roebucks when in hard antler.

Tine. Any one of the various branches from the main beam of an antler.

Tops. The tines of a red deer antler above the trez (tray) tine and forming the crown or cup of the antler.

Trade. The ground signs of deer activity in general.

Trail. Hoofmarks and associated signs of a deer's passage.

Tray tine. See *Trez tine.*

Trez (tray) tine. The third tine above the coronet on a fully developed red deer antler, the bez (bay) tine is sometimes absent, making the trez tine the second tine.

Trophy. The head, skull or part of a skull of a male deer with antlers attached. Trophy-hunting as a prime objective is counter-productive to sound deer management.

Tufters. Specially trained hounds employed in staghunting, and formerly in buck-hunting, to locate and separate from its companions a deer selected for hunting before the main pack is laid on.

Variety. A distinctive type of plant or animal within a given species or subspecies. For example, black, common, menil and white fallow deer are all varieties of one species.

Velvet. The combination of skin, hair, blood vessels and other elements which nourish and protect growing antlers and which dies and is rubbed off when antler growth is complete.

Venison. Muscle tissue and other elements forming the edible flesh of deer.

Wallow. A patch of moist and muddy ground where male red or sika deer 'go to soil', wallowing and rolling, especially during the rut.

Waster. A deer in poor physical condition which looks unlikely to improve.

Whistle. The characteristic rutting call of a male sika deer, most often uttered as a succession of three whistles (which are actually vocal sounds) followed by a period of silence.

White fallow deer. A colour variety of fallow which looks superficially white but which has a buffish tinge to its pelage which is most pronounced in fawns; such fallow deer are not albinos and retain full pigmentation in the eyes

Yeld. An adult female deer (especially a red deer) which fails to produce a calf, fawn or kid in any one year but may well do so the following year.

DISTRIBUTION MAPS

Locations of counties and administrative regions in Britain and Ireland. In the case of Great Britain and Northern Ireland, counties and regions are as defined following local government boundary changes in 1974 and include some counties and other administrative units which have since ceased to be administrative entities or have been subdivided into unitary authorities. (Andy Miles Illustration)

ENGLAND, SCOTLAND AND WALES
1   HIGHLAND
2   GRAMPIAN
3   CENTRAL
4   STRATHCLYDE
5   KYLE AND CARRICK
6   FIFE
7   LOTHIAN
8   BORDERS
9   DUMFRIES AND GALLOWAY
10 NORTHUMBERLAND
11 TYNE AND WEAR
12 CUMBRIA
13 COUNTY DURHAM
14 LANCASHIRE
15 CLEVELAND
16 NORTH YORKSHIRE
17 WEST YORKSHIRE
18 HUMBERSIDE
19 SOUTH YORKSHIRE
20 GREATER MANCHESTER
21 MERSEYSIDE
22 CHESHIRE
23 DERBYSHIRE
24 NOTTINGHAMSHIRE
25 LINCOLNSHIRE
26 CLWYD
27 GWYNEDD
28 POWYS
29 DYFED
30 WEST GLAMORGAN
31 MID GLAMORGAN
32 SOUTH GLAMORGAN
33 GWENT
34 SHROPSHIRE
35 STAFFORDSHIRE
36 WEST MIDLANDS
37 LEICESTERSHIRE
38 NORFOLK
39 CAMBRIDGESHIRE
40 NORTHAMPTONSHIRE
41 WARWICKSHIRE
42 HEREFORD AND WORCESTER
43 GLOUCESTERSHIRE
44 OXFORDSHIRE
45 BUCKINGHAMSHIRE
46 BEDFORDSHIRE
47 SUFFOLK
48 HERTFORDSHIRE
49 ESSEX
50 LONDON
51 KENT
52 EAST SUSSEX
53 WEST SUSSEX
54 SURREY
55 BERKSHIRE
56 HAMPSHIRE
57 ISLE OF WIGHT
58 WILTSHIRE
59 AVON
60 SOMERSET
61 DORSET
62 DEVONSHIRE
63 CORNWALL

NORTHERN IRELAND
1   LONDONDERRY
2   LIMAVADY
3   COLERAINE
4   BALLYMONEY
5   MOYLE
6   LARNE
7   BALLYMENA
8   MAGHERAFELT
9   COOKSTOWN
10 STRABANE
11 OMAGH
12 FERMANAGH
13 DUNGANNON
14 CRAIGAVON
15 ARMAGH
16 NEWRY AND MOURNE
17 BANBRIDGE
18 DOWN
19 LISBURN
20 ANTRIM
21 NEWTOWNABBEY
22 CARRICKFERGUS
23 NORTH DOWN
24 ARDS
25 CASTLEREAGH
26 BELFAST

REPUBLIC OF IRELAND
27 DONEGAL
28 LEITRIM
29 SLIGO
30 CAVAN
31 MONAGHAN
32 LOUTH
33 MEATH
34 DUBLIN
35 LONGFORD
36 ROSCOMMON
37 MAYO
38 GALWAY
39 CLARE
40 WESTMEATH
41 OFFALY
42 KILDARE
43 LAOIS
44 TIPPERARY
45 KILKENNY
46 CARLOW
47 WICKLOW
48 WEXFORD
49 WATERFORD
50 LIMERICK
51 KERRY
52 CORK

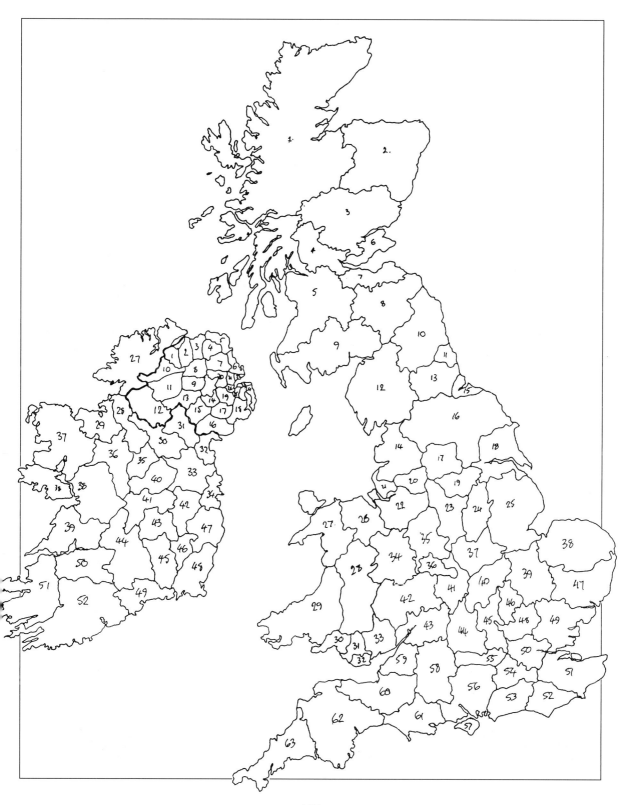

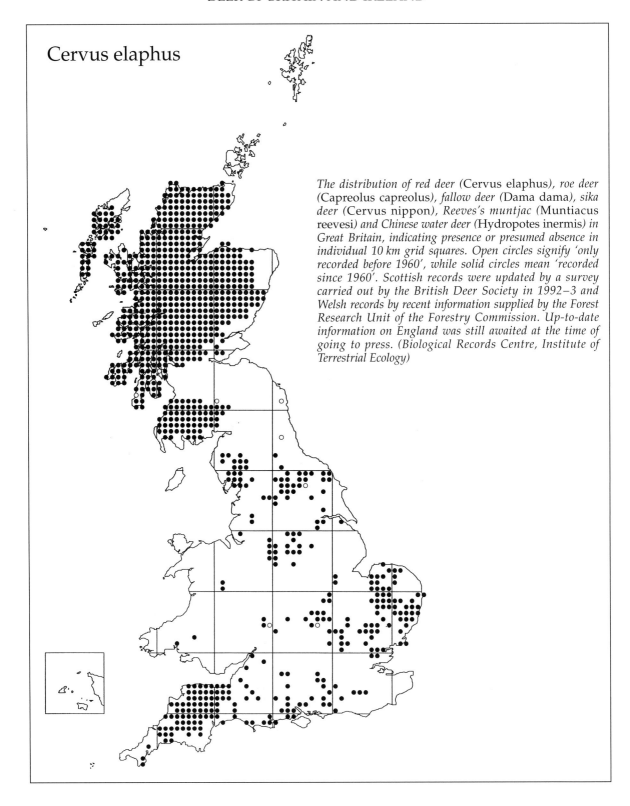

Cervus elaphus

The distribution of red deer (Cervus elaphus), *roe deer* (Capreolus capreolus), *fallow deer* (Dama dama), *sika deer* (Cervus nippon), *Reeves's muntjac* (Muntiacus reevesi) *and Chinese water deer* (Hydropotes inermis) *in Great Britain, indicating presence or presumed absence in individual 10 km grid squares. Open circles signify 'only recorded before 1960', while solid circles mean 'recorded since 1960'. Scottish records were updated by a survey carried out by the British Deer Society in 1992–3 and Welsh records by recent information supplied by the Forest Research Unit of the Forestry Commission. Up-to-date information on England was still awaited at the time of going to press. (Biological Records Centre, Institute of Terrestrial Ecology)*

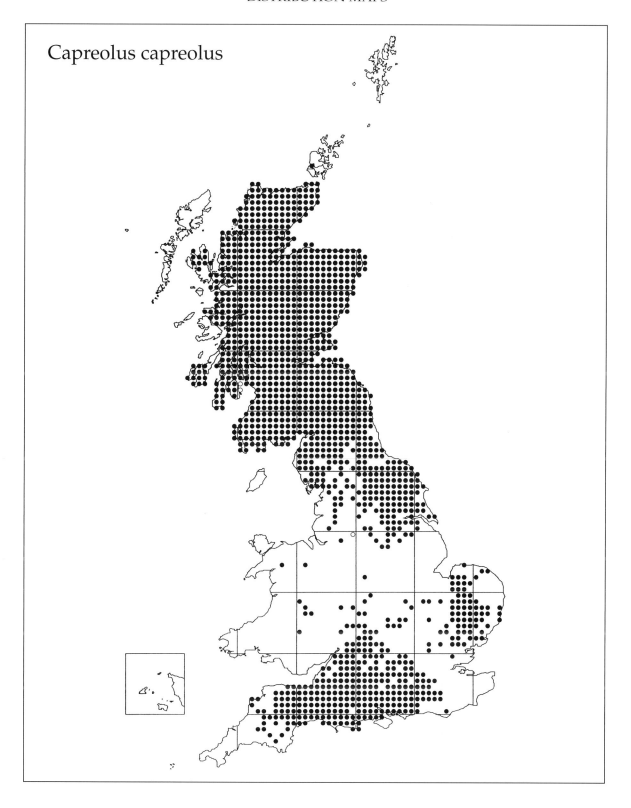

Capreolus capreolus

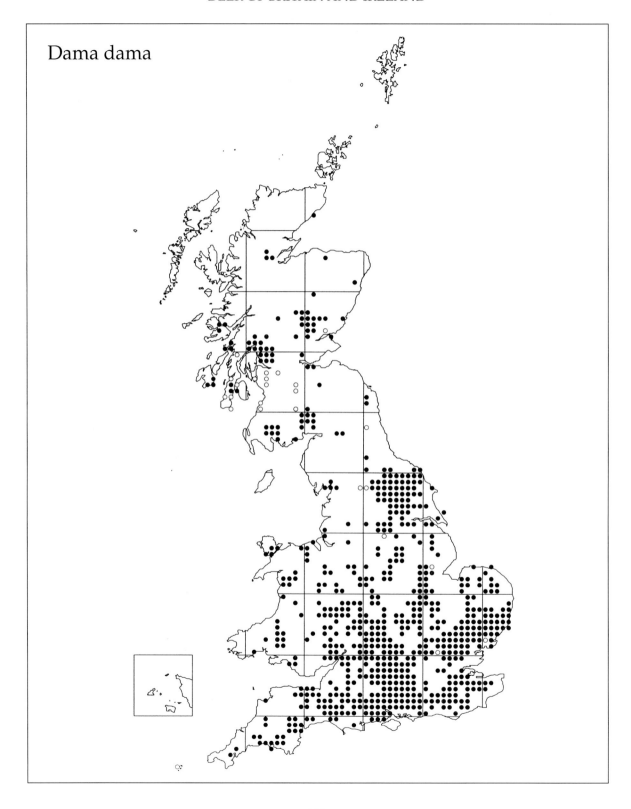

Dama dama

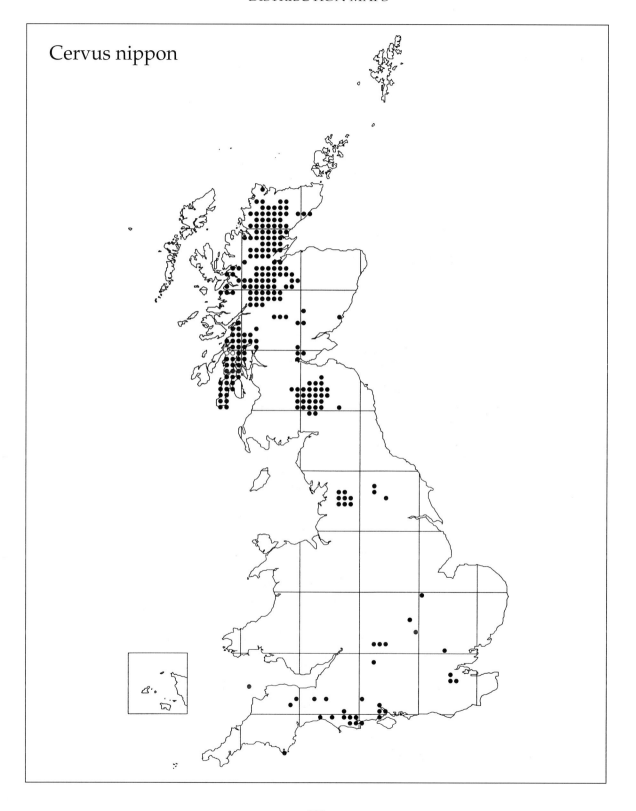

Cervus nippon

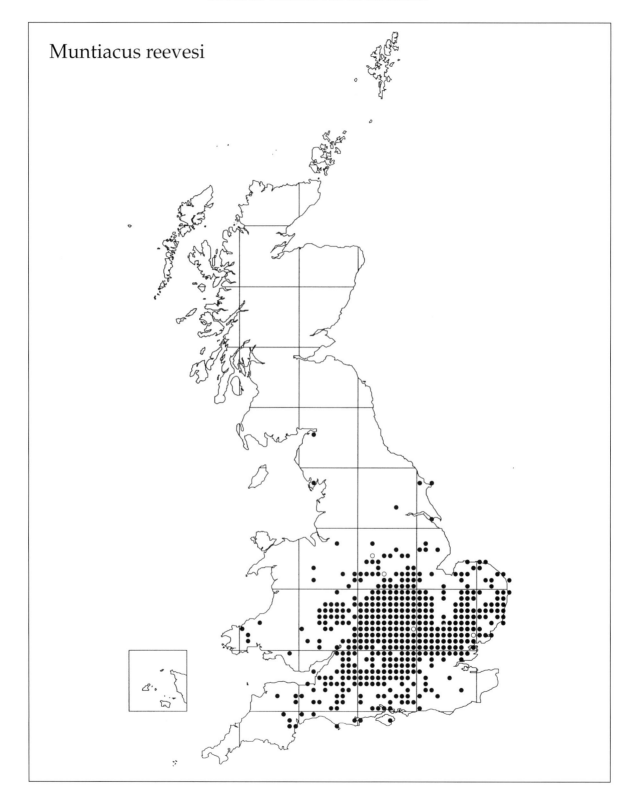

Muntiacus reevesi

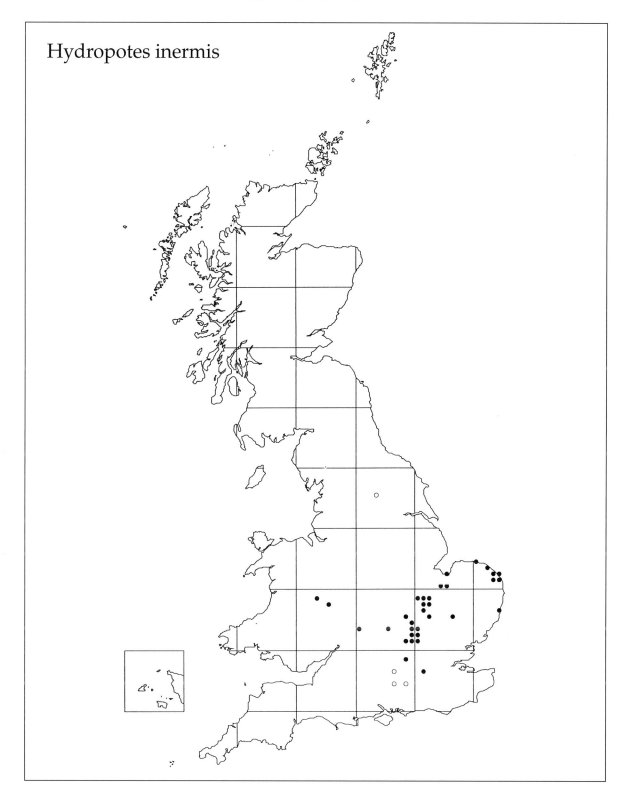

Hydropotes inermis

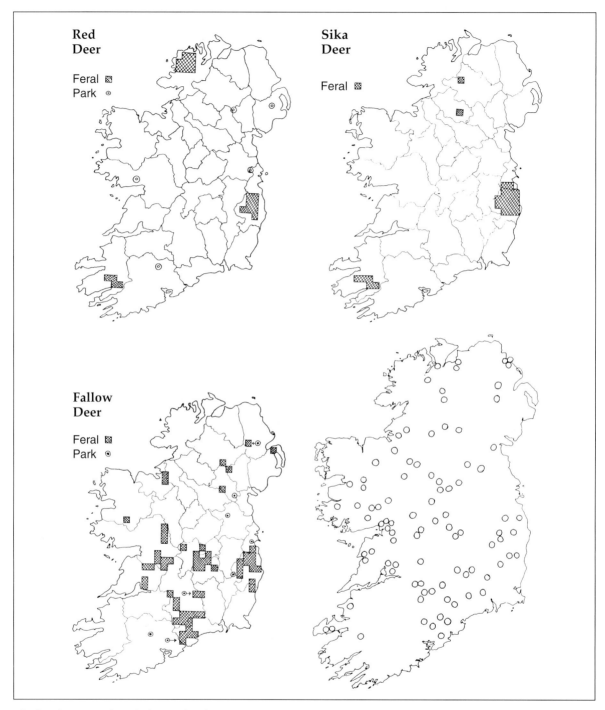

The first three maps show the known distribution in Ireland of red, fallow and sika deer respectively as recorded in 1970 by Fergal Mulloy of the Irish Deer Society. The fourth map shows the location of Irish townlands with the name 'deer park', signifying the bygone widespread occurrence of such parks.

BIBLIOGRAPHY

Prior to the Second World War literature devoted specifically to deer in Britain and Ireland was relatively sparse and was largely concerned with stalking red deer in Scotland or hunting them in south-west England. There were also a few historical studies and passing references to deer in books and articles on a more general range of subjects. The development of a more broadly based interest in the study of deer in these islands was generated in the immediate post-war period by a growing awareness of how little was known about these animals. Listed here is a wide range of literature bearing in one way or another on deer history, distribution, natural history and management, much of which has contributed source material for this book. Many articles cited were published in the British Deer Society's original newsletter *Deer News* or its successor journal *Deer*. Copies of these are held at the Society's headquarters office, Burgate Manor, Fordingbridge, Hampshire, SP6 1EF, telephone 01425 655434, fax 01425 655433. Photocopies of individual articles can be supplied at a small charge, and copies of some back issues of the journal are available.

Acton, C.R. (1936) *Sport and Sportsmen of the New Forest*. London: Heath Cranton Ltd.

Adams, A. Leith (1878) 'Report of the History of Irish Fossil Mammals'. *Proceedings of the Royal Irish Academy* (2), iii, Science, 91–2.

Alcock, Ian (1993) *Stalking Deer in Great Britain*. Shrewsbury: Swan Hill Press.

—(1996) *Deer: A Personal View*. Shrewsbury: Swan Hill Press.

—(1998) *Chasing the Red Deer and Following the Roe*. Aboyne, Aberdeenshire: Sauchenyard Press.

Alcock, Ian and McPhail, Rodger (1998) *Rodger McPhail, Artist-Naturalist-Sportsman*. Shrewsbury: Swan Hill Press.

Alexander, T.L. and Buxton, D. (Eds) (1994) *Management and Diseases of Deer A Handbook for the Veterinary Surgeon*. London: The Veterinary Deer Society.

Allen, D.R. (1952) 'Notes on some Mammals and Amphibians of Doubtful Status or Occurrence in the Isle of Man'. Contribution to *The Peregrine*, a publication of the Manx Field Club, Vol. 2, No. 1, September 1952, 16–18.

Almond, Richard (1994) 'Medieval Deer Hunting'. *Deer* 9(5), November 1994, 315–18.

Alston, E.R. (1880) 'The Fauna of Scotland, with Special Reference to Clydesdale and the Western District'. *Mammalia*, Natural History Society of Glasgow University, January 1880.

Andersen, R., Duncan, P. and Linnel, J.D.C. (Eds) (1998) *Roe Deer: The Ecology of Success*. Oslo, Norway: The Scandinavian University Press.

The Annals of Scottish Natural History (1892–1911) Various contributors. Edinburgh: David Douglas.

Annikin, Bernard P. (1977) 'The Macclesfield Forest Red Deer Project'. *Deer* 4(2), February 1977, 89–90.

Anon (1906) 'Deer Hunting in Lancashire'. *Country Life*, Vol. XX, No. 513, 3 November 1906, 641–2.

Arbuthnott, The Viscount of (1972) 'The Future of Red Deer in Scotland'. *Deer* 2(8), July 1972, 866–9.

—(1975) 'Red Deer in a Woodland Setting: The Red Deer Commission View'. *Deer* 3(6), February 1975, 341–2.

Aubrey, John (c. 1666–91) *The Natural History of Wiltshire*. Ed. John Britton, 1847, published for the Wiltshire Topographical Society. London: J.B. Nichols & Sons.

Baillie, Peter (1974) 'A Cull Buck as World Record'. *Deer* 3(5), November 1974, 262–3.

Bale, Jeffrey (1980) 'A White Stag on Exmoor'. *Deer* 5(2), July 1980, 88–9.

Balharry, Dick and Edgar, Audrey (1996) 'The Revival of a Deer Forest'. *Deer* 9(10), April 1996, 649–55.

Balharry, R. and Thompson, D.B.A. (1991) 'Deer Management: Shared Responsibility and Heritage Stewardship'. *Deer* 8(6), November 1991, 357–9.

Bang, Preben and Dahlstrom, Preben (1974) *Collins Guide to Animal Tracks and Signs*. London: Collins.

Bannerman, M.M. and Blaxter, K.L. (Eds) (1969) *The Husbanding of Red Deer*. Aberdeen: The Highlands and Islands Development Board and The Rowett Research Institute.

Banwell, D. Bruce (1994) *The Royal Stags of Windsor*. Auckland, New Zealand: The Halcyon Press.

—(1955) 'The Sikas'. *Deer* 9(7), July 1995, 446–50.

—(1996) 'The Sikas of Japan – Part I'. *Deer* 9(10), April 1996, 638–42.

—(1996) 'The Sikas of Japan – Part II'. *Deer* 10(1), July 1996, 38–43.

—(1999) *The Sikas*. Auckland, New Zealand: The Halcyon Press.

Barton, Brian (1979) 'Studying the Deer in South–West Essex'. *Deer* 4(8), February 1979, 418–20.

Bauer, Edwin A. (1995) *Antlers: The Antlered Animals of Europe and North America*. Shrewsbury: Swan Hill Press.

Bingham, J., Bradley, C.E., B.Sc., Bradley, C.G., B.Sc. and Yates, P.S. (1977) 'Mortimer Forest: Impressions of the Fallow Rut'. *Deer* 4(2), February 1977, 90–94.

Birkett, Alan (1996) 'Fallow Deer Behaviour in Tatton Park, Cheshire'. *Deer* **10**(2), October 1996, 93–7.

Blackwood, W.T. (1925) 'Fauna'. Contribution to *A History of Peebleshire*. (*See* Buchan, J.W.)

Blakely, Diane, Chapman, Norma, Claydon, Kathie and Mick, Harris, Stephen and Wakelam, Judy (1997) 'Studying Muntjac in the King's Forest, Suffolk'. *Deer* **10**(3), January 1997, 156–61.

Blamey, Graham and Curtis, Peter F. (1980) 'An Investigation of Problems Arising from Incursions by Fallow Deer on to Stansted Airport'. *Deer*, **5**(2), July 1980, 74–8.

Blaxter, Sir Kenneth, Kay, R.N.B., Sharman, G.A.M., Cunningham, J.M.M., Easie, J. and Hamilton, W.J. (1988) *Farming the Red Deer*. London: The Stationery Office.

Boate, Dr G. and others (1726) *A Natural History of Ireland in Three Parts*. Dublin: George Grierson.

Bolton, Douglas (1996) *Wild Deer in Galloway and the Red Deer Range*. Newton Stewart: Douglas Bolton.

Bowser, David (1991) 'Scotland's Red Deer at the Crossroads'. *Deer* **8**(6), November 1991, 337–8.

Bradley, Christopher (1989) 'The Fallow Deer of Wyre Forest'. *Deer* **7**(10), November 1989, 518–19.

—(1996) *The Realm of the Fallow Buck: The Deer of Wyre Forest*. Callow Hill, Worcs: Christopher Bradley.

—(1999) 'Wyre Forest Fallow: A Shed of Evidence'. *Deer* **11**(3), July 1999, 14.

Braine, A. (1891) *The History of Kingswood Forest*. London: E. Nister.

Bramley, P.S. (1970) 'Territoriality and Reproductive Behaviour of Roe Deer'. *Journal of Reproduction and Fertility* Supplement 11, March 1970, 43–70.

Brander, Michael (1986) *Deer Stalking in Britain*. London: The Sportsman's Press.

Bray, Derek W. (1978) 'A Day with *Dama dama springthorpeii*'. *Deer* **4**(5), February 1978, 281–2.

Breadalbane, The Marchioness of (1997 reprint) *The High Tops of Black Mount*. Crosby Ravensworth, Cumbria: David Grayling.

Brink, F.H. van den (1967) *A Field Guide to the Mammals of Britain and Europe*. London: Collins.

British Association for Shooting and Conservation (1995) *Deer Management in Scotland* (two-part paper). Rossett, Wrexham. BASC.

British Deer Society (1996) *Basic Deer Management*. Fordingbridge, Hampshire. British Deer Society.

Brown, Michael Baxter (1985) *Richmond Park: The History of a Royal Deer Park*. London: Robert Hale.

—(1988) 'The Historical and Ecological Significance of London's Royal Deer Parks'. *Deer* **7**(7), November 1988, 343–7.

—(1992) 'The Royal Parks'. *Deer* **8**(7), March 1992, 425–9.

—(1998) 'The Royal Venison Warrant'. *Deer* **10**(8), April 1998, 503–4.

Brown, Michael Baxter and Goldspink, C.R. (Eds) (1989) *Management, Conservation and Interpretation of Park Deer*. Manchester: Manchester Polytechnic.

Browne, Montagu (1889) *The Vertebrate Animals of Leicestershire and Rutland*. Birmingham and Leicester: Midland Educational Co. Ltd.

Buchan, J.W. (1925) *A History of Peeblesshire*, Vol. **1**. Glasgow: Jackson, Wylie & Co.

Buckingham, Walter G. (1981) 'Living with Muntjac'. *Deer* **5**(5), July 1981, 252–4.

Buckingham, W.G. and B.M. (1985) 'Keeping Muntjac in the Garden'. *Deer* **6**(6), March 1985, 202–4.

Buxton, E.N. (1884) *Epping Forest*. London: Edward Stanford.

—(1911) *Epping Forest*. (8th edition, revised.) London: Edward Stanford.

C.J.C. (1902) *The Oxenholme Hunt*. Kendal: Atkinson and Pollitt.

Cadman, W.A. (Arthur) (1967) 'Deer of the New Forest'. *Deer* **1**(4), November 1967, 121–7.

—(1969) 'Deer in a Sanctuary'. *Deer* **1**(9), June 1969, 362–3.

—(1989 reprint) *Dawn, Dusk and Deer*. London: The Sportsman's Press.

—(1994) Letter in *Stalking Magazine*, December 1994, 4.

Callander, Robin F. and Mackenzie, Neil A. (1991) *The Management of Wild Red Deer in Scotland*. Perth: Rural Forum Scotland.

Cambrensis, Giraldus (1188) *The Itinerary through Wales and the Description of Wales*. Translated by Sir R.C. Hoare, 1908. London: Everyman's Library.

Cameron, Allan Gordon (1984 reprint) *The Wild Red Deer of Scotland*. Weybread, Diss, Norfolk: Antony Atha.

Cameron of Lochiel, Lord, and others. (1997 reprint) *The Red Deer*. Dumfries: The Signet Press.

Canny, Michael (1991) 'Deer and the Republic of Ireland Wildlife Service'. *Deer* **8**(4), March 1991, 190–91.

Cardigan, The Earl of (1949) *The Wardens of Savernake Forest*. London: Routledge & Kegan Paul.

Carne, P.H. (Peter) (1965) 'Deer in Dorset – An Historical Outline'. *Deer News* **1**(6), January 1965, 25–7.

—(1967) 'History and Distribution of Deer in Dorset'. *Proceedings of the Dorset Natural History and Archaeological Society*, Volume 88.

—(1967) 'Deer of South-western England'. *Deer* **1**(2), February 1967, 42–4.

—(1968) 'Further Spread of Muntjac'. *Deer* **1**(6), June 1968, 190.

—(1969) *Wild Deer of the West Sussex Downs*. Elsted, Midhurst, West Sussex: West Sussex Deer Management Society.

—(1972) 'The Petworth Roe: Thoughts on their Origin – II'. *Deer* **2**(7), March 1972, 798–9.

—(1982) 'The Distribution of Wild and Feral Deer in Great Britain and Ireland'. *Deer* **5**(7), March 1982, 345–7.

—(1985) 'No Welcome for Roe in the Valleys?' *Deer* **6**(6), March 1985, 190–91.

—(1989) 'Quantock Red Deer Under the Microscope'. *Deer* **7**(8), March 1989, 390–92.

—(1991) 'West Country Red Deer: The Ongoing Debate'. *Deer* **8**(5), July 1991, 269.

—(1995) *Wild Deer of the West Sussex Downs* (new edition). Elsted, Midhurst, West Sussex: West Sussex Deer Management Society.

—(1995) 'Red Deer in the New Forest: An Historical Appraisal'. *Deer* **9**(8), October 1995, 499–502.

—(1999) *Woodland Stalking*. Shrewsbury: Swan Hill Press.

—(1999) 'A Sandy-White Roe and Deer at Sea'. *Deer* **11**(4), October 1999, 212–3.

Carter, Douglas (1967) 'The Haldon Fallow Deer'. *Deer* **1**(2), February 1967, 46.

Carter, N.A. (1984) 'Bole Scoring by Sika Deer (*Cervus nippon*) in England'. *Deer* **6**(3), March 1984, 77–8.

Cartwright, Roger (1980) *Deer of the Arnside Silverdale Area*. Fordingbridge, Hampshire: British Deer Society.

—(1998) 'Black Roe on the Morecambe Bay Limestone Hills'. *Deer* **10**(10), October 1998, 612.

Cassels, K.A.H. (1968) 'Traditional Deer Coursing in the Highlands'. *Deer* **1**(5), February 1968, 174–6.

—(1997) *A Most Wonderful Creature of Heaven: The Scottish Deerhound*. Wimbish Green, Saffron Walden, Essex: K.A.H. Cassels.

Chafin, William (1818) *Anecdotes and History of Cranborne Chase* 2nd edition. London: J. Nichols Son and Bentley.

Chalmers, Patrick A. (1984 reprint) *Deer Stalking*. Weybread, Diss, Norfolk: Antony Atha.

Chandler, G.M. (1982) 'Return of the Fallow Deer'. *Deer* **5**(9), November 1982, 454.

Chaplin, Raymond E. (1966) *Reproduction in British Deer*. London: Passmore Edwards Museum (London Borough of Newham).

—(1966) 'Staggers – A Disease of Red Deer'. *Deer News* **1**(10), June 1966, 49.

—(1972) 'The Antler Cycle of Muntjac Deer in Britain'. *Deer* **2**(9), November 1972, 938–41.

—(1977) *Deer*. London: Blandford Press.

Chapman, D.I. (1977) 'Deer of Essex'. *Essex Naturalist*, New Series, **1**.

Chapman, Donald I. and Chaplin, Raymond E. 'The Deer of Epping Forest'. *Deer News* **1**(5), October 1964, 25–6.

Chapman, D. and Norma (1972) 'Muntjac Deer Hybrids'. *Deer* **2**(7), March 1972, 803–4.

—(1973) *Deer of East Anglia*. Ipswich: F.W. Pawsey & Sons.

—(1997 reprint) *Fallow Deer: Their History, Distribution and Biology*. Machynlleth, Powys: Cochy-Bonddu Books.

Chapman, Norma (1984) *Fallow Deer*. Oswestry, Shropshire: Anthony Nelson Ltd.

—(1990) 'Milu Across the Miles'. *Deer* **8**(1), March 1990, 19–20.

—(1991) *Deer*. London: Whittet Books.

Chapman, Norma and Donald (1978) *Fallow Deer*. Fordingbridge, Hampshire: British Deer Society.

—(1980) 'The Distribution of Fallow Deer: A Worldwide Review'. *Mammal Review* **10**(2 and 3), June and September 1980.

—(1982) *The Fallow Deer*. Forestry Commission, Forest Record 124. London: Stationery Office.

Chapman, Norma *et al.* (1997) 'History and Habitat Preferences of Muntjac in the King's Forest, Suffolk'. *Deer* **10**(5), July 1997, 289–94.

—(1994) 'Muntjac in Britain: Is There a Need for a Management Strategy?' *Deer* **9**(4), July 1994, 226–36.

Chapman, Norma and Harris, Stephen (1993) 'The Spread of Muntjac in Britain'. *Deer* **8**(10), March 1993, 650–52.

—(1996) *Muntjac*. London: The Mammal Society and Fordingbridge, Hampshire: the British Deer Society.

Chapman, Norma and Whitwell, Katherine (1998) 'Skeletal and Dental Changes in the Old Lady of Richmond Park'. *Deer* **10**(7), January 1998, 405–8.

Chard, J.S.R. (1965) 'Sika and Fallow Deer in Kent'. *Deer News* **1**(6), January 1965, 42–3.

—(1966) 'Control of Fallow Deer at Mortimer Forest'. *Deer News* **1**(9), January 1966, 23–5.

—(1970) 'Deer and the Forester'. *Deer* **2**(2), June 1970, 510–14.

—(1976) 'The Red Deer of Furness: Their History, Biology, Status and Future – 1. The History of the Herd'. *Deer* **4**(1), November 1976, 22–6.

Clark, Michael (1965) 'Muntjac and Fallow Deer in the Northaw and Cuffley Area S.E. Herts.'. *Deer News* **1**(8), October 1965, 38–40.

—(1968) 'Roe Deer in Hertfordshire'. *Deer* **1**(5), February 1968, 179.

—(Ed.) (1971) *Deer of the World*. Fordingbridge, Hampshire: British Deer Society (East Anglian Branch).

—(1981) *Mammal Watching*. London: Severn House Publications Ltd.

—(1971) 'Notes on Muntjac in Southern Hertfordshire'. *Deer* **2**(6), November 1971, 725–8.

Clarke, Michael (ed.) (1974) 'Deer Distribution Survey, 1967–72'. *Deer* **3**(5), November 1974, 279–82.

Clarke, W. Eagle and Roebuck, W.D. (1881) *A Handbook of the Vertebrate Fauna of Yorkshire*. London: Lovell Reeve & Co.

Clutton-Brock, T.H. (1991) 'Red Deer and Sacred Cows'. *Deer* **8**(5), July 1991, 301–3.

Clutton-Brock, T.H. and Albon, S.D. (1981) 'The Roaring of Red Deer and the Evolution of Honest Advertisement'. Reprinted from *Behaviour*, LXIX 3–4. Cambridge: King's College Research Centre, University of Cambridge.

—(1989) *Red Deer in the Highlands*. Oxford: Blackwell Scientific Publications Ltd.

—(1992) 'Trial and Error in the Highlands'. *Deer* **8**(9), November 1992, 590–92.

Clutton-Brock, T.H., Guiness, F.E. and Albon, S.D. (1982) *Red Deer: Behaviour and Ecology of Two Sexes*. Edinburgh: Edinburgh University Press.

Coles, Charles (ed.) (1988) *Shooting and Stalking: A Basic Guide*. London: Stanley Paul.

—(1997) *Gardens and Deer*: A Guide to Damage Limitation. Shrewsbury: Swan Hill Press.

Collier, Raymond V. (1965) 'Fallow Deer in the Castor Hanglands Area, near Peterborough'. *Deer News* **1**(8), October 1965, 40–42.

Collyns, C.P. (1862) *Notes on the Chase of the Wild Red Deer*. London: Longman & Co.

Cooke, A.S. (1994) 'Is the Muntjac a Pest in Monks Wood Nature Reserve?' *Deer* **9**(4), July 1994, 243–5.

—(1998a) 'Colonisation of Holme Fen by Chinese Water Deer and Muntjac, 1976–1977' *Deer* **10**(7), January 1998, 414–16.

—(1998b) 'Some Aspects of Muntjac Behaviour'. *Deer* **10**(8), April 1998, 464–6.

Cooke, A.O. (1913) *The Forest of Dean*. London: Constable & Co. Ltd.

Cooke, Arnold and Farrell, Lynne (1998) *Chinese Water Deer*. London: Mammal Society and Fordingbridge: British Deer Society.

Coope, G.R. (1973) 'The Ancient World of Megaceros'. *Deer* **2**(10), February 1973, 974–7.

Corbet, G.B. (1966) *The Terrestrial Mammals of Western Europe*. London: G.F. Foulis & Co. Ltd.

Corbet, G.B. and Southern, H.N. (Eds) (1977) *The Handbook of British Mammals*. Oxford: Blackwell Scientific Publications Ltd.

Corfield, J.S. (1964) 'Grizedale Forest Deer and their Control'. *Deer News* **1**(4), May 1964, 26.

Cotter-Craig, T.D. (1975) 'Red Deer in a Forestry Setting: A Private Forestry View'. *Deer* **3**(6), February 1975, 343–5.

Cottrell, Helen (1987) 'The Royal Forest of Galtres'. *Deer* **7**(3), July 1987, 144–5.

Courtier, F.A. (1991) 'Sika Deer in the New Forest'. *Deer* **8**(6), November 1991, 367–70.

Coward, T.A. (1910) *The Vertebrate Fauna of Cheshire and Liverpool Bay*, Vol. 1. London: Witherby & Co.

Cowen, G.A., Ridley, The Viscount, and Tegner, H.S. (1965) 'Roe Deer in Northumberland and Durham'. *Transactions of the Natural History Society of Northumberland, Durham and Newcastle-upon-Tyne* **XV**(3) (New Series), 109–20.

Cox, J. Charles (1905) *The Royal Forests of England*. London: Methuen & Co.

Crealock, Lieut-Gen. H.H. (1892) *Deer-Stalking in the Highlands of Scotland*. London: Longmans, Green & Co.

Cronin, Doreen (1993) 'The Anti-Hunt View of Deer-hunting with Hounds'. *Deer* **8**(10), March 1993, 652–4.

Cross, Richard J. (1983) *Deer Antlers: Regeneration, Function and Evolution*. London: Academic Press.

Crossing, W. (1902) *A Hundred Years on Dartmoor*. 5th edition. Plymouth: The Western Morning News Co. Ltd.

Curtis, Peter F. (1994) 'Damage to Coppice in Blackwater Wood, Buckinghamshire: A Case Study'. *Deer* **9**(4), July 1994, 246–7.

Danilkin, A. (1996) *Behavioural Ecology of Siberian and European Roe Deer*. London: Chapman & Hall.

Dansie, Oliver (1966) 'Reeves's Muntjac (*Muntiacus reevesi*) in the Welwyn Area'. *Deer News* **1**(9), January 1966, 37–41.

—(1969) 'Red Deer in Hertfordshire'. *Deer* **1**(8), February 1969, 313–15.

—(1969) 'Are Muntjac Deer?' *Deer* **1**(9), June 1969, 373.

—(1971) 'The Spread of the Remarkable Muntjac'. *Deer* **2**(4), February 1971, 616–20.

—(1979) 'Live-Catching Sika Deer at Killarney, South-West Ireland'. *Deer* **4**(10), December 1979, 527.

—(1981) 'Are Muntjac Solitary?' *Deer* **5**(5), July 1981, 254–5.

—(1992) 'Red Deer in Scotland: Back to the Elrig?' *Deer* **8**(9), November 1992, 592.

Dansie, Oliver (1983) *Muntjac*. Cooke, Arnold and Farrell, Lynne (1983) *Chinese Water Deer*. (One volume.) Fordingbridge, Hampshire: British Deer Society.

Darling, F.F. (Sir Frank Fraser) (1937) *A Herd of Red Deer*. London: Oxford University Press.

—(1947) *Natural History in the Highlands and Islands*. London: Collins.

—(1972) 'Red Deer in the Highlands'. *Deer* **2**(9), July 1972, 834–6.

Darwall, George (1985a) '250 Years Ago'. *Deer* **6**(7), July 1985, 160–61.

—(1985b) '250 Years Ago: The Hart and Buck'. *Deer* **6**(8), November 1985, 316–17.

—(1986) '250 Years Ago: Hunting the Hart and Buck'. *Deer* **6**(9), March 1986, 360–61.

Davies, E.J.M. (1975) 'Red Deer in South Scotland: The Forestry Commission View'. *Deer* **3**(6), February 1975, 340.

Davies, John (1987) 'The History of the Red Deer of Galloway'. *Deer* **7**(3), July 1987, 132–4.

De Nahlik, A.J. (1959) *Wild Deer*. London: Faber and Faber.

—(1974) *Deer Management*. Newton Abbot, Devon: David & Charles.

—(1987) *Wild Deer: Culling, Conservation and Management*. Shedfield, Hampshire: Ashford Press Publishing.

—(1992) *Management of Deer and their Habitat: Principles and Methods*. Gillingham, Dorset: Wilson Hunt.

Deane, C. Douglas (1972) 'Deer in Ireland'. *Deer* **2**(9), November 1972, 920–26.

Deer Commission for Scotland. (1998) 'A Policy for Sika Deer in Scotland'. *Deer* **10**(9), July 1998, 551–2.

Deer Distribution Records. Various Sources. *Deer News* **1**(2), October 1963, 8–11; **1**(3), January 1964, 14; **1**(4), May 1964, 19–22; **1**(5), October 1964, 13–15; **1**(6), January 1965, 15–16; **1**(7), June 1965, 20–22; **1**(8), October 1965, 18–20; **1**(9), January 1966, 16–18; **1**(10), June 1966, 23–4. *Deer* **1**(1), November 1966, 26; **1**(2), February 1967, 58; **1**(3), July 1967, 100–2; **1**(4), November 1967, 159; **1**(5), February 1968, 186; **1**(6), June 1968, 233; **1**(7), November 1968, 278; **1**(8), February 1969, 326; **1**(9), June 1969, 381–2; **1**(10), November 1969, 425; **2**(1), February 1970, 474; **2**(2), June 1970, 531; **2**(3), November 1970, 582; **2**(4), February 1971, 645; **2**(5), July 1971, 700–1; **2**(6), November 1971, 767; **2**(7), March 1972, 829; **2**(8), July 1972, 891; **2**(9), November 1972, 951; **2**(10), February 1973, 1017; **3**(1), July 1973, 59; **3**(3), February 1974, 185–6; **3**(4), July 1974, 250; **3**(5), November 1974, 306; **3**(6), February 1975, 361.

Deer Herd Book Society of Great Britain (1925) *Register of Park Herds*. Edited by G. Tyrwhitt-Drake (Hon. Secretary). Maidstone: Deer Herd Book Society of Great Britain.

Delaney, M.J. (Ed.) (1985) *Yorkshire Mammals*. Bradford: University of Bradford.

Delap, Peter (1936) 'Deer in Wicklow'. *Irish Naturalists' Journal*, Vol. VI January 1936–November 1937, 82–8.

—(1960) 'Present Status of Lakeland Deer'. Contribution to *The Changing Scene*, No. 2, Transactions of the Eden Field Club, Penrith and District Natural History Society: Kendal Natural History Society: Grange Natural History Society.

—(1964) 'Inter-specific Association of Red and Sika Deer'. *Deer News* **1**(3), January 1964, 23.

—(1964) 'Deer of North-Western England'. *Deer News* **1**(4), May 1964, 25.

—(1964) '1964 Deer Census at Martindale Forest'. *Deer News* **1**(5), October 1964, 27.

—(1967) 'Hybridisation of Red and Sika Deer in North-West England'. *Deer* **1**(4), November 1967, 131–3.

—(1968) 'Some Thoughts Based on Deer in North-West England'. *Deer* **1**(6), June 1968, 205–7.

—(1970) *Roe Deer*. Fordingbridge, Hampshire, British Deer Society.

—(1970) *Red Deer*. Fordingbridge, Hampshire: British Deer Society.

—(1973) 'The World of the Martindale Red Deer'. *Deer* **2**(10), February 1973, 991–3.

—(1976) 'The Red Deer of Furness: Their History, Biology, Status and Future – 2. Some Aspects of their Survival'. *Deer* **4**(1), November 1976, 26–7.

—(1984) 'A Deer Trap in the Lake District'. *Deer* **6**(4), July 1984, 132–3.

—(1988) 'Rhum Goings-on'. *Deer* **7**(6), July 1988, 302–3.

Discovery Channel Online Website (1999) 'New Deer Species Found'. *Deer* **11**(4), October 1999, 213.

Dixon, Alexandra (1992) 'Rare Deer Programmes at Whipsnade Wild Animal Park'. *Deer* **8**(9), November 1992, 560–61.

Donnelly, Peter (1993) 'Coping with Deer on the Urban Fringe'. *Deer* **8**(10), March 1993, 668–9.

—(1998) 'Lyme Park: A Potted History 1398–1994'. *Deer* **10**(7), January 1998, 395–8.

Drabble, Phil (1970) 'Deer in an Urban Situation'. *Deer* **2**(2), June 1970, 517–20.

—(1971) *Design for a Wilderness*. London: Pelham Books.

Dubicki, T.E. (1985) 'Cross-Channel Deer!' *Deer* **6**(8), November 1985, 312–13.

Dulverton, Lord (1968) 'Red Deer and Forestry Development in the Scottish Highlands'. *Deer* **1**(5), February 1968, 169–71.

Edward, 2nd Duke of York (*c.* 1410) *The Master of Game*. (Edited by William A. and F. Baillie-Grohman, 1909) London: Chatto & Windus.

Eick, Ernst, König, Robert and Willett, John A. (1995) *Sika, Cervus nippon Temminck 1838*. Mohnesee, Germany: International Sika Society.

Elford, Colin (1988) *Practical Woodland Stalking*. Ramsbury, Wiltshire: Crowood Press.

Ellis, W.S. (1885) *The Parks and Forests of Sussex*. Lewes, Sussex: H. Wolff.

Ettinger, D.M. Turner (ed.) (1974) *Natural History Photography*. London: Academic Press.

Evans, A.H. (1911) *A Fauna of the Tweed Area*. Edinburgh: David Douglas.

Evans, A.H. and Buckley, T.E. (1899) *A Vertebrate Fauna of the Shetland Islands*. Edinburgh: David Douglas.

Evans, H. (1993 reprint) *Some Account of Jura Red Deer*. Borough Green, Newmarket, Suffolk: R.E. and G.B. Way.

Evans, W. (1892) *The Mammalian Fauna of the Edinburgh District*. Edinburgh: McFarlane & Erskine.

Fawcett, John K. (1986) 'The Art of Deer Photography'. *Deer* **6**(9), March 1986, 348–51.

—(1997) *Roe Deer*. London: The Mammal Society and Fordingbridge, Hampshire: British Deer Society.

Fforde, C. (1981) 'A Year's Cull of Red Deer on a Scottish Island'. *Deer* **5**(4), March 1981, 190–91.

Field Guide to the Animals of Britain. (1984) London: The Reader's Digest Association Ltd.

Field, The. Various contributors.

Fisher, W.R. (1887) *The Forest of Essex*. London: Butterworths.

Fitter, R.S.R. (1945) *London's Natural History*. London: Collins.

—(1949) *The Ark in our Midst*. London: Collins.

—(1968) *Vanishing Wild Animals of the World*. London: Midland Bank and Kaye & Ward Ltd.

Fitter, Richard and Maisie (1967) *The Penguin Dictionary of British Natural History*. London: Penguin Books Ltd.

Fletcher, John (1996) 'Deer Farming Twenty-Five Years On'. *Deer* **10**(1), July 1996, 31–3.

Floyd, G.C. (1998) *All His Rights: A Story of the Wild Red Deer of Exmoor*. Porlock, Somerset: G.C. Floyd.

Foll, John (1986) 'The Setting-Up of the Deer Collection'. *Deer* **7**(1), March 1986, 10–12.

Fooks, H.A. and Hotchkis, John (1964) *Deer Control*. Fordingbridge, Hampshire: British Deer Society.

Forde, A. 'Roly' (1992) 'Some Facts About Staghunting'. *Deer* **8**(9) November 1992, 565–6.

Forestry Commission (1964) *The Roe Deer*. Forestry Commission Leaflet No. 450. London: The Stationery Office.

Forestry Commission (1966) *The Fallow Deer*. Forestry Commission Leaflet No. 52. London: The Stationery Office.

Forestry Commission, S.W. England Conservancy (1966) 'Notes on Wyre Forest'. *Deer News* **1**(9), January 1966, 25–6.

Forrest, H.E. (1899) *The Fauna of Shropshire*. Shrewsbury: L. Wildling.

—(1907) *The Vertebrate Fauna of North Wales*. London: Witherby & Co.

—(1919) *A Handbook to the Vertebrate Fauna of North Wales*. London: Witherby & Co.

Fortescue, Hon. J. (1887) *Records of Staghunting on Exmoor*. London: Chapman & Hall.

Fortescue, Hon. J.W. (1897) *The Story of a Red Deer*. London: Macmillan & Co.

Fox, John (1967) 'The Ettington (Warwickshire) Fallow Deer Herd'. *Deer* **1**(3), July 1967, 97.

Fox, Levi and Russell, Percy (1948) *Leicester Forest*. Leicester: Roger Backus.

Fraser, A.F. (1968) *Reproductive Behaviour in Ungulates*. London: Academic Press.

'The Future for Red Deer on Exmoor and the Quantocks' (1991) *Deer* **8**(5), July 1991, 282–98.

'Gallowegian' (1977) 'Fallow Deer in the South of Scotland: An Attempt at Re-introduction'. *Deer* **4**(3), July 1977, 148–9.

Gardyne, Col. C. Greenhill (N.D.) *Records of a Quiet Life*. Privately printed.

Garner, Robert (1844) *The Natural History of the County of Stafford*. London: John van Voorst.

Geipel, Udo (1979) 'Rushmore: A Deer Shoot in Cranborne Chase, Southern England'. *Deer* **4**(8), February 1979, 420–23.

Geist, Valerius (1999) *Deer of the World: Their Evolution, Behaviour and Ecology*. Shrewsbury: Swan Hill Press.

Gibson, S.D. and Goldspink, C.R. (1988) 'A Note on the Distribution of Fallow Deer in Tatton Park, Cheshire'. *Deer* **7**(7), November 1988, 352–5.

Gibson, W.N. and MacArthur, K., BEM (1966) 'Roe Deer and Methods of Control in the Forests of South Scotland'. *Deer* **1**(1), November 1966, 10–15.

Gilpin, Revd William (1791) *Remarks on Forest Scenery*. London: R. Blamire (1973 facsimile reprint). Richmond, Surrey: Richmond Publishing Co. Ltd. (1834 edition) Sir Thomas Dick Lauder, Bt. (Ed.) Edinburgh: Fraser & Co. of Northbridge. London: Smith, Elder & Co. Dublin: W. Curry Junior & Co.

Gladstone, H.S. (1912) *A Catalogue of the Vertebrate Fauna of Dumfriesshire*. Dumfries: J. Maxwell & Son.

Goldspink, C.R. and Hoult, M. (1985) 'A New Stag to Lyme Park, Cheshire 1979–82'. *Deer* **6**(6), March 1985, 196–9.

Goodman, S.J. *et al.* (1996) 'The Introgression of Introduced Asiatic Sika Deer into Scottish Red Deer – Does Hybridisation Matter?' *Deer* **10**(2), October 1996, 86–90.

Gordon, Seton (1947) *A Highland Year*. London: Eyre & Spottiswoode.

Gordon-Duff-Pennington, Patrick (1996) 'Alec Angus – the Master Stag of North Uist'. *Deer* **10**(2), October 1996, 81.

Goss, Fred (1931) *Memories of a Stag Harbourer*. London: H.F. & G. Witherby.

Gough, John (1999) 'Observed Differences in the Muntjac Deer Populations of Kineton and Yardley Chase'. *Deer* **11**(4), October 1999, 185–7.

Grant W. (Bill), MBE. (1969). 'The Role of Forest Parks in Conservation'. *Deer* **1**(9), June 1969, 364–9.

—(1971) 'Deer: A Recreational Asset'. *Deer* **2**(4), February 1971, 605–7.

—(1976) 'The Red Deer of Furness: Their History, Biology, Status and Future – 4. Management of Red Deer at Grizedale Forest'. *Deer* **4**(1), November 1976, 33–7.

Graves, Lord (1814) *The Staghunting Establishment of the County of Devon*. A letter addressed to Lord Ebrington relating to this subject. Exeter: Trewman & Son.

Greswell, Rev. W.H.P. (1905) *The Forests and Deer Parks of the County of Somerset*. Taunton: Barnicott & Pearce, Athenaeum Press.

Grewcock, David (1985) *Deer*. London: A. & C. Black.

Grimble, A. (1896) *The Deer Forests of Scotland*. London: Kegan, Paul, Trench, Trubner & Co. Ltd.

Gunn, J.W.S. (1909) *A Vindication of the Deer Forests and Grouse Moors of Scotland*. Glasgow: R. Maclehose & Co. Ltd.

Hall, H. Byng (1849) *Exmoor, or the Footsteps of St Hubert in the West*. London: Thomas Cautley Newby.

Hall, Michael (1968) 'Roe Deer on the Mendip Hills'. *Deer* **1**(5), February 1968, 178.

Hamilton, Archibald (1907) *The Red Deer of Exmoor*. London: Hoare Cox (*The Field* Office).

Hannett, John (1894) *The Forest of Arden*. 2nd edition. Birmingham: Charles Lowe.

Hardie, P.A. (1974) 'The Deer Forests of Scotland'. *Deer* **3**(5), November 1974, 283–6.

Harding, Stephan P. (1982) 'The Muntjac Project: A Brief Progress Report'. *Deer* **5**(9), November 1982, 450–51.

Hare, C.E. (1997) *The Language of Field Sports*. Crosby Ravensworth, Penrith, Cumbria: David Grayling.

Harris, Roy A. and Duff, K.R. (1970) *Wild Deer in Britain*. Newton Abbot, Devon: David & Charles.

Harris, Stephen (1984) 'Roe Deer in the City of Bristol'. *Deer* **6**(3), March 1984, 87–9.

Harris, Stephen *et al.* (1995) *A Review of British Mammals*. Joint Nature Conservation Committee, Totnes, Devon: Natural History Book Services Ltd.

Hart, Cyril (1971) *The Verderers and Forest Laws of Dean with Notes on the Speech House*. Newton Abbot, Devon: David & Charles.

Hart-Davis, Duff (1978) *Monarchs of the Glen: A History of Stalking in Scotland*. London: Jonathan Cape.

—(1993) 'Deer-stalking and the Highlands'. *Deer* **9**(1), July 1993, 14–16.

Harting, J.E. (1880) *British Animals Extinct within Historic Times*. London: Trubner & Co.

—(1883) 'Hertfordshire Deer Parks'. *Transactions of the Hertfordshire Natural History Society*, Vol. 11, Part 3, 97–110.

Harvey, Lieut-Col. J.R. (1910) *Deer Hunting in Norfolk*. Norwich: The Norwich Mercury Co. Ltd.

Harvie-Brown, J.A. (1906) *A Fauna of the Tay Basin and Strathmore*. Edinburgh: David Douglas.

Harvie-Brown, J.A. and Buckley, T.E. (1887) *A Vertebrate Fauna of Sutherland, Caithness and West Cromarty*. Edinburgh: David Douglas.

—(1888) *A Vertebrate Fauna of the Outer Hebrides*. Edinburgh: David Douglas.

—(1891) *A Vertebrate Fauna of the Orkney Islands*. Edinburgh: David Douglas.

—(1892) *A Vertebrate Fauna of Argyll and the Inner Hebrides*. Edinburgh: David Douglas.

—(1895) *A Vertebrate Fauna of the Moray Basin*, Vol. 1. Edinburgh: David Douglas.

Harvie-Brown, J.A. and Macpherson, Revd H.A. (1904) *A Fauna of the North-West Highlands and Skye*. Edinburgh: David Douglas.

Hastings, 12th Duke of Bedford (1949) *The Years of Transition*. London: Andrew Dakers Ltd.

Hawkins, Desmond (1980) *Cranborne Chase*. London: Victor Gollancz.

Heath, Gerald (1971) 'Attingham Park and its Deer'. *Deer* **2**(4), February 1971, 610.

—(1977) 'The Midnight Cowboy of Attingham'. *Deer* **4**(2), February 1977, 96–7.

Heath, Veronica (1990) 'Kielder Restructuring: An Enlightened Approach by the Forestry Commission'. *Deer* **8**(3), November 1990, 155–6.

Heathcote, Terry (1990) *A Wild Heritage: The History and Nature of the New Forest*. Southampton: Ensign Publications.

Hendy, E.W. (1946) *Wild Exmoor through the Year*. London: Eyre & Spottiswoode.

Henshaw, Dr John (1997) 'Hunting Deer with Hounds and the Decision of the National Trust to Ban Hunting on NT Land'. *Deer* 10(5), July 1997, 299.

Hewitt, H.P. (1963) *The Fairest Hunting*. London: J.A. Allen & Co. Ltd.

Hickin, Norman E. (1971) *The Natural History of an English Forest: The Wild Life of Wyre*. London: Hutchinson.

Hinde, Thomas (1985) *Forests of Britain*. London: Victor Gollancz.

Hingston, Major F.B. (Frederick) (1987) 'The Deer of Donington Park'. *Deer* 7(4), November 1987, 195–6.

—(1988) *Deer Parks and Deer of Great Britain*. Buckingham: Sporting and Leisure Press.

Hitchmough, Howard and Morrison, K.C.G. (1968) 'The Deer of Thetford Chase'. *Deer* 1(5), February 1968, 160–62.

Holmes, Frank (1975) *Following the Roe*. Edinburgh: John Bartholomew & Son.

Hore, J.P. (1895) *The History of the Royal Buckhounds*. Newmarket, Suffolk: J.P. Hore.

Horwood, M.T. (1973) 'The World of Wareham Sika'. *Deer* 2(10), February 1973, 978–84.

Horwood, M.T. and Masters, E.H. (1970) *Sika Deer*. Fordingbridge, Hampshire: British Deer Society.

Hotchkis, John (1989) 'Ensuring Free Passage for East Sussex Fallow'. *Deer* 7(9), July 1989, 469–71.

Hudson, David (1989) *Highland Deer Stalking*. Ramsbury, Wiltshire: Crowood Press.

Hutchinson, Horace G. (1904) *The New Forest*. London: Methuen & Co. Ltd.

Hyland, Matt (1989) 'Wild Deer Management in the Republic of Ireland'. *Deer* 7(9), July 1989, 481.

—(1990) 'A White Red Deer in Ireland'. *Deer* 8(3), November 1990, 152.

Idle, E.T. and Mitchell, J. (1968) 'The Fallow Deer of Loch Lomondside'. *Deer* 1(7), November 1968, 263–5.

Insley, Hugh (1976) 'Deer and the Visitor to the New Forest'. *Deer* 3(10), July 1976, 542–5.

—(1977) 'The Wessex Branch Roe Deer Survey, 1976'. *Deer* 4(4), November 1977, 212–14.

—(1979) 'Deer in the New Forest: History, Heads and Freaks'. *Deer* 4(10), December 1979, 510–15.

Insley, Hugh and Clarke, Michael P.G. (1975) 'A Short History of the New Forest Deer'. *Deer* 3(7), July 1975, 376–81.

Ireson, The Revd David (1996) 'Celebrating Exmoor and its Wildlife'. *Deer* 9(9), February 1996, 565.

Jackson, J.E. and Moore, J. (1976) 'The Deer of North-West Somerset'. *Deer* 3(9), February 1976, 488–91.

Jackson, John (1977) *Deer in the New Forest*. Bradford-on-Avon, Wiltshire: Moonraker Press.

Jardine, Sir William (1835) *The Naturalists' Library, Mammalia*, Vol. III, 'Ruminanta', Part 1. Edinburgh: W.H. Lizars.

Jayes, Jon (1988) 'Wollaton Hall: 400 Years'. *Deer* 7(5), March 1988, 234–7.

Jefferies, Richard (1989 reprint) *Red Deer*. Lockerbie, Dumfriesshire: The Signet Press.

Jeffery, Victoria (1987) 'Staghunting: Doubts Dismissed in the Quantocks'. *Deer* 7(2), March 1987, 81–2.

Jeffery, W.G. (1974) 'The Galloway (Red) Deer Control Scheme'. *Deer* 3(4), July 1974, 226–31.

Jennison, George (1937) *Animals for Show and Pleasure in Ancient Rome*. London: Oxford University Press.

Jewell, Peter A. and Holt, Sidney (eds) (1981) *Problems in Management of Locally Abundant Wild Mammals*. London: Academic Press.

Johnson, Lieut-Col. A.L. (1982) *Notes on the Behaviour of Roe Deer* (Capreolus capreolus L.) *at Chedington, Dorset, 1970–1980*. Forestry Commission Research and Development Paper 150. Edinburgh: Forestry Commission.

Johnson, John (1989) 'Deer Park Restoration at Leonardslee'. *Deer* 7(9), July 1989, 468–9.

Johnston, Sir H. (1903) *British Mammals* (Woburn Library of Natural History). London: Hutchinson & Co.

Johnstone, Gerald (1950) 'Deer in the South-West'. *The Field*, Vol. 195, 14 January 1950, 48–9.

—(1950) 'Wild Deer in Sussex'. *The Sussex County Magazine*, Vol. 24, No. 11, November 1950, 472–8.

Kemp, Ernest (1975) 'Studley Royal and its Deer'. *Deer* 3(6), November 1975, 322–4.

Kilpatrick, Cecil (1986a) 'Deer in Ulster – I. *Deer* 6(9), March 1986, 358–9.

—(1986b) 'Deer in Ulster – II: The Eighteenth Century'. *Deer* 6(10), July 1986, 410–14.

—(1986c) 'Deer in Ulster – III: The Nineteenth Century'. *Deer* 7(1), November 1986, 35–6.

—(1987) 'Deer in Ulster – IV: The Twentieth Century'. *Deer* 7(2), March 1987, 87–91.

Kinahan, G.H. (1883) 'Notes on the *Cervus megaceros* (Megaceros hibernicus). *Transactions of the Edinburgh Geological Society*, IV, 343–5.

King, R.J. (1968) 'Fallow Deer in Savernake Forest'. *Deer* 1(7), November 1968, 268–70.

Knowlton, Derrick (1973) *The Naturalist in Central Southern England*. Newton Abbot, Devon: David & Charles.

—(1974) *The Naturalist in Scotland*. Newton Abbot, Devon: David & Charles.

—(1977) *The Naturalist in the Hebrides*. Newton Abbot, Devon: David & Charles.

—(1980) *Looking at Mammals: A Beginner's Guide*. Cambridge: Lutterworth Press.

Langbein, Jochen (1985) *North Staffordshire Deer Survey, 1983–1985. Vol. 1. Research and Development*. Stoke-on-Trent: British Deer Society, Midlands Branch.

—(1995) 'The Red Deer of Exmoor and the Quantocks'. *Deer* 9(8), October 1995, 492–8.

—(1998) 'The Ranging Behaviour, Habitat-Use and Impact of Deer in Oak Woods and Heather Moors on Exmoor and the Quantock Hills'. *Deer* 10(10), July 1998, 516–21.

Larsen, R.T.F. (1979) 'The Problems of Red Deer as They Affect Forestry in Scotland'. *Deer* 4(8), February 1979, 410–12.

Lascelles, The Hon. Gerald (1915) *Thirty-Five Years in the New Forest*. London: Edward Arnold.

Latymer, Lord (1997 reprint) *Stalking in Scotland and New Zealand*. Crosby Ravensworth, Penrith, Cumbria: David Grayling.

Laver, Henry (1898) *The Mammals, Reptiles and Fishes of Essex*. Chelmsford: Edmund Durrant & Co.

Lawrence, M.J. and Brown, R.W. (1974) *Mammals of Britain: Their Tracks, Trails and Signs*. London: Blandford Press.

—(1977) *Mammals of Britain*. London: Blandford Press.

Lawton, Jeanette (1983) 'British Deer Society Midlands Branch Deer Survey'. *Deer* **6**(2), November 1983, 52.

—(1987) 'Stress in Deer at Dunham Massey Park'. *Deer* **7**(4), November 1987, 188.

Le Fanu, T.P. (1893) 'The Royal Forest of Glencree'. *The Journal of the Royal Society of Antiquaries of Ireland*, Section 3, Vol. III, 268–80.

Leftwich, A.W. (1958) 'The Deer of Northamptonshire'. *Journal of Northamptonshire Natural History Society*, Vol. 33 (241), June 1958, 194–8.

Leland, John (1536–9) *Itinerary in Wales of John Leland in or About 1536–39*. Arranged and edited by L. Toulmin Smith, 1906. London: George Bell & Sons.

Leslie, Kim C. (1972) 'The Petworth Roes: Thoughts on their Origins – I'. *Deer* **2**(7), March 1972, 796–8.

Leslie, Roderick (1993) 'Managing Fallow Deer in South and West England'. *Deer* **9**(1), July 1993, 29.

Lever, Sir Christopher (1977) *The Naturalized Animals of the British Isles*. London: Hutchinson & Co.

—(1985) *Naturalized Mammals of the World*. London: Longmans, Green & Co.

Lewis, P. (1811) *The New Forest*. London: T. Payne.

Lewis, W.P. (1965) 'The Marking of Roe Deer at Chedington, West Dorset'. *Deer News* **1**(6), January 1965, 27–32.

Lincoln, Gerald (1975) 'A Deer Count on Rhum in October'. *Deer* **3**(6), February 1975, 337–8.

Lincoln, G.A., Youngson, R.W. and Short, R.V. (1970) 'The Social and Sexual Behaviour of the Red Deer Stag'. *Journal of Reproduction and Fertility* Supplement **11**, March 1970, 71–103.

Linnard, Dr William (1988) 'Llantrithyd Deer Park: Sport in the Late Eighteenth Century'. *Deer* **7**(5), March 1988, 257.

Lloyd, E.R. (1970) *The Wild Red Deer of Exmoor – a Microstudy*. Tiverton, Devon: The Exmoor Press.

—(1971) 'Red Deer on Exmoor: Their Relationship with Farming and Sport'. *Deer* **2**(4), February 1971, 607–10.

—(1984) 'Staghunting in the West of England'. *Deer* **6**(4), July 1984, 137.

Logan, George (1973) 'Journeying to Rhum'. *Deer* **2**(10), February 1973, 972–3.

Love, John A. (1980) 'Deer Traps on the Isle of Rhum'. *Deer* **5**(3), November 1980, 131–2.

Lowe, V.P.W. and Gardner, A.S. (1976) 'The Red Deer of Furness: Their History, Biology, Status and Future, 3 – The Implications of the Hybrid Deer (Red x Sika) on Cartmell Fell for the Future of the Native Deer of the Lake District'. *Deer* **4**(1), November 1976, 28–32.

—(1983) 'The Origins of the Petworth Roe Deer'. *Deer* **6**(1), July 1983, 17–19.

Loyd, Lewis R.W. (1925) *Lundy, Its History and Natural History*. London: Longmans, Green & Co.

Lubbock, Revd R. (1879) *Observations on the Fauna of Norfolk*. Norwich: Jarrold & Sons.

Lucas, C.J. (Charles) (1969) 'Chital at Warnham Park'. *Deer* **1**(9), June 1969, 371.

—(1971) 'Warnham Park: Some Notes on the Herd's History'. *Deer* **2**(4), February 1971, 600–1.

—(1973) 'The World of Park Deer'. *Deer* **1**(10), February 1973, 988–90.

Lumsden, J. and Brown, A. (1895) *A Guide to the Natural History of Loch Lomond and Neighbourhood*. Glasgow: David Bryce & Son.

Luxmoore, Edmund (1991) *Deer Stalking*. Crosby Ravensworth, Penrith, Cumbria: David Grayling.

Lydekker, R. (1898) *The Deer of all Lands*. London: Rowland Ward Ltd.

—(1915) *Catalogue of the Ungulate Mammals in the British Museum (Natural History*, Vol. IV: Artiodactyla. London: Trustees of the British Museum.

MacArthur, K.H. (1975) 'Deer in South-West Scotland'. *Deer* **3**(6), February 1975, 338–9.

Macdermot, E.T. (1911) *The History of the Forest of Exmoor*. Taunton: Barnicott & Pearce.

Macewen, W. (1920) *The Growth and Shedding of the Antler of the Deer*. Glasgow: Maclehose, Jackson & Co.

Mackenzie, Ewen G. (1907) *Grouse Shooting and Deer-Stalking*. London: Love & Malcomson Ltd.

—(1997 reprint) *Grouse, Salmon and Stags*. Lockerbie, Dumfriesshire: The Signet Press.

Mackenzie, A. (1946) *The History of the Highland Clearances*. 2nd edition. Glasgow: Alex. Maclaren & Sons.

MacNally, Lea (1970) *Highland Deer Forest*. London: J.M. Dent & Sons Ltd.

—(1972) *Wild Highlands*. London: J.M. Dent & Sons Ltd.

—(1975) *The Year of the Red Deer*. London: J.M. Dent & Sons Ltd.

—(1983) *Highland Year*. London: Century Publishing.

—(1985) 'The Scottish Deer Scene Today'. *Deer* **6**(7), July 1985, 255–7.

—(1992) 'Deer Management at Abernethy, an RSPB Reserve'. *Deer* **8**(9), November 1992, 587–90.

—(1993) *Torridon: Life and Wildlife in the Scottish Highlands*. Shrewsbury: Swan Hill Press.

Macpherson, Revd H.A. (1892) *A Vertebrate Fauna of Lakeland*. Edinburgh: David Douglas.

Macpherson, Hon. J.G. (1964) 'Red Deer in Essex'. *Deer News* **1**(5), October 1964, 44.

MacRae, Finlay M. (1986) 'Red Deer in Upland Forests: Yesterday, Today and Tomorrow'. *Deer* **7**(1), November 1986, 20.

Magnusson, Magnus, KBE (1993) 'Red Deer and Scotland's Natural Heritage'. *Deer* **9**(1), July 1993, 19–22.

Malcolm, G. (1912) *List of Deer Forests in Scotland*. Edinburgh: Douglas & Foulis.

Mammal Review **4**(3), September 1974, 61–124. 'Proceedings of a Symposium on the Biological Basis of Deer Management'.

Manning, Charles J. (1998) 'The Oldest Roebuck'. *Deer* **10**(10), October 1998, 616–17.

Marshall, Fred. (1970) 'Deer and the Farmer'. *Deer* **2**(2), June 1970, 514–16.

—(1972) 'An Introduction to Sussex Deer'. *Deer* **2**(7), March 1972, 793–6.

Martin, Martin (1703) *A Description of the Western Islands of Scotland*. London: Andrew Bell.

Matheson, Colin (1932) *Changes in the Fauna of Wales within Historic Times*. Cardiff: The National Museum of Wales.

Matthews, L. Harrison (1952) *British Mammals*. London: Collins.

Maxwell, H.A. (1967) 'Red Deer and Forestry with Special Reference to the Highlands of Scotland'. *Deer* **1**(4), November 1967, 126–30.

Mayle, Brenda A. (Ed.) (1995) *Muntjac Deer: Their Biology, Impact and Management in Britain*. Fordingbridge, Hampshire: British Deer Society and Edinburgh: Forestry Commission.

McCarthy, A., Baker, A. and Rotherham, I.S. (1996) 'Urban Deer, Community Forests and Control: Roe Deer in the Urban Fringe – a Sheffield Case Study'. *Deer* **10**(1), July 1996, 16–17.

McCavish, W.L. (1968) 'Roe Deer Management at Kielder, Forestry Commission'. *Deer* **1**(7), November 1968, 256–7.

—(1977) 'Dowsing Deer'. *Deer* **4**(3), July 1977, 138–9.

McConnochie, A.I. (1923) *The Deer and Deer Forests of Scotland, Historical, Descriptive, Sporting*. London: H.F. & G. Witherby.

—(1996 reprint) *Deer Forest Life*. Crosby Ravensworth, Penrith, Cumbria: David Grayling.

McCurdy, R.J. (John) (1982) 'Deer in the North of Ireland'. *Deer* **5**(9), November 1982, 434.

—(1988) 'Sika Deer in Ireland: A Success Story'. *Deer* **7**(5), March 1988, 239–40.

—(1991) 'Deer Management in Northern Ireland'. *Deer* **8**(4), March 1991, 229–30.

—(1991) 'Glenveagh: An Irish Deer Forest'. *Deer* **8**(5), July 1991, 311.

McDiarmid, A. (1969) *Diseases of Free-Living Wild Animals*. London: Academic Press.

—(1972) 'Enzootic Ataxia of Deer'. *Deer* **2**(8), July 1972, 864–5.

—(1979) 'The BDS Stag from Glenfeshie and its Introduction to Windsor Great Park'. *Deer* **4**(10), December 1979, 489–91.

McIntosh, Dr Bob (1991) 'Roe Deer Management in Kielder Forest'. *Deer* **8**(6), November 1991, 353–4.

Mech, L. David (1970) *The Wolf: The Ecology and Behaviour of an Endangered Species*. London: Constable & Co. Ltd.

M'Elfrish, A. (1903) 'The Red Deer of North Uist'. *The Annals of Scottish Natural History*, No. 45, January 1903, 4–7.

Millais, J.G. (1897) *British Deer and their Horns*. London: Henry Sotheran & Co.

—(1906) *The Mammals of Great Britain and Ireland*, Vol. III. London: Longmans, Green & Co.

Miller, Innes (1979) 'The Red Deer Problems as perceived by the Red Deer Commission'. *Deer* **4**(8), February 1979, 408–9.

Mitchell, Brian (1984) 'Effects of the Severe Winter of 1962–63 on the Deer (Hinds and Calves) in North-East Scotland'. *Deer* **6**(3), March 1984, 81–4.

Mitchell, G.F. and Parkes, H.M. (1949) 'The Giant Deer in Ireland'. *Proceedings of the Royal Irish Academy*, XLIV, Section B, No. **7**, 291–314.

Mitchell, W.R. (1984) 'Bowland Sika: Some Notes on the Deer and Their Habitat'. *Deer* **6**(3), March 1984, 76.

Mitchell, W.R. and Delap, Peter (1974) *Lakeland Mammals: A Visitor's Handbook*. Clapham, North Yorkshire: Dalesman Books.

Mitchell, W.R. and Robinson, J. (1971) 'The Bowland Sika: Their History, Status and Distribution'. *Deer* **2**(6), November 1971, 729–32.

—(1973) 'The Bowland Sika: Some Aspects of the Rut'. *Deer* **3**(1), July 1973, 21–5.

—(1974a) 'The Bowland Sika: Some Notes on Vocal Activity'. *Deer* **3**(3), February 1974, 150–53.

—(1974b) 'The Bowland Sika: Some Notes on Antlers'. *Deer* **3**(5), November 1974, 264–9.

—(1975) 'The Bowland Sika: Some Notes on Calving'. *Deer* **3**(7), July 1975, 382–5.

—(1978) 'The Bowland Sika: Some Notes on Pelage'. *Deer* **4**(5), February 1978 276–8.

Moffat, C.B. (1938) 'The Mammals of Ireland'. *Proceedings of the Royal Irish Academy*, Vol. XLIV, Section B, No. 6, 61–128.

Moncrieff, Lieut-Col. D.G. (1969) 'From the Deer Park to the Hill'. *Deer* **1**(9), June 1969, 360–61.

Monro, Dean (Sir Donald) (1549) *A Description of the Western Isles of Scotland called Hybrides*. Republished 1934. Stirling: Eneas Mackay.

Mooney, O.V. (1952) 'Irish Deer and Forest Relations'. *Irish Forestry*, Vol. IX, No. 1, Summer 1952, 11–27.

Morey, Frank (1909) *A Guide to the Natural History of the Isle of Wight*. Newport, Isle of Wight: The County Press.

Morris, Sir Daniel (Ed.) (1914) *A Natural History of Bournemouth and District*. Bournemouth: The Natural Science Society.

Morris, Paul G. (1985) 'Some Observations on North Oxfordshire Muntjac'. *Deer* **6**(8), November 1985, 315.

Morrison, Major K.C.G. (1988) 'Northamptonshire Roe'. *Deer* **7**(5), March 1988, 239.

Moryson, Fynes (1735) *The Description of Ireland, being 'An History of Ireland from the year 1599 to 1603, with a short narration of the State of the Kingdom from the year 1169', to which is added A Description of Ireland*. 2 Vols. Dublin.

Mutch, W.E.S., Lockie, J.D. and Cooper, A.B. (1976) *The Red Deer in South Ross A Report on Wildlife Management in the Scottish Highlands*. Edinburgh: Department of Forestry and Natural Resources, University of Edinburgh.

Nairn, Richard and Crowlet, Miriam (1999) *Wild Wicklow: Nature in the Garden of Ireland*. Dublin: Town House.

The New Forest (1966). London: Phoenix House.

New Forest Deer Monitoring Group (1998) Press release. *Deer* **10**(7), January 1998, 426.

The New Statistical Account of Scotland (1834–45). Fifteen volumes. Edinburgh: William Blackwood & Sons.

Newbigging, Thomas (1893) *History of the Forest of Rossendale*. 2nd edition. Rawtenstall, Lancashire: J.J. Riley.

Newton, E.T. (1903) 'The Elk in the Thames Valley'. *Quarterly Journal of the Geological Society*, Vol. LIX, 1903, 80–89.

Nicholls, H.G. (1858) *The Forest of Dean*. London: John Murray.

Noble, Martin (1980) 'The Deer of Mortimer Forest'. *Deer* 5(2), July 1980, 86–7.

Nolan, L.M. (Liam) 'Phoenix Park Fallow Deer: An Update'. *Deer* 9(8), October 1995, 424.

—(1996) 'Deer Farming in Ireland: Time for a Re-think'. *Deer* 10(1), July 1996, 34–7.

—(1997) 'Megaceros!' *Deer* 10(3), January 1997, 151–3.

—(1997) 'Wicklow Mountains National Park: Consultants' Survey Report'. *Deer* 10(4), April 1997, 256–8.

—(1997) 'Medieval Scottish Deer Forests'. *Deer* 10(6), October 1997, 354–6.

—(1999) 'Irish State Forestry Board Underestimate'. *Deer* 11(1), January 1999, 44.

Nolan, Liam V. and Liam M. (1995) 'Phoenix Park Deer Cull, 1942'. *Deer* 9(6), March 1995, 356–9.

Norris, J.R. (1982) 'A Note on Chatsworth Deer and their Management'. *Deer* 5(8), July 1982, 403–4.

North, F.J., Campbell, Bruce and Scott, Richenda (1949) *Snowdonia*, The New Naturalist. London: Collins.

O'Brien, Lieut-Col. E.J.K. (1998) 'The Roe Deer of Larkhill, Wiltshire'. *Deer* 7(6), July 1988, 311.

O'Gorman, Fergus (1965) 'A Note on the Status of Deer at Killarney, Co. Kerry, and a Programme for Research into their Management and Conservation'. *Deer News* 1(8), October 1965, 44–5.

Omand, Donald (ed.) (1981) *Red Deer Management*. Inverness and Edinburgh: Red Deer Commission (now Deer Commission for Scotland).

Orr, Willie (1982) *Deer Forests, Landlords and Crofters*. Edinburgh: John Donald Publishers.

Orwin, C.S. (1929) *The Reclamation of Exmoor Forest*. London: Oxford University Press.

Osborn, H.F. (1921) *The Age of Mammals in Europe, Asia and North America*. New York: The Macmillan Co.

Page, F.J. Taylor (1954) 'The Wild Deer of East Anglia'. *Transactions of the Norfolk and Norwich Naturalists' Society*, Vol. XVII, Part V, 316–21.

—(1968) 'Research on Roe Deer Damage in Thetford Chase, 1955–58'. *Deer* 1(5), February 1968, 164–6.

—(1971) 'The Capture and Handling of Deer in Ancient Times'. *Deer* 2(5), July 1971, 661–4.

Page, F.J. Taylor (ed.) (1970) *The Sussex Mammal Report, 1969*. Henfield, Sussex: The Sussex Naturalists' Trust.

—(1982) *Field Guide to British Deer* 3rd edition. Oxford: Blackwell Scientific Publications.

Page, J.L.W. (1890) *An Exploration of Exmoor and the Hill Country of West Somerset*. London: Seeley & Co. Ltd.

Pardy, Vic. (1975) 'The Finding of a Second Monster'. *Deer* 3(6), February 1975, 336–7.

Parkes, Charles and Thornley, John (1994) *Fair Game*. London: Pelham Books.

Peden, Joan D. (1988) 'Deer Poaching in Ancient Somerset'. *Deer* 7(5), March 1988, 256.

Peel, C.V.A. (1901) *Wild Sport in the Outer Hebrides*. London: F.E. Robinson & Co.

Pemberton, J.M. and Dansie, Oliver (1986) 'Fallow Deer: Do the Colour Varieties Differ in Size?' *Deer* 7(1), November 1986, 18–19.

Penistan, M.J. (1965) 'Deer Control in Wareham Forest'. *Deer News* 1(6), January 1965, 33–4.

—(1967) 'Deer in South and Central Devon'. *Deer* 1(2), February 1967, 44–5.

Pennant, T. (1774–6) *A Tour in Scotland*, 3 volumes. 3rd edition. Warrington, Lancashire: W. Eyres.

Pepper, Hubert (1970) 'Lydney Park and its Deer'. *Deer* 2(1), February 1970, 449.

Perceval, P.J.S. (1909) *London's Forest, Its History, Traditions and Romance*. London: J.M. Dent & Co.

Perry, Richard (1965) 'Notes on Red Deer in the Scottish Highlands'. *Deer News* 1(6), January 1965, 48–50.

—(1971) *The Watcher and the Red Deer*. Newton Abbot, Devon: David & Charles.

Petley-Jones, Bob (1997) 'Report from the Silverdale Deer Management Seminar'. *Deer* 10(3), January 1997, 165–7.

Phillips, Joan and Mutch, W.E.S. (eds) (1974) *Red Deer in Woodland*. Privately published.

Pickvance, T.J. and Chard, J.S.R. (1960) 'Feral Muntjac Deer (*Muntiacus spp.*) in the West Midlands with Special Reference to Warwickshire'. *Proceedings of the Birmingham Natural History and Philosophical Society*, Vol. XIX, Part 1, 1–8.

Pirrie, Tom D. (1993) 'Fallow Deer in Dumfriesshire'. *Deer* 9(2), November 1993, 89–92.

'Pitman' (M. Wright) (1933) *The Deer of Cannock Chase*. Wolverhampton: The Midland News Association Ltd.

Place, Lieut-Col. J.W. (1986) 'Deerstalking in Co. Wicklow'. *Deer* 6(9), March 1986, 356–8.

Platt, Margery I. (1935–6) 'Reindeer Antlers from Rousay, Orkney'. Reprint from the *Proceedings of the Society of Antiquaries of Scotland*, Vol. LXX (Vol X, sixth series), 435–41.

Plot, R. (1686) *The Natural History of Staffordshire*. Oxford: printed at the Theater.

Portland, Duke of. (1935) *The Red Deer of Langwell and Braemore 1880–1934*. London: Blackie & Son Ltd.

Potter, T.R. (1842) *The History and Antiquities of Charnwood Forest*. London: Hamilton, Adams & Co.

Powerscourt, Viscount (1884) 'The Acclimatization of Deer at Powerscourt'. *Proceedings of the Zoological Society*, London, 1884, 207–9.

Praeger, R.L. (1950) *Natural History of Ireland*. London: Collins.

Pratt, Robin (1986) 'Red Deer to Ramsey Island, West Wales'. *Deer* 5(1), March 1986, 24–5.

Price, Richard I.B. (1984) 'Management of the Deer at Petworth'. *Deer* 6(4), July 1984, 125–7.

Prior, Richard (1963) *Roe Stalking*. London: Percival Marshall & Co.

—(1965a) *Living with Deer*. London: André Deutsch Ltd.

—(1965b) 'Taking Stock of Roe Deer in Cranborne Chase'. *Deer News* **1**(6), January 1965, 32–3.

—(1968) *The Roe Deer of Cranborne Chase*. London: Oxford University Press.

—(1973) *Roe Deer Management and Stalking*. Fordingbridge, Hampshire: The Game Conservancy.

—(1983) *Trees and Deer*. London: B.T. Batsford Ltd.

—(1985) *Modern Roe Stalking*. Rhyl, North Wales: Tideline Books.

—(1987) *Roe Stalking*. Fordingbridge, Hampshire: The Game Conservancy.

—(1993 reprint) *Deer Watch*. Shrewsbury: Swan Hill Press.

—(1995) *The Roe Deer: Conservation of a Native Species*. Shrewsbury: Swan Hill Press.

—(1997) 'A Black Roe from Dorset'. *Deer* **10**(4), April 1997, 236–7.

Provisional Atlas of Suffolk Mammals (1992) Ipswich: Suffolk Biological Records Centre.

Putman, R.J. (Rory) (1986) *Grazing in Temperate Ecosystems: Large Herbivores and the Ecology of the New Forest*. Bromley, Kent: Croom Helm.

—(1988) *The Natural History of Deer*. Bromley, Kent: Christopher Helm.

Putman, R.J. and Clifton-Bligh, J.R. (1998) 'The Natural History of the Sika Deer of the Dorset Ranges'. *Deer* **10**(10), October 1998, 581–4.

Putman, R.J. and Hunt, E.J. (1993) 'Hybridisation between Red and Sika Deer in Britain'. *Deer* **9**(2), November 1993, 104–10.

Rackham, Oliver (1993) *The Last Forest*. London: J.M. Dent & Sons Ltd.

Rackham, Oliver *et al.* (1975) *Hayley Wood: Its History and Biology*. Cambridge: Cambridgeshire and Isle of Ely Naturalists' Trust.

Ramsay, Lord (1991) 'Deer, Mountains and Man: The Landlord's Role'. *Deer* **8**(5), July 1991, 298–300.

Ramsden, James (1975) 'Red Deer in a Yorkshire Valley'. *Deer* **3**(6), February 1975, 325–6.

Ratcliffe, Philip R. (1986) 'Forestry Conservation and Japanese Sika Deer'. *Deer* **7**(1), November 1986, 15–17.

—(1987) 'The Future of the Red Deer of Galloway'. *Deer* **7**(3), July 1987, 134–6.

Ratcliffe, P.R. and Mayle, B.A. (1992) *Roe Deer Biology and Management*. Forestry Commission Booklet 105. London: The Stationery Office.

Rawle, Edward J. (1893) *Annals of the Ancient Royal Forest of Exmoor*. Taunton: Barnicott & Pearce.

Red Deer Management (1981) Inverness and Edinburgh: The Red Deer Commission.

Reynolds, Sidney H. (1929) *The Giant Deer: A Monograph on the British Pleistocene Mammals*, Vol. III, Part III, December 1929. London: Palaeontographical Society.

Ribblesdale, Lord (1897) *The Queen's Hounds*. London: Longmans, Green & Co.

Richardson, H.D. (1846) *Facts Conserning the Natural History of the Gigantic Irish Deer*. Dublin.

Ridley, Viscount (1968) 'Roe Deer at Blagdon, Northumberland'. *Deer* **1**(7), November 1968, 237–8.

Rintoul, L.J. and Baxter, E.V. (1935) *A Vertebrate Fauna of Forth*. Edinburgh: Oliver & Boyd.

Ritchie, J. (1918) 'Roe Deer in Bute'. *The Scottish Naturalist*, No. 21, September 1918, 212.

—(1920) *The Influence of Man on Animal Life in Scotland*. Cambridge: Cambridge University Press.

—(1927) 'Red Deer in Selkirkshire in Prehistoric Times'. *The Scottish Naturalist*, No. 165, May–June 1927, 65–8.

—(1929) 'Prehistoric Red Deer's Antlers in Roxburghshire'. *The Scottish Naturalist*, No. 175, 8.

—(1930) 'Red Deer Remains from Orkney'. *The Scottish Naturalist*, No. 184, July–August 1930, 126.

Robinson, J. (John) (1973) 'The World of Bowland Sika'. *Deer* **2**(10), February 1973, 984–7.

—(1975a) 'Deer in North-West Yorkshire'. *Deer* **3**(6), February 1975, 320–22.

—(1975b) 'Deer in South Yorkshire'. *Deer* **3**(6), February 1975, 322.

Rodgers, Joseph (1908) *The Scenery of Sherwood Forest, with an Account of Some Eminent People once Resident There*. London: T. Fisher Unwin.

Rose, Hugh (1991) 'Deer, Mountains and Man: A Conference Report'. *Deer* **8**(4), March 1991, 206–8.

—(1994) 'Scottish Deer Distribution Survey 1993: Final Report'. *Deer* **9**(3), March 1994, 193–5.

—(1999) 'Wytham Woods: A Deer Management Project'. *Deer* **11**(3), July 1999, 119–23.

Rose, H.R. (Ed.) (1995) *Deer, Habitat and Birds*. Fordingbridge, Hampshire: British Deer Society and Sandy, Bedfordshire: Royal Society for the Protection of Birds.

Rose, R.R. (1978) 'Some Aspects of Wildlife Management in a Border Forest'. *Deer* **4**(5), February 1978, 283–6.

Rowe, Judith (1966) 'Deer Research in the Forestry Commission'. *Deer News* **1**(10), June 1966, 34–7.

Rowe, Samuel (1896) *A Perambulation of the Ancient and Royal Forest of Dartmoor and the Venville Precincts*. Exeter: James G. Commin.

Rowland, R. (1967) 'A History of the Deer at Beaulieu, Hampshire'. *Deer* **1**(4), November 1967, 125–6.

Rudge, A.J.B. (Ed.) (1985) *The Capture and Handling of Deer*. Attingham Park, Shrewsbury: Nature Conservancy Council (now English Nature).

Rutty, Dr John (1772) *An Essay towards a Natural History of the County of Dublin* 2 volumes. Dublin: Privately printed by W. Sleator.

Ryan, Sean (1998) *The Wild Red Deer of Killarney*. Dingle, Co. Kerry: Mount Eagle Publications.

Saberton, Ian A. (1980) 'The Royal Venison Warrant'. *Deer* **5**(3), November 1980, 134–6.

Sage, Bryan L. (Ed.) (1966) *Northaw Great Wood*. Hertford: Hertfordshire County Council.

St John, C. (1878) *Sketches of the Wild Sports and Natural History of the Highlands*. London: John Murray.

—(1884) *A Tour in Sutherlandshire*, 2 volumes. 2nd edition. Edinburgh: David Douglas.

Sauer, Wolfgang (1989) *The Red Deer*. London: J.M. Dent & Sons Ltd.

Scharff, R.F. (1918) 'The Irish Red Deer'. *The Irish Naturalist's Journal*, Vol. XXVII Nos. 10 and 11, October–November 1918, 133–9.

Scott, W.A. (1967) 'Fallow Deer in the Teign Valley'. *Deer* **1**(2), February 1967, 45.

Scott, W.A. and Yeo, Colin (1967) 'Development and Problems Arising from Deer Control on Estates in Central and East Devon'. *Deer* **1**(2), February 1967, 46–7.

Scottish Field. Various contributors.

Scrope, William (1839) *The Art of Deer-stalking*. London: John Murray.

Sharman, G.A.M. (1974) 'The Farming of Red Deer'. *Deer* **3**(3), February 1974, 135–9.

Shaw, R. Cunliffe (1956) *The Royal Forest of Lancaster*. Preston: The Guardian Press.

Shields, J. Gillies (1976) 'The Deer of Donington, Leicestershire'. *Deer* **3**(9), February 1976, 486–7.

Shirley, E.P. (1867) *Some Account of English Deer Parks*. London: John Murray.

Shooting Times and Country Magazine. Various contributors.

Simper, Ian and Frances (1993) 'Some Observations on Norfolk Fallow Deer'. *Deer* **9**(2), November 1993, 93–4.

Smith, Eric (1991) 'Fallow Return to the Deer Park at Hagley Hall'. *Deer* **8**(6), November 1991, 371–3.

Smith, John A. (1873) 'Notice of Discovery of Remains of the Elk (*Cervus alces* Linn., *Alces malchis* Gray) in Berwickshire, with Notes of its Occurrence in the British Islands, more Particularly in Scotland. Also Notes of the Remains of the Irish Elk (*Megaceros hibernicus*) Found in Scotland'. Edinburgh: *Proceedings of the Society of Antiquaries*, Vol. IX, 1870–71, 297–350.

Smith, Stephen (1995) 'New Forest Sika Deer, Part I – Antlers'. *Deer* **9**(6), March 1995, 366–9.

—(1996) 'New Forest Sika Deer, Part II – Vocal Behaviour'. *Deer* **9**(1), April 1996, 643–5.

Smith, W. McCombie (1904) *The Romance of Poaching in the Highlands of Scotland*. Stirling: E. Mackay.

'Snaffle' (1987 reprint) *The Roedeer*. Shedfield, Hampshire: Ashford Press Publications.

Soper, Eileen A. (1969) *Muntjac*. London: Longmans, Green & Co. Ltd.

Southern, H.N. (Ed.) (1963) *The Handbook of British Mammals*. Oxford: Blackwell Scientific Publications Ltd.

Springthorpe, Gerald (1966) 'Long-Haired Fallow Deer'. *Deer* **1**(1), November 1966, 15–16.

—(1980) 'Long-Coated Fallow Deer'. *Deer* **5**(2), July 1980, 83–5.

Springthorpe, G.D. and Myhill, N.G. (Eds) (1994) *Wildlife Ranger's Handbook*. 2nd edition. Edinburgh: Forestry Commission and London: The Stationery Office.

Springthorpe, G. and Voysey, J. (1969) 'The Fallow Deer of Mortimer Forest'. *Deer* **1**(10), November 1969, 407–9.

Squire, Mike (1997) 'Deer Control in the Urban Fringes'. *Deer* **10**(3), January 1997, 162–4.

Stadtler, Stephen G. (1988) 'Observations on the Behaviour of Chinese Water Deer (*Hydropotes inermis* Swinhoe, 1870)'. *Deer* **7**(6), July 1988, 300–1.

Stalking Magazine. Various contributors.

The Statistical Account of Scotland (1791–9) Edited by Sir J. Sinclair from the communications of the Ministers of the different parishes. 21 volumes. Edinburgh: William Green and J. Donaldson and J. Guthrie *et al.*

Steelfox, A.W. (1934) 'The Problem of the Irish Elk'. *The Irish Naturalists' Journal*, Vol. V, No. 4, July 1934, 74–6.

Stephens, Martin (1936) *Fair Game*. London: John Murray.

Street, Philip (1953) *Whipsnade*. London: University of London Press Ltd.

Stewart, David (1988) 'The Quantock Hills Red Deer'. *Deer* **7**(7), November 1988, 358–9.

—(1997) 'New Urban Woods and Rising Deer Populations'. *Deer* **10**(3), January 1997, 165.

Stringer, Arthur (1977 reprint) *The Experienced Huntsman*. Belfast: The Blackstaff Press Ltd.

Stuart, J. Sobieski and Stuart, C.E. (1848) *Lays of the Deer Forest*. 2 volumes. Edinburgh: William Blackwood & Sons.

Sutcliffe, A. and Zeuner, F.E. (1962) 'Excavations in the Torbryan Caves, Devonshire'. *Proceedings of the Devon Archaeological Exploration Society*, Vol. V, Parts 5 and 6, 1962 for 1957–8, 127–45.

Sutton, Revd C.N. (1902) *Historical Notes of Withyham, Hartfield and Ashdown Forest*. Tunbridge Wells: A.K. Baldwin.

Symposium on Red Deer and Forestry. (1968) *Scottish Forestry*, Vol. 22, No. 1 January 1968.

Tabor, R.C.C. (1999) 'The Effects of Muntjac Deer, *Muntiacus reevesi*, and Fallow Deer, *Dama dama*, on the Oxlip, *Primula elatior*'. *Deer* **11**(1), January 1999, 14–19.

Talbot, Dennis (1980) 'Reeves's Muntjac at Woburn: Their Habits, History and Management', *Deer* **5**(1), March 1980, 27–8.

Tattersall, W.M. (Ed.) (1936) *Glamorgan County History*, Vol. 1, Natural History. Cardiff: William Lewis (Printers) Ltd.

Taylor, Keith (1971) 'The Red Deer of Wollaton Park, Nottingham'. *Deer* **2**(5), July 1971, 184–7.

—(1973) 'The Deer of Bradgate Park, Leicester'. *Deer* **3**(2), November 1973, 85–8.

—(1981) 'The Northerly Spread of Muntjac in the Midlands'. *Deer* **5**(4), March 1981, 185–6.

Taylor, Michael Bradley (ed.) (1996) *Wildlife Crime: A Guide to Wildlife Law Enforcement in the UK*. London: The Stationery Office.

Taylor, Sir W.L. (1939) 'The Distribution of Wild Deer in England and Wales'. *The Journal of Animal Ecology*, Vol. 8, No. 1, May 1939, 6–9.

—(1948) 'The Distribution of Wild Deer in England and Wales'. *The Journal of Animal Ecology*, Vol. 17, No. 2, November 1948, 151–4.

—(1949) 'The Distribution of Wild Deer in Scotland'. *The Journal of Animal Ecology*, Vol. 18, No. 2, November 1949, 187–92.

Tegner, Henry (1953) 'The Present Distribution of the Roe Deer in Great Britain'. *The Naturalist*, January–March 1953, 19–21.

—(1964) 'The Roe at Blair Drummond'. *Deer News* **1**(5), October 1964, 27–9.

—(1970) *Charm of the Cheviots*. Newcastle-upon-Tyne: Frank Graham.

—(1971) *A Naturalist on Speyside*. London: Geoffrey Bles.

—(1981) *The Roe Deer*. 2nd edition, revised by Richard Prior. Rhyl, North Wales: Tideline Books.

Thompson, William (1841) *Report on the Fauna of Ireland*, Div. Vertebrata. London: R. & J.E. Taylor.

—(1856) *The Natural History of Ireland*, Vol. IV. London: Henry G. Bohn.

Thrower, Ruth (1973) 'Red Deer Control and Preservation in the West Country'. *Deer* **2**(10), February 1973, 970–72.

Thurlow, Frank (1967) 'A Red Deer Stag among Cattle'. *Deer* **1**(2), February 1967, 50–51.

Tickner, Pamela (1986) 'A Roebuck in Suburbia'. *Deer* **6**(9), March 1986, 362.

Tubbs, Colin R. (1986) *The New Forest*. London: Collins.

Turberville, George (1576) *The Noble Art of Venerie of Hunting*. Tudor and Stuart Library edition, 1908. London: Clarendon Press.

Turner, G.J. (1901) *Select Pleas of the Forest*. London: Bernard Quaritch for Selden Society.

University of Southampton (1994) 'Exmoor and Quantocks Deer Research Project: The Impact of Deer and Sheep on Woodland and Moorland Regeneration and its Relationship to Surrounding Land Use Patterns'. *Deer* **9**(3), March 1994, 156–7.

Ussher, R.J. (1882) 'Notes on Irish Red Deer'. *The Zoologist*, **VI**(3), 81–4.

Utsi, Mikel (1975) 'Reindeer in Scotland'. *Deer* **3**(7), July 1975, 390–91.

Veal, Vyvyan (1996) 'The Fallow Deer of Parndon Wood'. *Deer* **9**(9), January 1996, 566–72.

Venner, B.G. (1970) 'Fallow Deer in the Forest of Dean'. *Deer* **2**(1), February 1970, 446–8.

Vesey-FitzGerald, Brian (1946) *British Game*. London: Collins.

—(1996) *Portrait of the New Forest*. London: Phoenix House.

Viccari, R. (1978) 'Deer of Mid to East Sussex: A Sample Area'. *Deer* **4**(7), November 1978, 370.

Vowles, Alfred (1936) *Wild Deer of Exmoor*. Minehead and Williton, Somerset. Cox, Sons & Co. Ltd.

Wallace, H. Frank (1913) *British Deer Heads*. London: Country Life Ltd.

—(1935) *A Highland Gathering*. 2nd edition. London: Eyre & Spottiswoode.

—(1944) *Happier Years*. London: Eyre & Spottiswoode.

—(1949) *Hunting Winds*. London: Eyre & Spottiswoode.

Wallace, H. Frank and Edwards, Lionel (1927) *Hunting and Stalking the Deer*. London: Longmans, Green & Co. Ltd.

Warner, Leonard J. (1972) 'A Muntjac in Windsor Forest'. *Deer* **2**(8), July 1972, 876–9.

—(1977) 'The Roe Deer of Windsor Forest: A Preliminary Survey'. *Deer* **4**(4), November 1977, 208–11.

—(1978) *Mammal Photography and Observation: A Practical Field Guide*. London: Academic Press.

Waterson, H.A. (Ed.) (1987) *Going to the Hill: An Introduction to Red Deer Stalking in Scotland*. Oswestry, Shropshire: Anthony Nelson.

Waterson, H.A. and MacArthur, K.H. (1977) 'The Wild Red Deer of Galloway'. *Deer* **4**(4), November 1977, 198–202.

Watson, Dr Adam (1983) 'Eighteenth Century Deer Numbers and Pine Regeneration near Braemar, Scotland'. *Deer* **6**(2), November 1983, 52–3.

—(1977) 'Human-induced Changes in Numbers of Red Deer in the Cairn Gorm Area'. *Deer* **10**(5), July 1997, 278–81.

—(1997) 'Changes in Use of the Cairn Gorm Area by Sheep and Reindeer'. *Deer* **10**(6), October 1997, 346–7.

Watson, J.M., Marshall, K. and Chapman, D.I. (1966) 'A Study of the Epping Forest Fallow Deer, 1964–65'. *Deer News* **1**(9), January 1966, 49.

Wayre, Philip (1968) 'Deer in the Norfolk Wildlife Park'. *Deer* **1**(5), February 1968, 168–9.

—(1969) 'The Role of the Wildlife Park in Education'. *Deer* **1**(9), June 1969, 359–60.

Wegner, Robert (1992) *Wegner's Bibliography on Deer and Deer Hunting*. DeForest, Wisconsin, USA: St Hubert's Press.

Wemmer, Christian M. (1987) *Biology and Management of the Cervidae*. Washington DC, USA: Smithsonian Institute Press.

Weston, F., DFC, BSc. (1975) 'Deer in the Forestry Commission Areas of Yorkshire'. *Deer* **3**(6), February 1975, 318–20.

Whitaker, James (1892) *A Descriptive List of the Deer-Parks and Paddocks of England*. London: Ballantyne, Hanson & Co.

White, Gilbert (1989) *The Natural History and Antiquities of Selborne in the County of Southampton with Engravings, and an Appendix*. Facsimile reprint 1970. Menston, Ilkley, Yorkshire: Scolar Press Ltd.

White, Robert (1875) *Worksop, 'The Dukery', and Sherwood Forest*. London: Simpkin, Marshall & Co.

Whitehead G. Kenneth (1950) *Deer and their Management in the Deer Parks of Great Britain and Ireland*. London: Country Life Ltd.

—(1960) *The Deer Stalking Grounds of Great Britain and Ireland*. London: Hollis & Carter.

—(1964) *The Deer of Great Britain and Ireland*. London: Routledge & Kegan Paul.

—(1964) *Deer Stalking in Scotland*. London: Percival Marshall & Co.

—(1969) 'Deer Parks: Their History and Present Day Management'. *Deer* **1**(9), June 1969, 349–54.

—(1972) *Deer of the World*. London: Constable & Co.

—(1973) 'Woburn and its Deer.' *Deer* **3**(2), November 1973, 72–6.

—(1973) 'Roe from Sussex Introduced to Seafields Sporting Club Estates'. *Deer* **3**(2), November 1973, 82–4.

—(1980) *Hunting and Stalking Deer in Britain through the Ages*. London: B.T. Batsford Ltd.

—(1981) *The Game Trophies of the World*. Hamburg: Paul Parey.

—(1982) *Hunting and Stalking Deer Throughout the World*. London: B.T. Batsford Ltd.

—(1984) 'Sika Deer in Britain'. *Deer* **6**(3), March 1984, 75–6.

—(1986) *Practical Deer-Stalking*. London: Constable & Co.

—(1993) *The Whitehead Encyclopaedia of Deer*. Shrewsbury: Swan Hill Press.

—(1996) *Half a Century of Scottish Deer Stalking*. Shrewsbury: Swan Hill Press.

Whitlock, Ralph (1979) *Historic Forests of England*. Bradford-on-Avon, Wiltshire: Moonraker Press.

Wigan, Michael (1991) *The Scottish Highland Estate: Preserving an Environment*. Shrewsbury: Swan Hill Press.

—(1993) *Stag at Bay: The Scottish Red Deer Crisis*. Shrewsbury: Swan Hill Press.

Wildlife in the Forest (1967) Supplement to *Forestry*. London: Oxford University Press.

Willett, J.A. (John) (1985) 'Hog Deer or Para (*Axis porcinus* Zimm.)' *Deer* **6**(6), March 1985, 200–1.

—(1988) 'Bald-Faced Red Deer'. *Deer* **7**(6), July 1988, 303–4.

Willett, J.A. and Mulloy, Fergal (1970) 'Wild Deer: Their Status and Distribution, 1970'. *Deer* **2**(2), June 1970, 498–504.

Williams, W. (1881) 'On the Occurrence of the Great Irish Deer *Megaceros hibernicus*, in the Ancient Lacustrine Deposits of Ireland'. *Geological Magazine*, August 1881.

Williamson, Henry (1931) *The Wild Red Deer of Exmoor*. London: Faber & Faber.

Williamson, Richard (1978) *The Great Yew Forest: The Natural History of Kingley Vale*. London: Macmillan.

Wilson, John (1964) 'Deer at Ashridge – Past and Present'. *Deer News* **1**(5), October 1964, 23–5.

Winans, Walter (1913) *Deer Breeding for Fine Heads*. London: Rowland Ward Ltd.

Wise, John R. (1863) *The New Forest, Its History and Its Scenery*. London: Henry Sotheran.

Witchell, Arthur (1983) 'Badminton Deer Park'. *Deer* **6**(1), July 1983, 19–21.

Witchell, C.A. and Strugnell, W. Bishop (1892) *The Fauna and Flora of Gloucestershire*. Stroud, Gloucestershire: G.H. James.

Woodcock, N.J. (Norman J.) (1964a) 'Some Data on Wyre Forest Fallow Deer'. *Deer News* **1**(3), January 1964, 20–22.

—(1964b) 'The Fallow Deer of Wyre Forest'. *Deer News* **1**(4), May 1964, 33–4.

Woodford, M.H., MRCVS (1967) 'The Henley Park Fallow Deer Translocation'. *Deer* **1**(4), November 1967, 134–6.

Woodruffe-Peacock, Revd E. (Ed.) (1898) *The Natural History of Lincolnshire*. Horncastle, Lincolnshire: W.K. Morton.

Woodvine, Keith (1982) 'The Deer of Chatsworth, Derbyshire'. *Deer* **5**(7), March 1982, 333–4.

Worsfold, S.R. (1978) Photograph of a roebuck on the Stonor estate, in the Oxfordshire Chilterns near Henley-on-Thames, and believed to be the first of its kind north of the Thames in that part of England. *Deer* **4**(5), February 1978, 249.

Wray, Stephanie (1994) 'Competition between Muntjac and other Herbivores in a Commercial Conifer Forest'. *Deer* **9**(4), July 1994, 237–42.

Wright, M.A. (1913) 'The Red Deer in Glamorgan'. *Report and Transactions of the Cardiff Naturalists' Society*. Vol. XLVI, 1913, 95–6.

Yerex, David (ed.) (1982) *The Farming of Deer: World Trends and Modern Techniques*. Penruddock, Penrith, Cumbria: British Deer Farmers' Association.

Yerex, David and Spiers, Ian (1987) *Modern Deer Farm Management*. Carterton, New Zealand: Ampersand Publishing Associated Ltd.

Young, Colin D. (1980) 'Deer Farming in Britain Today'. *Deer* **5**(1), March 1980 22–3.

INDEX